LIGHT AND DARK is the story of a mother and daughter, the one bound in the sexual slavery of nineteenth century marriage, the other fighting free from a childhood of neglect to battle for the rights of women in the poor areas of Edinburgh.

Lorianna Blackwood is married to a considerably older man, a man who is cold and cruel, unable and unwilling to satisfy the desires which day by day are building up in his beautiful wife. Into this situation walks Robert Kelso, quite simply the most attractive man Lorianna has ever seen, and between them builds an inevitable, dangerous and forbidden attraction.

As their relationship builds towards an explosive and tragic climax, Lorianna's daughter Clementina is quietly growing up, more or less ignored, and running wild. In the second part of the book it is Clementina who emerges, determined, strong, resolved to fight the kind of subjugation to which her mother was condemned, but through her fight for women's rights confronted – just as her mother was – with the passion of a strong and seductively attractive man.

Light and Dark

Margaret Thomson Davis

CORGI BOOKS

LIGHT AND DARK

A CORGI BOOK 0 552 12700 0

Originally published in Great Britain by Century
Publishing Co. Ltd.

PRINTING HISTORY
Century edition published 1984
Corgi edition published 1985

This book is set in 10/11 pt Sabon

Corgi Books are published by Transworld Publishers Ltd.,
Century House, 61–63 Uxbridge Road, Ealing,
London W5 5SA, in Australia by Transworld Publishers
(Aust.) Pty. Ltd., 26 Harley Crescent, Condell Park,
NSW 2200, and in New Zealand by Transworld Publishers
(N.Z.) Ltd., Cnr. Moselle and Waipareira Avenues,
Henderson, Auckland.

Made and printed in Great Britain by
Hunt Barnard Printing Ltd., Aylesbury, Bucks.

To my agent and friend
Fiona Morrison

Acknowledgements

There are many people whom I would like to thank for their kindness in helping me with my research – most especially Mr Joseph Beltrami, who so generously gave of his time and expertise to authenticate the legal aspects of the story and the courtroom scene.

Part 1

INNOCENCE

CHAPTER ONE

Lorianna wondered how she could seduce Gavin. Was it right to go to him now with her dark brown hair piled up and secured with ivory combs? Was she looking her best in her enormous cartwheel hat festooned by two winged birds and posies of spring flowers to match the season? Would her elegance attract him as she paraded slowly along the path, her furled parasol piercing the soft earth? She hoped he would prefer her like this, silent and stately, her tightly laced corset emphasising her curves, forcing bosom forward and hips back under her violet velvet dress and short cape.

She paused for a moment to listen for the light clip-clop and heavy rattle of his horse and trap, but there was nothing; silence brooded over the lane, deeply rutted with carriage wheels, that led between Blackwood House and the Drumcross Road. It was as if the place had been forgotten by humanity and was now the sole domain of the animal world. The white tails of rabbits bobbed in and out of the hedgerows. A stoat with swift, stealthy movement scurried across her path. Birds flitted high over trees alive with darting squirrels. Butterflies like rainbow-coloured fans fluttered low.

Eventually the trees thinned out and it was possible to see some of the fields of the home farm on the left. Further on, where the lane met the Drumcross Road, there would be the signpost pointing right to the village of Littlegate and the market town of Bathgate further on at the foot of the hill. To the left the signpost pointed to Edinburgh.

For the moment Lorianna felt a reluctance to move from this silent forgotten place with the high beech hedges, the woodruff sparkling in damp places under the trees and everything sweet-smelling. Here she would like to make love with Gavin — here she would enjoy blending with nature. A vision came to excite her . . . She saw herself, hair unpinned and flowing wild around her face and body, her skirts enveloping him, sucking him into her. She revelled in the wave of sensuousness fanned by the animal movements around her and by the earthy smell of the place. With the sensuousness came the memory of the farm where she had spent her childhood. Great shaggy-fetlocked cart-horses stamped across her mind's eye, led by great shaggy men, walrus-moustached and walnut-skinned.

She forced herself to continue walking, the rustle of her taffeta petticoats dominating the silence. Reaching the crossroads at last, she gazed along the Drumcross Road shading her eyes with a white-gloved hand. There was no sign of anyone. She stood uncertain now of what to do, the cool breeze teasing the birds' wings on her hat making them quiver as if about to take off, and lifting her cape and gently ballooning it out. She was tempted to go on walking and only with difficulty managed to resist the temptation. It would only make Gavin angry with her. She had a regrettable streak in her nature which often pushed her beyond her limits of physical endurance. Her instincts were always to walk too far, even to run; to talk too much, to give too much, to try to please too much, to want to make love too often. As far as possible she controlled these instincts, but it was a constant uphill battle.

Lorianna's dignified elegance was a fragile shell through which harsh and desperate longings were forever struggling and all too often succeeding in smashing through. She envied the poise and serenity of her friends and their contented acceptance of their role as lady of the manor. She felt guilty and ashamed because she was not content with the quiet daily routine of her life. She knew she ought to feel grateful that she was so respected and cherished. From morning to night she was cosseted and tended like a fragile hot-house plant. Gemmell, her personal maid, opened the curtains in the morning and allowed the daylight into her bedroom. Then Gemmell helped her to sit up in bed and arranged the pillows to support her back before giving her a tray set with delicate fluted china. While she was sipping tea and nibbling wafer-thin pieces of bread and butter, the housemaid would attend to the fire so that the room would be warm and her clothes heated before she rose and dressed. Gavin – out of consideration for her, he said – slept in a bed in his dressing room. He would have risen earlier and now be downstairs in his study choosing the morning readings from the bible.

When she appeared downstairs to join him for prayers he would greet her with his usual polite, 'Good morning, my dear. You slept not too badly, I hope?' And she would murmur, 'Yes, thank you, dear.'

It was understood that she suffered from nervous restlessness which prevented her from sleeping.

After breakfast, when Gavin and Gilbert had left for the factory, the carriage would come round to take her on routine calls to other ladies in the area. Or they would arrive to pay calls on her. Either way, the time would be passed sipping tea and tutting over local gossip or discussing the latest fashions. Other than that there was absolutely nothing to do all day but embroidery and a little piano playing and singing to herself to practise these accomplishments.

All the time, a secret part of her rebelled, rioted recklessly about and was in constant danger of escaping. She terrified herself. The rawness of her emotions bewildered her and for self-protection she had acquired a habit of keeping her eyes modestly lowered. By looking directly at anyone she feared they might detect the wanton creature she was struggling so desperately to conceal and then she would be shamed.

11

Every morning at prayers she pleaded with God to purge her of her wicked longings and unladylike hungers. But God never answered her prayers and she was left to struggle alone with the traitor inside her. Today she had been fighting a losing battle. She could not bear to remain a moment longer at her embroidery in the sitting-room of Blackwood House. She wanted to scream out loud and crash the wretched frame into the fire, or lurch madly about the room sending all the silver-framed photographs flying from the tables and all the ornaments splintering to the floor. Yet she had nothing against the place. Indeed, what could be more pleasant than her large sunny sitting-room at the back of the house with its wide windows looking across the croquet lawn and fields to the distant shimmering waters of the Firth of Forth? Often she flung down her embroidery to gaze through Gavin's powerful binoculars at the ships passing on the Firth. Sometimes she found pleasure in this and dreamed of being whisked away on one of the ships to romantic faraway places where exciting and erotic adventures awaited her. But at other times, like today, watching the ships only increased her restlessness and frustration.

Lorianna sighed. If only Gavin would come . . . she wanted him. Her need stretched through her veins, tightened in the pit of her abdomen and tormented her with its lack of fulfilment. She could have doubled up and nursed herself in anguish with it as she had often done alone in bed.

In one of the fields across the road from where she stood, sheep slowly moved, heads down and intent on keeping the grass clipped neat. Around them lambs gambolled. In another field cows came ponderously jostling towards the fence in order to have a closer look at her. And still there was neither sight nor sound of Gavin! In the cows' field a great hawthorn tree, its many flowers making it look like a giant ball of snow, filled the air with exquisite perfume and increased her feeling of sensuousness until she could hardly endure it. Then faintly in the

12

distance she heard the scraping of horses' hooves and wooden wheels on the loose stones of the Drumcross Road. Her heart began to pound with confusion and distress as well as with passion. Gavin was a man of uncertain temper, a stern man, who might not take kindly to her coming to meet him like this and loitering at the crossroads like a common milkmaid. Nervously she retreated to the shelter of the high beeches. Blind now to the beauty of her surroundings, divorced from any sensitivity to the animals, she walked quickly; her velvet skirts brushed against the grass and bushes, caught on twigs and had to be jerked by hand and swished free. A fox, curled up asleep in a ditch under thick overhanging greenery, awakened at her passing and quickly disappeared.

But as the sounds of the approaching horse and trap came nearer Lorianna slowed her pace. It wouldn't do for Gavin to see her rushing either. He would consider it unbecoming and unladylike, as indeed she knew it was.

At last she stopped and turned to face him.

'Gavin, my dear! How fortunate to meet you. I was out for a stroll, but became somewhat fatigued I'm afraid.'

Without replying he put down his hand and helped her on to the seat beside him. As usual his silence made her feel more guilty than any words he might have said. With a clicking noise of his tongue and a jerk of the reins he set the horse in motion again. His silence was a reprimand.

She stole a glance at him. He was a thin, neat man with expressionless blue eyes behind gold-rimmed pince-nez, yet there was an anger about him that simmered continuously beneath his quiet manner.

As she sat beside him, aware of the heat of his body even through the velvet skirt and the taffeta petticoats, she was unsure whether it was fear or passion which made her pulse keep fluttering unevenly. He sat very straight, his legs together, his hands resting on the reins as he held them. The thigh nearest to her had a hypnotic effect as it moved to the jerky rhythm of the trap and eventually she slid her hand over it, at the same time glancing sideways at Gavin's face. She saw it tighten under his pointed red beard, but could not be sure if this was with passion or disapproval. She almost broke the silence by asking him how things had been at the factory, but stopped herself in time – he would only tell her that the factory was no concern of hers and there was nothing about it that she would understand.

What could she tell him about *her* day? It had been so dull! There had been no visitors and when she had called on Euphemia Argyl there had been no one at home and she had merely left her card and then returned to Black-wood House and her embroidery. How wearisome it had been. Nurse had taken Clementina out for the day, and Gavin's two sons by his previous marriage were away about their business. Gilbert managed the factory under his father's supervision and Malcolm was at university in Edinburgh where eventually he hoped to take a divinity degree.

Gavin's first wife, Kirsty had died of consumption when Gilbert was ten and Malcolm was nine, only a year older than Clementina was now. Once, on her way to school in Bathgate Academy, Lorianna had seen Kirsty sitting in this same carriage beside Gavin as she was sitting now. She still remembered the tiny shrunken figure, and the haunted look about the large, sad eyes.

A year after Kirsty's death and still barely more than a schoolgirl at sixteen, she had become Mrs Gavin Black-wood.

At the time, she had been almost as flattered and excited as her mother at such a wealthy man's attentions. And the thought of breaking free from parental restriction and being mistress of her own had proved a very attractive proposition.

Now, all too often she felt as she did today, that her life had become empty and hopeless. Yet it was spring. The sun was shining and life was stirring outside and everything was new and fresh.

'Is Gilbert still at work?' she murmured eventually.

'The least he can do is a full day at the factory. I seldom ask him to help me run the estate.'

Gavin had a solemn voice that would have suited a minister and she had noticed that already Malcolm was trying to copy it. Gavin would have made a good preacher; he was a very devout religious man, who regulated his household along strictly Christian lines. All the family and staff gathered early every morning for prayers which he led and each day he gave verses of the bible to study. He said she was much in need of self-discipline as well as a husband's firm hand and of course she agreed. She admired his strong character and his capacity for self-denial. Her weaknesses and unruly passions were a constant source of concern to them both and guilt forever dogged her heels. Ladies did not feel passion, Gavin said. Only low and vulgar women had sexual appetites.

Then the woods on either side of the road suddenly cleared and they were at the open gates of Blackwood House and speeding up the curving drive. At first the drive was like a country lane between meadows with grazing cattle. Then the trees closed in again. On the left a chestnut tree dipped towards a pool in the hollow formed by an old quarry. On the right a path led to the glade, thickly surrounded by rowans and hollies, lilacs and rhododendrons.

The drive curved round by the pool and there was the house with its two distinct periods of architecture: the tall, sturdy, sixteenth century tower house with its tiny slits for windows, and the two-storey wide-windowed extension built in the nineteenth century.

Gemmell, smart in her long black dress and frilly white apron and cap, had the door open for them both before Gavin had pulled the horse to a halt. Lorianna swept past her, into the tiled entrance hall, up the stone stairs, across the small landing, through the open doors with their stained-glass panels and into the reception hall. Gemmell pattered after her with skirts hitched and once through in

15

the bedroom divested her of cape and hat and gloves. She impatiently dismissed the maid, who seemed to be taking an excruciatingly long time to hang the cape in the wardrobe, smooth the gloves into a drawer and arrange the hat in its box. Lorianna felt she could never forgive Gemmel if the maid's lingering presence caused Gavin to go to the sitting-room or his study instead of coming to the bedroom. But just as the maid left, Gavin entered; it was then that she saw the maniacal fire in his eyes and knew she was afraid. She had forgotten what he could be like, perhaps because she had wanted to forget. It was nearly a year since they had made love and, like the pangs of childbirth, time had diminished the anguish of it.

Only her passion remained, growing gradually over the weeks and months like a torturous thirst that had to be assuaged. With fumbling fingers she unbuttoned the bodice of her dress and stepped out of it, then her petticoats, every now and again smiling across at her husband coquettishly and yet with an underlying shadow of timidity and apprehension in her eyes.

She wanted to plead with him to tell her he loved her. She longed for him to take time to be tender. She needed sweet words and caresses. But her pleas withered in her throat as Gavin came towards her and she saw something more like fury than love contorting his face.

'Oh Gavin, please don't hurt me,' she gasped as he knocked her back against the bed and came on top of her. 'Gavin . . .'

She opened her mouth, soft and yielding, but he immediately savaged it with teeth and tongue. His hands were hard and bruising too and, gasping now and giving high-pitched moans, she tensed against them, struggling to protect herself from injury in her softest and most vulnerable places. Soon in mindless turmoil as Gavin's brute force and animal grunts became wilder, her passion disintegrated to his animal level. They became like a couple of wild beasts, writhing and growling and squealing and groaning until she was rampaged into an

16

orgasm that left her sick and exhausted. But Gavin went on and on without mercy. All the time it was as if he was punishing her rather than making love to her, until she was sobbing and then crying out in pain. His hand immediately clamped over her mouth, silencing her as her agony continued. Eventually she must have fainted, because when she opened her eyes he had gone. She lay for a long time with waves of pain tumbling over her, drowning in hopelessness.

She sat up and began to weep. Surely love wasn't meant to be like this? Surely every married woman didn't suffer the torture that she did? Weeks or even months of enforced chastity, then this agonising experience! She longed to ask someone, but her mother was dead and in any case had never spoken of such things except to impress on her the superiority of men, especially one's husband and how it was a wife's duty to concur with her husband's wishes at all times. On her wedding day her mother had drawn her aside and said, 'There's just one thing I must tell you, Lorianna. Remember, whatever Gavin does to you is *right*.'

No one discussed the more intimate aspects of marriage and the secrecy made the intimate experience all the more bewildering and distressing.

Love and marriage, it seemed, bore no resemblance to the romantic novels she had read with such wistful eagerness. Even the most shocking of these had not prepared her for the brutality and physical pain of love. And yet she needed physical passion, her body kept crying out for it. She felt trapped in confusion and uncertainty. In a fever of pain and unhappiness she struggled from the bed and, oblivious of her torn underwear and tangled hair, went over to the window. Still sobbing, she pressed her burning cheeks against the cool glass, until suddenly she became aware of someone watching her from outside. Down in the garden at the side of the house stood the tall figure of the grieve, Robert Kelso. He supervised the Blackwood home farm and grounds and she had seen him occasionally striding across meadow or field, his hair glistening like a raven's wing and his skin as smooth and brown as leather. They had never spoken and she had never looked him in the eye, but now their eyes locked for a minute – his grey and thoughtful and questioning, hers anguished. Then, more distraught than ever, she shrank away from the window and hid her face in her hands.

CHAPTER TWO

'Give us strength, O Lord,' Gavin's solemn voice intoned, 'to fight against our baser impulses.'

He leaned against the gilt marble mosaic table as if he had all the world's sin on his shoulders and was bowed down by it. Before him in the reception hall, heads lowered, were two lines of servants. Mrs Musgrove, the housekeeper, stood stiff-backed with hands folded in front of her long black skirts. They were big hands, with only the fingers showing from the black silk mittens she always wore.

Beside her Mrs Prowse, the cook, at forty-five looked at least ten years younger than Mrs Musgrove although there was, in fact, only five years between them. Despite the rolls of fat she carried about, Mrs Prowse was energetic and merry-eyed. She had such a capacity for getting the most out of life in all its aspects, but especially those concerning men, that Mrs Musgrove had to continuously lay down the law and lecture her about proper behaviour and her duty to show a good example to younger members of staff. Mrs Musgrove, who had been jilted many years ago, had such a hatred of men that she refused to work in any establishment where there were male members of staff. She only managed to be icily polite to Jacobs, the coachman or to Robert Kelso, the grieve who managed the home farm, because they were not house staff and she seldom saw them. The gardeners and the farm workers she completely ignored except when she had to instruct the head gardener as to the fruit and vegetables she wished brought into the house.

She would have preferred also to icily ignore the head of Blackwood House; this not being possible, however, she avoided laying her sharp, snappy eyes on him whenever she could. This morning she at least approved of the theme of his prayer and the text for the day, which was Romans VIII, verse 6: 'To be carnally minded, is Death.' She felt sure his prayer and text were aimed at Mrs Prowse and hoped the disgusting woman would take Mr Blackwood's words to heart. She could never bring herself, even in her thoughts, to use the words 'the Master'. No man was fit to be *her* master. Men were lower than animals, cunning, devious, heartless, faithless, disgusting, despicable creatures.

Little Mrs Henning, the nurse – 'Henny' to her small charge – kept stealing proud and affectionate glances at Clementina from beneath lowered lashes. She adored the child, despite the fact that she found the little girl's precociousness and wild tomboy ways a constant source of anxiety. At the moment Clementina was dutifully standing next to her mother, who was sitting beside the table. She was an engaging, perky child with eyes of the most startling emerald green and at eight years of age it was already obvious that she had the makings of a beautiful woman. Not the same dark-haired, smouldering-eyed beauty of her mother; Clementina had a luxurious mop of hair like polished amber that softly framed her face, loosely curled at the ends over her shoulders and looked quite exquisite against her green satin ribbons. The brown long-sleeved dress she wore was protected by a white muslin dress-pinafore frilled at the shoulder and hem and tied at the waist by a broad green satin ribbon which exactly matched the narrow hair ribbons.

Mrs Henning was suffering agonies of pride and suspense, her pride in Clementina spilling over into the only pride she had of herself. A gentle-eyed woman who had originated from an Edinburgh orphanage, she had never quite got over her incredible good fortune in not only obtaining the position as nanny in Blackwood House but also having as her charge such an adorable infant who was now fast growing into a very special young lady. Mrs Henning would challenge anyone (and often did) to show her any child in the whole of the Lothians, including Edinburgh – indeed in the whole of Scotland – so quick, so clever, so stunningly beautiful, as *her* young lady.

Her suspense arose from fear that Clementina might become restless and say or do something which other people, particularly her father, might not appreciate or understand. The master, Mrs Henning felt, was cruelly severe on the poor child and totally lacking in understanding. She closed her eyes and silently prayed, not the master's prayer – which, by the by, she regarded as quite unsuitable for eight-year-old ears – but one of her own: 'Dear, dear Miss Clementina, stand still, please do! Don't dig at the carpet with the toe of your shoe. And please, oh please, no matter how scratchy your petticoats are, don't tug them about or lift them up to examine underneath!'

Standing next to Mrs Henning, bulbous eyes reverently closed, stood Gemmell, Lorianna's personal maid. She was dreaming of Robert Kelso and wondering if he would call at the big house today or if she would see him on her way home this afternoon. It was her afternoon off, when she always went home to visit her parents in the village and made a point of making a detour past the farm buildings – a very long detour, because the farm was actually in the opposite direction.

In the evening she sometimes went to the Picturedrome in Bathgate or to the dancing class. She lived in hope that she would meet Robert Kelso in Bathgate but so far this had never happened. She would never forget, however, dancing with him at the Christmas party at Blackwood House. The sensation of being held in his arms was as vivid and exciting now, months later, as it had been at the time. She still felt the hard whipcord muscles and the musky-male smell of him clung in her nostrils. She remembered the strange feeling of having him close against her, yet knowing he was not really there at all. His grey eyes, when he was unaware he was being observed, had a distant look as if he was thinking about someone else, but as soon as he became conscious that she was watching his face he looked down at her and smiled, his eyes like slivers of silver set deep under black brows. Polly Gemmell shivered with delight at the memory of that silver stare. She dare not tell her mother and father of her interest in the grieve, because her father worked under Kelso and found him a hard task-master. 'The iron man', he called him and, like the other farm labourers, waited to be spoken to, never daring to speak to him first. Awesome tales about his work capacity, strength and endurance ran rife. Her father with his own eyes had seen the grieve lift down a plough from a farm cart single-handed. Kelso had the strength of an ox and could tackle any of the work better than his men could when he had a mind to, but it was not that which kept them in awe of him and forced them to work like slaves at his bidding; it was the sheer force of will that the grieve possessed, from which her father was glad to escape to his one-room cottage in the village as often as he could. He would never even consider the idea of Kelso as a prospective son-in-law — horseman Murdo McGregor was her parents' choice and Murdo wanted her. Her mother said, 'This'll be your last chance. You're twenty-eight. An old maid already!' She didn't want to end her days as a dried-up old spinster, but at the same time she felt she was made for better things than sharing the rest of her life with the coarse ruddy-faced, bushy-moustached Murdo McGregor.

Robert was in a different class from Murdo and his tall athletic build and strength had won him every prize at the annual Highland Games for the Blackwood Estate. To see him throwing the hammer and tossing the caber was a magnificent sight. His shoulder muscles looked especially powerful, sloping up his neck and shortening it. Once she had spied on him as he swam in the river, shockingly naked. She would never forget those rippling muscles, the hard, flat stomach and smooth brown skin.

22

A deep sigh crackled the starched bib of her apron and caused Ella Baxter, the head housemaid, to steal a sly glance round at her. It was as much as she could do to suppress a giggle. Polly Gemmell would be sighing over Robert Kelso. She never stopped talking about him and obviously fancied her chances. Polly had quite a tip for herself and imagined she was a cut above the rest — God knows why, she was nothing much to look at with her long nose, bulbous eyes and frizzy hair which she fought to smooth with a dripping-wet comb before securing it with pins and covering it with her cap. They didn't need to wear a cap with their morning blue cotton dresses and aprons, only with their formal black from lunchtime onwards. But Polly Gemmell was never without a cap, or of course a hat when she went out. She always made sure it was a brimmed hat and wore it flat on top of her head with never a curl nor a wisp showing at the front. But no matter how tightly she pinned her hair back into some semblance of a bun, it soon straggled out like the stuffing from a horsehair sofa. She was always longing surreptitiously to tuck stray wisps back from the front of her ears and up from the nape of her neck.

Ella shifted her feet and her weight to a more comfortable position and prayed that the master would not take much longer. He did go on so — he was worse than the minister! She didn't much like the look of him either, with his pale blue eyes blinking behind his pince-nez and the way he fussed with his little red goatee beard. His son Gilbert, also red-haired, was just as unprepossessing, she thought, only taller and with a moustache.

The mistress looked as pale and delicate as a lady should. Her eyes were lowered at the moment. Sometimes they seemed a strange tawny colour; at other times they just looked dark brown like her hair. Now *her* hair was the kind that Polly Gemmell would dearly love to have, thick and satiny and long enough to sit on when it was brushed out.

Polly Gemmell said it was all very well for her of

23

course. 'If my hair got the care and attention hers gets, mine would look like that as well.' She said the same thing about the mistress's creamy skin and her shapely figure. 'It's all very well for her!' was one of Polly's favourite gripes.

Behind the senior staff were grouped the nursery-maid, the second housemaid, the under-housemaid, the kitchen-maid and the scullery-maid. Other staff like the coach-man, the grieve, the gardeners and the farmworkers had cottages on the estate (of which the village of Littlegate was part) and didn't come to the house for prayers. Nor did the two laundry-women.

At last the 'Amen' sighed across the top of their heads, releasing them from boredom but not escape until the master and Mr Gilbert and the mistress had disappeared into the dining-room for breakfast. After breakfast the mistress would go into the high-ceilinged sitting-room with its red wall-hangings offset by oyster and ivory paintwork, and have her daily discussion with the house-keeper. The master and Mr Gilbert usually went into the oak room to finish reading their newspapers and enjoy the first cigar of the day before leaving for the factory.

All the main apartments and the main bedrooms either led directly from the reception hall or the corridor off it. The other apartments were situated in the tower house and were reached by a spiral staircase off one side of the hall but hidden by an oak door. At the opposite side of the hall a long corridor eventually reached the library. Along this corridor all the staff crowded, then filed through the doorway (past the dining-room) that led down another stone stairway to the kitchen premises and staff bedrooms. But Mrs Henning, Tait the nursery-maid and of course little Clementina bustled away towards the tower stair at the very top of which were the nurseries.

Both the spiral stairs to the nurseries at the top of the tower house and the stairs down to the rabbit warren of domestic quarters at ground floor and basement level had to be trod with great caution. There was no lighting at all

24

during the day and at night there were only tiny oil-lamps flickering at alternate twists of the spiral up to the tower and only candles downstairs to the domestic quarters. This meant one dark curve to be essayed by groping hands and feet, then one faintly lit curve quickly dousing into darkness again, as cautious steps shuffled round and round, up and up, or descended down and down.

Lorianna seldom visited the downstairs part of the house more than once a year, when she and Gavin graced the servants' party for a brief half hour. The party was held in the servants' hall situated underneath the library, but she preferred to go out of the house and enter by the yard door at the side rather than risk the steep spiral in her long dress and train. For the same reason she seldom went up to the nursery, preferring to have Mrs Henning or Tait bring Clementina to the sitting-room each evening for her bedtime story and good-night kiss.

Mrs Musgrove she also saw in the big bow-windowed sitting-room, where each morning they discussed the menus for the day and any other household business. There were seldom any domestic crises to warrant her personal attention, for the housekeeper was a very capable woman who ensured that no ripples disturbed the smooth and efficient running of the house. She was aware, of course, that Mrs Musgrove disapproved of Cook, but as Mrs Prowse produced excellent, mouth-watering food which gave Blackwood House such a good reputation for dinner parties, Lorianna did not take her objections too seriously.

Usually she checked Gavin's dressing-room and his wardrobe to make sure that everything had been properly cleaned, his clothes laundered and pressed and in good repair. It was Lorianna's one domestic worry that Mrs Musgrove might allow or condone some neglect of Gavin, for she had a regrettable idiosyncrasy about men. The mere mention of a man – any man – caused her nose to pinch in and the little muscles round her mouth to tighten. At the best of times she was a severe and daunting-looking woman with her straight black hair sleeked tightly down from its centre parting and pinned in a bun at the nape of her neck. Her skin was sallow and rather coarse, her eyes as black as her dress and mittens.

Lorianna, as if afraid that Gavin might – despite her conscientious scrutiny and care – feel in any way neglected, made other special efforts on his behalf too. On long winter evenings she knitted his socks; she kept a secret supply of collar studs in case he lost any and an emergency arose; she took special cognisance of his preferences in food and saw that his likes and dislikes were always accommodated.

The only other household task for which she took special responsibility was the floral arrangements. She did all the floral arranging for the house, even gathering the flowers herself which could be a long and arduous job considering the number of flowers required. Gavin said that to do the job herself was a typically extravagant gesture and quite unnecessary – surely one of the maids could bring her all the flowers she needed? But Lorianna loved going out with her flat wicker basket to gather lupins, dahlias, roses, antirrhinums, calendulas and delphiniums – whatever was in perfect bloom in its season. It was not easy to crouch or bend in her stiff corset, but she managed this with elegance and grace. Yet all the time in her imagination she was running free of all restrictions, the blood coursing warmly through her body and her hair streaming loose in the wind. And it seemed only in a dream that she sedately moved about, ignoring the raging hunger inside her as if it never existed.

After she had gathered the flowers, a sheet would be spread on top of the grand piano or on one of the sideboards and she would spend a pleasant hour or more constructing extravagant pyramids and peacock-tail fans of flowers. In summer sweet peas were her favourite and she would create enormous sun-bursts of them, their colours radiating from deepest pink to rose to mauve to purple to blue – scenting every room of Blackwood

House with their dreamy sweetness.

Gavin was always guarded in his compliments to her lest she might be encouraged to let loose her baser impulses, but she had heard him speak with pride to admiring guests about her talent for flower arrangements. She found it very touching when he boasted about her; it helped her to forgive other aspects of their relationship which she found so bewildering and distressing.

Her husband believed that 'coupling', as he called it, was only for the purpose of creating children, and that carried out for any other reason it was not only a weakness but a wicked indulgence. They should be pure in the eyes of God, not defiled by selfish lusts. It worried her terribly because she could see that he too had a desperate struggle to contain his passions and when, through what he deemed weakness, they spilled over, he was afterwards racked with guilt and regret and spent many anguished hours at the praying stool in his dressing-room. He knelt there, his arms leaning on the heavy oak support carved like a miniature pulpit around the stool, his head lowered over his arms, his fingers arching and twisting together as he muttered prayers. Often he wept. But she dare not approach him or try to comfort him, in case her touch or nearness or even her sympathetic words might be misinterpreted and put a further strain on him and his terrible struggle with himself.

After one of these spells they would gradually settle down to their normal routine again: he shut away every night in his dressing-room, she alone in the big four-poster bed; he at one side of the dining-room table or the sitting-room fire, she at the other. Everything indeed would become quite civilised and pleasant once more. Gavin and Gilbert would talk about the running of the factory or the estate and, while her head was bent over the canvas of her embroidery, she would listen. Sometimes if Malcolm was at home she would chat with him, or the four of them would enjoy a game of whist. Often they entertained in the evening and sometimes in the

27

afternoons she called on friends or had visitors call for tea.

Days, weeks, months would pass in this way, but with only a surface pleasantness and peaceful contentment. Secretly, passion would be burning through her body again, stronger and stronger as if some tormenting devil had taken possession of her and was playing havoc with her very blood and bones. Then it became a pain nagging mercilessly at the base of her abdomen, pulsating, stretching and aching deep within; a madness from which she had to find release.

Yet she had begun to dread the consummation of her passion, taking the ultimate assault on her body as a punishment for her wickedness. In an effort to cool her thoughts and refresh her spirits she had acquired the habit of enjoying walks in the garden and grounds, sometimes covering considerable distances and purposely tiring herself so that she would no longer be able to feel anything but exhaustion.

Now she wandered into the sitting-room after morning prayers and looked up Gavin's text for the day: 'For to be carnally minded is death; but to be spiritually minded is life and peace. Because the carnal mind is enmity against God.'

Dutifully she read the words over and over again, sincerely indeed, desperately trying to make them sink into her mind and soul in order that she would be purged and cleansed of all wickedness. But all too soon her attention began to wander and her eyes drifted round the room, across to the pink silk damask sofa and beyond it on the opposite wall to the huge cabinet displaying Gavin's collection of Blue John urns and ornaments. Then her gaze drifted round to the painted Sheraton secretaires on either side of the fire; to the oyster silk chairs and the leather chairs with their rich reddish glow; the variety of tables — some in rosewood, some in oak — scattered around, some cluttered with brass candlesticks and bric-à-brac, some with framed photographs. The heavy, gilt-framed mirror

28

above the marble mantelpiece reflected the scene, including the crystal, many-candled chandelier hanging from the mushroom-coloured ceiling.

Lorianna's wistful face turned to survey the window and the great expanse of lawn. It was too early in the day for the languid crack of the croquet mallet against a ball. All was still and silent outside except the swifts speeding through the sky in screaming groups before swerving up under the eaves. She longed to speed with them, noisy and free. Suddenly, for no apparent reason, she felt like weeping but was saved from doing so by hearing the rustle of bombasine and sensing the chilling presence of the housekeeper.

Sometimes Lorianna wondered where the custom had originated that senior women servants had to be known as 'Mistress' whether or not they were married. And usually, like Mrs Musgrove, they were not. It seemed especially inappropriate and incongruous in her case, for surely no man had ever come within touching distance of this tight-lipped, cold-eyed creature with a spine like a steel rod. She was carrying her usual maroon hard-covered notebook with its matching pencil, attached by a narrow black tape to the chatelaine round her waist. They discussed the day's luncheon and dinner menus and then as usual went to inspect Gavin's dressing-room and check through all his things, except of course his writing set where he kept his personal letters and the diary he meticulously wrote in every night. This task was one that made Mrs Musgrove bristle with icy spikes, but her attitude only succeeded in making Lorianna all the more conscientious.

'These windows look somewhat cloudy,' she pointed out now. 'They should be sparkling.'

'I'll inform Baxter immediately, madam.'

'Goodness, is that a broken bootlace? Have that replaced at once! And inform the housemaids, Mrs Musgrove, that I will not have the master inconvenienced or neglected.'

'Very well, madam.'

The inspection over, Lorianna allowed Mrs Musgrove to go about her business in whatever way she wished, for she never interfered in any other sphere of the housework. There was never any need – Mrs Musgrove kept everything running with admirable smoothness.

After the housekeeper had left, Lorianna forced herself to stitch at her embroidery until she could have screamed with boredom. Time seemed to move so slowly. After a while she moved through to the library and wrote some letters at the flat-topped desk. Then she put them on the hall table for the maid to post. Gavin seldom came home for lunch; he usually ate something with Gilbert in the Dreadnought Hotel in Bathgate and returned home during the afternoon. So she lunched alone at the big round table in a dining-room dark with oak-panelling, in which were hung black and brown and green Flemish verdure tapestries. Afterwards she rang for Gemmell, who helped her to change into a white and black striped dress, nipped in at her tiny waist, which flounced out wide from a black velvet band from knees to floor. The dress was topped by a short-bodiced black jacket with a high neck and long sleeves, trimmed with black velvet.

'I think the pink straw hat, Gemmell,' she murmured, slowly turning with hands on hips in front of the mirror.

The hat had a wavy brim with a cluster of white roses and green leaves under it at the front. Black velvet bows decorated the crown. Gemmell pinned the colourful creation on her thick nest of hair, then enquired, 'Your pink parasol, madam?'

'Yes, it's the same shade as my hat.'

Again she surveyed herself in the mirror. How dark and luminous her eyes were, too large and emotional-looking for her otherwise small, even features and pearly skin.

'Ah well,' she said without enthusiasm. 'Now I'm ready to take the air.' As her skirts swished across the reception hall and down the stairs, she decided she would stroll by the home farm. Some of her happiest memories were of farm life when she was a child and now, more than ever, she needed to seek the comfort of her roots.

CHAPTER THREE

Because of narrow tower windows, the nursery was shadowy even during the day. Light arrowed in, leaving dark corners and misty patches. It flickered spasmodically on stone walls and bare wood floors and across the faded drugget in front of the fire, spotlighting the dancing dust on the round table and the stools and chairs. The white clothes closet and toy cupboard were ambered with it.

The day nursery, like the night nursery, was a spartan room bare of curtains, cushions or pictures. Gavin Blackwood had always believed that nursery discipline should be based on the evangelical sense of sin, maintaining that his children must be repressed, corrected, withheld by all means from temptation. He insisted that it was dangerous to provide children with luxuries to foster their vanity, to gratify their carnal desires. So the nursery food was plain and not always palatable, a cold bath every day was the rule except on Friday when a hot bath was allowed. Hard chairs were for forcing Clementina to sit upright. He ordered that the child should have lessons every day instead of games. Hymns had to be learned by heart, also the text for each day and several verses from the bible.

Once a week – on a Sunday evening – her father tested her by asking her questions not only on religion but also on arithmetic, spelling and nature study. Henny dreaded the day approaching every week, but Clementina seldom thought of the ordeal until it was almost upon her and she was led by a shivering Henny down and down, round and round the dark spiral stairs. Then, hand in hand, they crossed the reception hall with its wool mosaic pictures, chiming clock and Blue John urns. Along the narrow corridor they went in anguished silence, with not a glance at the clutter of pictures crowding the walls on either side. Eventually they reached the library, corridor-shaped itself but wider and book-lined, with the portion at the far end jutting out at the bay window like a separate small room. It was here on one of the big greyish-green plush armchairs that the fiery-haired figure of her father awaited Clementina. Her heart immediately raced with apprehension at the sight of him, a mixture of desperation to please and fear that she would not.

But it was not Sunday yet and after lessons at the round table had been completed and inky fingers scrubbed in the wash-bowl which was left for Alice Tait the nursery-maid to empty, Clementina accompanied Henny downstairs. After pausing for a few moments to listen at the door to make sure there was no one about, they slipped out and across the hall to the stained-glass-topped doors that opened on to the carpetless stairs. Clementina raced down to the entrance hall with Henny hurrying after her in twittering agitation. To open the big front door was always a struggle, but Clementina managed it and escaped outside before Henny could catch her. It was not that she wanted to escape from the nurse; just that she was so impatient to enjoy the freedom of the gardens and grounds, although she was careful not to tumble about on the grass or try to climb trees until she was some distance from the house in case her mother or father might see her. Not that her mother ever beat her, but her father did quite frequently and she could see it upset her mother who always tried to restrain him but when she failed – as she invariably did – she ran from the room. Afterwards, as Clementina lay sobbing on Henny's arms in the nursery, they would hear mother playing beautiful music on the piano and Henny said that was her way of comforting her daughter.

Clementina hesitated outside the front door, hopping

from one foot to the other, petticoats ballooning out. She was unsure whether to fly straight ahead to the pond or further away to the bluebell woods, or to the left towards the stables and the dairy and the home farm. Or she could race right round the house to the back where she could have fun with the croquet mallets or play hide-and-seek with Henny among the high rhododendron bushes.

Or perhaps she could persuade Henny to take her to the village. She loved that most of all, because there were more children to play with there. Sometimes she managed to hide from Henny and then escape with some of the boys to their secret place in the Littlegate woods near the village. There was an oak tree there which they used as one of their hide-outs; it had a hole in its giant trunk and quite a few children could squeeze in. The boys hadn't wanted to play with her at first, far less show her their secret hideout, and she had had to prove that she wasn't 'soft' like other 'stupid girls'. This she did by giving Sandy Campbell a black eye that sent him howling home to his mother. In any game, no matter how tough, she was never knocked down. No matter who thumped her or bumped her, she stood four-square, as firm as a rock and always ready to use her little sharp teeth, or fists or feet as weapons. The sons of the local farm workers, or blacksmith, joiner, shepherd or carter came to respect her despite her fancy clothes and satin hair bows, and the fact that she came from the big house.

'Can we go to the village, Henny?' She swished back her hair and gazed wide-eyed at the nanny, knowing full well how much Henny adored her and seldom could refuse her anything. 'Please, please?'

Henny nibbled at her nails in wretched indecision. 'You'll play with the village children and get all dirty and dishevelled. Oh dear, it's just that I don't want you to get into trouble, you see. If the master or mistress saw you . . .'

'How will they see me?' Clementina scoffed. 'They never go to the village. Please, Henny?'

34

She didn't say she would try not to get dirty or that she'd not play with the village children. She had at times what some of the staff of Blackwood House were forced to regard as a regrettable streak of stubborn honesty. Many a black look and beating it got her and anyone below stairs who loved her prayed that she would grow out of it.

'All right,' Henny capitulated, still anxious-eyed. 'But you will learn something on the way, won't you, Miss Clementina?'

It was Henny's way, unknown to the master of Blackwood House, to teach lessons as a game or at least to make them as pleasing and informal as possible.

'Oh Henny, I love you!' Clementina flung herself at the nurse and hugged her round a waist which any high-born lady might have envied. Henny was not pretty – it was Lorianna's policy, something shared by most of her friends, that one should never employ a pretty servant if it could be avoided – but the nurse had a certain delicacy of appearance with her brown hair softly waving back into a bun and her gentle brown eyes and birdlike features. She was tiny, half-child, half-woman, it seemed.

She patted Clementina's head and was immediately worried because she had forgotten the child's straw hat. Before she could announce that they ought to go back for it, Clementina had darted away down the drive like a sturdy little bird, white pinafore flapping. Henny fluttered breathlessly after her.

'Nature study. Nature study, Miss Clementina!'

Clementina came skipping back with the same stiff bounciness she had when dancing. At a children's ball at a neighbouring mansion she had been the most beautiful child there, but even Henny had to admit – only to herself of course – that she danced with as much grace as an awkward young foal. But she had not the slightest doubt that Clementina would grow into a most graceful young woman.

'Nature study, nature study!' Clementina sang.

'Isn't it a lovely lovely time of the year, Miss Clementina? Remember Mr Wordsworth –

Then sing ye birds, sing, sing a joyous song
And let the young lambs bound as to the tabor's sound
We in thought will join your throng . . .'

Clementina, skipping at the nurse's side now, joined in,

'Ye that pipe and ye that play
Ye that through your hearts today
Feel the gladness of the May.'

'You remember!' Henny was delighted. 'What a clever girl!'

They veered a little to the right, tempted to go round the other side of the pond to inspect again the moorhen's nest they had seen on the stump of an alder tree just out of reach of the bank. The nest had been neatly put together with sticks and dead reeds and had contained one egg.

Already Henny was hitching up her skirts and picking her way through the long dewy grass, but Clementina tugged her back to the drive. 'You promised, Henny.'

The nurse straightened her straw boater with one hand after it had been tipped slightly askew by Clementina's jerky enthusiasm.

'Don't you remember the nest, dear?'

'There are nests in the hedges further down.'

'Oh well . . .' Henny's face peeked up under the straw brim. 'Ah yes . . . Mr Browning . . .

Hedgerows all alive,
With birds and gnats and large white butterflies
Which look as if the Mayflower had caught life
And palpitated forth upon the wind.'

Back on the drive, Clementina began skipping again.

'Oh dear, oh dear, what energy you have, child! But it's not very ladylike, is it? What would your mother say? She's so graceful and elegant and proper and . . .'

'Butterflies!' The little girl was not much interested in her mother. She seldom saw her – just for a half-hour or so each day in the sitting-room or drawing-room and more often than not there were other people there including her father and it was something of an ordeal, especially if the half-hour stretched to an hour. Mother was nice, of course. She had a nice smile and soft hands and she smelled of rose-petals. When she thought about it, which she didn't very often, she supposed she quite liked her mother. But she loved Henny.

Henny put a finger to her mouth and they both tiptoed stealthily across to where the butterflies were busily gathered as if for a gossip under the trees.

'Speckled wood butterflies,' Henny said, peering forward. 'See how the broken sunlight matches the pattern of their wings?'

There had been a heavy shower earlier and the trees were still dripping. Drops of water rainbowed by the sun plopped to the ground every now and again, making the wild forget-me-nots suddenly quiver. Rain still glistened on the russet backs of cows as they munched contentedly, and the rich odour of rain-moistened cowpats filled the nostrils.

Out through the big iron gates at the end of the drive now and along the dirt road with the giant beeches on either side, Henny and Clementina proceeded with little hurrying spurts and leisurely stops.

Sometimes Henny would put her finger to her mouth and her brown eyes would widen. Clementina would hunch up her shoulders conspiratorially and listen with Henny to the purr-purr of the turtle-dove through the thick hedges. Or they would watch young blackbirds and song thrushes hopping under bushes, beaks wide, desperately calling out to be fed.

Out at the crossroads at last and over to the Dumcross

Road, with rabbits getting up on their hind legs, and with cocked ears and two dainty forefeet hanging in the air, listening and watching suspiciously, ready if necessary to dart quickly into their holes. The road was coggly with loose stones and more than one person had gone down on their ankle here, only saved from serious injury by strong lacing or button-up boots. A white dust covered the grassy verge on either side and Henny said that was caused by the men who broke up the stones to throw on the road.

The Littlegate woods at last! A mysterious green and shady place with firs and sycamores, beeches and oaks. Clementina said it was like being under the sea and Henny giggled. 'Under the sea!' She had a habit of echoing everything clever or imaginative that Clementina said with incredulous admiration.

The little girl was in her element now, darting around trees, jumping up with arms high, fingers grasping at branches, sometimes catching a low one and wildly swinging. Henny stumbled about after her with a mixture of hilarity and terror.

'Only little monkeys do that! Oh, Miss Clementina, look, your pinafore's caught. It's all right, dear, I'll loosen it. There we are! But careful, careful now. You don't want to tear it, do you? Oh, Miss Clementina, little ladies don't do that! What are you doing now . . .' Suddenly she gave a shriek, snatched up her skirts and ran back to the path. Clementina had found a dead mouse and was holding it up by the tail, examining it with interest.

'It's dead, Henny. It can't hurt you. You told me dead things can't hurt anyone. You said it was just sad when . . .'

'Yes . . . yes, dear. I know mice are really harmless little creatures and couldn't hurt anyone even when alive. Silly old Henny doesn't know why they make her shiver, but they do. So please put it down, Miss Clementina.'

'I think we should bury it.'

'No . . . no, just throw it away, oh please do!'

'They buried Grandmother when she was dead.'

Hysterical laughter bubbled up in Henny's throat. 'They buried Grandmother!'

'But they *did*!'

'I know, dear, but a mouse is a rather different matter, don't you think?'

'No!'

'Anyway, you've nothing to dig with.'

'I can dig holes with my fingers. See . . .'

'No, no, please!' Henny pleaded. 'You'll get so fearfully dirty. I know! Just lay it down and cover it with leaves and twigs. They do that sort of thing in other countries. Not every country buries its dead. No. No, there are lots of different customs and practices. Of course there are.'

Already Clementina was hunkered down, knees splayed wide in a most unladylike way, enthusiastically scrabbling about for leaves and twigs. 'Will that do, Henny?'

The nurse peered cautiously forward, holding on to her hat with one hand and her skirts with the other as if in readiness to run.

'I'm sure that's very appropriate and proper. Yes . . . very proper.'

'Now we must say a prayer.'

Really, Henny thought in helpless exasperation, yet with hysterical laughter not far away. Miss Clementina was a most . . . a most . . . she searched for a word that would not be disloyal . . . a most amusing child.

'I . . . I . . . don't know. It could be impious.'

'What's impious?'

'Wanting in respect for God.'

'I don't understand.'

'You know . . . using God's words to . . . to . . . bless a mouse.'

'But God made it, didn't he?'

'Yes, but . . .'

'Well, it must be all right.'

39

Still down on her haunches, Clementina put her hands together and squeezed her eyes tight shut.

'Our Father which made this mouse, show it the way to heaven, for Jesus' sake. Amen.'

Then she sprang up and went loping along the path with Henny trotting in her wake.

Sunshine was shafting through the trees as they approached the village end of the woods, bathing everything in shimmering gold. Henny's high tremulous voice sang out:

'From the Welsh of Dafydd ap Gwillym –
An angel mid the woods of May
Embroidered it with radiance gay –
That gossamer with gold bedight
Those fires of God – those gems of light.'

Clementina had found a stick and was prodding at something. Too late Henny saw that it was a wasps' nest and as she ran forward, a vicious explosion of wasps sent Clementina screaming away. Ignoring the wasps, Henny flung her wide skirts around the child, covering her and holding her protectively close as they ran together out of the woods and along the grassy path through the fields. They ran until, conscious that the angry buzzing had stopped, Henny stopped too and uncovered her small charge.

'They're gone now. There's nothing to be afraid of, nothing at all! Are you all right, dear?'

Clementina looked pale but stubborn. 'I wasn't afraid.'

'But sometimes it's only sensible to be afraid.'

'I *wasn't*.'

'If you met a lion for example, you would, anyone would – be afraid. It would be perfectly proper.'

'I'd fight the lion until it was frightened and *it* ran away. It would not frighten *me*.'

She tossed her hair and it caught the sun and became for a magic moment like shining sunlight itself, before she went clambering over a wooden stile with a flash of woollen stockings and frills at the knees of her knickers. Then she was away, defiantly skipping towards the village.

It was only then that Henny became aware not only of the pain of wasp stings, but of another more alarming pain. It took her breath away and she had to sit down on the stile. There, hidden by the long grass, she clasped at her chest and struggled to gulp in air.

'Henny, Henny, where are you? I don't want to play at hide-and-seek.'

Recognising the undercurrent of fearful uncertainty in the child's voice, Henny immediately rose up and, despite her agony, called back. 'It's all right, Miss Clementina. Everything's all right. I'm here!'

CHAPTER FOUR

Lorianna was acutely, pleasurably conscious of silk whispering over her skin as she walked, caressing and fondling it. She had had her dressmaker fashion several Japanese silk lace-trimmed chemises, camisoles, drawers and petticoats, preferring always to have the sensual softness rubbing against her. She could then suffer the tightly laced corset and the cotton petticoats before donning the top skirt of taffeta needed to give a smooth base for her gown and make the delightful rustling, swishing noise every time she moved.

The sun was shining as she picked her way carefully along the grassy path, earth-ridged by cart-wheels. She decided she didn't need the protection of her parasol, because the trees and bushes afforded enough shade although they kept opening to reveal fields of waving grass or stiffening corn, and rolling meadows lemon-dotted with dandelions and buttercups.

A breeze softly hissed and sighed through the branches of the trees, approaching and receding like the sea. The farm was visible now beyond the meadow with a great hawthorn tree roofing the grass underneath, making it a darker, moister green in the pool of shadow.

The farmhouse, built of solid grey stone with walls three feet thick, sat sturdily in front of a cluster of out-houses. There were stables for the horses, barns for the hay, sheds for the farm wagons and byres for the sheep and cattle. And a little further away past some bushes were the hen-houses.

The sight of the place so similar to the farm of her

childhood — except that her farmhouse home had been much bigger — awakened vivid memories in Lorianna. Memories of still, shadowy places suddenly bursting into life with hens or cockerels flying out from dark corners, a herd of mooing cows crowding in for milking; a pair of buzzards circling slowly in the sky, distant from each other but communicating with sharp vibrant cries. She had been happy then, waking up in her sunny bedroom to the sound of the cock crowing loud and near and knowing that she had a ride into Bathgate with her mother to look forward to. Or it might be the day when cook did the baking and would allow her to help roll the biscuits on the kitchen table. She could still smell the hot spicy aroma from the big black oven beside a kitchen fire that made sweat bristle from cook's red face.

Was she not happy now? Lorianna sighed, unsure of what to think. Her mother had said she was lucky that such a man as Gavin Blackwood wished to marry her. She had been sixteen, a worry to her mother with her wicked ways and had been caught with one of the squire's sons rolling in the hay. She blushed now at the memory: nothing had happened really; the boy had stolen a few kisses and she had fallen giggling to the ground in the struggle. But her mother had wrung her hands and wailed: 'I dread to think what you might have made the poor young gentleman do if I hadn't come along.'

Woman, since Eve in the garden of Eden, was a temptress, her mother said, and it was no use trying to blame the man. The instigation of all evil came from the woman.

Not that her mother was unkind or unloving; quite the reverse. Born in far-off Italy and rescued from a life of poverty by Lorianna's father, she was a devout and passionate woman whose relationships were as sincere and intense as her prayers. She was always hugging and kissing the child and had once physically attacked a nurse, literally flinging her from the house after she had discovered her smacking four year-old Lorianna. Poor Mamma! Lorianna thought, so desperate to be a lady and do the proper thing, but letting herself down so often by such volatile emotions. How vigilant she had been trying to prevent her daughter from suffering the same impediment! How delighted when Gavin had come to court her.

'Such a wealthy Christian gentleman, Lorianna! And so much older and more sensible than you, my dear. He'll be able to guide you in the ways of the Lord and take good care of you. Praise be to God for being so merciful to us!'

Mamma had been embarrassingly grateful to Gavin, almost obsequious. But then of course, Mamma had always been like that to Papa as well. 'Thank the good Lord every night for your good husband, Lorianna, as I do for mine.'

Lorianna sighed. She had never failed to do as Mamma said, but she couldn't help feeling a little cheated. Marriage was not quite as wonderful as her mother had always made out. Not that it was Gavin's fault of course. He was still the upright Christian gentleman Mamma had always said he was, and he had provided her with a beautiful home in which she could indulge herself in any whim and fancy. If she wanted a new maid she could have one, providing of course that she asked Gavin's permission. Perhaps a little womanly pressure was required, but this was only to be expected. If she wished for a day in Bathgate or even in Edinburgh Gavin, while frowning on any frivolous or unnecessary 'gadding about', would arrange that her wish should be granted. She did struggle to control and contain her restlessness, her wicked and wayward emotions and her most regrettable discontent. Only sometimes it was painfully difficult. She felt imprisoned inside herself, beating at invisible bars, distressed and bewildered, not knowing what she was trying to escape from or what she longed to run to.

As she neared the farm she opened her pink parasol and turned it lazily over her head. Two black and white collie dogs came to meet her – Jess the old one, fat and plodding and Ben the pup, with his tail wagging his entire body. She leaned forward to pat the old dog's head and was somewhat disconcerted by the enthusiasm of the pup which kept bouncing against her like a dusty rubber ball. She had to take little steps back and then back again, hand protectively outstretched in an effort to shield her dress from the dirty paws.

Suddenly a smooth rich voice commanded, 'Ben, down!' The dog dropped like a stone and lay with its face between its paws.

Lorianna felt embarrassed by the appearance of the grieve and annoyed at herself for being embarrassed. She had expected him to be out working in the field at this time of day, or supervising the other workers.

She kept remembering that she had recently caught him standing staring up at her bedroom window. That day he would have been at the house for the legitimate purpose of seeing Gavin of course. Gavin really knew nothing about farm work and did nothing about the running of the estate except to ride around it occasionally and demand regular reports from the grieve. He didn't seem to like Kelso and she had heard him complain to Gilbert about the man not knowing his place. Gilbert had asked if he had said anything impertinent and Gavin had replied that on the contrary, it was his silences accompanied by a certain look in his eyes that he found most offensive.

Admittedly there was something disturbing about Kelso's eyes, grey like a winter's sky under jet-black brows. Such a striking-looking man could cause unrest among the female staff.

'Good afternoon, Mrs Blackwood!' His low-pitched voice was automatic, almost absent-minded, but his eyes were sharp and searching. She smiled in acknowledgement, then tipped up her chin and gazed around. He had not saluted her, she noticed.

'Can I help you in any way?' he was asking now.

'No, I'm just enjoying a stroll,' she said, turning aside, parasol lightly twirling over her shoulder.

'The farm must bring back happy memories. You were brought up on a farm, I believe?'

'Yes, indeed,' she agreed before sauntering away. She was slightly unnerved that he should have read her mind so accurately. The farm drew her like a magnet on her lonely perambulations, but she had seldom seen Kelso there. He was usually keeping the men hard at work in the fields. Sometimes she saw the dairymaid, who would give her a pretty curtsey. Or the odd-job-man might be somewhere around and he never failed to doff his cap and stand respectfully still until she passed.

The farm with its sights and smells and sounds acted like a buffer to her growing sense of unfulfilment. The atmosphere soothed her with its memories of happy times. Yet it made her sad too. The loving response she had had to love in her childhood was reawakened now in her maturity, eager and aching and open-armed.

She walked round the farm buildings, which formed a three-sided square at the back of the farmhouse and faced on to a duck pond where fat ducks fished with tails up in the shallows, and moorhens darted about. The stables faced the pond and not only housed the giant slow-moving farm horses, but the riding horses too.

The dairy was shadowy and cool, with buckets of milk and flat pottery bowls with cream rising thick to the surface and being skimmed off by the dairymaid and thumped into butter in a barrel-shaped churn.

'Afternoon ma'am.' The maid curtseyed.

Lorianna favoured her with a smile before passing on to the cow-shed where placid cows stood in semi-darkness munching chopped turnips as they awaited the arrival of the milkers with their three-legged stools.

The door to the boothy for the unmarried farm-labourers was open wide, and Lorianna caught a glimpse of the widow-woman from the village who fed the men and looked after the place. A smell of carbolic soap overflowed from the shadowy interior as, taking advantage of the men's absence, she rubbed and scrubbed at the stone floor. So intent was she on her task that she did not notice Lorianna's presence.

The bothy looked out on to a central midden where all the manure from the stables and cowshed were dumped. The steamy morass had such a pungent odour that many of Lorianna's genteel lady friends would have fainted at the stench — not to mention the sight — of such a place. But to Lorianna it was part of the earthy texture of her happy childhood memories.

She turned at the cart shed where the wooden-wheeled carts lay back, shafts up, strangely bereft and vulnerable without the harnessed, brass-decorated farm-horses. Her usual walk back was through the fields and then into the garden through what she liked to think of as her secret gate. She was glad of the parasol, because in the great rolling fields there were fewer shady places. When she did approach cool shadows, rooks loudly cawed at her and rose up in protest at her audacity for coming so near to the trees where their nests were built.

Once she turned round for another glimpse of the farm and was taken aback to see, over to her left, Robert Kelso on horseback on a raised bank of ground, his tall figure silhouetted darkly against the pale sky. He was watching her, she felt sure, and it was a disturbing intrusion. She had been treasuring her solitude and her ability to soak up sensations of the past which had become so necessary to her present survival.

The swish of her skirts quickened as she walked towards the stile and then the shelter of the narrow path that led to her secret gate into the garden of Blackwood House. The path was almost overgrown with plants and hedges. Horny roots of trees clawing up from the earth were liable to trip the unwary; hedges were thick and high and full of flowers and the rustle and hum of living things. Flecks of sunshine danced up and down the bark of the trees. Closer to her gate the foliage became denser, a dark earthy-smelling tangle through which she had to dip and duck and tread with extra care. Then the gate was stiffly creaking, squeaking under the spicy shade of a huge walnut tree. There were ash trees too and a beautiful copper birch. Then she was into the garden, past the blaze of rhododendrons and round to the right on to the croquet lawn.

But instead of feeling buoyant with gladness at being home and safe from prying eyes, depression snatched the heart from her, leaving her empty and exhausted. She sighed at the same time as chastising herself; she must try to stop these wistful wanderings into the past and instead seek calmness and contentment in the present.

Gavin was in the sitting-room when she arrived, comfortably ensconced in a chair by the window. It occurred to her that compared with the deep red wall-hangings of silk damask, Gavin's hair and beard looked glaringly orange. Somehow the sight of him increased her depression, but she managed to smile a response to his polite, 'Good afternoon, my dear.' Instead of going over to sit at the window beside him, however, she went through to the adjacent drawing-room and sat down at the grand piano. The piano had been given to her by Gavin on her marriage and the case had been painted with roses with the letter 'L' on one side within a wreath.

Gently Lorianna caressed the keys, the clear tinkling notes seeming to come from another age and match the eighteenth-century furniture and continental pieces in the room. In contrast with the plainer, darker and more solid furniture of the sitting-room and its clutter of sepia photographs, the drawing-room was light, ornate and colourful with its Chinese tapestry panel over the chimney-piece, paintings and elegant French sofa and chairs.

When the last note died away a polite clapping made her turn in surprise, thinking it was Gavin. But it was Gilbert lounging in the connecting doorway.

'Thank you, kind sir,' she said with a mock curtsey. And then as she joined him in the sitting-room, 'Everyone seems to be home earlier than usual today. First your father and now you.'

48

Gilbert smoothed two fingers down over the middle silky section of his moustache.

'Oh? I thought we left the Dreadnought at the usual time. I to go back to the factory and father to come home.'

'Usual time indeed!' Lorianna laughed. 'Your father is hardly ever home by early afternoon, are you, my dear?'

Gavin neatly folded his newspaper and laid it aside. 'Not when I have to go to Edinburgh first.'

'Edinburgh?' Gilbert echoed, his face puzzled.

Gavin sprang up lightly from his chair. 'Kelso was telling me there's trouble with the potatoes in the North end field. Some blight or other, he thinks. Don't just stand there, come on with me and have a look.'

After the two men had gone, Lorianna felt a vague unease . . . something she could not put her finger on. Alone in the high-ceilinged room she hovered absent-eyed as if she had forgotten what it was she had come in for.

CHAPTER FIVE

'A', her father monotoned from his green chair and Clementina, standing sturdily in front of him in her brown dress and white pinafore with lacy cap sleeves, piped up, 'A soft answer turneth away wrath but grievous words stir up anger.'

Henny had brushed her honey-coloured hair so that it hung softly from a middle parting, framing her pert little face, loosely curling over her shoulders and tumbling down her back. Her eyes were wide with a mixture of desperation and defiance. She had an awesome admiration for her father and was in a fever to please him, but if she did get things wrong and incurred his wrath she was determined not to shame herself further by flinching or weeping.

'B.'

'Be . . . be . . .'

'Come on! Come on!'

'Be ye kind to one another, tender-hearted, forgiving one another.'

'C.' Her father leaned forward to fire his words at the fragile target of her face.

'C . . . C . . . C . . .' Her heart pattered up to her throat, but she must *not* stutter. To stutter could be fatal, Henny said. Clementina had terrible visions of one day dying of a stutter, choking to death over words that just wouldn't come out.

'Come ye little children,' she managed in an excited rush, 'hearken unto me. I will teach you the fear of the Lord.'

She was acutely tuned in to Henny's tension and could see the nervous twitch in the nurse's eye without looking round at her. The library was a shadowy nightmare place, long and windowless except for the far corner. Its ceiling-high shelves of maroon, brown and black books were intimidating, as were the bulky high-backed chairs and big gold-fringed, blood-coloured light shades that always seemed to darken rather than lighten the room. Even so, the library did not have such frightening associations as the oak room which was her father's study. There she would be punished and there Henny would be made to wait outside the door.

'D.' Her father's voice continued and Clementina noticed his eyes had begun to twitch behind his pince-nez.

Hands tightly clasped behind her back, she tossed her head as if she was not a bit frightened.

'Depart from evil and do good, seek peace and pursue it.'

'E.'

'Em . . . em . . .'

'E.'

'Enter not into the paths of the wicked and go not in the way of evil men.'

If she was very good and answered every question promptly and correctly, she was rewarded with a pat on the head which made her quiver with pride and pleasure. It was not only the alphabet that had to be faced of course. There was adding and subtracting, spelling and singing.

If she did not do well in her testing, or if she had been particularly naughty in any other way, she could be punished in a variety of ways from being locked alone in a dark windowless cellar where rats scraped and rustled, and beetles scurried to and fro, to the humiliation of having to unbutton and pull down her knickers and be thrashed on her bare bottom until she felt faint but never cried. Only later, safely back in the nursery at the top of the tower with Henny, would she broken-heartedly sob

51

into the nurse's apron. More than anything else it was incurring her father's displeasure that distressed her.

Henny would cradle her close, hush her and kiss her and sing —

'Hush-a-ba, birdie, croon, croon,
Hush-a-ba birdie, croon;
The sheep are gone to the silver wood,
And the goats are gone to the broon, broon.'

Then of course there was the other ordeal of the visit to the sitting-room or the drawing-room every night. The drawing-room was always the worst, because that meant there would be other people there as well as her mother and father.

Special dolls were kept there for the occasion, hard-faced dolls with cold, uncuddly china limbs. Mother or one of the visitors would pretend they were having a marvellous time playing with her. They would dress and undress the dolls and keep repeating, 'Oh look, how sweet! Oh, just look at those little shoes. Oh, isn't it a darling dolly in that sweet little hat?'

Or her mother's rose-petal fingers would lightly stroke Clementina's cheek and she would smile and say to the others, 'Isn't she beautiful?' And Clementina would blush and toss her hair.

If father was there her mother didn't say such things — or if she did, she quickly lapsed into guilty silence; Henny said this was because father didn't believe it right to praise children to their faces. He didn't think it was good for them.

Picture books would be brought out, pages turned and questions asked. 'And what is that, darling? and that . . . and that?'

And Clementina would stand with chin pressed stubbornly down into her pinafore, only raising her eyes to steal yet another look at the clock on the mantelshelf. When the big hand and the little hand were straight up and down, Henny would come and fetch her and take her up to the nursery.

Today there was no one there but her mother and Gilbert. But she didn't like Gilbert very much.

'How's the little tomboy?' he asked.

'Gilbert!' her mother scolded. 'She's not; she's mother's little angel, aren't you, pet?'

'Angel, my foot!' Gilbert chortled. 'I've seen her shinning up trees like a squirrel and fighting with the gardener's son.' Then, bending over Clementina and lowering his voice, 'Will I tell father? By George, you'd get some licking for that, eh?'

'Gilbert! Don't torment her!'

She didn't simply dislike Gilbert, she hated him.

'You mustn't get upset, darling,' mother said, offering her a sweet from a little silver dish half-hidden between framed photographs on the pedestal table. 'Gilbert's only teasing.'

To get a sweet was such a novelty that Clementina forgot her hatred in the intense enjoyment of the treat. 'Thank you, Mother.'

Gilbert grinned under his moustache. 'Old-fashioned as well. She's never once called you "Mama," has she?'

'She's a very clever girl, aren't you, my pet?'

Clementina felt irritated and impatient to be away. Mother was very beautiful, but she did ask silly questions at times. If she were to answer 'Yes' she would be regarded as vain. If she answered 'No' she would be chastised for being cheeky.

Ignoring the question, Clementina chewed earnestly at her sweet and wondered what story Henny would tell her tonight. Sometimes it was a story about history like the glories of Queen Elizabeth, Francis Drake and Walter Raleigh or the escapes of Charles II and Bonnie Prince Charlie. At other times it was a story about animals. She liked all Henny's stories and had no special preferences.

At last she was removed from the spotlight of mother's and Gilbert's attention and escaped with Henny outside to the hall. Henny was getting slower at climbing the stairs and Clementina, racing on in front, had to call to her to hurry. The oil lamps had not yet been lit in the tower and the small voice echoed down through the darkness.

'Henny! Henny!'

'Watch now, dear. Watch you don't fall. Be careful. Please do!' The nurse called breathlessly back but couldn't hurry. Hand leaning on the rough stone wall, she took the steps as a very small child would – one foot first, then the other hoisted up to stand beside it before repeating the process. At the top of the stairs at last, she had to lean against the wall for a few minutes to recover. Alice Tait, the nursery-maid, came out of the day nursery and peered along through the shadows of the wooden-floored corridor.

'Are you all right, Mrs Henning?' Alice, barely sixteen years old, had a wobbly barrel of a figure and a broad moon face framed with the big frill of a mob cap always worn well pulled down to hide her hair because she was self-conscious about her outrageously thick curls. Some days she didn't bother to comb it, for it was such a struggle to get the comb through her curly mop.

'Put on the kettle, Alice,' Henny's words escaped in little puffs.

'Right you are.' Alice bustled away to balance the kettle behind the big iron fireguard on the nursery fire. There was no means of cooking in the nursery and Mrs Musgrove insisted that all food had to be carried up from the kitchen. But a kettle was allowed and Henny kept a tea-caddy and a tin of biscuits on one of the shelves of the toy cupboard. Sugar and milk tended to be a problem, but they usually managed to save some from the meal trays that Alice brought up from the kitchen at breakfast, lunch and tea times.

It was not that Cook grudged extra milk or sugar, but Mrs Musgrove kept such an eagle eye on the stores and every grain, drop, crumb or ounce of everything had to be accounted for. It was a terrible harassment to Cook and a state of war continually simmered under the surface between her and the housekeeper which was liable to erupt violently and unexpectedly at any time and send everyone scurrying nervously from the kitchen. Mrs Musgrove never lost her temper; she became icy calm which, as Cook said, wasn't natural and enough to put the wind up anybody. Cook always lost her temper and tended to take it out on lesser mortals like Mima, the kitchen-maid, or Janet the scullery-maid, or any other maid – or even Clementina if she happened to be handy.

Her temper, however, flashed across the blue sky of her sunny nature and just as quickly fizzled out. She was sorely tried, she said, by that monstrous woman. But then she'd say, 'Oh, to hell, let old beady eyes have her own way. Why should I care? I've better things to think about!' Meaning her secret tryst in the long grass by the river with poacher Wattie McLeod.

Now Henny collapsed into the rocking chair by the fire and it creaked helplessly back and forth for a minute or two. Alice didn't like the look of her. Mrs Henning was wiry and as energetic as a grasshopper, but she seldom had much colour except patches of freckles on her cheeks and now her skin looked proper sickly.

'Are you sure you're all right, Mrs Henning?' she asked again, in a lower more dramatic voice.

The nurse put out both hands for her cup of tea and after a few sips managed to nod and say, 'Yes, of course, of course. Stop asking me that. You're worrying Miss Clementina.' And then to the child, 'It's all right, dear. Henny's just a little tired. I think after we've had our tea we'll both go to bed.'

Clementina slept in the same room as Henny and loved to watch her dress and undress. The nurse was a perpetual wonder to her and no less when she was performing these feats. She always dressed and undressed under the bell-tent of her long-sleeved flannelette nightdress. In the morning she would first of all extricate herself from the sleeves, after which a hand would grope out from under the hem and snatch her combinations from the bedside chair. Then her stays, bust-bodice, black stockings, knickers – everything disappeared under the nightdress! Then suddenly it was whipped off and there would be Henny almost fully clothed.

Later, when putting on her hat to go out, she would perform another feat of magic. She wore two huge hat-pins and Clementina always thought she stuck them right through her head.

The procedures occurred in reverse at night and on this occasion Clementina, cosily tucked up in bed, watched wide-eyed with interest as usual.

'Tell me a story,' she asked as soon as Henny's feat of undressing had been accomplished. Henny sat down on the bed breathless and smiling.

'Just a small one, Miss Clementina, while I brush out my hair.'

Clementina thought Henny had the most beautiful hair in the world. Maybe it wasn't a pretty colour like her mother's, or even as glossy, but it was comfortable hair – hair that didn't mind being touched or twined round small fingers or messed about. Fuzzy and warm to the cheek, when you buried your nose in it, it tickled and made you laugh. It seemed an enormous amount of hair for such a delicate little face and no matter how it was screwed back and pinned, it still remained bushy enough to make hats rise and wobble precariously on top of it.

Entranced, Clementina watched the way an overall fuzz refused to be brushed down and the shaft of light from the narrow window at Henny's back shone through it, giving her a kind of halo in the child's eyes.

Sometimes, as a special treat, she was allowed to clamber into Henny's bed and cuddle in beside her. Clementina loved to mould into Henny's back and feel the bony ridges of her spine and the soft flesh about it and the long hair tickly against her face. Sometimes she would tickle Henny and then Henny would grab the child's foot and drag it over her hip until they struggled and laughed together. Clementina became entangled and enveloped in Henny's hair and voluminous nightgown and it was as if she and the nurse had become one person. Eventually, an exhausted Clementina would fall blissfully asleep in the nurse's arms.

Sometimes, if her mother and father were going out to dinner or to some important function, she and Henny would creep down the tower stairs and open the door just a crack so that they could peer through into the hall and, unseen, watch her mother and father come out of the bedroom in all their finery, cross the hall and disappear through the stained-glass doors. Then she and Henny would rush upstairs and watch from the nursery window. It was especially exciting on a winter's evening when the gardens and all the estate were in darkness and only a slice of light from the entrance hall and the lamp on the brougham illuminated the scene of father helping mother into the carriage. Father would be in his black evening suit and silk top hat. Mother with her hair dressed with long combs studded with pearls and a large rose set low on the nape of her neck. Her delicate lace gown with its trimming of frills and beads would spread over the ground in her wake and her bare shoulders would be covered by her sable evening cloak with a broad insert of guipure lace. Or perhaps she would have feathers in her hair and wear her shiny satin gown and diamond collar and velvet cloak.

Whatever mother wore would send Henny into gasps and excited whispers of admiration and she would say to Clementina, 'Aren't you a lucky girl, to have such a beautiful mother?'

Clementina would feel quite excited too, but her excitement stemmed more from the secret game she and Henny were playing of running up and down the stairs and spying on the event. She took some pride and pleasure at the dazzling sight of her mother, but both her parents were soon forgotten in a story-telling session with Henny as she sat on Henny's knee and they sipped their bedtime tea or hot milk, isolated close together in the shadowy candlelit nursery at the top of the tower. Her parents were strangers belonging to a different world.

In truth, Clementina preferred Henny's clothes even if her dresses were always light blue cotton and didn't have a train. And even if her jackets were not fur, but short black cloth with leg-of-mutton sleeves. And Henny wouldn't be Henny without boots that always seemed slightly too clumpy and heavy for her.

Alice the nursery-maid was not altogether of their world. She was always grumbling because she had so much work to do, like clearing out the day nursery fire (father didn't allow fires in the night nursery) and polishing the grates and washing the floors, and running up and down the stairs with bath water and meals, not to mention the coal. She just lived for the afternoons and evenings off when she could be away from the nursery. It was strange to see her then without her big frilled cap but instead a frill of untidy curls dangling around her plump face.

Sometimes when Alice became too harassed and Clementina was in her way she would give her a vicious push or punch, then hiss at her, 'If you tell Henny, the gipsies'll get you and burn you alive in their camp fire!'

Alice had made so many threats about what the gipsies would do to her that Clementina always clung close to Henny if they passed gipsies on one of their walks to Littlegate or Bathgate.

Small though Henny was, Clementina was sure that the nurse would never let anyone hurt her.

As long as Henny was there to protect her, she was safe.

CHAPTER SIX

'Sometimes I hate father,' Gilbert said. His lower, fleshy lip protruded childishly and the corners of his mouth dragged down.

'You mustn't say such a thing,' Lorianna protested.

'Damn it, it's true! All his church friends in Bathgate and thereabouts think he's such a saintly and generous gent, but to me he's just a beastly old skinflint.'

'Your father provides you with a good home and everything you need.'

'He may provide you with everything you need, stepmamma, but not yours truly.'

They were on their bumpy way down to Bathgate, where she was to pay a call on Mrs Forbes-Struthers and Gilbert had to visit his tailor.

'It's a frightful humiliation for a chap having to beg and plead for every suit or shirt he needs,' Gilbert continued. '*And* having to justify the need. I work hard in that factory, damn it – not to mention the estate – and I don't get a penny.'

'Surely that can't be true?'

'Not a penny to call my own. I'm twenty years of age and not a penny to call my own!'

'Your father does give you some money,' persisted Lorianna.

'I'm telling you, only when I beg and plead and justify to his approval why I need it, and he always impresses on me that it's his money and he's doing me a great favour by giving me anything – which is always much less than I ask, incidentally.'

Lorianna sighed. Gavin was the same with her, but she accepted it as the normal way of a careful and conscientious husband. She realised, however, that it could be a humiliating situation for a young man to be in.

'Have you spoken to him about a salary?' she ventured tentatively.

'Oh, I've tried,' Gilbert said bitterly, 'and got nothing but one of his dreary sermons for my trouble. *And* more work and less money into the bargain! He puts on his preacher's voice and quotes Thessalonians at me – "For even when we were with you, this we commanded, that if any would not work, neither should he eat." And who was talking about not working, for Christ's sake!'

'Gilbert!'

'I apologise for my language, step-mamma, but can you blame me for feeling so ill-used? I work jolly hard and he knows it.'

Lorianna sighed and looked away. She had no wish to become embroiled in any quarrel Gilbert had with his father, for she had as much as she could cope with in treading the prickly path of Gavin's moral rectitude as it was. He would not regard it as a proper or indeed a Christian thing for her to take anyone else's side against him. As he had reminded her many times, he was not only her protector and provider but also her Lord and master in the eyes of God and man. Her loyalty and gratitude were qualities that Gavin insisted on to an obsessive degree. Not that he had any need to question her complete devotion to him, as she so often tried to tell him. But he could work himself into such a state of moral indignation and outrage that it didn't matter what she said.

Indeed, it was more often than not her devotion that sparked off his worst criticism of her. Or at least, what she had thought of as devotion but he had regarded as her 'habitual and wicked pursuit of sensual pleasures'.

'The human soul,' he explained to her, 'is in its own nature, a spiritual and sin compounded substance, incapable of full enjoyment of anything that is not pure and spiritual like itself. But by its union with material organs, it comes to be contacted also with objects of sense and appetite and so is allied to the inferior and brutal . . .'

They were in the open victoria carriage with Jacobs perched like a statue up front in his navy-blue and crimson livery; as they came to the end of the long avenue of trees on the Drumcross Road she could see the market town of Bathgate tucked down in the valley below. The tall spire of St John's rose on the left side of town. The crown-topped St David's dominated the centre and the clock tower of the grey stone Parish Church looked over the town from the right. Around these three edifices clustered the shops and stables, houses and cottages – all looking like a toy town from this height and distance. On the far side, beyond trees and fields, the occasional pit bing rose up like a black pyramid. Beyond them again were the rolling hills. Bathgate was, in fact, surrounded by hills and looked a clean and pleasant place with the sun frosting the grey roof tiles of the houses into silver and flaming the square red tower of St David's.

Soon muted sounds began filtering up the steep hill; the distant whistle of a train and the iron clatter of a bread van vied with the lowing of cattle and the soughing of the wind.

Mrs Forbes-Struthers lived in Marjorybanks Street, a quiet street of imposing villas at the upper end of the town. Lorianna was not particularly looking forward to the call. The woman did go on so about her servants, always complaining about them. Sometimes it was the sole topic of conversation. But her husband, like Gavin, was an elder in the church and Gavin liked to have them to dinner occasionally and encouraged her to return Mrs Forbes-Struthers' calls.

'Just drop me off at the corner, Jacobs,' Gilbert raised his voice, then dropped it again. 'I don't suppose you've any spare cash on you just now, Lorianna?'

Without hesitation she opened her reticule and took out the coins she had in her purse. 'That's all I have, but you're welcome to it.'

'Bless you!' He lifted one of her gloved hands and dropped a kiss on it before alighting from the carriage. 'I'll see you later.'

She watched his slim figure, jaunty now because he had some money jingling in his pocket, disappearing away down Hopeton Street. Then she instructed the coachman to turn left along Marjorybanks Street.

The Forbes-Struthers' mansion was not as big as Blackwood House, but it was square and solid looking and the maid who opened the door was very smart in a long black dress with leg-of-mutton sleeves and lace-trimmed apron, and a cap with long streamers down the back. Nevertheless Lorianna could not help noticing that there was a strained look about her.

The hall was gloomy and smelled too strongly of wax polish and Brasso. She could see her reflection on the floor and she stepped nervously on the rugs in case they slithered away under her feet and caused her to fall. The 'Wag-at-the wa' clock had been so vigorously polished with Brasso that its numbers and pendulums dazzled hypnotically through the shadows and its ponderous 'tick-tock, tick-tock' seemed very slow and loud.

'What name please, ma'am?' the maid whispered. Then after a timorous knock at the drawing-room door her hand jerked back in anguish, obviously remembering too late that it was extremely vulgar to knock at a drawing-room door.

'Mrs Gavin Blackwood, ma'am,' the maid announced.

'Mrs Blackwood, how nice to see you!' Mrs Forbes-Struthers flashed a glower at the servant before her face smoothed into a smile of greeting.

Lorianna allowed the girl to take her feather boa, gloves, silk muff and long parasol, but of course kept on her hat, an enormous creation of straw with a seagull and a great froth of net on top.

'Do sit down, my dear,' Mrs Forbes-Struthers said as the maid left the room. 'Tea will be served in a few minutes. That is, if the stupid creature remembers – I don't know what I've done to be tormented so.'

Lorianna tried to make herself reasonably comfortable on the slippery horsehair sofa. 'Servants can be a prob lem,' she murmured.

'Problem? My dear, they are the bane of my life! I've told Brown – the parlourmaid – that if she doesn't smarten herself up she will be out on the street without a character.'

Mrs Forbes-Struthers was a large-bosomed woman who was much older than Lorianna, nearer Gavin's age in fact, as was her husband. They were childless and Lorianna sometimes thought that if Mrs Forbes-Struthers had had a child she might not have been so obsessed with the lower orders. At least it might have given her something else to talk about. On the other hand, she might simply have added a nanny and a nursery-maid to her list of tormentors.

Thinking of a nanny reminded Lorianna of Mrs Henning. Gavin had been complaining that she was a stupid ditherer of a woman and quite incapable of instructing Clementina or disciplining her. No doubt he was right, but it was such a pity because Clementina was obviously so fond of the nurse.

'Are you feeling all right, Mrs Blackwood?'

'Pardon?' Lorianna suddenly realised that Mrs Forbes-Struthers had been speaking. 'Oh yes, I'm quite well. Perhaps a little fatigued . . .'

'Ah, here's tea at last! No wonder you're fatigued my dear – having to wait so long.' And then in a lower tone and with narrowed eyes, 'I'll speak to you later, Brown!'

The maid, looking paler and more nervous than ever, was arranging everything on the table in front of Mrs Forbes-Struthers: a hanging silver kettle on a stand, a silver teapot, cream jug and sugar basin and dainty cups and saucers of fine porcelain. The tea consisted of thin slices of white and brown bread and butter, small macaroons and iced sponges. Everything always had to be nibbled very neatly because it was not the done thing to provide plates or serviettes at afternoon tea.

Mrs Forbes-Struthers poured the tea and handed the cup to the maid, who carried it over to Lorianna in both hands and with excruciating care.

'And how is your dear husband?' Mrs Forbes-Struthers enquired after the maid had been dismissed.

'Very well thank you, I'm glad to say.'

'Will he be at the feeing fair today? Or does he leave the engaging of farm servants and estate workers to his grieve?'

'Oh, the feeing fair! I had forgotten about that. Is it today?'

'Yes, it's a wonder you didn't catch a glimpse of it. Sometimes it spills over from Engine Street into Hopeton Street and as for the Steel Yard, it's always absolutely packed I'm told. Then of course there's the shows and roundabouts down Whitburn Road, where they all go at night and fritter away their fee. And the public houses do a roaring trade, I believe. My dear, a lady wouldn't dare put a foot out of her carriage anywhere near the centre of the town on a day like this. Why, I remember once . . .'

Mrs Forbes-Struthers launched into a story that Lorianna had heard more than once before about how she had been insulted by a drunken ex-gardener of hers.

Lorianna had a sudden wicked urge to go and watch the feeing fair – perhaps even steal a glance at the shows. Many a time when she was a young girl she had enjoyed the crush and bustle and excitement of such occasions when her father used to stroll along Engine Street looking for new farmhands, horsemen and maids. She remembered how he used to examine the men like oxen for strength and fitness by feeling their back, shoulder and arm muscles. He even used to prise open their mouths and examine their teeth. Then as the day went on bargains were struck by each farmer placing a shilling or a half-crown in his palm, spitting on it and then holding it out for the man or woman of his choice to smack his or her palm on top and seal the bargain. Bargains could also be sealed with a dram, and the back room of the licensed grocers as well as all the inns did a continuous and noisy trade.

She doubted very much if Gavin would be there. For one thing he was one of the leading lights of the Temperance Society and so would certainly not seal any bargain with a dram.

When at long last she was able to make a polite escape from Mrs Forbes-Struthers and the carriage was taking her back along Marjorybanks Street, Lorianna impulsively instructed Jacobs to turn down Hopeton Street instead of going up the other way. In a matter of minutes they were at the end of Engine Street and she called on him to stop for a few minutes.

Sitting in the carriage gently twirling her parasol, she gazed along at the moving mass of farm folk so densely packed in both Engine Street and the town square at the other end — for some unknown reason called the Steel Yard — that it was a mystery how farmers could crush a path through in order to select new employees. Then as she watched she suddenly noticed a tall athletic figure instantly recognisable even in the smart tweed suit and hat tipped slightly back on his head.

Not wanting to be seen by Robert Kelso, yet somehow unable to drag herself completely away from the spectacle, she ordered Jacobs to carry on down Hopeton Street, then turn down the continuation of North Bridge Street. At the foot of North Bridge Street they turned left along South Bridge Street, only to discover that some of the fair had even spilled round there. Like the Steel Yard the street was dotted with stalls protected by umbrella covers of white canvas and offering for sale everything from safety pins and sewing needles to huge horned gramophones. The air was spiced with the aroma of smoked haddock and hot newly-baked gingerbread.

'It's going to be very difficult for us to get through the Steel Yard, ma'am,' Jacobs said. 'Do you wish me to try?'

'I cannot see that we have any choice now that we've come this far, Jacobs.'

'Very well, ma'am.'

She regretted her foolish whim to tour the streets on such a day now that her carriage was in danger of being jostled and her horse beginning to whinny in fright and paw at the air. But more than anything she began to panic in case Kelso might witness her predicament. As they pushed their way slowly across the Steel Yard she glanced along Engine Street, praying that he would not be there. She saw that he was, but his back was towards her.

'For pity's sake *do* something, Jacobs! If I don't get away from here immediately I shall faint,' she said, surprised herself at the keenness of her agitation.

'Very well, ma'am.'

Jacobs cracked his whip and there were screams of fright from people milling nearby as the horse's hooves clattered on the cobbles and sped forward. Lorianna held on to the side of the carriage with one hand and her parasol with the other. Her cheeks were burning and she felt guilty and ashamed of herself – so much so that as soon as she got safely home she went straight to Gavin's praying stool and knelt at it with eyes closed until she felt calm again.

66

CHAPTER SEVEN

Clementina and Henny had climbed the Knock Hill. It was breezy up there and Henny had to cling on to her hat, the skirts of her blue cotton dress flapping and cracking in the wind like a flag and strands of her hair tugging out and streaking across her face. Sometimes the hair tickled her nose and made her sneeze and Clementina nearly laughed herself silly. She loved to come up the Knock and feel the wind frolicking her own hair and clothes and tingling her cheeks. She gambolled about in it like a young lamb, laughing and jumping up and down flinging up her arms and racing about pretending she was a kite.

'You can see five counties from here on a clear day,' Henny called out. 'And look, Miss Clementina, what's that away over there?'

'*You* know,' Clementina giggled.

'Ah, but do *you* know, Miss Clementina? Do you know?'

'The Forth Bridge.'

'And what, I wonder, is that sparkling underneath it?'

Clementina rolled her eyes. 'That's too easy. The Forth, of course!'

Suddenly Henny grabbed the little girl's hands and whisked her round. 'London Bridge is falling down, my fair lady . . .'

Clementina skipped quickly, jerkily, her long hair streaming out behind her. Then Henny stopped, suddenly breathless.

'Oh dear, oh dear,' she panted. 'Poor Henny must be getting old. I run out of puff so easily these days.'

She sat down on the grass, chest heaving. Clementina's round green eyes fixed worriedly on the nurse. Henny had a nice chest, not big and sticking out like her mother's or her mother's friends. They even wore big frills on their dresses and blouses and pouched them out over their skirts, to make their chests look huge. Henny said everyone did this because it was fashionable to have what she called 'a voluptuous, bendy-forward figure'.

Clementina was glad Henny didn't have a figure like that. Henny was neat and straight and small enough to cuddle.

'You'll never get old,' she told the nurse, pouncing on her and hugging her round the neck.

'Don't dear, please don't! I feel I'm choking as it is. That's better.' She straightened her hat. 'Everyone gets old, you know. But of course it takes a *long*, long time, so there's no need to worry . . . no need at all.'

She took some slow deep breaths, closing her eyes as she did so; then suddenly they were open wide again and full of mischief and her mouth, turned up at the corners even in repose, was smiling. 'There, that's better. All I needed was a little rest. Now, fetch your hat, Miss Clementina and we'll descend. But Henny will go down slowly if you don't mind. What an old nuisance I'm getting these days — always puffing and blowing.'

'Like a steam engine.'

'Yes indeed. Just that, exactly. Your hat, Miss Clementina!'

'Oh pooh! I hate hats.'

'You hate Henny's hats? Oh dear, oh dear!'

'No, not your hats, Henny. I love *your* hats.'

'Well, then.'

'It's just my hats I hate.'

'Fetch it, Miss Clementina. Please do! You should never have taken it off and flung it aside like that. What would your father say?'

'He wouldn't say anything, he'd just beat me. Or lock me away somewhere horrid.'

The nurse winced. 'Do fetch it, dear, and put it on before we walk back.'

The child scrambled across some boulders to a clump of long grass where the hat had landed. Retrieving it, she tugged it on to her head and then sat on the boulder for a few minutes, legs dangling, face brooding on the restriction of the stiff crown and flopping brim.

'You look very pretty in it, Miss Clementina. You really do.'

'I don't want to look pretty.'

'Tut-tut, of course you do.'

'Don't! *Don't!*'

'Do! *Do!* Oh dear, I sound like a pigeon, don't I?'

Clementina caught a giggle in her hands and then, forgetting about her hat, scrambled down beside the nurse.

'Oh my,' Henny said. 'Aren't you lucky your dress is green? It won't show any grass stains, will it? Only I do wish your pinny was green too and your petticoats and knickers.'

'Don't worry, Alice will take them to the laundry-women,' Clementina said cheerfully. 'Mother and father will never know.'

'Well, maybe so, but still, do try to be a little more careful with your pinny, Miss Clementina. If we met your mother or father they would certainly see that. I tell you what! You be careful with your pinny and I'll carry your gloves until we come to the drive.'

This was joy indeed to Clementina. A hat was bad enough but in the country on a summer's day, gloves were sheer purgatory. She couldn't even see the sense in wearing them. But her mother had been shocked when she had seen her out walking hatless and gloveless with Henny one day. She had been angry with Henny and Clementina had hated her for what she had said.

'Mrs Henning, I expect a child's nurse to know better than this. It is not proper for any respectable girl to be seen out walking without hat and gloves. She has plenty of hats and gloves, I take it?'

'Oh yes, madam, yes indeed. She has very pretty hats and gloves, but you see the point was . . .'

'The point is, Mrs Henning, that if you don't do your job properly I shall be forced to report you to the master.'

All the time Clementina had stood with head bowed, clinging into Henny's skirts, just waiting for the horrid woman to go away. As soon as Lorianna had gone she burst out to Henny: 'I hate her!'

'Oh, no, no, no, you mustn't!' Henny had cried in alarm. 'Not your own mother. That'll never do. No, no, no, Miss Clementina!'

'She said she would tell father.' The child began to tremble. 'That's wicked.'

'No, no, not on you, dear; never on you. Your mother would never get you into trouble.'

'I wasn't thinking about me. I'd rather she told on me. I'm used to getting into trouble with father and I don't mind.'

This was a lie, she knew. It distressed her beyond words to be at the receiving end of her father's wrath, but equally it was the truth that she would rather have mother tell on her than on Henny. The thought of Henny being subjected to the torture of a beating or the terrors of the cellar was unendurable.

'You're a brave girl,' Henny had said, kissing her warmly. 'A very brave, good and loving little girl and Henny loves you dearly. Oh, very dearly. But you mustn't think badly of your mother; all she wants is for you to grow up to be a fine lady.'

Now, as they prepared to leave Knock Hill, the nurse said, 'Come, take Henny's hand and help her down this steep slope. I'm liable to tumble if you don't!'

So they picked their way down the hill hand in hand, with the wind clawing at their clothes and snatching their breath away. Henny had to stop for a few minutes at the foot until she recovered once more. Then they crossed the meadow where groups of small butterflies swooped around and gnats danced in long columns in the still air; then on to the path where cow parsley, as high as Henny's shoulders, turned the roadside white.

It seemed then, more than ever, that Clementina and Henny were alone in the world.

'Look!' Henny said. 'The hawthorn flowers are beginning to turn pink.'

'I wish they stayed all white all the time.'

'Oh, but pink is such a pretty colour too, don't you think? Look at the briar bushes and remember what Mr Scott said: "All twinkling with the dewdrops' sheen, the briar rose falls in streamers green." '

Henny suddenly danced forward, boots clumping on the stony road, hands holding out her skirts.

'For the rose, ho, the rose!
Is the eye of the flowers,
Is the blush of the meadows that feel themselves fair
Is the lighting of beauty that strikes through the bowers . . .'

Clementina laughed out loud and clapped her hands and then went dancing after the nurse, hat flopping so much that it eventually fell off.

'Oh dear, oh dear!' Henny said. 'What am I going to do with this hat!' She perched it on top of her own and made tears of hilarity pour down Clementina's face. Never had there been anything so funny as Henny dancing along the road in two hats and clumpy boots, faded blue dress hitched up to reveal thick woollen stockings.

But before they turned the next corner Henny stopped, took off the small floppy hat and placed it on Clementina's head. 'Right now! We'll soon be back home. We've had our fun and now we must behave very properly. That's much easier once you've had some fun, don't you think?'

Clementina nodded and rubbed the tears of laughter from her face with a fistful of pinafore.

71

'I wonder,' said Henny, 'if we slipped in the side door and along to the kitchen, would Cook be able to give us a glass of her delicious lemonade?'

Clementina knew that it all depended on whether or not Mrs Musgrove was in the vicinity. If they were very quiet going along the stone-flagged corridor and if the housekeeper was upstairs or even in her sitting-room, they would be all right. Cook was a kindly person and wouldn't normally grudge the lemonade. The only danger with her was she could be what Henny called 'volatile'.

'It all depends, you see,' Henny had explained once, 'if Mrs Musgrove has been picking on her. Oh yes, sometimes Mrs Musgrove pick-pick-picks and that makes Cook very volatile.'

It was a dangerous and tricky business, but worth it if success was rewarded by a drink of lemonade, or by the even rarer treat of one of Mrs Prowse's home-made barley bannocks, liberally spread with equally mouthwatering home-made jam. Such delicacies were never seen upstairs in the nursery except for Sunday or birthday teas.

The side door had to be reached first of all by entering the yard where the gardeners had their cottages and even here there could be the danger of meeting Mrs Musgrove. It wouldn't be the first time they had come across her in the yard; formidable figure with its heavy key-laden chatelaine hanging round her waist, hair parted in the middle and screwed back tighter than tight at the back of her head. Her sharp daggers of eyes missed nothing and even though she was intent on issuing orders to the gardener about the vegetables or fruit she wanted brought in, she would see Henny and Clementina trying to sneak past. And then she'd want to know immediately why they were not using the front door.

But on this occasion they were lucky. The walled yard was silent and empty and they were able to slip into the house without any trouble.

The long flagged passage was cold and dark compared

with the sunny garden and along one side stood a row of filled coal-scuttles and the zinc liners for the wooden scuttles with sloping lids which were in most of the rooms. There were also some tin-lined white wooden boxes with sloping sides which were used for cleaning grates and laying fires. Each had a tray on top containing brushes, black-lead powder for iron work and special cloth gloves kept for the job. The gardeners were supposed to keep up the supply of dry kindling and the under-housemaid to keep the scuttles filled with coal.

Off this long corridor were different doors that fascinated Clementina and she always explored behind each as she and Henny tiptoed along. There was the store-room which was kept locked and only Mrs Musgrove held the key. But Henny said that inside it had a red tiled floor and grey painted shelves and cupboards. In the cupboards and on the shelves there was everything from bars of yellow soap for rough scrubbing and soft soap like green jelly for washing up, to marmalade in great stone jars and bottles of gooseberries and plums, raspberries and blackcurrants to be used for dishes of stewed fruit and Sunday tarts throughout the year.

All the good china and silver cutlery were kept under lock and key in huge, ceiling-high glass-fronted cupboards in the housekeeper's sitting-room next door. Opposite there was the red-tiled larder with slate shelves and pierced metal fly-proof windows. A similar place was kept especially for hanging game. Then there was the servants' hall in which stood a small table with an aspidistra on it and a long table at which all the staff ate except Mrs Musgrove; she ate alone and in state in her housekeeper's room. Henny and Alice Tait had their meals upstairs in the nursery. There were no carpets in the servants' hall, but a rug lay in front of the fire around which some rather saggy-seated armchairs were grouped and above the fireplace hung a sepia engraving of Landseer's 'Monarch of the Glen'.

A side corridor leading off the main one led to the

servants' bedrooms and in the main passageway between the kitchen door and the laundry were ranged six or seven flat-irons used for all the domestic ironing.

'Hello, wee ruffian!' Cook greeted Clementina when she and Henny reached the kitchen. 'And what have you been up to today, eh? Something wicked I'll bet! Oh, you needn't give me that big green-eyed innocent stare. I know you of old, I do. And I know what you've come in here for and it's not to enquire after Cook's health, is it now?' Mrs Prowse was an almost incessant talker, another thing about her that infuriated Mrs Musgrove who was very tight-lipped. Mrs Prowse talked while she worked, while she ate, while she was taking a so-called rest in one of the armchairs in the servants' hall and when there was no one to talk to, she talked to herself.

'Oh no, little missy. I know you're here for some of Cook's lemonade. Mima, don't just stand there grinning like a hyena,' she whirled round to the kitchen-maid. 'Away through to the pantry and fetch some for the little lady and her nanny. Little lady, indeed. Did you hear what I said, eh?' Back to Clementina again: 'You're no lady, are you? What are you, eh?'

'A wee ruffian,' Clementina answered dutifully.

Henny tutted at the cook. 'Oh dear, you shouldn't make her say things like that, Mrs Prowse, you really shouldn't . . .'

'She doesn't mind,' Cook said, giving Clementina's hair a gentle tug as she bounced past her to reach the huge black range that occupied almost all of one wall. 'Do you, eh?'

'No,' Clementina agreed truthfully.

The range fascinated her. It had a central grate and two ovens on either side and everything about it was made of heavy iron and was always extremely hot – which was why, no doubt, Cook's face was always fiery pink and dripping with sweat and she had to keep mopping at it with her big white apron.

Housemaids flitted about in the corridor outside, their

feet clicking up and down the stairs from the passageway to the upper region of the house. Sometimes the scullery-maid emerged from the scullery that opened out from the kitchen, only to be shouted back by the cook who Henny insisted wasn't really very unkind, but had a terrible burden of work to get through and everything had to be on time. As a result she dare not allow either herself or anyone else to waste a minute. She never even stopped to fight with Mrs Musgrove, but just kept bouncing back and forth past her, talking all the time as she struggled to get the baking done or dinner ready before the dinner gong was rung.

The lemonade proved as delicious as ever and to Clementina's joy a coconut-covered madeleine was delivered to her with another friendly tug of the hair.

'Ooh!' Her eyes widened in disbelief at her incredible good fortune.

'Now, now, what do polite little girls say?' Henny prompted.

'Thank you very much, Cook.'

'Just hurry up and eat up, the pair of you, then get out of my way. As well as tea I've a five-course meal to get ready. They're having dinner guests tonight.'

Clementina felt happy in the kitchen with its warmth and bustle and its delicious smells. She wished that she and Henny had a bedroom along the corridor beside cook and the other staff. It was so much better down here than away at the top of the tower, where even in the summer the wind howled and moaned continuously under the eaves and in the winter it was icy cold and extremely draughty.

Alice Tait said the tower was haunted and ghosties and ghoulies came out at night to gobble up human sacrifices. Once when Henny had heard Alice, she had boxed her ears and warned her that she'd better not dare to frighten Miss Clementina again or she would be sent packing.

'I'm going to be a cook when I grow up,' Clementina suddenly announced. 'And have a kitchen of my own.'

Cook and Henny laughed at that and Cook said, 'You've a lot to learn, wee ruffian.'

And Henny looked down at her with love and echoed: 'A kitchen of my own!'

CHAPTER EIGHT

The dinner party had gone well, so why did she feel such a sense of let-down?

Depression lay heavy on Lorianna. Standing in all her finery in front of the bedroom mirror, she saw that she looked beautiful but felt only sadness. Gemmell deftly unhooked the mauve chiffon dress with its off-the-shoulder neckline, bead trimming, satin bows and many-tiered train of satin frills. Then she helped her out of her petticoats and corset and other undergarments and into her lace-trimmed nainsook nightdress. As soon as Lorianna seated herself at the dressing-table, the maid began unpinning her hair which tonight had been elaborately puffed out in front. At last, the brushing task completed and all the clothes put away, Gemmell bade her goodnight and she was left once more to contemplate herself sadly in the mirror.

What had been wrong tonight? Cook had excelled herself with the food. The Fausse Fortue Claire, the Filets de Sole à la Cardinal, the Jambon de York à la Macedoine, the Sherry Trifle – everything had been perfection. The conversation had never once flagged; Mr Wyndford, Mr Binny and Gavin had spoken at length about their latest game of golf, and how they would conduct the war with the Boers.

Mrs Wyndford, Mrs Binny and Lorianna herself had discussed the merits and demerits of the minister's last sermon and what everyone had been wearing at church. The guests had eventually taken their leave contentedly smiling at having passed such a pleasant evening. After they had gone, Gavin had actually remarked on how successful the dinner party had been — normally she would have felt most grateful at receiving the nearest thing to a compliment that Gavin ever gave her.

What *had* gone wrong?

Looking back with her mind's eye, Lorianna suddenly realised how old everyone had been. Gavin was forty, sixteen years her senior, but as far as his friends and acquaintances were concerned he seemed to gravitate to even older people. Mr Wyndford, the banker, must be at least fifty-five and his wife not much younger. Mr Binny, one of the most important businessmen in Bathgate, was probably older still and rumour had it that his wife could give him a few years.

So old, so staid, so dull. The men pontificating in their high stiff collars. The women piously gossiping. It wasn't that she had been bored — it was more serious than that. She had felt oppressed. She had looked at Gavin with his short red hair neatly parted on one side and his V-shaped beard perfectly clipped and his fine gold-rimmed pince-nez primly set on the bridge of his nose, and she had felt sad. She tried to trace her sadness to its roots, but felt so hopelessly depressed she could hardly be bothered. She had always been so full of life and love and so eager to give freely of that love, but over the years of marriage to Gavin somehow life and love had become despoiled and eroded until now, suddenly, she knew she no longer wanted to share anything with him. She felt a folding into herself, a shrinking, a shrivelling. And it grieved her that she should feel like this.

Lorianna looked at herself in the mirror, gazed bitter-eyed at the satin cloak of her hair reaching down past her hips, her full red lips and the firm voluptuousness of her breasts and she thought — what a waste. She forced herself to rise and go over to climb into the big double bed and lie staring up at the ceiling, not bothering even to blow out the lamp.

She must have fallen into an exhausted sleep eventually, because she awoke with Gemmell tapping on the bedroom door.

'Enter.'

'Good morning, madam.'

The maid put the tray on the bedside table, tugged the curtains open, then piled extra pillows behind Lorianna so that she could be comfortably supported when she sat up and had the tray on her lap. The tea and thinly-cut bread and butter refreshed her physically, but failed to reach her deep inner core of grief.

She chose a morning frock of white muslin with a handsome top tunic effect embroidered in ruby red and sapphire blue, and after morning prayers she had a silent breakfast with Gavin and Gilbert in the dining-room. No one ever spoke at breakfast; Gavin and Gilbert just concentrated on their newspapers. The room faced the front of the house and Lorianna could see part of the drive and a bushy wall of willow, beech, ash and birch trees, their branches dipping and quivering.

The clock on the mantleshelf tick-tocked relentlessly as she toyed with her egg and sipped at her tea. Later she tried to summon enough energy to appear interested in Mrs Musgrove's report on the stores and what needed to be ordered from the grocer, the butcher and fishmonger in Bathgate. Then there was the question of the menu for dinner. All this took some considerable time, because Mrs Musgrove was particular about the stores and kept a meticulously detailed record of everything in the store-room and pantries. Lorianna was left in no doubt that Mrs Musgrove thought it the duty of the lady of the house also to check on every detail. This Lorianna conscientiously did, but only with Mrs Musgrove's lists and cash book and files of tradesmens' accounts. She never ventured downstairs to inspect the shelves or the interiors of cupboards. Relieved of the housekeeper at last, she rang for Gemmell.

'It's such a lovely day, Gemmell, I think I shall go for my walk now.'

Gemmell pinned on a creamy straw hat decorated with a huge crimson bow the whole width of the brim.

'Your crimson parasol, madam?'

'Yes, the one with the satin frill.'

She decided not to go near the farm buildings today, but instead to walk to the meadow at the other side of Badger Hill and gather some wild flowers for pressing. She had already created some pretty designs with honesty, polyanthus, goose-grass and buttercup, and incorporated them into the base of a paperweight and a ring box. Now she planned to be more ambitious and decorate a dressing-table set and also make a framed picture.

Her flat basket held in one gloved hand and her parasol in the other, she set off slowly through her secret gate.

★ ★ ★

It was a very hot day and the flies had been particularly troublesome to Black Baron as he cropped the succulent grass in the corner of the long field.

Black Baron was the home farm bull, two tons of solid flesh and bone. Normally he was as gentle as a lamb, but if anything annoyed him he could become a very mean and dangerous beast. Today he was slightly annoyed by some particularly nasty and persistent flies that buzzed around his eyes and nostrils. In an effort to rid himself of their persistent attentions, he rubbed his face vigorously against the thick and thorny hedge dividing the long field from the meadow.

The disastrous effect of this was not only to collect a deep painful scratch on the most tender part of his colossal anatomy – his nose – but also to get his horns caught in the thickest parts of the hedge. This was altogether too much to bear, so he set about demolishing the offending hedge. The more he attacked it, however, the more he tore his muzzle and face until he looked a real fearsome sight with his bloodshot eyes and blood-spattered face. Standing back he pawed the ground in rage, then launched his massive bulk in a furious charge at the offending barrier only to finish up on his knees in the meadow. Snorting with fury, he looked up to find something else on which to vent his temper.

★　　★　　★

There was a sunny glade at the side of the meadow where a little stream gurgled along. Nearby in the trees blackbirds whistled and willow-wrens plaintively sang. Lorianna picked a few flowers beside the stream before sauntering to some hedgerows further on, where she discovered white violets and grey blue-veined ones as well as the more ordinary purple variety. Further on again she found short-stemmed cowslips with a delicious honey-sweet scent and had just placed some in her basket and was continuing her stroll, twirling her parasol over her shoulder in an effort to create a cooling breeze, when she heard the angry bellow. She was only slightly startled at first, thinking that the bull must be safely secured in the long field. But when she turned she screamed in terror at the sight of the enraged animal pounding towards her. Dropping both basket and parasol, she began to run, but tripped over her long skirts and fell, painfully twisting her ankle.

Her screaming became panic-stricken as she struggled unsuccessfully to get to her feet and run again. Then suddenly she heard a gruff command and a loud barking mixed with her screams as Ben and Jess came racing between her and the bull and stopped it in its tracks. While they were jumping up, barking and snapping at the bull, she felt herself being swept off her feet and carried away.

'You're all right now,' the calm deep voice of Robert Kelso assured her. He climbed over the stile and into the next field with her in his arms as coolly and effortlessly as if she had been no heavier than a feather.

He was wearing an open-necked shirt with the sleeves rolled up and she could feel the warmth and strength of him emanating through his skin, and smell the musky male smell of him. Still holding her, he turned and whistled to the dogs to come.

'Thank you, Kelso,' she said, her voice trembling with the shock she had had. 'You can put me down now.'

But when he did so she cried out in pain. 'My ankle! I think I must have broken it.'

Firmly he sat her down on the grass and, kneeling in front of her, he lifted her skirt and put his hands round her ankle. Her heart pounded at the impropriety of the situation, but she refrained from saying anything because after all it was an emergency and he was only trying to help her. Watching him, her face contorted in pain, although his big hands were so gentle that he looked as if he was caressing her.

'No it's not broken,' he said eventually. 'It's probably a bad strain. You'll need to rest it.'

'How am I going to get home?'

He shrugged. 'We're nearer the farm. I can carry you there, put you on a cart and drive you home. Or I can carry you all the way back if you prefer.'

The embarrassment of arriving at Blackwood House in the arms of the grieve for all to see didn't bear thinking about.

'No, just get me to the farm please,' Lorianna asked.

Without another word he slid one hand under her legs and the other round her waist and hoisted her up. She was forced to cling round his neck as he strode along the hard ridged path through the field. Somehow the silence between them intensified the touch of his hand on her legs and waist and the feel of her left breast against the hardness of his chest. Her face was close to his shoulder and she became aware of the rich tan of his skin and the way the development of his shoulder muscles gave a shortened effect at the sides of the neck. She noticed the thick glossy texture of his inky black hair and how it grew thickly

82

down in front of his ears and a smooth black lock of it had slid over his brow. He had very deep-set eyes and when they suddenly stared down at her she noticed they were a cool silvery-grey colour, before she hastily directed her attention to the path ahead. They were nearing the farmhouse and when they reached it Kelso kicked the door open and carried her through a cool shadowy passage and into a low-ceilinged room which was obviously the farm kitchen.

There was an oak settle by the fire covered with a long cushion, and it was on this that he laid her.

'I ought to get that shoe off now,' he said. 'It would be agony for you to get it off later.'

'Very well. But do be careful, Kelso. It's quite painful enough as it is. Oh!' She bit her lip and gripped his shoulder as he bent over her, loosened and then removed the shoe. Her foot was now so swollen that she felt quite faint at the sight of it.

'You look pale,' he said. 'Try to relax while I make you a cup of tea.'

He was relaxed enough, she thought, as she watched him move about the room putting the kettle on the fire and fetching a cup and saucer from the dresser.

'Do you live here alone?' she asked.

'Yes. I've been a widower now for nearly seven years.'

'Who looks after you?'

He smiled round at her, surprising her with strong white teeth and the way the smile made his eyes glimmer. 'I don't need anyone to look after me.'

The smile had a most disturbing, melting effect on her. It made her feel more faint and weak than the pain of her ankle and she was thankful that she was reclining back on the settle.

'I mean who cleans the house?'

He shrugged. 'The woman who does the bothy scrubs it once a week.'

'I see.' Lorianna could also see black hairs on his brown arms and chest and the way his shoulders tapered down to a flat abdomen and long muscular thighs. He was a big man, but without an ounce of soft or superfluous fat on his body. She remembered now: 'the Iron Man', they called him. She had heard Gavin and Gilbert call him that when they had spoken of his enormous capacity for work and his amazing strength – how he could handle the hundred-weight sacks of barley with consummate ease, how he could lift a plough from a farm cart single-handed.

'Drink this,' he said, now.

Never before in her life had she been ordered to do anything by a servant. But in the silence that followed, she found herself accepting the cup from his hands and putting it to her lips.

CHAPTER NINE

Clementina had never had such a gloriously happy day in her life. She was dazed with the joy and wonder of it. Henny had taken her to Bathgate to watch the procession and had then decided to let her march with the other children through the decorated streets. They both knew that this was an outrageous and dangerous thing for Henny to do, and if found out would be the means of getting her instantly dismissed.

Young ladies did not jostle through the streets hatless and gloveless with the *hoi palloi*.

The streets were beautiful with their rainbows of bunting looped across from one side to the other and flags sprouting from every window. But loveliest of all were the floral arches made from hundreds of blooms. In the procession there were many floats, most of them supplied by local tradesmen and all vivid splashes of colour, the result of hours of enthusiastic and conscientious labour.

The reason for the procession was to honour the memory of John Newlands, once a citizen of Bathgate, who had gone out to the West Indies and made a fortune which he left to be used to build a school in which the poor children of the town were to have free education. This had been the origin of the Bathgate Academy, the imposing pillared building perched at the top of the hill in Marjorybanks Street.

'Newlands Day', however, had become mixed with the ancient history of the town. There were now Royal Proclamations and trumpet-blowing Heralds in colourful regalia and Robert the Bruce rode at the head of the procession on a frisky black stallion. He was followed by an open carriage in which sat his daughter, the lovely Princess Marjory, with a crown on her head and a purple velvet and ermine-trimmed cloak draped round her shoulders. On horseback or in carriages there were also a velvet-cloaked Walter, Lord High Steward of Scotland who had lived in Bathgate Castle and who had married Princess Marjory; the Abbot of Holyrood, Lord Lyon, King-of-Arms, the Earl of Moray and spearmen and others too many to mention all in colourful and dashing costume. There were pipe bands too and lines of enthusiastic drummers. The noise of the procession was ear-splitting especially when, each time the children reached one of the floral arches, they cheered at the tops of their voices.

Clementina yelled with the rest and was so hysterically excited that she kept skipping instead of marching and wildly waving to Henny, who was pushing desperately along through the crowded pavements trying to keep up and not lose sight of her.

All the children wore their best pinafores and had what they called 'tinnies' hanging round their necks on pieces of string; when they eventually reached the field where the sports and games were to take place, their tinnies were filled with milk and they were given a paper bag containing a cheese sandwich, a bun and an apple or an orange.

Clementina won two races and was given a sixpence and a bar of Highland toffee which she shared with Henny and they chewed for most of the long walk home up the hills. They stopped half-way up the Drumcross Road at the horse-trough, where horses always needed to be watered after the steep climb before being able to continue any further. Henny washed Clementina's sticky face and hands and dried them on the skirt of her blue cotton dress. She had been carrying the little girl's hat and gloves all day and now she put them on the child before anxiously inspecting her. Oh, how beautiful she looked with her long sunny hair shimmering from underneath the white lacy trim of her hat and her emerald eyes jewel bright with joy and love as she gazed up at her. She was glad she had given her the chance to be in the procession. Children, she believed, should have lots of memories of love and happiness to look back on and Clementina, she knew, would never forget this day. But of course it had been an outrageous thing for them to do and something that could yet be discovered with terrible consequences. After all, they still had to get safely into the house and upstairs to the nursery without being seen.

Certainly Henny knew that the master and mistress were out to dinner, which was why she and Clementina had been able to stay away for so long without needing to rush back for Clementina's usual evening visit to the drawing-room. But anything could have gone wrong by now – the master and mistress might have returned early; Master Gilbert might be in; or Mrs Musgrove could catch them. Sometimes Henny wasn't even too sure about some of the maids.

Still, all the fear and tension and harassment of the day had been worth it, she knew, when she looked at the child's upturned, happy and adoring face.

'There now,' she said, dropping a quick kiss on Clementina's nose. 'All nice and clean!'

Hand in hand, they began trudging up the hill again, and along the avenue of trees which dwarfed them. The evening sun dappled their plodding figures as well as the dusty road through the archway of branches. High banks now, hedgerows dark with the shadows of trees and rolling fields with corn bending as if nodding off to sleep. Above, there was the serene blue sky with snowy clouds wisping into bars of gold and pink.

Along the road in front of Henny and Clementina a white butterfly floated. How quiet and content everything was.

Henny announced suddenly, 'Mr Arnold:

The evening comes, the fields are still,
The twinkle of the thirsty rill.
Unheard all day ascends again,
Deserted is the half-mown plain,
Silent the swathes! the singing wain,
The mowers cry, the dogs alarms,
All housed within the sleeping farms!'

Clementina sighed with happiness almost too much to
bear. To finish such a day with poetry! Only Henny could
think of such a thing. And of course it was because of
Henny's love of poetry that she had grown to love it too.
Taking her cue from Henny's inviting pause, she began to
recite:

'The business of the day is done,
The last left hay-maker is gone,
And from the thyme upon the height,
And from the elder blossom white,
And pale dog-roses in the hedge,
And from the mint plant in the sedge.'

Now Henny joined in and they spoke together:

'In puffs of balm the night air blows,
The perfume which the day fore-goes,
And on the pure horizon far,
See, pulsing with the first-born star,
The liquid sky above the hill!
The evening comes, the fields are still.'

Past the Littlegate woods now, where already the interior
was dusky and impenetrable. For a minute or two as they
walked along they heard a loud though distant clamour
of rooks and daws, restlessly moving in their roost-trees
before settling for the night. The cawing and dawing rose

to a crescendo, then fell into silence.

By the time they had reached the crossroads both Henny and Clementina's feet had slowed considerably and Henny had become breathless.

'It's lovely living in such a hilly place,' she managed eventually, 'but oh dear, oh dear, when I say it takes my breath away I mean it literally. I'm puffing like a steam engine again, aren't I?'

'Shall we stop and rest a while?' Clementina asked.

'Better not, Miss Clementina. We're so very late as it is. I dread to think what the master and mistress would say if they knew.'

'I don't care. I don't care about them.'

'Oh, Miss Clementina, you must care about your mother and father.'

'They don't care about me.'

'You mustn't say such a thing. You mustn't even think such a thing! Of course they care about you, dear.'

They turned off the Drumcross Road and along the rough dirt path between some fields and a few scattered trees. Then the trees thickened until on either side there was a thick wall of beech trees with trunks bushy-leafed all the way down. At last there were the big gates of the drive, with meadows opening out at either side. This was where Henny and Clementina felt exposed and apprehensive in case they could be seen from any of the upper windows of the house, although the house was not yet visible to them.

'Run!' Henny whispered, clutching at her hat and trying not to make too much noise with her boots. Round the curving drive they flew, keeping to the right and the shelter of the rhododendron bushes until they reached the side entrance to the gardeners' yard and ran into the darkness of the corridor. This was a very tricky and dangerous part, because the corridor was very poorly lit with only an occasional candle. But with great care and quietness they managed to reach the servants' stair up to the library corridor; from there, with a prayer in their fast beating hearts, they tiptoed along to the reception hall and across to the door of the tower. Despite her breathlessness Henny still hurried agitatedly up the tower stairs and did not relax until they were both safely shut inside the night nursery.

'Oh dear, oh dear! What a relief, Miss Clementina. Oh, you'll never know what a relief! Oh dear, oh dear.' She clutched at her chest, closed her eyes and took a couple of deep breaths.

Clementina looked at Henny, at her shabby hat askew with flowers drooping over one eye, her short tight jacket, faded blue dress, her black dusty boots; then at her dear face with its sweet turned-up-at-the-corner mouth and delicate dusting of freckles, and an enormous wave of gratitude engulfed her.

At first she was speechless with it and Henny, suddenly aware of the child's intense concentration on her, said, 'What's wrong, Miss Clementina?' Her thin hands fluttered up over her shabby clothes and then tried to tidy back stray wisps of hair and tuck them behind her ears.

'Do I look an awful sight?'

Clementina suddenly fell on her and clutched her fiercely round the waist. 'Thank you.' The words were muffled against the nurse's body, but she heard them and was touched.

'Come now,' she said. 'We're both tired – happily tired, thanks be to God – and it's time we went to bed.'

Henny helped Clementina to undress first and then tucked her in one of the two iron bedsteads. There Clementina watched Henny enact her magic trick of undressing under her flannelette nightgown.

'Do you mind, Miss Clementina,' she said, sitting down at last on Clementina's bed as she brushed out her thick wavy hair, 'if we just have a little poem tonight instead of a story? I'm so tired, you see.'

'A poem will be perfectly all right,' Clementina said kindly.

'All right, dear, close your eyes now and I'll say it very softly. That's a good girl . . .

A cloudless sky; a world of heather,
Purple of foxglove; yellow of broom;
We two among it, wading together,
Shaking out honey, treading perfume.
Crowds of bees are giddy with clover,
Crowds of grasshoppers skip at our feet,
Crowds of larks at their matins hang over,
Thanking the Lord for a life so sweet.'

Clementina drifted off to sleep with a peaceful smile on her face, happy in the knowledge that Henny would sleep close beside her on the other iron bedstead with the patchwork quilt that she had made with her own hands. That night she dreamed of walking hand in hand with Henny round the garden and down to the river bank where the grass was dew-laden and the water sparkling. Bees were humming and brilliant butterflies shimmered in the heat of the early morning sun. The mist had risen from the Bathgate hills and they stood out sharp and clear and higher than before. The bluish mistiness about the woods had also been blown away and everything was bright and beautiful. Everything was clearly defined, even the smells: the sweet smell of the grass and flowers, the pungent aroma of greenery. She awoke with the smell of the flowers strong in her nostrils, only to discover that it was Henny's familiar toilet water.

Whenever Henny felt hot or faint, she always refreshed herself with a dab or two of this magic water and then she would take a couple of sniffs of it and say happily, 'There now, I'm fine again.'

Clementina had never smelled it so strongly before and when she peered round she immediately saw why. The bottle had fallen from the bedside table and spilled on to the floor.

'Oh dear, oh dear,' she cried out, unconsciously

mimicking Henny as she scrambled up in bed. 'Henny, your magic water's all spilled out! You must have knocked it over in your sleep.'

Henny did not answer and that was unusual. Indeed, it was unusual for Henny to be in bed at all in the morning. She was always up, bustling about and singing when Clementina wakened – ready to report on what a beautiful, interesting day it was, full of wondrous things to learn about and explore.

'Henny, I'm wakened!'

Clementina bounced from the bed and pattered across to clamber in beside the nurse. But even then Henny didn't move; she just lay cold and still.

'Henny?'

Clementina leaned over her to peer into the fragile bird face, almost invisible in its nest of tousled brown hair. And as she continued to stare, the terrible truth began to dawn on her.

'Oh, Henny, please don't be dead!'

She was too shocked to weep. Clinging to the flannelette nightgown, she pressed her face hard against it and kept on repeating, 'Don't be dead. *Please* don't be dead.'

CHAPTER TEN

'. . . I shall not return even to the land of darkness and the shadow of death. A land of darkness as darkness itself and of the shadow of death, without any order and where the light is as darkness . . .'

The servants had gathered in the hall for morning prayers the day after the funeral and stood in silence with heads bowed – except for Janet the scullery-maid, who kept sniffling and noisily blowing her nose, irritating everyone. She was only thirteen and cursed with the affliction of never doing anything right and sniffling at the slightest provocation. Her eyes were constantly bloodshot and her face blotchy with weeping in her scullery dungeon.

Gavin Blackwood eyed her reprovingly over his pince-nez. Then as Clementina suddenly began to make strange high-pitched animal noises and jerky moans, his face darkened with annoyance. He managed to continue, but had to slightly raise his voice in order to be heard, something he scrupulously avoided as a rule. He liked to keep a tight, smooth rein on himself at all times, just as he liked to be punctual, orderly, organised and tidy.

'Oh death, where is thy sting? Oh grave, where is thy victory? . . .'

Clementina had lifted the front of her pinafore and hidden her face in it, but even this failed to completely muffle the shrieking sobs that racked her body.

Gavin's eyes hardened with fury. Clementina's dress had become partly caught up with the pinafore, revealing black woollen stockings and the legs of white knickers.

However, he managed to keep his voice smooth: '. . . Therefore, my beloved brethren, be ye steadfast, unmovable, always abounding in the work of the Lord, forasmuch as ye know that your labour is not in vain in the Lord.'

The servants waited for the master and mistress and Master Gilbert to disappear as usual into the dining-room. But today, before doing so, the master addressed Alice Tait the nursery-maid.

'How dare you allow your charge to behave in such a disgraceful manner? When is your next day off?'

'This afternoon, sir.'

'You will stay on duty instead and instruct Miss Clementina on how to behave.'

'Yes, sir.'

Alice could hardly choke out the words. To lose her time off today of all days was like a death knell. Worse in fact, for today she was going to meet the new ploughman. She had never found it easy to get a man although she was always eager and willing, but she wasn't as pretty as some with her plump face and barrel body. Eck McColl was the ploughman's name and he had asked her to meet him in the corner of the hayfield at half-past two. It was unthinkable that she should miss the chance; she had thought and dreamed of nothing else all week.

'Take her upstairs just now and see that she washes her face and makes herself respectable. Then after breakfast, bring her to me in the oak room.'

'Yes, sir.'

Alice waited until he had gone into the dining-room before grabbing Clementina and dragging her up the tower stairs.

'See what you've done?' she said, punching the child's back all the way. Quite apart from being tragically deprived of probably the only chance she would ever have to get a man, she felt harassed beyond endurance by the unexpected burden of responsibility and extra work involved in having to look after Clementina. As

94

if she hadn't enough to do, making beds and lighting fires and scrubbing the nursery floors and running up and down the stairs for Miss High and Mighty's meals and bath water and God knows all what. It was all right for some, wasn't it? Some had all the luck, with all that blonde hair and those big green eyes. *And* with somebody to run after them into the bargain!

Once they were safely in the nursery and all the doors shut, she peered close into Clementina's face and said, 'Stop your howling.' Then she began to violently shake the child while repeating over and over, 'Stop your howling, stop your howling!' Suddenly she hustled Clementina over to the basin and, after splashing water into it from the jug, commanded her, 'Wash your face!'

Clementina stood helplessly buffeted by her grief, unable to concentrate on any action other than finding enough breath between sobs. She could not accept that Henny had gone forever. It was too terrible to contemplate . . . impossible to be endured.

'Come on!' Alice punched her again. 'You heard what he said.' But still Clementina did nothing.

'All right, then,' Alice shouted in exasperation, near to tears herself at the loss of big Eck McColl. 'I'll do it for you.' And forcing Clementina's head over the basin she dipped the sponge in the water and smacked it over the little girl's face, holding it hard against her nose and mouth. A moment or two later she threw aside the sponge in horror, for Miss Clementina was choking and making the frightening noises that Alice had heard from babies with whooping cough. And Alice had known babies with whooping cough die. In terror now and filled with remorse, the nursery-maid dragged Clementina over to the open window and held her near to it to get more air.

'Miss Clementina, I'm sorry. Honest to God I am! Miss Clementina, for pity's sake! Do you want to see me arrested and dragged off to jail and hanged for murder?' She rubbed energetically at the child's back. 'And me just newly sixteen and never laid a finger on a soul in my life.'

She could see that Clementina was recovering and beginning to breathe normally again, but dregs of horror remained to stir Alice's already over-active imagination.

'Fancy!' she said, running to fetch a towel to dry Clementina's face and a brush to tidy her hair. 'I nearly murdered you there and that's the God's truth. That would have meant another funeral. No, two! A funeral from here for you, with flowers all over your beautiful white coffin and everybody weeping and wailing. And a hanging for me in a prison in Edinburgh and then do you know what they'd do? They'd shove me in any old box, dig a hole in the prison yard and stick me down there with not a soul to shed one tear.'

Clementina, exhausted now, was staring up at Alice with a pathetic, pleading expression.

'Come on through and have breakfast,' Alice said. 'I'm so hungry I could eat a horse, tail and all!' She took Clementina's hand and led her along the tiny windowless passageway into the room that served as a day nursery.

'You sit there at the table and I'll run downstairs and fetch it.'

Already her fury and frustration had spent itself and she was sure that something could be worked out. One way or another she would manage to keep her tryst with big Eck. By the time she had reached the kitchen she was whistling.

'How is the young mistress?' Cook asked. 'Poor wee ruffian, she took it bad, didn't she? Like two peas in a pod, her and her nanny was. Doted on each other, they did, and she's bound to miss her.' She gave a quick furtive glance around. 'Here's an extra bit of toast for the wee soul. And now the master wants to see her in his study. Surely he's not going to give her a beating at a time like this?'

'There's a devil in him,' Alice said. 'Honest to God, there is! Evil spirits gets into some folks and makes them do wicked things and he's wicked all right. He's going to thrash poor Miss Clementina to shreds, I just know it.'

'Evil spirits indeed!' Cook scoffed. 'The trouble with you, Alice Tait, is you've got far too much imagination. It'll get you into trouble yet, you wait and see — you'd better not let the master hear you say such terrible things about him. He's a fine Christian gentleman who does his duty as best he thinks fit, although I do think myself that at times he's a bit too severe with the child. Mind you, she's wild at times and needs putting right. She'd rather race about kicking a ball with the village lads than sit prim and proper at her sewing as any nice young lady should, and something has to be done about that but not at a time like this. At a time like this she should be left in peace to grieve for her nanny. Here, take another piece of toast up to the poor wee soul.'

Alice clumped happily back up to the nursery, her sense of drama now fully aroused. The poor mistress, grieving and pining for a favourite servant, was going to be martyred like Joan of Arc or Mary Queen of Scots. The master was a wicked, evil tyrant, (hadn't he stopped her from getting her time off?). Worse, he was a dracula, thirsty for the blood of a helpless and innocent victim.

Clementina couldn't eat any toast, so Alice wolfed it down instead. Then she inspected her charge to make sure she was clean and tidy enough for her visit to the master's study.

'Oh, you poor innocent young lady!' she kept saying. 'Honest to God, he's going to thrash you to shreds, I just know it. And you grieving for your nanny that's not yet cold in her grave. It's wicked, so it is.' She lowered her voice conspiratorially and bent down to peer closer at Clementina's face. 'One day he'll burn in the hell-fire and roast like a plucked chicken on a spit.'

She nodded with satisfaction and straightened up. 'Like a plucked chicken on a spit, turning and turning over red-hot flames.'

★　　★　　★

Downstairs in the dining-room Lorianna broke the

normal breakfast silence.

'Gavin, do you think you're being wise?'

He lowered his paper and, shocked, stared at her over his pince-nez.

'I beg your pardon?'

'Are you certain you're doing the right thing in having Clementina brought to you? You're surely not going to punish her?'

'Why not? She behaved disgracefully.'

'I told you she was very fond of Mrs Henning.'

'That is no excuse for bad behaviour. She was worse than that idiot scullery-maid, instead of setting a good example to the servants.'

'But when you lose someone!'

'Really, my dear, I cannot see what all the fuss is about. Even the best of servants can be easily replaced. And Mrs Henning was not the best; she was a weak, stupid and completely disorganised woman who obviously never was able to exercise sufficient control over our daughter. It is a great pity that you engaged her in the first place and I only hope your regrettable error of judgement has not done Clementina irrevocable harm. I will see to it that Mrs Henning's replacement is a more suitable person — a governess who can discipline and instruct the child properly. Meantime, I have an added responsibility and I do not intend to shirk it.'

'Gavin, please, surely a little kindness . . . when she's so upset . . . *please*, for my sake . . .' Lorianna trembled with the strength of her feelings, a strength that seemed to outrage her husband.

'I forbid you to say another word on the subject. You are not qualified to express an opinion.' He folded his newspaper and rose, his eyes twitching behind his pince-nez.

She could see how angry he was and trembled all the more at the thought that instead of helping Clementina she had made matters infinitely worse for her. Later she could barely concentrate on what Mrs Musgrove was

98

saying, but tried to gain some peace of mind from what Gilbert had whispered to her before he had left for the factory.

'Don't worry, dear step-mamma. Our little Clementina is tougher than you think.'

But still she could not banish the memory of the child's sobbing. It was an added distress with which she felt ill-equipped to cope. Already her emotions were in such a turmoil that her mind dared not consider them and she had been desperately trying to keep herself busy so that she would have no time to feel anything. Her embroidery, her flower pressing, her floral arranging, all these activities failed to stem the frightening tide that was threatening to roar over her and rampage with her to dangerously deep waters from which there could be no return.

She had gone out to pay calls and had calls returned. She had gone to Bathgate and looked round Hardy's and McNaughton's. She had bought a new pair of black stockings with a pattern of red roses going up one side of each leg. And still she felt guilty and afraid. The added worry about Clementina was too much and she paced about the sitting-room wretchedly wringing her hands. Then she hurried through to the drawing-room to try to soothe her distraught emotions at the piano, but even this did not have its usual calming effect. She returned to the sitting-room and suddenly, seized by an irresistible impulse, she lifted the silver sweet dish and — heart pattering at her temerity — hastened across the hall with it and up the tower stairs.

In the night nursery Clementina was standing staring at Henny's bed. Then suddenly she flung herself on to it and grabbing fistfuls of Henny's patchwork quilt, clutched it up against herself, burying her face in it and stuffing lumps of it into her mouth.

'Miss Clementina!' Alice came bursting excitedly into the room, jerked her from the bed and tugged the quilt free from Clementina's rigid fingers. 'You'll never guess who's in the day nursery. You'll *never* guess who's come all the way up here to see you. Now you remember to be on your best behaviour and not be getting me into trouble again. Hurry up, come on!'

When Clementina entered the day nursery she saw, standing by the window, the figure of her mother, vividly out of place in the small starkly furnished, carpetless room. She was wearing a dress of brilliant blue taffeta with pearls looped across it and pearls hanging from her ears.

This was the woman who had spoken unkindly to Henny!

'How are you, my dear?' The blue dress loudly rustled forward. 'See, I've brought you some of the sweets you're so fond of.' The silver dish was held out.

With a vicious sweep, Clementina knocked the dish and sweets flying.

'I hate you!' she said.

CHAPTER ELEVEN

Lorianna was still white and shaken when she emerged from the tower stair and before she could recover, she received another shock. Robert Kelso was standing there, thumbs hooked in the front of his belt, a giant of a man making the hall look cramped. The rows of wool mosaic pictures on every wall, the three Louis XV commodes, the big glass-fronted display cabinet, the two Italian tables, the Chippendale chairs, the chiming clock, the ornaments – everything was reduced to a useless clutter. He was the only beautiful and real thing there with his broad shoulders, muscular brown neck and deep-set, penetrating eyes.

She stopped abruptly, vaguely aware that the maid, Gemmell, was there too. Immediately she saw her, the maid's long-nosed face flushed with what looked more like annoyance than embarrassment.

'The master says for Kelso to wait here, madam,' she said before disappearing away downstairs.

Kelso said, 'How are you?'

'Very well thank you, Kelso.'

'You look pale.' His grey eyes smiled down at her. 'Perhaps you need some more of my tea?'

Coming from a servant this was an impertinence. Yet she couldn't feel angry with him. Neither did she feel able to move away.

After a second or two he said, 'Your ankle?'

'Completely recovered, thank goodness. I must be more careful in future.'

101

He smiled again. 'Yes, it's dangerous to go around chasing bulls.'

Just then Gavin emerged from the oak room and said, 'Ah, Kelso. Come in.'

The difference between the two men was startling and Gavin looked small, almost effeminate next to Robert Kelso. Even the way they walked was different. The grieve had a slow, easy stride, in comparison with which Gavin's steps were quick and fussy.

The oak room door shut behind them and Lorianna was left standing in the hall alone. She felt faint and it took all her will-power to reach the sitting-room and sink into a chair at the window. After a few minutes, however, she rose and rustled back across the hall and into the dining-room. Closing the door quietly behind her, she went over to stand near the dining-room window.

The sitting-room and drawing-room looked out on to the back of the house and the croquet lawn and fields beyond and in the far distance the Firth of Forth. The dining-room, however, like the oak room, was at the front and faced the drive; from there she could see the patches of lawn, the bushes and trees and the shady pool with the chestnut tree dipping over it.

There were various ways to return to the farm, but the most usual route from the house would be to take the cut-off to the left a few yards down the drive. This was a path fragrant with rhododendron bushes and trees and it led to a five-bar gate and a stile which in turn led to a footpath across fields. If he knew of the secret gate, he could of course go round the side of the house through the rhododendron bushes and then away through the trees.

Time passed slowly as she stood watching. Its slowness stretched her nerves and made her whole body taut. Even her eyes felt tense and strained.

Then at last she heard his heavy tread on the stairs. She surreptitiously moved nearer to the window and, slightly edging the curtains aside, saw him leave the house and saunter away down the drive. After he had disappeared she turned worriedly back into the room. Every now and again she experienced tremors of fear as if something terrible was about to happen over which she had no control – as if the whole secure and respectable fabric of her life was in danger.

She kept dismissing these feelings as being foolish figments of a neurotic imagination and tried with an effort of conscious will to calm down and concentrate on thoughts of her lunch guest. Today her best friend Jean Dalgleish was calling and Lorianna was very much looking forward to her visit. She never managed to see enough of Jean, for she was always either pregnant or unwell or both. Often Jean's husband either took her or sent her away with the children, a couple of nurses and a few maids for long months to the seaside or to the highlands, so that she could enjoy the benefit of the air.

'But, heavens above,' Jean always rolled her eyes in exasperation. 'What better air could there be right here in the Bathgate hills?'

Jean seemed very knowledgeable about life and Lorianna had always suspected that her friend would welcome confidences about her own intimate problems and even give her some enlightenment, if not provide solutions. But somehow Lorianna could never bring herself to tread such delicate ground. It was one thing to gossip daringly about other people's predicaments; quite another to reveal one's own to the mercy of prattling tongues.

However, on this occasion, tense and worried, she did attempt to confide in her friend, in a careful roundabout way of course. They had settled in the sitting-room with their after-lunch coffee and she had admired Jean's hat of ostrich feathers and stiffened satin bows.

'You look lovely in it, Jean.'

'Thank you, my dear. You're looking beautiful yourself – perhaps a trifle paler than usual, though.'

'Well,' Lorianna forced a laugh. 'It's not because I'm

in an interesting condition.'

'Oh, I'm sorry,' Jean said. 'Fancy, only one child in – what – eight years of marriage? Have you seen a doctor?'

'Well, I . . . no . . . you see . . . Gavin doesn't seem . . . I don't think he wants any more children. At least, not yet.'

'Oh well, I suppose at your age you've still plenty of time.'

'I don't know. I must confess that sometimes . . .' She felt herself flushing with embarrassment and confusion. 'I worry – I mean about . . . about Gavin not . . .'

'Do you mean he doesn't make many demands on you?' Jean laughed. 'My dear, aren't you lucky?'

'Am I?'

'But of course. As good wives we must do our duty whenever called upon to do so, but to be called as often as I am, my dear, I do assure you can be frightfully exhausting.'

'I suppose so,' Lorianna murmured unhappily.

'No supposing about it, Lorianna, my pet! Why do you think I've to go away for my sojourns to seaside and mountains so often? Between you and I, my dear, it's not really to take the air – at least, not as far as I'm concerned. It's just to get a rest. I get so exhausted. But of course it seldom happens that way. As often as not Duncan comes with me or at best he visits me as often as he can.' She gave another trilling laugh before finishing her coffee. 'Men can be beastly at times, can't they? So demanding! It's really quite frightening to ladies of our sensibility isn't it? I mean, how different gentlemen are as compared with ladies. Like a different species altogether. How interesting, though, that your husband doesn't insist on his rights every night.'

Already Lorianna felt guilty and disloyal and keenly regretted her indiscreet disclosure. 'That's not what I said, Jean. All I said was that Gavin didn't seem to want more children at the moment.'

'Ah well,' Jean sighed. 'As I say, my dear, you've still plenty of time. Alas, I haven't any more time to spare at

104

the moment. I must be off. Duncan's invited hordes, absolutely hordes of people to dinner!'

'Oh, Jean,' Lorianna gave a helpless laugh as she crossed the room to ring for the maid to fetch her friend's parasol. 'I do admire you; I don't know how you manage.'

'It's life, my dear. A woman's lot. We've just got to manage.' They kissed warmly before bidding each other goodbye.

After her friend had left the afternoon stretched endlessly before Lorianna. She felt restless and unfulfilled. Yet Jean had indicated that she ought to feel lucky and in a way, now that she came to think of it, maybe she was. To have to suffer a physical attack — for that was how she regarded love-making — to have to suffer physical attack from Gavin every night was indeed a frightening prospect. Poor Jean! It sounded as if her husband subjected her to this painful and fatiguing ordeal as often as that. No wonder she suffered from exhaustion and had developed such a delicate constitution.

She went through to the sitting-room, thoughts following her, pestering her like a cloud of insects. Why had the intimate side of the marrage to be so painful, so frightening? Jean had said men were beastly. But surely beasts didn't savage each other when they coupled? At least, not domesticated beasts. But perhaps wild beasts did and men became like wild beasts when their passions were aroused.

The memory of her wedding day came back to her and of her mother taking her aside and saying, 'There's something I must tell you. Whatever Gavin docs to you is *right*.'

There was also the indisputable fact that she always tried to arouse Gavin's passions and encourage him to couple with her. Could she really blame him for trying to resist her baser impulses and to control his own, if it was to spare her the pain and exhaustion and deleterious effect on her health that Jean, for instance, had to suffer?

Gavin was a good husband. Lorianna had never been more sure of that than now. Determined to work through her emotional confusion and impose order on her thoughts, she vowed to try to be a better, more dutiful wife. She must endeavour to be more ladylike and control her wicked passions. No doubt she had inherited this regrettable weakness in her nature from her mother, who had come from working-class stock in Italy and, although she spent the rest of her life in Scotland desperately trying to forget her past and act like a lady, had never quite succeeded. She must not fail as her mother had failed.

The more she thought of how Gavin managed to control his passions for months on end – the last time for almost a year – the more ashamed she felt of herself. She told herself now that she ought to sit quietly down with her sewing and be content. Yet still her body rebelled. Her restlessness was like a fever.

Fortunately, Gavin came home early and she welcomed him with impulsive warmth. He seemed to bristle at her sudden rush of affection and quick kiss on his cheek.

'Good afternoon, my dear.' It was strange how he could make even these innocent words sound like a reprimand.

'I'm so glad you didn't go to Edinburgh today,' she said. 'Why do you have to go to Edinburgh so often anyway?'

He took off his pince-nez and polished it briskly with his handkerchief. 'Business, nothing you would understand.'

She sighed. 'I wish we could talk more about things – even business.'

'You're being foolish. Why should I talk to you about business? You have no need to know about such things – even if you could understand them.'

'Well, we could talk about other things then.'

'What things?' he said, his voice testy.

'About our marriage, for instance. Are you happy, Gavin? Happy with me, I mean?'

106

He neatly replaced his pince-nez and then made a bridge of his fingers, tapping their tips lightly together.

'I think I can say that I am tolerably satisfied with the way you grace my home, the way you take your place at my side when we entertain friends here for instance. Although even there, there could be room for improvement.'

'In what way?'

'I should prefer you to be more circumspect.'

'I don't quite understand, dearest.'

'You have a most regrettable emotional streak in your nature, Lorianna, that is a constant worry to me, even – or I might go as far as to say, especially – in public.'

She was shocked. 'Oh Gavin, I behave emotionally in public? Surely not!'

'It is something for which you must constantly be on the watch and take the most stringent means to suppress!'

'But I do, I do!'

'You must try to behave with calmness, dignity and modesty at all times.'

'Oh, surely I do Gavin, in public at least?'

'There have been occasions when a certain excitability has suddenly surfaced and I have been forced to catch your eye in order to quell it and silence you.'

It could not be denied that at times enthusiasms had bubbled up inside her and threatened to spill over in a vivacious monopolisation of the conversation. Now that she came to think of it, she had even caught reproving glances from ladies in the company – older, quieter, much more dignified ladies, respectable wives of Gavin's business and church friends from whom, Gavin always said, she should take an example.

'I'm sorry,' she said, lowering her eyes. Then after a few seconds, 'Shall I ring for afternoon tea?'

'Very well.'

Over the delicate, fluted china tea-cups they spoke about Clementina's future. Gavin repeated that this time he would choose who was to be in charge of her and this

time it would be a governess, someone who would educate the child properly and develop in her character the
necessary Christian virtues. 'She has been allowed to run
wild for long enough. It's time she learned self-discipline.'

Lorianna agreed, but did not tell her husband just how
wild and lacking in self-discipline Clementina had
become. The incident in the nursery had distressed and
saddened her but she would never consider for a moment
causing Clementina distress in return because of course
Gavin, had he known, would have severely punished their
daughter. The child had behaved very badly to her, but
the poor little thing had been upset about the loss of her
nanny. She forgave her gladly and when Clementina came
that night for her usual visit to the sitting-room, she tried
to be extra attentive to her. She brought out the pretty
dolls which were kept there especially for the purpose and
tried very hard to appear enthusiastic.

'Oh, look, darling, isn't it sweet? Just look at those
little shoes! Oh, isn't it a darling dolly in that sweet little
hat?'

But all the time Clementina stood stubborn and
uncooperative, chin pushed down into her pinafore and
hands clasped behind her back. Picture books were no
more successful in eliciting a response and Lorianna was
quite relieved when Tait, the nursery-maid – now pro-
moted to nanny – came to take the child away.

It had been a most disturbing day one way and another
and she was glad eventually to blow out the lamp and
collapse into bed. No sooner had she done so, however,
when she experienced the biggest shock of all – she heard
the connecting door to the dressing-room open and then
Gavin entered the bedroom carrying a candle and clad
only in his robe.

Surely she had done nothing to provoke him? She
cringed back in the shadows of the bed with rapidly racing heart, too afraid to speak or move as he came across
the room and laid the candle on the bedside table. In its
flickering light she saw the flame in his eyes and was more

afraid than she had ever been before. He snuffed out the candle and immediately the madness was let loose. There had been times during her long months of celibacy when she had forgotten what the pain of coupling was like. This time she remembered, but even her memory did not prepare her for the savagery of Gavin's passion. She closed her eyes and tried very hard to be a good wife and not to struggle or cry out.

CHAPTER TWELVE

'You know what to do?' Alice said.

Clementina nodded. A pattern had been established and at least twice a week on their afternoon walks she had to lie, face down, behind one of the bushes in the dirt road outside the main gates of Blackwood House.

'You lie there,' Alice always said. 'And don't move a muscle until I come back or else the cannibal man will get you. I'll go and see if I can chase him away.'

Clementina would lie very still on her stomach on the damp brown earth, mouth tightly shut, tongue rolled back behind her teeth, eyes on ground level, ears straining for the terrible sounds of the cannibal man who always carried a long knife with which to cut out little girl's tongues and take them home to boil them for his tea.

There was the added terror that he might eat Alice and then Clementina would be left with no one to protect her. But Alice always returned, flushed, breathless and dishevelled, but happily victorious.

'You can come out now,' she would call cheerily. 'I've made short work of *him*.'

Alice always had to help her up because she got so stiff and earth and twigs, even insects and beetles clung to her pinafore and hair.

'Lord's sake, what a sight you are!' Alice would say. 'We'd better get you back to the house and cleaned up before the master or mistress sees or they'll be disowning you.'

That meant being thrown out on her own to the mercy of the cannibal man.

'Or,' Alice said, nudging her, 'maybe they'd just banish you forever to the cellar. Or let the ghosties have you!'

There were several ghosts haunting the tower, according to Alice. One was a big black slave who had once worked in the silver mines. Another was a green lady who had been locked in the tower by a wicked husband and starved to death. Yet another was a young servant who had dropped a lamp and accidentally set fire to himself.

'Sometimes,' Alice said, 'he can be heard screaming, sometimes moaning in agony round and round the tower stairs.'

Today the ordeal of lying behind the bushes was endured and then the suspense of hustling back to the nursery in case anyone saw her. Hand in hand they scrambled as quickly as their legs could carry them up the tower stairs, often stumbling in the dark in their panic to get to the top before any of the ghosts appeared. Alice, although fearless in her dealings with the cannibal man, was terrified of ghosts and at times could work herself into near hysteria. On more than one occasion she had fallen on the stairs in her rush to get up or down them.

However, Cook had laughed at Alice's wild tales of being chased by the green lady. 'You and your imagination!' she had told Alice. 'It'll be the death of you yet.' And then aside to Mima the kitchen-maid. 'She enjoys it, you know. Ordinary things and folks are too dull for our Alice. She's got to keep making up exciting things like ghoulies and ghosts and God-knows-all-what.'

And then Cook had turned to Clementina. 'Don't believe a word of it, young missy. Not a word!'

But it was very difficult not to believe Alice, especially when her big bumpy mob-cap and large moon face pushed close, eyes bulging, wide nostrils quivering, voice low and husky with drama. And especially when they were cut off alone together at the top of the tower for long evening hours.

Sometimes Clementina was left alone at night and not just in the night nursery. She was always alone there, because Alice said that wild horses wouldn't make her sleep in a dead woman's bed. Sometimes, however, she would hear Alice tiptoe along the passageway and then race away down the stairs. Clementina never knew if she had just gone down on some errand to the kitchen, or had run right out of the house – whether she would be back in a few minutes or a few hours or would never return again.

Life became as insecure as walking a tightrope over a pool of crocodiles. Even a special birthday tea gave no comfort or ease of tension because Alice, who had a voracious appetite, had to gobble up most of the birthday food before the cannibal man got a smell of it and was tempted to come rampaging indoors.

'Honest to God, it's your own fault!' Alice said. 'You're far too slow.'

But on days when the cannibal man was not on the loose, Alice would take her to the village and they would visit Alice's granny and auntie Bella.

Alice said she had never had a mother and father, only a granny and an auntie Bella. Auntie Bella wasn't there very often, because she worked as kitchen-maid over at the Main's Farm, but granny always welcomed them with a drink of ale and a bit of bread and cheese which Clementina ate as greedily as Alice, because she never seemed to get enough to eat now and was always hungry. Granny's cottage was one of the end houses in the village and all its walls were uneven and its ceilings very low. It was even darker than the nursery in the tower, because the cottage windows were smaller and hardly allowed in any light at all. Granny always knew when they arrived because all her doors loudly creaked; they were made of heavy oak and hung on big iron hinges. The doors were warped by damp and let in so many draughts that, winter and summer, granny wore a dark grey shawl pinned round her ample shoulders and a cotton bonnet tied under her many chins. She smoked a clay pipe and looked like one of the gipsies that Clementina and Alice had met

112

at the other side of the woods near the river. Only bigger. Alice said high-born girls like Clementina had to watch out for gipsies, because gipsies could kidnap girls from big houses if they took it into their heads.

As they had supped their ale and chewed at their bread and cheese in Alice's granny's cottage, Clementina had asked her about this habit of gipsies and the old woman had said, 'I wouldn't put it past them. They've nerve enough for anything, that lot.'

'They'll have stolen more than one of your father's cows and sheep already,' Alice informed Clementina. 'Isn't that right, Granny?'

'They've been hanged for sheep stealing before now,' Granny agreed.

'Tell Clementina about how they have battles with each other . . . and how that man got his hand cut off and he rushed into the farmhouse kitchen and stuck the stump of his arm up against the bars of the fire to stop the bleeding!'

But there were times when Granny couldn't be bothered and just wanted to enjoy a puff at her pipe. Then they would have to leave the uneven brick-floored cottage and go to seek diversion elsewhere. Sometimes Alice stopped in at Mrs Stodges' corner sweetie shop and if she had any money she would buy a small bag of toffee balls and lounge outside, arms folded across her broad bosom and cheeks bulging as she chewed the sweets. She always gave Clementina one, sometimes two. For a time Clementina would stand sucking and chewing beside her, but she would soon get bored with just standing and watching the world go by and would join in a game with the village children. Sometimes, however, the village children would be in a tormenting mood and then they would gang up against her and Alice and shout insults like, 'Fat Alice! Fat Alice!'

On these occasions Clementina became enraged and rushed at the tormentors, fists clenched and hard-hitting in Alice's defence. Alice, still with arms comfortably folded and still chewing, would roll out words nearly drowned in saliva.

'That's right, Miss Clementina, you get stuck into them.'

But if she saw that Clementina was getting the worst of the fight, she would wade in herself, plump red hands slapping in all directions, mouth spraying out angry words.

'Rotten wee bastards! I'll murder the lot of you. I'll hang for you, so I will!'

Occasionally Alice took her to watch the blacksmith at work and as they went through the wide doors of the forge, she said, 'This is what it's like going through the gates of hell.'

'How do you know?' Clementina asked.

'Your father told us about hell, didn't he?'

Inside it was murky with smoke and Alice pointed to the figures of the smith and his boy outlined against the glow of the fire as they heated a strip of iron held in long pincers.

'They're like devils with tridents.'

'What's a trident?' Clementina enquired.

'Don't you ever listen to your father?' Alice burst out in exasperation.

When a horse was brought in, it stood patiently on three legs while the smith unclinched the nails which held on the old shoe. Clementina winced when the new shoe, hot from the fire, was nailed into place, but the horse didn't seem to mind. Soon it was clattering away over the cobbles with only the hair of its fetlocks singed.

Sometimes, instead of going to the village they would walk through the fields, but Clementina didn't like doing that because it reminded her of Henny and made a terrible sadness drag at her heels. Then Alice would say, 'What's up with you? Cat got your tongue?' Or, 'Cheer up, you'll soon be dead!'

Often Clementina had wanted to die so that she could be with Henny again. 'Kill yourself! Kill yourself!' she had often repeated in her mind. But when it came to the crunch, as Alice would say, she just didn't know how.

She was never sure which was her worst time – night or day. Night-time, lying alone in bed listening fearfully for ghosts. Or day-time when she was hungry.

Then one day Alice said that there was going to be a dinner party downstairs and it was a damned disgrace that more food would be left on plates and wasted than was allowed for the nursery for a week. A lot better food too, because of course nursery food was never anything like what was eaten downstairs – even by the servants.

'It's all that Mrs Musgrove's fault,' Alice grumbled. 'It's her that says what we've to get. Or what we've not to get more like. I think she hates us and wants to starve us to death.'

'Couldn't we somehow take what's left on the plates?' Clementina suggested, trembling at the enormity of her suggestion.

'You mean steal it?' Alice said with alarming plainness of speech.

Horror struggled with hunger in Clementina and prevented her from saying any more, but Alice quickly warmed to the idea.

'The best time would be after the ladies go into the drawing-room and the gentlemen go through to the library to smoke their cigars. And you must do it – just cram whatever you can into your pinny and run back upstairs with it.'

'Why can't you come with me?'

'Because I'd get the sack, I would, if Mrs Musgrove caught me and I'd never be able to get another place as long as I lived. Then I really would starve. She couldn't put you out now, could she? You're the young lady of the house. You'll never need to find a place, so you'll always be all right.'

So it was arranged and when Alice thought it was safe, Clementina tiptoed down the tower stairs and out into the reception hall. Then, mouth dry with terror, she approached the dining-room door but before she could touch the handle, the door suddenly opened and she nearly fell in against her father's legs. She would never forget the horror and then the cold fury in his face.

'You have been eavesdropping!' he accused. Then, turning to the two grey-bearded men at his back, he said, 'Just go on to the library, gentlemen. I will join you there in a few minutes.' After the gentlemen had passed along the library corridor he pointed in the direction of the oak room and Clementina walked across the hall towards it, cold and shivering from head to toe.

Her father's study or oak room had originally been the principle apartment of the sixteenth-century tower house and Clementina guessed the nursery apartments must be somewhere high above it. Not immediately above, though, because Henny had once told her that first of all a secret passage led from behind one of the window shutters in the far corner, up a mural stair to a room above. This secret chamber was equipped with a listening hole or spy-hole through which, in the olden days, conversations in the room below could be overheard. Then above the secret room was a floor of apartments which had originally been used as a schoolroom when Gilbert and Malcolm had been young and for their governess's accommodation. Now they lay empty.

Immediately her father shut the door behind them he said, 'Prepare yourself for punishment.'

Clementina awkwardly bunched up her dress, pinafore and petticoats and fumbled with the buttons of her knickers. Her father was looming so closely over her in such eye-twitching impatience that she was beginning to panic and her fingers were shaking so violently and her skirts and petticoats were so much in the way that she was finding it difficult to accomplish the feat. Upstairs, first Henny and now Alice always helped her with her knickers.

'Do as I say!' her father said. 'Do as I say!'

'Yes, father.'

116

The colour had completely gone from her face and she was nearly fainting. Then suddenly the buttons came loose and she was able to pull the knickers down and stand, ankles pinioned by them, arms clutching the bunched-up skirts obediently high to show her nakedness. This was the part of her punishment that she dreaded as much, if not more than, the pain of the thrashing. This terrible, long-drawn-out humiliation of standing there exposed while her father walked round and round and round, examining her.

CHAPTER THIRTEEN

Round and round went the reaping machine, pulled by two hefty black Clydesdales with snowy fetlocks and gently jingling harness. The machine's long arms were like red windmill-sails and added a splash of colour in the golden field. The glistening grain slowly shrank to a square and then an oblong and as she watched, a summer hum of bees and insects surrounded Lorianna. The day hung hazed with warmth as she stood, her flower basket over her arm, her mauve silk dress with its green pleated train making her look like a flower herself.

Following the machine were crowds of women with weather-beaten faces and hooded bonnets, their long skirts kilted up with safety-pins to reveal striped petticoats. They were busy making bands of straw which they laid at intervals on the stubble beside the row of mown corn. Men came after them, each collecting an armful of corn from the row together with its band of straw; then they twisted the band deftly round the armful, the ends twisted together and tucked down inside the tight band. After that the sheaf was thrown down and another made. Behind them came other men who picked up a sheaf in each hand and, as though knocking two people's heads together, brought the heads of the sheaves close, at the same time propping the stalks on the ground at an angle of about thirty degrees so that they leaned against each other.

In a nearby field a similar procedure was going on, except that here there was no machine. Instead, a row of men were whetting their scythes and mowing by hand in powerful, rhythmic sweeps. When Lorianna strolled nearer she saw that the leader was Robert Kelso and he was smiling to himself, obviously revelling in the gruelling pace he was setting, enjoying the sheer hard physical work. He did not see her, so intent was he on his labours and she hastily moved to the shade of a tree, its dipping branches hiding her from view as well as affording her a cool respite from the sun.

In the field with the reaping machine, men were waiting with their ash sticks, dogs quiet at their feet. Then suddenly rabbits – driven into the centre of the field by the noise of the swirling red-armed machine – raced out. Men and dogs immediately fell on them and very few escaped. Soon a pile of grey-brown twitching bodies grew by the gate, waiting to be shared out among the helpers when the reaping was completed.

In the shade of a tree near the gate of the other field, Robert Kelso's horse was tethered. Lorianna turned her attention on the grieve once more. As she stood motionless, the hot slumbrous melody of harvest-time floating in the air, she sensed a great joy about him, a celebration of strength and virility and the freedom and beauty of the countryside. This filled her with a wistfulness that moved her almost to tears and she forced herself to walk, tipping her green parasol to one side to hide her face in case he should turn in her direction and see her.

She had already collected a beautiful variety of flowers and berries, including golden rod, campanula, white roses, purple heather, red poppies and sweet-scented honeysuckle, but every now and again she stopped to gather others. It was when she was passing the farmhouse that an idea came into her head which she could not resist the impulse to put into practice. Going up to the farmhouse door, she lifted the latch and went in.

How dark and still it was compared with the bright yellow world outside with thistledown and butterflies floating in the air. The kitchen was clean and tidy, but so depressing with its dark woodwork, dark grey stone floor and black-barred cooking range. The whole place cried out for a woman's touch, something to brighten it and make it look more special. He had shown her kindness, indeed had saved her life. It would be little enough to create a floral arrangement to make his home more tasteful and attractive. So great was her pleasure in arranging the flowers into a delicate and artistic shape that she felt she had never enjoyed such a happy few minutes in her life.

It was not until she had finished the job to her satisfaction that she realised exactly what she felt and what she had done. She was standing back admiring her transformation not only of the old stone jar she had found in a cupboard in the scullery but also of the corner of the room where she had placed it – opposite the door over at one side of the window, where misty beams of light were caught and colour-shimmered. The flowers shone gently through the light, beautiful and peaceful in their intertwining relation to one another. She had created with such generosity of spirit, giving all of herself with such devotion that the dark corner, the stone jar, the flowers – everything seemed to have taken on an aura of love. All at once she was embarrassed; shocked and surprised too. She just wanted to leave the farmhouse and hurry away home.

All the way back Lorianna chastised herself. Foolish, silly woman! What on earth had possessed her to do such a thing? Goodness knows what Kelso would think. He would be justified in feeling resentful and angry, to say the least. After all, even servents were entitled to some privacy and she had had no right to enter his home when he was not there.

The more she thought of what she had done, the more horrified she became, until nearing Blackwood House she was almost running in her desperation to hide herself away in her bedroom. Even Gemmell, normally efficient but never solicitous, remarked how hot and flustered she looked and after divesting her of her hat, gloves and parasol, suggested that she might be wise to lie down for a few minutes to recover from the heat. Lorianna took her advice and lay back on the gold silk cushions of the pink damask settee that stood against the foot of the bed. It took her a long time to relax but eventually she recovered her composure, helped by the glass of Cook's delicious home-made lemonade which Gemmell brought up.

On the surface she was able to assure herself that her action had constitued the merest token of appreciation to the grieve. She kept reminding herself that after all, he had saved her life, and that what she had done had been in no way unladylike nor over-stepped the bounds of proper circumspection. Yet all the time in her heart of hearts she knew it had been terribly wrong and in the secret core of herself she shuddered.

Lorianna ventured no further than the croquet lawn next day, where she enjoyed a leisurely game with Gilbert's young brother, Malcolm, who had recently arrived home after staying with a friend, Alistair Geddes, since the University term had finished. Alistair's father had done missionary work in Africa and Malcolm had been interested to hear about Mr Geddes's experiences.

'Do you think you would like to do missionary work eventually, Malcolm?' Lorianna asked after their game when they were enjoying a stroll round the garden.

'I used to think so before I went to Edinburgh.' Malcolm shook his head. He was a smallish, delicate-boned young man with the same neat features as his father, but with spectacles instead of a pince-nez and black hair parted in the centre. Apparently his mother had been dark-haired. 'But oh, after what I've seen in our capital city, Lorianna, I realise that there is more than enough missionary work to do here.'

'Really?' Lorianna was intrigued. On her few visits to Edinburgh it had seemed to her a very civilised and respectable place.

'I couldn't tell you what sin goes on in that city.'

121

'Oh, Malcolm, and I thought Gilbert was the tease of the family.'

'It's not fit for a lady's ears, Lorianna.'

'Oh pooh! Just between us and in strict confidence – where's the harm? You have aroused my curiosity, Malcolm. Oh, do tell me about this sinful city of yours!'

'Well . . .' Malcolm bent his head nearer to her like a gossiping girl-friend. 'There are certain areas where crowds of women mill about and quite shamelessly accost men. They . . . they . . .'

A blush reddened his ears and neck and lowered his voice. 'They lift the fronts of their skirts. Lift the skirt hems slightly you understand, but this constitutes a proposition.'

The thought of women inviting the unleashing of men's dangerous passions in such an indiscriminate way appalled Lorianna.

'How dreadful! The foolish, ignorant creatures!'

'I would have thought sinful was the more appropriate word.' For a moment she detected a slight echo of his father's tone in his voice. 'And there are so many of them, Lorianna. Do you know – of course you don't, how could you? But I do assure you that it is a fact that there are no fewer than eight hundred full-time professional prostitutes in Edinburgh.'

'Eight hundred? Oh, surely not, Malcolm.'

'Indeed, that isn't all. It will shock you even more, Lorianna, to learn that in addition – *in addition* – there are no fewer than three hundred servants working part-time at the same trade.'

'Servants?' She was truly horrified now. 'You mean servants actually employed by ladies in respectable houses?'

'Indeed yes. It just goes to show that one cannot be too careful.'

'I can understand now why you say there's plenty of missionary work for you to do in Edinburgh, Malcolm. I never realised that such awful things went on.'

'Oh, it's a wicked world, Lorianna. A wicked world.' He shook his head and it occurred to her how old and serious he was for his nineteen years.

They walked in silence for a few minutes and then suddenly she asked – she didn't know why, 'Do you remember your mother, Malcolm? You'd be – what – nine when she died, about Clementina's age now?'

He nodded as he walked along, eyes concentrating on the ground in front of him, hands gripped behind his back.

'Yes, she was very small and frail.'

'That's how I remember her too. Poor woman!' Lorianna sighed. 'It's strange but I often think of her you know. I do hope that in some small way I was of some comfort to you.'

He patted her hand. 'Yes, indeed.'

'I was young myself of course. And very unversed in the ways of the world. I'm sure I must have made many mistakes, Malcolm.'

'I have always held you in the highest regard. Indeed, I used to boast about having such a beautiful young step-mamma.'

She laughed. 'Thank you, my dear. By the way, have you seen your beautiful half-sister yet?'

'No, what with all of us dining at the Drummonds last night . . . and then when I called up to the nursery this morning, she was out with her nanny for a walk.'

'Your father still hasn't decided on a governess. He has interviewed quite a few, but hasn't seen yet anyone who would be good enough. He's so very conscientious about the child's welfare.'

'Is she as sturdy as ever?'

'Yes, she's keeping very well. Tait is doing a splendid job as nanny; she's a solid, reliable person, but alas not of very high intelligence and certainly not qualified to tutor Clementina.'

'Don't worry, I'm sure Father will find someone eminently suitable.'

'I hope so. Anyway, you will see her when she's brought down to the sitting-room tonight. I hope you won't tease her like Gilbert does.'

'I'm not a bit like Gilbert.'

She laughed again. 'No, of course you're not!'

And they turned, still arm in arm, to go into the house. Lorianna was relaxed and happy now, her earlier embarrassment over the floral arrangement in the farmhouse forgotten, although it would return to her unexpectedly from time to time in little shivers of disbelief. Nevertheless, she was sufficiently confident to venture out as far as the Drumcross Road to meet Gavin the following day, and had just turned on to the rough, stony road, when, to her consternation, she saw Robert Kelso, not Gavin, approaching. He was on foot, his hat tipped jauntily back on his head. His collar had been tugged open at the neck, his waistcoat was unbuttoned and his suit jacket was hitched over one shoulder. He had obviously been to Bathgate for some reason or another. She stood transfixed to the spot until he reached her, her mind a blank, panic-stricken.

'Good afternoon, Mrs Blackwood,' he said in the voice that never failed to surprise her with its deep, rich timbre.

'Good afternoon, Kelso,' she managed faintly.

His silver-grey eyes always surprised her too. Against his black brows they were most unusual and compelling. Thoughtful, knowing eyes. There could be no doubt of course that he knew who had done the floral arrangement. Apart from anything else, he had seen her talents in this art displayed often enough in Blackwood House. But it was his eyes that convinced her that he knew. The few seconds during which she waited in agony for him to remark on her foolish indiscretion and shame her, seemed like an eternity. Of course she would make light of it, brush it aside with a nonchalant remark.

'Oh, that?' she would say. 'I had forgotten all about it. Just a little thank-you for coming to my rescue the other day.'

But those eyes, so cool, so calm, so penetrating, would *know*.

To her indescribable relief, however, he said nothing but merely smiled and passed on. She could hardly believe it. A wave of gratitude nearly brought tears to her eyes and it was only with difficulty that she was able to compose herself when she heard the sounds of horses' hooves in the distance. Gavin, she discovered when he came into view, was on horseback and so she couldn't get a lift as she expected. Gavin didn't believe it was ladylike for her to ride, not even side-saddle. Although many a horse she had enjoyed riding when she had been young on the farm and her father had given her a pony of her own when she was younger than Clementina. There had been a time when she had pleaded with Gavin for a pony for Clementina, but he had always stubbornly refused.

'You do far too much walking,' he told her when he reached her. 'You will overtire yourself, especially in this heat. Stay there in the shade and I'll send Jacobs back with the carriage.'

'No, please, dearest. I enjoy walking. I'm perfectly all right,' she assured him.

He was annoyed but said, 'Very well.' And spurred his horse away along the dirt path.

Lorianna was glad to be alone again. She needed to think and to savour the relief she felt and the gratitude to Robert Kelso that was flowing with the warm blood through her veins.

CHAPTER FOURTEEN

'Alice!' It was a wail of terror. 'Don't leave me. Please take me with you!'

Clementina had stumbled through from the night nursery in the dark just in time to catch Alice, candle in hand, crossing the passageway towards the stairs. By the candle's puny flicker Clementina could make out that she was wearing her jacket, which confirmed the child's worst fears. Alice wasn't just going downstairs – she was leaving the house.

'Bloody hell!' Alice exploded. 'I'm stuck with you all day and every day. Is that not enough? Am I not entitled to a few hours peace at night on my own?'

'I won't be any trouble Alice, God's honour. Don't leave me here alone. The Green Lady and the Black Slave and the Burning Man will all come howling up the stairs. That's when they're supposed to – when people are alone.'

Despite her extreme irritation, Alice couldn't help being affected by such an awful vision. 'Bloody hell!' she repeated. 'But what am I supposed to do with you?'

'Take me with you, oh please, Alice!'

'I'm meeting somebody and that's a secret, mind. I'll slit you up and feed your innards to the pigs if you tell a soul.'

'I won't tell, honest to God, Alice.'

'I'd have to leave you somewhere outside and collect you on my way back, so you'd be on your own then, outside in the dark.'

'I'm not frightened of outside. There are no ghosts outside, only in the tower.'

'Away and get some clothes on then and be quick about it. Bloody hell, I need my head looked at. If you make me late, I'll feed the whole of you to the cannibal man.'

Stumbling back to the night nursery in the dark with Alice hurrying after her, holding up the candle, Clementina said, 'You told me he slept sound as a rock at night and that it was only during the day he came out.'

'I'd feed you to him during the day, then.'

'Help me with my buttons, Alice.'

'It's high time you learned to do your bloody buttons up yourself. Nobody helps me with my buttons – nobody *ever* helped me with my buttons.'

'I *can* do them myself,' Clementina said indignantly. 'It's just that it's too dark and I can't see them.'

'Oh, come here!' Alice put down the candle and tugged Clementina towards her by her liberty bodice. 'I don't know what I've done to deserve being tormented by you. Never mind your petticoats, just shove your dress on and a jacket or something. What a bloody carry-on. I need my head looked at, so I do!'

At last some clothes were thrown on higgledy-piggledy and shoes buckled over drooping half-secured stockings. Then, clutching each other's hands, the pair set off.

Not a word passed between them until they had tiptoed safely through the sleeping house. Nor did they dare speak until they had hurried down the winding drive and had reached the shelter of the bushes and trees to the left where the path led to a five-bar gate and a stile.

'Where are we going?' Clementina whispered.

'Over here.'

'Then where?' she asked breathlessly as she scrambled across the stile.

'The high woods near the cornfields, but I'll leave you in the lane.'

Clementina knew this place well during the day. The path through the little meadows they now hurried along had oak trees that she had clambered up on other occasions and the meadows were rich with flowers too. But further up, nearer the wood, the lane became hollowed out between high banks. The banks at first were clothed with fern and then, when the hill became steeper, with fir trees standing tall and thick together, barely allowing the sunbeams misty with dust to fall aslant between them.

'You wait here,' Alice said. 'Settle yourself down behind that briar bush so I'll know where to find you if you drop off to sleep.'

Clementina did as she was told and as she crouched into a tight little ball, Alice's solid bulk merged away into the shadows and eventually disappeared.

During the day there was always something to see in the lane. Squirrels darted about and she had spied stoats as well. She had gathered ferns and flowers while birds sang noisily overhead. Now everything was eerily quiet and all she could see was an occasional bat and a white owl gliding down the slope.

Alice was taking such a long time that Clementina found herself nodding off to sleep, despite the cold evening air and the cutting draughts her lack of petticoats allowed in. Then suddenly she was alerted with relief and joyous expectation at the sound of a crackling twig. She was about to cry out when just in time she noticed that the shadowy figure approaching along the lane was taller and thinner than Alice and indeed not a girl at all but a man. As he came nearer she held her breath in an anguish of suspense in case he detected her presence. He was wearing a battered felt hat with a feather sticking from it, a scarf loosely knotted at his throat and a dark jacket and corduroys. Across his shoulder he carried a long ash stick on which a load of hares was slung, an equal number balanced back and front.

Clementina had never been so relieved in her life as when he passed within yards of where she was crouching and seemed completely unaware of her existence. Long after he had disappeared she was still weakly shaking and when Alice did return at last she clung to her in a sudden rush of tears.

'A man nearly got me,' she sobbed. 'He was carrying a whole lot of hares. Was that the cannibal man taking them home for his breakfast?'

'Don't be daft,' Alice scoffed. 'That was only Wattie McLeod, the poacher. He's out most nights killing something or other – he wouldn't hurt a fly!'

Bewildered and weary beyond any more words, Clementina allowed herself to be dragged away. By the time they reached the house she was sleeping on her feet and had no recollection of going to bed in the nursery, although she faintly remembered the dreamlike effort of staggering up the twisting tower stairs and bouncing painfully off the walls. She awoke in bed next morning with all her clothes on, even her shoes, and her hair in such a tangle that Alice complained it would take them all day to get it presentable for her to go into the sitting-room to visit her mother. Clementina said she didn't want to go to the sitting-room anyway and didn't like her mother, so what was the point?

'She pays my wages, that's the bloody point,' said Alice. 'So we've got to be nice and clean and tidy and polite for her every night.'

'Bloody hell!' said Clementina.

At last between them they got her cleaned up and after breakfast they gave the nursery what Alice called 'a bit of a tidy'.

'It's all it needs,' Alice explained. 'There's no use scrubbing floors and wearing ourselves out doing daft things like that when there's only the two of us. We're better to get out and about and enjoy ourselves, sure we are?'

Clementina wholeheartedly agreed. 'Will we go to Granny's today?'

'No, this is her day for going down to Bathgate to visit Mrs Munn.'

That was a disappointment. Clementina had been looking forward to the bread and cheese, not to mention her drop of ale.

'I'm hungry,' she said.

Alice sighed. 'What do you think I am?'

'You always eat more than me.'

'Well, I'm bigger than you, aren't I? There's more of me to fill. Honest to God, you'd have me disappear away to a shadow!'

'Maybe if we went down to the kitchen and told Cook, she'd give us something?' Clementina suggested. Although even as she spoke she knew it was like describing cloud-cuckoo land, as Alice would say. The nursery and the rest of the house were kept strictly separate. Clementina was never quite sure why; it was as if they had bloody leprosy, Alice said. Or just didn't exist.

'Maybe pigs will fly,' Alice said mournfully.

'Couldn't we try?' Clementina's hunger was making her reckless. 'I'll do the asking. Cook likes me.'

'Only if she's in a good mood, and only if she's not too busy to be bothered with you. And if Mrs Musgrove's sniffing around, then what will we do?'

'I'm hungry,' Clementina glowered stubbornly.

'Honest to God, you'll be the death of me yet. Come on! I need my head looked at, so I do.'

They raced down the stairs, but stopped at the oak door to quietly listen first and then cautiously open it a crack to peer into the hall. Great care had to be taken. They knew Clementina's father and Gilbert had gone, for they had watched them ride away down the drive from the nursery window. But they had no idea of the where-abouts of her mother and Malcolm. Housemaids were bustling about, but they didn't matter. They wouldn't tell – probably would neither notice nor care, so harassed were they in trying to keep up with their load of house-work. At 6.30 in the morning they had to start cleaning out the fires and then the whole of the drawing-room, sitting-room, dining-room and library, including the carpets which were sprinkled with tea-leaves to keep down the dust before they were brushed. After breakfast they turned out all the bedrooms, which was what they were sweating and puffing over now.

'All right,' Alice whispered and they made a dash for it across the hall and along the library corridor to the doors that opened on to the kitchen stairs.

Effie Summers, the under-housemaid – an undersized skinny thirteen-year-old, all big cap, big boots and knobbly elbows – was struggling up the stairs lugging a scuttle of coal. She just gave them a pained half-grimace, half-smile in passing.

Clementina stopped outside the kitchen door and Alice punched her on the shoulder and hissed, 'It was your idea, not mine.'

Mustering all her courage, Clementina opened the door and went in, Alice following closely at her heels.

Cook was pummelling pastry at the kitchen table as if it was Mrs Musgrove and at the same time shouting at Mima, the kitchen-maid, who was running around in circles like a creature demented.

'You're always the same, Mima Fairley. You never know where anything is. If you don't smarten yourself up you'll have to find that box of yours, that's what you'll have to find, and then pack it and get out of my sight for good. And now what?' she bawled, catching sight of Clementina and Alice. 'Can I not get a minute's peace in my own kitchen? This isn't Hopeton Street in the middle of Bathgate, you know. People aren't supposed to come in here. This is private, this is, in case you didn't know. Do I come up trespassing in your nursery? No, never! So why should you two dare to put a foot in here?'

It was obvious, as Alice said later, that Cook was at the end of her tether and that Mrs Musgrove, without a doubt, had been at the kitchen before them. They retreated in silence, knowing that today their case was hopeless and left by the yard door to scuff their feet down the drive heavy-hearted with disappointment. But

Alice was never down for long, any more than her imagination ever failed her.

'How about berries?' she announced suddenly.

Clementina's eyes widened: you had to admire Alice. 'I never thought of that.'

'You need your head looked at, that's why. Come on!'

Alice hitched up her skirts and ran, rocking from side to side on her fat legs, heavy as a miniature carthorse, followed by Clementina frisking and skipping like a young foal at her heels.

CHAPTER FIFTEEN

Wild flowers never lasted long and it seemed a pity to allow the corner in the cottage to become dark again with sad and dead blooms. So, daringly, Lorianna returned. The stone jar was exactly where she had left it but as she had thought, the flowers were beginning to wither. With a light heart she set about removing them, washing the jar and then creating a fresh arrangement. How beautiful it looked, even more beautiful than the last time.

Afterwards she once more suffered misgivings. It was perhaps excusable and understandable to do such a thing once, but to repeat the occurrence was somehow a different matter. Again, however, Robert Kelso made no reference to what she had done. He passed her on the stair of Blackwood House after one of his meetings with Gavin with no more than a fleeting smile and a deep rumbling 'Good morning.'

Bold now, she began to visit the cottage regularly to attend to the flowers. It was the highlight of her week, the one thing she genuinely looked forward to, that gave her a sweet and simple pleasure with which no grand dinner party or 'At Home' could begin to compete. Sometimes she sat down on the settle at the fireside gazing at the flowers. Sometimes, just enjoying the farmhouse kitchen with the sounds of the animals drifting in from outside, she would close her eyes in the solitude and find a deliciously soothing peace. She was sitting like that one day when suddenly she sensed she was no longer alone in the room. Jerking open her eyes, she nearly fainted with shock to see Robert Kelso watching her from the doorway. One of his powerful looking arms was stretched up against the lintel, his big hand resting on it as he lounged there calmly surveying her. The sleeves of his striped shirt were rolled up, showing black hair on his arms; black hair was also revealed by the wide-open front of his shirt. Leggings covered his trousers from just below his knees down to the heavy boots he wore.

Lorianna rose, heart thudding painfully, aware only that she was in what could be construed as a compromising situation with a rough and common workman. Never before had she felt so appalled at herself.

'Thank you for taking so much trouble with the flowers,' he said.

She swished the train of her dress round. 'It was the merest token of appreciation for rescuing me that time from the bull.'

One gloved hand rested elegantly on the handle of her furled parasol, while the other held her skirt against her hip.

'Actually you have a right to feel angry, Kelso. I have been invading the privacy of your home.'

'Yes, I would have felt that way with anyone else,' he said quietly, 'but not with you.'

Her heart began thudding again. 'I must go now.'

He dropped his hand from the lintel and moved aside, but he was still near enough the doorway as she passed for her to feel the heat from his body and to sense the rich earthy maleness that emanated from him.

'Good afternoon,' she said, without daring to look round.

He made no answer, but she could feel his eyes on her all the time until she reached the shelter of the trees. It was only then, away from any danger, that she realised the full extent of her shock. Her legs were suddenly so weak that they could hardly support her and she had to lean heavily against a tree for a few minutes until she could summon up the strength to move. At last she managed to get back to Blackwood House and, pushing through her secret gate, had the strange feeling of stepping from one world into another which was completely different.

In this different world Lorianna willed herself to be particularly pleasing to Gavin. She was quiet and reserved in company, her eyes kept modestly lowered whenever possible. Her loyalty to him was conscientiously guarded and not one word would she allow Gilbert to say against him. To her friends she praised him unstintingly.

But at the same time she found it impossible to wrench herself free of her secret world.

Comparatively few wild flowers flourished now except on the river bank. Roadsides had become dry and brown and large dead stems of hogweed stood wanly about. Nearly all the flowering grasses had turned to seed. Around the farm swallows gathered in large numbers as they prepared to leave for far off-places. Willow-warblers and chiff-chaffs sang as they drifted away towards the Southern coast.

Now was a time of change, of partings. The knowledge stirred in Lorianna unexpected ripples of apprehension. She knew that a choice would have to be faced and a decision taken, but even within the privacy of her inmost thoughts she dared not formulate her vague intuitions in concrete terms. She simply knew that something would have to be done.

Then one day she returned to the farmhouse a second time, as if in her growing anxiety she might find it had gone. Drawn by an irresistible force, she lifted the latch and went in.

He was sitting at the small table, and with barely a glance in her direction he went on eating a succulent-looking steak and a heap of boiled potatoes in their skins. The peppery smell of the steak pervaded the low-ceilinged room and she could see the big iron frying pan in which he had cooked it discarded at one side of the hob. The fire crackled cheerfully against the silence as she went over to stand facing it, with her back to him. She knew by the occasional scraping sound of his knife that he was still calmly cutting up his food, still continuing to eat. Eventually his deep voice broke the silence. 'You realise what you're doing?'

She turned then. 'I don't know what you mean. I was out walking and I simply thought . . .'

'You're a married woman,' he interrupted, tossing down his fork and knife then tipping himself back slightly in his chair. 'You can't possibly be that naive.'

She ought to have left then but instead she stood helplessly pinned under his stare, helpless as a butterfly in her white dress with its beautiful embroidery and her satin hat afroth with russet and green bows.

There was a need in her to know more about him. 'You told me you were married once,' she heard herself say. 'Were you happy?'

'Yes.'

'You must miss her.'

'I do. But I'm never short of a woman, if that's what you mean.'

His remark was like a slap in the face and she gasped at the insult behind his words. Praying that she would not shame herself even further by bursting into tears, she ran blindly towards the door, no longer caring about anything except the need to escape from the room.

He rose without apparent haste and firmly caught her arm, detaining her only long enough to say, 'I'm sorry. But it's better this way.' Then he allowed her to continue her flight.

Her heart wept as she hastened through the autumn countryside, wept and wept until her chest was tight and her throat painfully constricted. At last the mellow autumn evening slowed her down and soothed her. The sun was still shining and the fields were full of butterflies. Goldfinches were feeding in fluttering parties on the downy thistle-heads, while on the stubble fields a solitary cock pheasant was stalking along with two hens nearby. Soon the red deer stags would join the hinds in the lowland woods and the battle for mates would begin.

Nature and the cycle of the seasons continued no matter what happened. Somehow its constancy steadied her and reduced her shame to more manageable proportions.

★　★　★

'Lorianna!' Malcolm met her in the hall. 'We wondered where you had gone.'

'It was such a lovely evening.'

'I wish you had told me you were going for a walk. I would have joined you.'

She smiled. 'I promise I shall not go out for any more evening strolls without you, Malcolm dear.'

In the bedroom she sat staring listlessly in the mirror as Gemmell unpinned her hat.

'Will that be all, madam?'

Lorianna's gaze strayed to the maid's reflection. Gemmell's eyes were slightly protuberant, she had a longish nose and strands of hair wisped down in front of her ears; her best feature was her beautiful strong white teeth. Lorianna did not like her much and more than once had been tempted to dismiss her, but a sense of fairness had dissuaded her from doing so. After all, the woman was efficient enough at her job; it was merely that there seemed to be a hidden resentment about her nature which grated on the sensibilities. Lorianna suspected that the maid nursed dreams above her station which allowed a certain element of jealousy to take root. She had seen the look in those eyes when Gemmell had handled her jewellery.

Once when she had come into the bedroom, Gemmell had been standing with one of her best hats in her hands, twisting it round and admiring it. She looked as if she was about to try it on and had Lorianna caught her doing so, then she would have dismissed her.

But the maid had quickly said, 'I thought the ribbon needed a few stitches, madam, but no, I see it's all right.'

And the hat had been hastily replaced in its box.

'Yes, you may go,' she told Gemmell now.

Alone in the room, she remained seated at the dressing-table, depression wearying her. Why couldn't she be the kind of wife that Gavin wanted? What was wrong with her? Why did she seem intent on shaming him as well as herself by this irresponsible and disgraceful behaviour? And with a servant!

She thought she heard Gavin moving about in the dressing-room and in a surge of contrition she decided to take the opportunity to speak with him in private. She never entered his dressing-room after he came home, but they were rarely alone now that Malcolm was on holiday from university and so she decided to risk going in. She urgently needed to talk to him and be strengthened by his strong moral sense and unshakeable uprightness. Perhaps he could set her longer passages of the bible to study every day as a help towards self-discipline. She knew that at least it would please Gavin if she made such a request.

As well as the connecting door between the bedroom and dressing-room, there was a door from each into the hall and when she went into the dressing-room its door to the hall lay open. Gavin had obviously been called away unexpectedly and his diary still lay open on the small writing table over near the fireplace. She sat down on the chair beside it, the only chair by the fire, to wait for his return. She had not meant to look at the diary and her eyes strayed to it only in boredom as they wandered over all the other items in the room. But something leapt to her eye, riveting her attention and making her lean forward to look closer. Then incredulously she devoured page after page until suddenly she threw the book aside as if it was contaminating her. She felt so sick she could not stand up, but leaning forward with her head on her knees she tried to control the waves of nausea that jerked through her. At last, breathing slowly and deeply, she leaned her head back on the chair.

The instant Gavin came into the room and saw what

had happened, he became agitated and furtively hastened to shut both doors. Then, wringing his hands he began to weep, his pince-nez becoming wet and blurred until he had to remove it from his nose and rub at it with his handkerchief.

'Every day I plead with God to give me the strength to resist the temptation of evil women,' he sobbed. 'I ask him to strike them down, to remove the filth of them from the face of the earth so that I can keep to the paths of righteousness . . .'

'And to think . . .' Lorianna interrupted in gathering mindless rage, 'that you made *me* feel ashamed and guilty! You hypocrite! Talk about filth! You're the filth! To think how you have been lecturing and tormenting me for years and years, all in the cause of chastity and purity; yet all the time on every day you've gone to Edinburgh . . . all those other women . . .'

She could not bear to remain in the same room as Gavin and, sick at heart, she stumbled through to her bedroom. All those wasted years, she kept thinking. The nausea welled up again and this time she had to run to the wash-bowl and noisily vomit into it. Afterwards she dipped a corner of the towel into the jug of water and dabbed at her mouth and brow.

'No one matters to me but you, Lorianna. Look, I'll burn the diary if it will make you feel any better.' Gavin had followed her into the room and was stabbing the book into the fire. 'You're my wife. I was only trying to help you and protect you from yourself . . .'

'Oh, for God's sake!' Lorianna interrupted in disgust. 'Just go away and leave me alone.'

'I didn't want you to be like them. A wicked temptress . . .'

'Go away . . .'

'A modest woman should not desire sexual gratification or crave excitement. Only low and vulgar women . . .'

'If you don't leave me immediately, I shall scream for

Gilbert and Malcolm and tell them exactly what a filthy, perverted, hypocritical madman you are.'

Later, lying alone in bed, she tried to come to terms with her horror, to somehow salvage a reason to go on living and seek some kind of rules or understanding by which her life could be lived. Everything was confusion. Malcolm had said that there were over a thousand fallen women in Edinburgh alone. How many men were needed to keep so many women in such business? Solid, respectable, church-going family men like Gavin, no doubt. Thousands and thousands of them. The whole structure of society as she thought she knew it crumbled under her feet, allowing her to sink into a black pit of bitterness.

Did all men gloat and drool in secret over every sordid, sickening detail of their liaisons as Gavin did?

She could feel nothing but pity for the women when she thought of the physical pain she had suffered during coupling. But most of all she thought and thought of the wasted years she had already endured and the empty years still to come.

CHAPTER SIXTEEN

'I feel it is my duty to tell you, madam, that I do not consider Alice Tait is a suitable person to have sole charge of Miss Clementina.'

'Oh?' Lorianna looked up at Mrs Musgrove's sallow face. 'Why not?'

'I caught them coming in from their walk the other day. Miss Clementina looked an absolute disgrace, madam, if you will forgive me for saying so. She was wearing neither hat nor gloves and she had obviously been eating berries. The lower half of her face was covered in a purple sticky mess and her pinafore was also stained. I thought you ought to know.'

'Yes, you are quite right, Mrs Musgrove. I . . . I don't see any point in mentioning it to the master, though. I believe he has already engaged a governess, who is to start in a couple of weeks. So she will take over the responsibility for Miss Clementina – during the day at least. Tait will go back to her usual nursery-maid duties and will be answerable to the governess – Miss Viners, I believe she is called. Meantime, I will have a word with Tait myself.'

'Very well, madam. Do you wish to inspect Mr Blackwood's dressing-room now?'

'No.' Lorianna could not hide the hint of bitterness that touched her mouth and voice. 'From now on I shall leave the master's dressing-room in your capable hands, Mrs Musgrove.'

The housekeeper's quick sharp eyes missed nothing. 'Is everything all right, madam?'

'Oh yes!' Lorianna's bitterness still clung. 'What could be wrong. Mrs Musgrove? A slight touch of the vapours, perhaps?'

The housekeeper remained standing before her like a rock. It was as if she were determined not to budge until she knew the truth. There was suddenly something comforting about her.

For a long moment silence stretched between them, then Lorianna said, 'Do sit down for a few minutes, Mrs Musgrove. I must admit that I do feel somewhat low in spirits today. Perhaps if you stay and talk to me it will divert my mind a little.'

Mrs Musgrove sat down, straight-backed and with chatelaine jangling. Then silence hung over the room again.

'You never married?' Lorianna opened cautiously.

'No, madam.'

'You never wanted to?'

Mrs Musgrove's mouth assumed a slight tilt of mockery, which was the nearest she ever got to a smile.

'Once when I was young and foolish, I was engaged to be married. The man jilted me.'

'I'm so sorry.'

'I'm not. He's probably dead now – I hope so.'

Lorianna felt a chill go through her blood. It was the odd tilted travesty of a smile more than the words.

Another silence. Then the housekeeper said, 'They're like animals.'

'It does seem that,' Lorianna picked her words carefully, 'some do not possess the same degree of refinement and sensitivity as women.'

'Worse than animals.'

'I suppose one could say that some have a certain coarseness that could be the cause of much female suffering.'

'Wicked suffering!'

'I take it from the strength of your sentiments, Mrs Musgrove, that your personal experience . . . I mean you obviously know what we are talking about.'

The older woman's dark eyes held Lorianna's. 'Yes, I know what we're talking about.'

After a moment the housekeeper rose. 'You don't look well, madam.'

'Oh, I'm all right.

'No, you need to be better looked after.'

At any other time Lorianna would have regarded a contradiction, especially such an emphatic one, as an impertinence that could not be tolerated. But now she accepted it almost with relief.

'I shall get Cook to make you up a tonic drink of switched egg and brandy. I'll bring it up to you myself.'

She paused at the door before saying, 'An interesting thing about an indisposition, madam, is how it can be turned to a lady's advantage.'

Left alone, Lorianna mulled over the conversation, not quite sure what the housekeeper meant but aware that it did have significance. The brandy and switched egg seemed to strengthen her, although Mrs Musgrove later insisted that she rested for half an hour after she returned from her afternoon walk.

'I shall be waiting to attend to you, madam, and see that you are comfortably settled.'

'Oh, I can ring for Gemmell if I . . .'

'Gemmell is tolerably efficient, madam,' Mrs Musgrove interrupted smoothly and firmly. 'But she has not the understanding and caring attitude which I believe is necessary when madam is in such a highly-strung and nervous state.'

It was true that she was feeling taut and overstrained. She was trying to carry on with some semblance of normality, but every time she looked at Gavin a flame of hatred burned inside her and her nerves tensed to breaking point. She was grateful to Mrs Musgrove for stubbornly insisting on remaining in the bedroom during her afternoon rest; every day the housekeeper stationed herself on the sofa at the foot of the bed, to all appearances

143

intent on her knitting but obviously alert to any sound of Gavin. The moment she detected his footsteps approaching either door she was on her feet, striding across the room and barring his entry.

'I'm sorry, sir. Madam is sleeping and cannot be disturbed.'

Gavin, it seemed, was carrying on exactly as usual. He was politely solicitous; he enjoyed his silent breakfast and perusal of the newspaper; he left for work with the same courteous, 'Good morning, my dear'. In the afternoon he returned, sometimes earlier, sometimes later.

Lorianna never knew whether his later arrivals meant that he had been visiting Edinburgh or that he had been putting in extra hours at the factory, because sometimes he and Gilbert returned home together. She never asked him because she no longer cared what he did. Nevertheless thoughts of the ruin he had made of her life tormented her and her hatred never failed to be fanned by his unchanging piously reproachful attitude towards her.

'How dare he,' she thought, 'look on me with a reproving eye? Gavin of all people!'

When he behaved in this way or tried to lecture her, she simply stared sardonically back at him or else excused herself from the room on the pretext of a headache. She was beginning to understand now what Mrs Musgrove had meant. A lady had so few weapons and no protection at all, especially if she had no mother or father to run to in order to seek help and advice.

It had become a habit now that Mrs Musgrove sat while every morning they discussed the daily menus or the week's ordering of provisions. Afterwards she remained seated for a few minutes – sometimes saying nothing; sometimes making a suggestion for the improvement of the general running of the house; sometimes discussing the merits or demerits of one of the servants. Yet there was an almost visible will about her which invested even the smoothest-voiced suggestion with the authority of a command.

It was during one of their silences that Lorianna burst out, 'Life has to go on somehow, I suppose.'

'It will go on as smoothly as possible so long as I am here, madam.'

Lorianna looked at the big-boned, straight-backed woman seated opposite her. 'Yes, I know I can depend on you, Mrs Musgrove.'

'Indeed you can, madam.'

'The knowledge is a comfort.'

Sometimes, however, perhaps because of the tight-rope of nervous tension she was on, she took issue with the housekeeper. The woman was a servant, after all, and must not be allowed to forget her place. For instance, Lorianna had resisted the suggestion that Alice Tait should be summarily dismissed without a character.

Mrs Musgrove had been keeping an eye on the comings and goings of Alice and also had made a few enquiries about her and decided that she was not of good character – there was some talk of an association with a plough-man. But Lorianna had said sharply that what the servants did during their time off and what friends they had was their own affair, so long as it did not affect the efficient and conscientious carrying out of their duties. And she would hear no more about it.

Irritably she told herself that Mrs Musgrove would have her left without a servant if she was allowed to have too much of her own way. No doubt the woman would get rid of her excellent cook, for instance, and for much the same reasons. Strangely enough, at the same time she could not help feeling a deep resentment against Cook's unknown paramour, and now Alice's secret ploughman. Men caused nothing but worry and trouble, not to mention pain both physical and spiritual.

On her walks now Lorianna avoided going near the farm, keeping to the hills and woods and the green shade of the trees. But her solitary walks only served to depress her and one day, seeing leaves flutter from one of the trees, she began to weep to herself. They represented the measure of her wasted years. She stopped against the tree, leaning her folded arms against it and weeping helplessly into them until she was startled by a firm hand on her shoulder which was pulling her round. The next thing she knew she was being held against a man's chest, a hand was at the back of her neck pressing her face to its hardness. She could feel the coarse texture of the waistcoat against her cheek and the smell of wool cloth was strong in her nostrils.

At first she was too astonished to move or make a sound. Then she began to tremble with outrage at the audacity of the grieve – she knew it could be no one else but Robert Kelso, since no one else would dare. Pushing her hands against his chest now, her eyes flashed up at him, but before she could sear him with indignant words his face came slowly down until his lips touched hers – softly at first, softly at each corner, with his breath warm against her cheeks. Softly, softly over her mouth but still moving a little from side to side and up and down. A soft, hypnotic exploration.

All her anger, all her will melted under his mouth, which seemed to be feeding her with a magic potion that gently stimulated the nerve endings in her mouth and throat and gradually began reaching down to swell her breasts with sweet pain.

When he let her go and she looked dazedly up at him, he said, 'I can't bear to see you cry.'

Then he was walking away, his boots stepping on a twig and echoing in the silence of the woods like the crack of a pistol. She watched his tall figure recede into the green-black shadows, a painfully familiar stranger in his striped shirt with sleeves rolled up and his knee-breeches. His hair, unlike the short crop of the other workmen or indeed of any gentlemen she knew, was rather long and was one of the things that she had heard Gavin criticise about Robert Kelso. Any tendency to long hair was always looked on askance, marking a man as 'poetic' or 'artistic' and therefore not quite reputable.

146

She remembered how Gilbert had laughed at Gavin's disapproval. 'What? The Iron Man? I'm sure he wouldn't recognise a poem if he saw one, father. He just goes his own way, that's all. The more you complain about his hair, the more he will quietly defy you.'

'The trouble is,' Gavin had said, 'that he's such a good man at his job. Had he not been, I would have dismissed him long ago.'

'Yes,' Gilbert agreed. 'No one else could keep the men working at the pace he does. They must surely hate him.'

Lorianna walked back to the house with her nerve ends still tingling, her mind a whirlpool of confusion and uncertainty.

Mrs Musgrove noticed her agitation immediately. Under her watchful eyes a tight-faced Gemmell helped Lorianna out of her corset and into a tea-gown with a long plain fourreau of maize satin and a little bodice of maize chiffon crossed at the breast and held by two satin bands. The full chiffon sleeves were simply tied at the elbow with maize velvet ribbon. Over the satin robe went a long sleeveless coat of coarse filet net, edged all round with a band of mink fur and embroidered all over with a large pattern of conventional roses of every shade of brown and copper that enriched the dark colours of her hair.

Mrs Musgrove adjusted the neckline of the coat and plucked at the skirt of it to show its graceful lines. Then she said, 'That will be all, Gemmell.'

The maid's face was dark with barely repressed fury as she flounced from the room. Later she was to ask all and sundry in the servants hall, 'What's that old devil up to? That's what I'd like to know. And what's the mistress thinking about, letting her get away with it? It's no skin off my nose, of course,' Gemmell assured everybody, bulbous eyes bulging with emotion, 'I couldn't care bloody less!'

The tea-gown was loose and comfortable and Lorianna was able to lie on top of the bed in a relaxed manner for the half-hour which Mrs Musgrove insisted was the minimum requirement needed to recover her composure. Lying there, far from composed, Lorianna was tempted for a rash moment to confide in the housekeeper about Robert Kelso, but as soon as the idea entered her head a rush of fear banished it. She suddenly imagined Mrs Musgrove's horror – not because of her hatred of men, not because of any moral reason, although her reaction would include these things. But the worst horror would undoubtedly be the fact that Robert Kelso was a servant. It would be bad enough having a liaison with a gentleman – any gentleman – but with a *servant*! That was unthinkable, too shocking for words. It occurred to Lorianna that this reaction would be shared by all her friends, even her best friend Jean.

She warned herself that she must never put herself in such an invidious position. But her body kept betraying her, opening up to delicious new sensations, crying out, thirsting for more.

CHAPTER SEVENTEEN

For Clementina it had been a frightening day right from the start. First of all she had awakened too early and the wind had been howling and moaning round the tower. It was dark in the night nursery, but unexpectedly every now and again a shaft of moonlight would beam in straight and cool. Then suddenly it would melt and waver like a candle flame, sending a flurry of strange shapes across the opposite wall.

It might be the tall trees outside throwing shadows. But then again it might, as Alice would say, be witches and warlocks flying about on their brooms.

She was too afraid to get up out of bed and go through to Alice's room. For one thing, Alice didn't like her to do that; she had tried before and Alice had got such a fright when she had awakened to see a white-gowned figure climbing into bed beside her that she had screamed in the most alarming way. Then when she had discovered it was not a ghost and only Clementina, she had given the child a good punching and told her that if she ever did such a thing again, she would throw her out the tower window.

They had gone out early for their walk and while she was lying on her stomach waiting for Alice to go and make the way ahead safe from the cannibal man, a giant spider had dropped from its dew-laden web and skittered across her hair. She jerked up, making the bushes shower her with dewdrops which left her uncomfortably damp.

Later, when she and Alice had been trying to steal turnips in the turnip field, they were shouted at by the grieve

– a giant of a man with a shock of raven-black hair who was striding along some distance away, but near enough for them to see that he was carrying his gun. For a fat girl, Alice could cover the ground at remarkable speed and Clementina was often hard put to it to keep up with her. However, they both managed to escape into a wooded area, but turnip-less.

Then Alice had another idea: they would steal eggs from the henhouse. The grieve was walking in the opposite direction from the farm buildings, so there should be no danger from him. There was another danger, though, one which they had encountered before when merely walking past the hen-houses; there were about twenty hens and a fierce cockerel and it was the cockerel that was the trouble. He always rushed at them as they approached, running at full tilt, neck stretched forward, feathers ruffled to make him look bigger, spurs sharpened – for all the world, Alice said, like a knight in armour. There were tall wild rhubarb plants near the hen's hut and sometimes she and Alice broke off a piece and hit out at their cockerel enemy with the large umbrella-like leaf. Sometimes quite a noisy fight ensued, with the cockerel squawking, Alice shouting, 'You bloody rotten bastard! I'll hang for you, so I will!' and Clementina doing her best with her rhubarb leaf, but at the same time sobbing in absolute terror.

'Steal eggs from the hen-house?' She was appalled at Alice's suggestion, not because of the stealing but because of the cockerel. 'How could we?'

'I'll fight him off,' Alice said, obviously reading her mind, 'if you creep in and take the eggs.'

'But what if the hens won't let me?'

'They will, unless they're all broody.'

'What's broody?'

'When they sit on the eggs all day and won't budge; then they get bad-tempered and peck at anyone who tries to reach under them to collect the eggs.'

'Bloody hell!' said Clementina.

'Are you hungry or are you not?' Alice wanted to know.

'Yes, but . . .'

'Well, then.'

Clementina took up her stubborn stance, chin stuck forward, eyes glowering, fists clenched.

'I'm not going to go in there and put my hand under any broody old bad-tempered hen.'

'There's a knack to it if you'd give me a chance to explain.'

'How do you know?'

'I've stolen thousands of eggs in my time. It's easy. Hens are stupid – all you need to do is put your hat over it and it won't know where it is. It will just sit there confused and wondering and won't think about pecking you any more.'

The thought of a hen wearing her straw hat with the blue ribbons stunned Clementina into speechlessness for a minute. Then, recovering a little, she echoed incredulously, 'My *hat*?'

'No, mine would cover it better.'

As usual, Alice was wearing her frilly cotton mob-cap pulled well down and covering all her hair. It bulged up as if it contained a big plum pudding and admittedly looked adequate to house a hen.

'But what if you can't keep the cockerel away?' persisted Clementina.

'Don't you worry!' Alice's round face grimaced fiercely and she began tugging up her sleeves in readiness for battle. 'I'll soon make short work of that rotten old feathery freak!'

However, when it came to the point, it looked as if neither Alice's weapon nor her hat were going to be necessary because as they tip-toed into the cockerel's territory, holding their breath, neither he nor his wives were to be seen. Then suddenly he came racing wildly out from the bushes.

'Quick!' yelled Alice, looking like a wild creature herself with her hair sticking up on end and flying about.

Clementina, sobbing in terror, dived into the hen-house and flung Alice's cap over the nearest hen, which just had time to jerk its head up in astonishment before it disappeared under white cotton and frills. Its underside felt fat and soft and hot to Clementina's trembling hand, but she managed to retrieve a couple of eggs and the cap and scramble back outside to where Alice was almost invisible in a mad whirl of feathers and rhubarb.

'I've got them!' Clementina shouted, running like the wind past Alice and away down the path.

But even this episode ended in disaster, because she didn't manage to suck her egg as successfully as Alice. All she got for her trouble was a big yellow stain down the front of her pinafore. She had to wash her face and put on a clean pinny as soon as she got back to the house and then let Alice tug at her hair with the brush so that she would, as Alice said, 'look the part'. She had always to 'look the part' for 'that mother', as Clementina called her now, and 'that mother' was nothing but a nuisance. But as it turned out she was to wish that it had only been her mother whom she had to see. She found, however, that the governess her father had threatened had finally arrived and that evening in the sitting-room he introduced her to a tall, skinny woman with grey-streaked side-braids and a sickly white face. The woman gave her a sugary smile, patted her head and murmured, 'So this is the dear little lady.'

Clementina pushed her chin into her pinafore and refused to respond with a smile. She had no wish for a governess, nor for the lessons that the woman's arrival would inevitably involve.

Her father was annoyed. 'Where are you manners? Say "how do you do" to Miss Viners.'

Miss Viners gave a light little laugh and plucked a handkerchief from her sleeve with a whiff of mothballs to dab at the corner of her mouth with it.

'Don't worry, Mr Blackwood. Young missy and I will

get along splendidly once we get to know one another. These things take time, as I am sure a wise gentleman like yourself will appreciate.' Then to Clementina: 'And is my young lady going to show me to the nursery quarters?'

'Well, go on then,' her father urged impatiently. 'Show Miss Viners the nursery.'

As soon as the sitting-room door shut behind them, Miss Viners' smile disappeared. 'Your head will drop off,' she warned, 'if you keep it hanging down like that all the time. Walk properly. Shoulders back!'

As they climbed the tower stairs her voice acquired a note of interest. 'This place is surely very old?'

'It's the sixteenth-century tower house,' Clementina informed her, proud of her knowledge of the subject. 'And it has a secret room on a secret floor above father's study.'

'Yes, I sense a very powerful atmosphere.'

Clementina pointed along the first passageway they came to. 'The school-room's along there, but I'll show it to you afterwards. I know you'd like to meet Alice first and she's upstairs in the nursery.'

As soon as they reached the day-nursery Clementina made the necessary introductions, but Miss Viners did not seem much interested in Alice. She just kept looking around and repeating, 'Amazing, amazing! I have never tuned into a place so quickly before. Everywhere I feel the past reaching out to me . . . beckoning me.'

She moved back towards the door, dropping her handkerchief as she went. 'And those other doors off the passageway, I take it, are the night-nursery and the nursery-maid's bedrooms. Amazing! Amazing!'

Alice and Clementina stole a look at each other from behind Miss Viners' back and began giggling into their palms.

'Yes, Miss Viners,' Clementina managed after a struggle with her facial muscles. 'You've dropped your hanky, Miss Viners.'

But the governess was too intent on looking around.

Clementina nudged Alice. 'Is this your handkerchief, Miss Viners?'

'Oh, oh yes, thank you. Oh, even in the passageway I feel it. How fascinating!' She dabbed at her mouth. 'I can hardly wait.'

Alice nearly exploded in her efforts to suppress her giggles. Sometimes she could be taken with such painful fits of the giggles that they brought tears to her eyes.

'Wait for what, Miss Viners?' Clementina enquired.

'That is none of your concern.' Miss Viners patted the plaited hair over her ears. 'You can show me my apart-ments now, Miss Clementina.' Then she said to Alice, who was moving forward with Clementina as if they were Siamese twins, 'You can fetch the nursery tea and set the table.'

Alice was obviously relieved to go racing away down the stairs so that she could explode in private and Clementina was left to make her frustrated way to the school-room with the governess. This room was similar to the day-nursery, with painted stone walls and a ceiling-high cupboard, but the school-room had an upright piano with brown candle-stands that hung out from its front. There were several cane chairs and a table on which lay pens and pencils, an ink-stand and a large blotter. A blackboard – balanced on an easel with pegs stuck in holes – stood in one corner and in another there was a stand of rolled-up maps. A damp, fusty smell of disuse hung about the place.

Miss Viners looked round. 'Yes,' she said enig-matically. 'Even here.'

Clementina sighed with exasperation. 'Do you want to see your sitting-room and bedroom now?'

But the governess was walking about, apparently in such raptures about something that she failed to hear the question.

'Miss Viners?'

'Mmh? Yes?'

'Your bedroom and sitting-room are off this passage-way.'

'Ah, yes.' With an obvious effort of will, Miss Viners sharpened her attitude. 'At nine o'clock we start lessons, Miss Clementina. From 9 am until 4 pm – those are the hours I am on duty. After that my evenings are sacrosanct; you understand?'

'Yes, Miss Viners.'

'Do straighten up. Good deportment is such an important requisite for a lady.'

'Yes, Miss Viners.'

In the sitting-room Miss Viners stood with her thin hands on her thin chest, looking at nothing in particular, it seemed, for such a long time that Clementina grew restless.

'Can we go upstairs for tea now, Miss Viners?'

'Please,' said Miss Viners with another sudden switch in concentration.

'What?'

'You should have said: "May we *please* go upstairs for tea now, Miss Viners?" '

'May we please go upstairs for tea now, Miss Viners?' Clementina repeated dutifully.

'And ladies do not say "What?" They say, "I beg your pardon?" ' With that she hurried from the room and upstairs with Clementina hastening at her back.

As soon as Clementina's eyes met Alice's again, merriment bubbled to the surface and nearly spilled over when Miss Viners said, 'You have set the table for three.'

'Yes, miss, that's right. One, two, three.' Alice cheerfully pointed to Miss Viners, Clementina and herself in turn.

'You cannot eat with us,' Miss Viners said. 'You are only a servant and you must sit over there until we are finished. After we have left the table, you may eat.'

The merriment drained from Alice's eyes and she seemed to deflate back to the chair in the corner rather than walk. There she sat, with even the frill round her cap drooping as she watched, first in hurt and then in anguish and hunger as Clementina guiltily drank cocoa and ate bread and butter and Miss Viners sipped tea, every now and again rapping out, 'Elbows off the table!', 'Sit up straight!', 'Shoulders back!' or 'Deportment!'

Clementina was furious with Miss Viners for hurting Alice and after the governess had retired downstairs to her sitting-room she said, 'I hate everything about her. I hate her silly plaited hair and her flat chest and her stinky black moth-balls dress.'

'She's stupid, isn't she?' Alice said.

'I've never met anyone so stupid,' Clementina agreed.

'If you ask me, too much book-learning never did anybody any good.'

'I hope the Green Lady and the Black Slave and the Burning Man all go into her room tonight and frighten the living daylights out of her,' said Clementina. 'She even spoiled us from getting out this afternoon.' Clementina was glowering now.

'Never mind,' Alice cheered up. 'We're free now and we can go out wherever we like.'

'But it's nearly my bedtime. She surely wouldn't let me go out if she knew?'

'She *won't* know if we tiptoe quietly downstairs.'

So it was agreed and after Alice, as usual, had made sure that the coast was clear in the reception hall, they slipped out of the house.

It was not a very nice evening, however. The wind was rushing through the trees and drawing strange sounds from them, sometimes like groans, sometimes almost a shrieking. Clementina didn't like the wind – at least, not at night.

'Don't go away and leave me alone, Alice. Please don't!'

'Oh, all right.'

By the time they had reached the edge of the woods where a stream splashed over a line of stepping-stones, the wind seemed to have dropped. Hardly a leaf rustled. Alice was just about to do her usual balancing act over the stream when she spied a figure approaching. It was Wattie McLeod, the poacher. Tonight, as well as his hat with the tall feather, he was wearing a long overcoat that came down over his legs. Alice said it had secret pockets where hares and pheasants could be hidden. He was walking with a slight limp, but Alice said this was not because he had any injury but simply because he was carrying a sawn-off rifle down his trouser leg.

'What's the likes of you doing out at this hour?' he asked in a gruff voice and then spat to one side.

'Walking,' Alice said. 'And we've more right to be here than you.'

'You'll have the right to a kick up your cheeky arse in a minute.'

'Honest to God!' Alice said, rolling her eyes and deciding to keep to the path instead of risking the river in the dark. 'The nerve of some people!'

They had not gone much further, however, when they were forced to turn and start running as fast as they could for home, with Wattie McLeod's derisive laughter ringing in their ears. The storm had come with a crackle of thunder, bringing a deluge of rain like liquid pellets that cut through to their skin within a few minutes.

They had left the side door unlocked and were able to creep into the shadowy corridor. The candles were getting low and barely gave them enough light to grope towards the stairs, feel their way up to the hall and then into the tower stair. They had just reached Miss Viners' floor when they thought they heard a faint moan coming from the direction of her sitting-room.

They stopped in their tracks to listen, shivering, rain dripping from them on to the bare boards. There it was again!

'Maybe she's ill,' Clementina whispered. 'Perhaps we should go and see.'

'Maybe pigs should fly!'

157

'But what if she died?'

Alice rolled her eyes. 'Oh, all right, come on!'

Hand in hand they approached the door. Alice knocked, gently at first and then a little louder but there was no reply except another moan.

Then Alice opened the door and they both peered in to see the governess sitting on the chair at the table and facing the door. A candle on the table illuminated her face with a flickering light, a yellow oasis in a room of darkness, and they could see that her eyes were closed.

Alice cleared her throat. 'Are you all right, Miss Viners?'

Miss Viners gave a spine-chilling groan.

'Bloody hell!' Clementina whispered.

'Miss Viners!' Alice raised her voice. 'Is there anything me and Miss Clementina can do?'

Another groan, even worse than the first, tore across the room.

'Would this not put years on you?' Alice said. 'We'd better go in.'

Keeping close together, they made their way across to where the governess was sitting. From what they could see through the gloom, she looked a most peculiar colour.

'I think she's having a fit,' Alice said.

'What's a fit?' asked Clementina.

'It's a . . . it's a . . . Do you think I've nothing to do but stand here answering your stupid questions?' Alice burst out in exasperation.

'What are you going to do then?'

'Slap her face I suppose!'

Alice never ceased to astonish Clementina. 'Slap her face?' the child echoed.

'To bring her round – that's what you're supposed to do.'

Then to Clementina's horror Alice suddenly gave Miss Viners not just one, but two, hefty blows across the face.

Immediately all was chaos and terror as Miss Viners jumped up and her chair crashed noisily to the ground.

'Oh, how could you, how *could* you?' She clawed at Alice, her eyes rolling like those of a madwoman. 'You have spoiled everything just when I was making contact. I was in touch with the spirit world ... I was speaking with the dead. They are here in this room ...'

Alice and Clementina didn't listen to any more. They were clinging tightly to each other and crying in high-pitched, hysterical sobs.

CHAPTER EIGHTEEN

As usual, Mrs Musgrove appeared to be proved right and had her own way in the end. Alice Tait was dismissed. The outrageous accusation from the governess could not be ignored – it seemed that the dreadful girl had actually attacked the poor woman.

'I must admit I am surprised,' Lorianna told the housekeeper. 'Tait always seemed quite a good-natured creature. Not very intelligent of course, but kindly.'

'There is more to people than meets the eye, madam.'

'We cannot give her a character, I suppose?'

Mrs Musgrove's mouth tightened. 'Certainly not, madam.'

Lorianna sighed. 'Now we shall have to worry about finding another nursery-maid.'

'Effie Summers, the under-housemaid, can clean the nursery apartments and wait on Miss Viners and Miss Clementina,' stated Mrs Musgrove.

'Oh, very well. I will leave you to see to it.'

'Yes, madam.'

Lorianna was too depressed to concern herself overmuch with staffing problems. She had stopped going for her daily walks, fearing that even a stroll in the gardens might lead to a dangerous encounter. Instead, she had Jacobs take her for a drive every day, not in the open victoria but in the closed carriage; she kept the window down so that she could enjoy the air, but leaned well back in order that she would not be seen from outside.

Never had she felt so isolated, so alone. It was as if she had cut herself off completely from the rest of humanity.

Even when she was entertaining visitors or making calls, she did not feel in the same world as her guests or her hostesses. Jean Dalgleish had remarked on her sad abstraction.

'Are you feeling all right, my dear? You've been looking so terribly wan recently – is there someting wrong?'

Lorianna shrugged. 'I hardly know what's wrong with me any more. Everything? Nothing?'

Her friend concentrated on pouring tea from an elegant silver teapot. 'Well, if you were not a happily married woman I should say you were in love. But of course – forgive me, my dear, but I did get a certain impression that all was not well in your marriage. As I understood it, your dear husband was not as keen as you about having another child. I would try to speak to him again about it, if I were you. That's what is wrong with you, I am sure, and you must make it perfectly clear to him.'

Lorianna sighed. 'You don't understand.'

'Now, now, I know what you are thinking – that because Gavin makes few demands on you, he does not love you. But, my dear, I am sure it's quite the reverse. Anyone can see he adores you. So put that silly idea out of your mind and cheer up! A little heart-to-heart with Gavin will put everything right, I am sure.'

Afterwards Lorianna considered what Jean had said about being in love. Was it love that made her, even from the shadows of the carriage, keep hoping that she would catch a glimpse of Robert Kelso, striding up the hills on foot or cantering along on horseback, his alert eyes watching the men at work? Even in the streets of Bathgate her eyes kept straying hopefully around.

And there was such an ache inside her.

Then one day she felt she could not bear it any more. The house, the carriage, Gavin, Mrs Musgrove – her whole life became suffocatingly restrictive. She flung a fur-lined cloak on top of her tea-gown and flew from the house.

Her secret gate creaked. Leaves ankle-deep rustled all

around her and the lanes were lined with hazelnuts and hips and haws. Further on the cherry leaf was scarlet, the oaks like old parchment, the beech deep bronze.

From somewhere drifted a smell of wood-smoke and the smoke-scent seemed to emphasise the general stillness around her. And in the centre of that stillness she was a vale of tears. Yet the bronze beauty of the countryside affected her, enlarged her spirit and gave it room to breathe.

As if pulled by an invisible cord she continued in the direction of the farm. When she eventually entered the kitchen Kelso was on the settle, leaning forward with elbows on knees, staring into the fire. Closing the door behind her she collapsed against it, suddenly drained of energy again and deploring her outrageous behaviour.

He looked round at her without saying anything, forcing her to break the silence.

'I felt so depressed.' She closed her eyes, aware of the inadequacy of the words.

'You came for comfort?'

'I don't know why I came.'

He approached her with slow, easy strides. 'Don't you?'

She felt his fingers at her neck unfastening her cloak and they brought a pulse throbbing to her throat. He flung the cloak aside and his hand smoothed round to the warm, vulnerable nape of her neck. It was then that terror engulfed her. Looking up at him, she was aware as never before what a powerfully built man he was; when he 'attacked' her, surely it would mean an agony far beyond even what Gavin had subjected her to, far beyond anything she could bear? Yet she could not run away now — it was as if she was hypnotised.

Both his big hands were sliding down over her shoulders now. 'You're trembling.'

'Please don't hurt me!'

'Hurt you?' He raised a quizzical eyebrow. 'Why should I hurt you?' His hands moved up to cup her head

162

and tilt it back to accommodate his lips. Once more she found herself melting sweetly under him, absorbing the magic of him, becoming dizzy with him, dangerously light-headed, as if drinking too much champagne.

Before she had time to recover from his kiss she was swept off her feet and carried from the room. Without a word he strode along the passageway and up the narrow stairs, swinging her to one side and ducking his head because of the lack of height.

The bedroom was tiny and camceiled and the high brass bed with its fawn valance and patchwork quilt took up most of the space. He laid her down on the bed and said, 'Take that thing off.'

Already he was unbuttoning his waistcoat and shirt and tugging out the striped cotton material from his trousers. She averted her head in a panic of conflicting emotions, fumbling inexpertly with the ribbons of her tea-gown and trying not to think, to blot all thought from her mind.

He had to help her to undress, so unused was she to attending to her own needs. By the time they were both naked and he had come into the bed beside her, Lorianna was trembling again even more violently than before. She was tensing herself and silently weeping with the knuckles of both hands pressed hard against her mouth.

'My flower,' he said. 'What's wrong? You want me to make love to you, don't you?'

'I'm so afraid.'

'What's there to be afraid of about making love?'

'It hurts so dreadfully.'

There was a moment's silence and then he tipped up her chin so that she had to look straight into his eyes. 'With him,' he said. 'Only with him.'

Very gently he kissed her on the lips. Then he murmured against her mouth, 'Trust me.'

Afterwards she could hardly believe it. The tender stroking, the sensitive tongue, the large fingers exploring so gently. Even when he came on top of her he supported

163

his heavy body with his palms resting on the bed on either side of her, so that she would not feel the weight of him.

Nevertheless, when he entered her she tensed and drew back, but he continued to move smoothly, rhythmically inside her, deeper and deeper and all the time repeating softly, huskily, 'My flower, my flower . . .' Until she was hypnotised by him and drunk with him again and she began to moan in time with his movements, until her moans quickened into breathless gasps and suddenly she was left exhausted and he was lying at her side, forcing himself to take deep smooth breaths.

She could feel the slight tremor of his body. And she could hardly believe the beauty of what she had just experienced. She turned her head to look at him and after a few seconds he turned too and he smiled.

'All right?'

In answer, she leaned her head a little closer to him so that her mouth could touch his shoulder. He stretched one arm around her and cuddled her to him.

'All you needed was a bit of proper loving.'

Lorianna half-laughed, half-cried. 'You sound like a doctor who has just had his diagnosis proved correct.'

'Nothing in a bottle will make you feel as good as that, flower.'

'I do believe you are conceited.'

'Haven't I a right to be after possessing a beauty like you?'

'Am I beautiful?'

'Well . . . let me see . . .' He flung aside the bedclothes, making her grab at them immediately to cover her nakedness. She felt happily shy.

'You must leave me now so that I can get dressed.'

He threw back his head in a burst of laughter and glanced sideways down at her, his silvery-grey eyes glinting. '*Must?*'

She looked at him in genuine bewilderment. 'Yes.'

'No.'

'What do you mean?'

'You don't give me orders while you're lying in my bed.'

'Oh!' she gasped in mock annoyance and gave him a playful punch. "What do you want me to say – please?'

'Why not?'

'Oh!'

He was an impossible, shocking, impertinent, quite dreadful man. And he had the most wicked eyes she had ever seen.

'Say it!' he ordered her.

'Certainly not.'

'Say it, or I shall put you over my knee right now and thrash your beautiful arse.'

'*Oh!*' She flushed scarlet at his coarseness. 'How dare you talk to me like that!'

He tossed the cover aside, swinging his legs from the bed as with one arm he caught hold of her and began dragging her round.

'No,' she cried in panic. 'Please!'

He smiled down at her, then let her go and got up to saunter over and pick up his clothes. She thought he looked beautiful; she watched him put on the coarse, cheap clothes and even then he still looked beautiful. She wanted to weep at the sight of him, yet she had never felt so happy. Never in her life.

'I'll go down and make a pot of tea,' he said.

For a while she lay alone in the mountainous bed with the straw mattress that fustled and rustled with every move. She just lay listening contentedly to his heavy tread in the room below, savouring how wonderful her body felt, how soothed her spirit. At last she forced herself to get dressed and go downstairs. A steaming cup of tea awaited her and she sipped it with sensuous enjoyment. Everything seemed wonderful.

'I'll take you home,' he said when she had finished.

Only then did a shaft of darkness fall over the bright wonder of the day and she sighed.

'No, I ought to go back alone.'

He saw her to the door.

'Sweet dreams, flower.'

Already she was in a dream – walking back through the dewy wood-scented evening, a smile softening her mouth and shining in her eyes.

CHAPTER NINETEEN

Lorianna's ears now sharpened at any mention of him. From various conversations between Gavin and Gilbert spaced over a period of time, she pieced together different aspects of his character and different scenes. Even at dinner parties the general conversation would occasionally turn to boasting or, more often, complaining about servants. Usually it was the grieves and their feats of strength which were boasted about, although as far as the Blackwood estate was concerned it was Gilbert who did the boasting. Gavin more often complained about Robert Kelso — he never went to church, for instance, and apparently Gavin had once tackled him about it and said that he did not agree that people in his employ should not be regular churchgoers. Robert Kelso had not said anything until Gavin had pressed him for a reply; then he had simply shrugged and said, 'Then you must disagree.'

Gavin also frowned on the fact that Kelso was not a temperance man. Indeed at harvest time there had apparently been a serious clash of wills.

It was the custom for a bucket of ale to be brought to the fields for the workers who worked all day in the heat, sometimes until the harvest sun disappeared down over the horizon. Gavin had been against the supply of ale, insisting that good spring water would serve the purpose. The grieve had been equally insistent, not arguing so much as stubbornly refusing to agree.

'A most infuriating man,' Gavin said, angrily polishing his glasses as he recalled the incident. 'I told him that if we were to remain on good terms, indeed if he were to

167

remain in my employ, he must concur with my wishes in this matter.'

Robert Kelso had apparently thought for a minute or two and then said, 'I have no wish to find a new place, but if that's to be the way of it I shall be leaving your service come the term day.'

'Nothing would have pleased me better than to have allowed him to leave,' Gavin said. 'But at the same time I am not a fool and I know his services are too good to part with. So ale it was.'

Someone at the dinner table had laughed. 'Well, I suppose he's not called the Iron Man for nothing.'

Lorianna later had occasion to witness evidence of Robert Kelso's lack of temperance principles and she had to admit to herself that she was surprised and shocked.

She and Gavin were returning from an evening at Mr and Mrs McKeiller's house in Edinburgh. They had gone by train and alighted at Bathgate station where Jacobs was waiting for them with the coach. The station was down Whitburn Road, off the Steel Yard, and as they approached the Steel Yard, the horses clip-clopping and the light from the coach lanterns swaying and flickering, she had heard a burst of deep laughter and seen – under the pool of gas-light in front of the Railway Tavern – Robert Kelso and two or three other men in roistering mood. She could not be sure if they were actually drunk, but there was no doubt that they had been drinking.

The scene made her feel unexpectedly afraid and insecure. She had thought she knew him: a thoughtful man, a man who did not believe in wasting words; a man closely attuned to nature; an independent man whose life was regulated only by the unalterable cycle of the year. Only the turn of the seasons imposed their order on his life.

A dependable man, she had considered him. But now, seeing him in a coarse, noisy scene outside a public house, she suddenly realised he was a stranger.

The next time she visited the farmhouse she had tackled him about it, worriedly, indignantly. But all she had got for her trouble as he moved about the farm kitchen, dishing potatoes from the iron barrel of a pot on to his huge willow pattern dinner-plate, was a dismissive, 'Be quiet, woman!'

He was, as Gavin said, a most infuriating man.

Yet she loved him. Oh, how she loved him!

She wanted to do things for him and sometimes she even tried, to his amusement, to prepare his meal — she who had never made a pot of tea in her life.

Every afternoon she went to the farmhouse, eager to be with him for the most precious hour of her day. All she lived for was to be with him. Sometimes he was not there and she would sit alone or pace the floor, listening anxiously for his heavy leisurely tread along the passage. When there was only the slow relentless tick of the clock and no sound of him, she wept with disappointment and desolation.

Next day she would angrily upbraid him. 'I depend on your being here always,' she would say.

And he would shake his head. 'Don't do that.'

'Why not?'

'There's no future in it.'

'What do you mean?'

And he would look at her sadly and say. 'There is no future for you and me.'

She would not accept that. It was impossible to accept it.

'But I love you.'

'And I love you, flower.'

Lorianna was full to overflowing with hopes and plans: they would run away together!

Robert always smiled at her wild enthusiasms. 'Where to?'

'Another farm.'

'Not around here. Your husband would see to that.'

'Miles and miles away, then.'

'You underestimate the farming grapevine.'

'We would be together, no matter where.'

169

'Ah, yes, I can just see you marching along at my side up hill and down dale, your parasol held high to protect your beautiful skin from the sun.'

'Please don't laugh at me, Robert. You surely know that I would do anything, suffer anything and gladly, so long as I could be with you all the time.'

And suddenly he would be serious again. 'I don't want you to suffer, flower. That's the whole point.'

'We could lose ourselves in the city – in Edinburgh, or better still – Glasgow. No one knows us there.'

The twinkle returned to his eyes. 'Work in the city? You mean you want *me* to suffer?'

Thinking of it afterwards, she realised it was a ridiculous suggestion. He was a countryman with not merely a feel for the land and its changing scene, but a love for it etched deep into his soul.

She suspected that when he did not turn up at the farmhouse during some afternoons, he was just walking or riding through the fields and hills on his own, savouring the freedom and independence that seemed as necessary to him as breathing.

Sometimes it hurt her to see him buoyantly happy, apparently revelling in his own company. She would catch a glimpse of him as she passed in the carriage with Gavin or Gilbert or Malcolm. There he would be striding easily along, perhaps cheerfully whistling, his hat on the back of his head, his gun under his arm, the collies Jess and Ben panting along at his side.

'How can you be happy without me,' she asked him, 'when I am so miserable without you?'

And he could give her no answer. Except that once he tossed a poem on her lap and said, 'I know how he feels.'

It was a poem by Robert Louis Stevenson and began:

Give to me the life I love,
Let the lave go by me.
Give the jolly heaven above,
And the byway nigh me.

170

Bed in the bush with stars to see,
Bread I dip in the river –
There's the life for a man like me,
There's the life for ever . . .

She had read the poem over and over again until the last verse brought tears to her eyes.

Let the blow fall soon or late,
Let what will be o'er me.
Give the face of earth around,
And the road before me.
Wealth I ask not, hope nor love,
Nor a friend to know me;
All I ask, the heaven above,
And the road below me.

The day after he had given her the poetry, she had come across him cursing at some horsemen in the most coarse and shocking way. He had seen her but ignored her and she had been forced to hasten away in acute distress, his deep voice still rasping obscenities in her ears.

Sometimes he seemed a strange mixture of coarseness and tenderness. Once she had been shocked and upset when, after making love, he had smiled down at her and said, 'There's only one thing better than a good energetic fuck. That's a good loving fuck.' She wept because she loved him, no matter what he said or did not say – or did or did not do – or what he was or was not. She tried to show how much she loved him by being as passionately loving as she could, entwining herself around him, fingers twisting in black hair, legs around legs. She showered him with kisses from the top of his head to the soles of his feet. She wound her long hair around him, binding him to her. Reverently she buried her mouth in the palm of his hand. Reverently she fondled and kissed his manhood.

And he loved her with equal passion in return. He said he knew her so well and yet sometimes, catching a glance from his grey, guarded eyes, she felt she hardly knew him at all. There were depths to him that he would not allow her to reach, no matter how she tried.

As the days, weeks and months passed and autumn changed to winter, winter to spring and summer returned in all its glory, she pleaded with him to allow her to leave Blackwood House for ever and come to him for good. But he just shook his head and said, 'Flower, flower!'

She went on and on and eventually he said, 'What can I offer the likes of you?'

'I don't want anything except you.'

'One of us has to be practical.'

'All I care about,' she cried out to him, 'is that I love you!'

'I care about *you*,' he said.

Lorianna began to feel bitter. Not at him. Never at him! She could feel nothing for him except love. But often, sitting in Blackwood House, she would look at Gavin and feel bitter. 'Madman,' she would think. 'Sadist, pervert! How you have made me suffer. And might have gone on making me suffer, had it not been for Robert Kelso.'

She no longer felt she had anything in common with any of their 'friends', even Jean Dalgleish with her talk of good wives 'doing their duty' and 'submitting to a husband's demands'. Was that all love meant to Jean and women like her? Did they not know what love could really be like? But how could they with the solemn-faced excuses for men that they had as husbands? What could these stiff-collared, black-coated creatures have in common with her beautiful man, stripped to the waist, brown body rippling with strength as he wielded the axe in the farmhouse yard to chop wood for the kitchen fire? Or when he washed, dipping his head in the icy water of the rain-barrel and then jerking it heavenwards with a gasp like a hallelujah! Or when he was swimming naked in the river — his powerful arms, shoulders and long thighs smoothly cleaving through the water with the grace and joyous freedom of one of nature's own creatures.

She would look at Gavin with his short slicked-down red hair with its neat side parting, his neat pointed beard and his fussy little pince-nez and she would detest and despise him.

During the past year since she and Robert had become lovers, Gavin had twice attempted to come to her bed. She had fought him off tooth and nail with all the strength that was in her. The last time when she had feared that neither her strength nor clawing nails would be sufficient to stop him, she had resorted to screaming filthy obscenities. That had stopped him all right. Apart from fearing that she would awake the whole house, he was overwhelmed with horror that she should know such words.

The next day he had tried to make her kneel with him at the praying stool. She had merely given him a sarcastic look, excused herself with a headache and rung for Mrs Musgrove before he could do anything more.

Mrs Musgrove's big-boned, sharp-eyed domineering presence was a match for any man. Her overpowering devotion could have been an embarrassment as well as an irritation had Lorianna not been so glad of her strength as a buffer against Gavin. More and more she felt in danger of succumbing to the temptation to tell the housekeeper about her love for Robert and to ask for her help. Not to protect her against Robert, of course. On the contrary, somehow to help her to be with him for always. But some intuition still held her back, although there were times when she suspected that Mrs Musgrove must know. There seemed very little she did not know.

One day the housekeeper was sitting silently on the sofa at the foot of Lorianna's bed, knitting as usual, when she suddenly said, 'Men cause nothing but trouble and you will find the most handsome and attractive ones are the worst.'

'What makes you say that?' Lorianna was startled.

'It has been my experience, madam.'

'Was the man you were going to marry handsome and attractive?'

'Yes. As a matter of fact, he was very like Robert Kelso. Every time I see that man I am reminded of him.'

Another day Mrs Musgrove said unexpectedly, 'Watch Gemmell, madam.'

Puzzled, Lorianna asked, 'Why?'

'Just be careful. She is not to be trusted.'

'Dishonest, you mean? Surely not?'

'She would do you harm if she could. She ought to be dismissed now before it's too late.'

'After all these years of service? And for no apparent reason? Really, Mrs Musgrove, I thought you knew me better than that.'

The woman's sallow jowls darkened. 'There is a reason, madam.'

'Oh?'

Lorianna felt herself become wary. There was something ominous as well as intimidating about Mrs Musgrove's expression, and her eyes so black they looked like pupils with no irises. The tone of her voice was resonant and harsh, although she never forgot her place and always said, 'madam'.

'It's rather a delicate matter, madam, and one that might cause you distress. I suggest you leave everything in my hands.'

Broad hands like a man's folded in front of the black bombasine waist, looked incongruous in their lace mittens.

Lorianna felt uneasy, even a little afraid. Worriedly, absently, she said, 'I am sure I can trust you to do what is best, Mrs Musgrove.'

'Yes, madam.'

CHAPTER TWENTY

Miss Viners had large dark eyes that filled Clementina with terror. But her eyes were not the only terrifying thing about her, for the governess had a morbid obsession with the dead. On their afternoon walks, which were supposed to be for nature instruction as well as exercise, they went to explore parts of the countryside where there were remains of Roman forts. 'Roman soldiers have fought and died here,' Miss Viners would say. 'One might be lying under our very feet.'

Or they would visit different graveyards. 'That black gravestone,' Miss Viners would say, 'is lying flat like that to protect the grave against body-snatchers.'

As they walked across the damp spongy graves Miss Viners would say, 'Can you imagine it? All those bodies of real people under our very feet! Dozens and dozens of them – all with spirits longing to speak to us . . . to make contact with us.'

And then to Clementina's horror Miss Viners would try to summon them up. Her large eyes would grow larger, her nostrils would quiver and she would stretch out her skinny arms beseechingly.

'Members of the spirit world, allow me to be your medium.'

When nothing happened except the rustling of a bush or the sad swirl of some leaves in the wind, she would sigh and say, 'It's never any use in daylight; it has to be during the hours of darkness.'

Clementina longed for Alice and the close camaraderie they had once enjoyed. Alice had been her protector, friend and fellow-sufferer in a life fraught with vicissitudes, dangers and deficiencies. Then suddenly she had been summoned downstairs and dismissed. She had come puffing up the stairs, her round face scarlet, her eyes swollen with tears.

'I've to pack my box and go without even a bloody character. Where am I going to get another place without a character? Honest to God, I'm done for! I might as well just jump out of that window right now.'

Clementina had not bothered about this threat, because Alice was obviously too fat to squeeze through the tower window, but the fact that she was leaving shocked her into speechlessness. She stared at Alice in disbelief as the girl packed her few belongings into a battered tin box.

'It's that bloody Mrs Musgrove who's behind this,' Alice sobbed. 'She's had it in for me all along. Just been waiting for a chance to pounce, so she has. Rotten, evil old hag! No wonder she never got married. Can you imagine any man taking that big Frankenstein?'

'What's Frankenstein?' Clementina's curiosity got the better of her.

'Bloody hell!' Alice exploded. 'Fancy asking questions at a time like this!'

Ashamed, Clementina lowered her head.

'A monster,' Alice said, relenting. 'And a lot of use that mother of yours is.' A fresh gush of tears overflowed from her red and swollen eyes. 'She's bloody well ruined me for life, not giving me a character.'

Tearing off her frilly mob cap, all her unruly curls sprang loose. It was then that Clementina began to cry too. It was awful to see Alice capless and apronless, fat wobbling loosely about as she struggled to tie her tin box together with a piece of thick string.

'Don't leave me, Alice! Take me with you, please. Oh, please, Alice.'

'Bloody hell!' Alice roared broken-heartedly. 'Would this not put years on you!'

Clutching her box under her arm, she dashed away down the tower stair with Clementina howling at her heels. The noise brought Miss Viners running from her room to grab the child and pull her struggling and kicking all the way back up to the nursery, where she soundly boxed her ears. Then, before she returned downstairs, the nursery door was firmly shut and the key turned in the lock.

Clementina rushed to the window just in time to see Alice disappearing down the drive like a little pink barrel in her striped cotton dress.

Miss Viners, as if in perpetual mourning for the dead, always wore black. A black hat decorated only by black ribbons perched above the sidebraids that were tightly pinned over her ears. She wore either a long black dress or a black blouse and skirt, a long coat and black gloves even in summer. In the midst of all this black, her pale sickly face and large eyes acquired a certain ghostly luminosity.

The governess turned Clementina's childhood into an unrelieved nightmare. Even during the mornings in the school-room fear hedged round her, making her shrink permanently into herself in cautious stillness.

Like a young animal which, sensing danger, freezes and is silent . . . so even her mind froze.

Every lesson was tinged with morbidity and Queen Victoria's death and funeral were dwelt on with endless detail and relish. The death a few months later of the Queen's eldest daughter, the Dowager Empress of Germany, was seized on with the same obsessive fascination. How they would be dressed in their coffins, the skills of the undertakers – everything was discussed and even illustrated on the blackboard.

At least one could be certain that they would be dead, Miss Viners said. But there were others – in the old Bathgate cemetery for instance – who, when their coffins were dug up for some reason, had obviously been less fortunate.

177

'One woman's coffin,' Miss Viners said, her voice dropping in awe, 'had terrible scratch marks on the inside of the lid. She had been buried alive and trying desperately to get out.'

The days were frightful for many reasons. Clementina's frozen wits could not cope with the intricacies of arithmetic or indeed with anything that precluded instinct, intuition or imagination and required the sharpness of critical, calculating or reasoning faculties. Her mind was no longer bright and quick and clear; no amount of rapping over the knuckles with Miss Viners' ruler could make it so. Indeed, the more punishment that was meted out, the more stupid Clementina both felt and appeared.

'You stupid, stubborn child!' Miss Viners would say. 'How many times must I tell you? It's like trying to teach a moron. Or one of the living dead.' Sometimes Miss Viners would report her stupidity to her father and she would receive punishment from him.

After four o'clock, when Miss Viners went off duty and either disappeared into her room or away to Bathgate on some mysterious business of her own called a séance, Clementina would sit alone in the tower, her mind mercifully blank.

Effie Summers cleaned the day- and night-nursery and Miss Viners' room while the governess and Clementina were in the school-room – and then cleaned the school-room after four o'clock. By that time she was too harassed and exhausted to suffer Clementina hanging about trying to speak to her. And she continued as she had always done to sleep downstairs in the servants' quarters, after having had such hysterics at the mere suggestion of sleeping in the 'haunted tower' as she called it, that even Mrs Musgrove had agreed for the sake of peace and quiet. Clementina had hopefully sought some contact with Alice through Granny in the village, but Granny said Alice had gone to try her luck in Edinburgh and Clementina had better steer clear of the cottage in future

178

because Granny didn't want to be the next one getting into trouble.

'This cottage belongs to your father, don't forget,' she told Clementina.

The days were bad enough, but it was at times of darkness that terror wormed its way into the mind and awakened it. Not so much the darkness outdoors in the garden and fields; that wasn't nearly so bad as the darkness inside the house. No matter how many lamps were carrjed up from the servants' passageway; no matter how many candles were wedged, guttering, into candlesticks, there were always dark corners and shadowy places. Even in the sitting-room or the drawing-room when she went to visit her mother, Clementina's eyes kept straying fearfully to the black places under tables and chairs, behind screens and sofas.

But it was in the tower that the darkness was worst: around the bends of the stairs, in the quiet empty passageways, in the pitch black of the night-nursery. Stiff with terror, she would feel for the pewter candlestick with its pewter saucer and snuffer. The rasp of the match was like a sharp needle scraping over her exposed nerves, followed by the ominous wavering shadows flung out by the candle-flame in the draught.

Violently trembling in her mad haste Clementina undressed, leapt into bed and burrowed down, hiding her head beneath the blankets. Even then she could still hear the moaning of the wind or the trailing branch of ivy tap-tapping against the window pane, or the soot pattering down into the empty grate.

She was thankful for the return of summer when everything was bright and warm and colourful, when there was the cosy hum of bees and the cheerful sound of the farm-horses clop-clopping along with jingling harness.

Sometimes she walked about the hills with only the curlew, the snipe and the peewit for company, the lark rising and floating far away in front of her. Or she would wander along lanes fragrant with wild rose and honeysuckle, with the perfume of the grassy meadows wafting over the hedges in the breeze. At other times she met some of the village children and went with them all the way down to Bathgate.

That was a busy place, mostly because of the railway and the sounds of its clanking and whistling and chuff-chuffing all day long. But it was also busy with cattle on market day, when perhaps a wave of sheep like silver-grey froth would fill the streets, or cattle the colour of rich red earth. Cattle-men would herd the cows from Whitburn Road, growling coarse unintelligible noises at them while thumping them from behind with a stick, making them moo loudly in protest as their wandering, crushing, bumping bodies filled the Steel Yard before overflowing along the Edinburgh Road.

There was a picture-drome in Bathgate on the same side of the Steel Yard as the Railway Tavern and often the village children would go in to see the picture. Not having any money for a ticket and being too proud to admit it, Clementina would toss her hair and say, 'I don't like stupid pictures. I'm not wasting my time going in there.'

Left alone, she would stand for a while in the doorway listening to echoes of the dramatic piano accompaniment to the film that was showing inside. Or she would watch the traffic going by. Horses and buggies came spanking by and away up Engine Street; carriages lumbered along, rattling noisily over the cobbles; railway carts trundled past pulled by slow, plodding horses.

Sometimes Clementina couldn't be bothered to go anywhere and just stayed in a quiet corner of the garden, listlessly making daisy chains with only the droning honey-bees for company. Sometimes, lying on her stomach, elbows digging into the grass and head supported in her hands, she read a book purloined from the schoolroom cupboard. She liked the poetry books best, the beauty and rhythm of the words somehow giving her comfort.

But no matter what she did, another night had to be endured alone and then another day with Miss Viners.

Often she dreamed desperate dreams of running away to Edinburgh to try her luck with Alice. But she had no money — although at last it seemed that she might be able to save up enough and make the dream a reality. Out of the blue during one of her daily visits to the sitting-room, her mother had said to her father, 'Clementina should get pocket money. I had pocket money when I was a child. I'm sure you did too?'

Clementina had waited with bated breath. Her father had not seemed very enthusiastic but — miracle of miracles — he had agreed. She still couldn't believe it and carried her precious pennies about with her in the pocket of her pinafore. Every now and again she would finger them just to make sure they were there and that she hadn't been dreaming.

She began to take a special interest in everything connected with Edinburgh, asking Miss Viners endless questions about where it was and what it was like. So desperate was her need to like the city and belong there that she even managed to surmount some of Miss Viners' ghoulish descriptions of it.

'The houses are all built of hard grey stone like tall tombstones crowded together on steep hills, with the castle on its craggy rock towering over them like an ancient mausoleum.' Quickly warming to her subject, Miss Viners went on to say that Edinburgh was the place where the body snatchers were most active and where Burke and Hare lived and plied their evil trade.

However, the story that most affected Clementina and brought tears of distress to her eyes was the one about the little dog, Greyfriars Bobby, who after his master died lay on his grave every day keeping faithful watch over it for fourteen years until his own death.

'Now he is buried near his master in the graveyard of Greyfriars Church,' Miss Viners said.

There were pictures of the capital city in one of the

school-room books and Clementina avidly studied them. She discovered that the city, although admittedly having a certain grey grimness, was enthroned on a grand scale on rocky hills with glorious views of the sea. It boasted of a palace as well a castle and had so many beautiful historic buildings that it was known as 'the Athens of the North'. She made up her mind that she was going to escape to this beautiful place. This knowledge was the only thing that helped her to survive.

CHAPTER TWENTY-ONE

Polly Gemmell was as frightened of Mrs Musgrove as were the rest of the servants, but underneath the fear a deep resentment burned. Mrs Musgrove knew all their ways and was forever on the watch. Her vigilance and tyranny made a menacing shadow over the house that even succeeded in affecting Cook, making her more and more bad-tempered and edgy. She literally jumped with nerves if, turning from the kitchen range, she unexpectedly encountered the tall black-clad figure of the housekeeper. The rustle of her bombasine dress or the metallic jangle of the huge bunch of keys that she carried was enough to make the housemaids tremble and everyone within hearing distance fall silent and wait apprehensively for her approach. Her shadow only needed to cross the entrance to the scullery to make Janet, the scullery-maid, burst into tears.

Even in the servants' hall everyone kept their voices down in case Mrs Musgrove could hear. Off duty, books were read or whist played with an air of furtiveness. Only well away from the house could any of the servants breathe easily. Mrs Prowse often told Wattie McLeod that if it was not for her weekly meetings with him, she would go mad. Like the others, Polly Gemmell clung to the safety of, 'Yes, Mrs Musgrove. No, Mrs Musgrove.' Like the others, she kept her eyes safely and respectfully lowered in the formidable presence of the housekeeper. But inwardly she seethed with resentment.

Life was so unfair, she fumed. Why should she have to spend all of her time kow-towing to a sour-faced so-and-so like Mrs Musgrove? She shouldn't have to take orders from her at all – she was a lady's maid and as such was second to the housekeeper in rank. By rights she should take orders only from the mistress – not that she enjoyed that either. Why should *she* have so much of everything and such a life of ease? She wasn't a *real* lady anyway – only a jumped-up farmer's daughter; a wealthy farmer, maybe, but still only a farmer. As for the master with his boring prayers and sanctimonious texts! She knew what she would like to do with them. His latest had been, 'She looketh well to the ways of her household, and eateth not the bread of idleness.' And he had used his lesson to lecture the servants on their duty to have 'profound reverence for your superiors, submission under your trials and a spirit of thankful contentment with your lot'. Well, *she* wasn't content with her lot. Far from it! Everything about it beat up to her head in bitter discontent. So many things infuriated her in Blackwood House, upstairs and downstairs; not the least of these was the text of advice and rules of behaviour stuck up in the servants hall:

Don't think too much about wages, serving in a good home is of greater consequence.

If something has been lost, offer to have your own possessions searched.

Don't gossip with tradespeople or servants.

Don't read silly, sensational stories or poisonous publications which are brought to the back doors of respectable homes.

Don't let candles flare away for hours without being of use.

Remember to pray carefully and regularly.

Mr Blackwood was a great one for the Christianity,

thought Polly. He had once said, 'Rest assured of this, that we can never be truly happy or comfortable in this world till God gives us grace not only to submit to the position in which He has placed us but to be heartily contented and thankful for it.'

All very well for him and his pampered young wife to be heartily contented with their lot — it was easy enough for them. But why should she, Polly Gemmell, be contented with a life of intimidation and drudgery? There was so much in her which was fighting for expression; so much she wanted to have and enjoy; so much she itched to do.

For a long time, of course, she had accepted that the only escape from demeaning servitude was in marriage. All female servants knew that. And indeed she would rather marry Murdo McKay than be doomed to run up and down stairs fetching and carrying for a pampered doll like Mrs Blackwood, dressing and undressing her and God-knows-all-what.

But, damn it, why should she marry Murdo McKay when Robert Kelso was the man she wanted and she failed to see why she should not have him. They had never actually walked out together, but they had known each other for a long time. They had often talked together, they had even danced together. After all, he had no one else. Or that's what she had always thought until recently.

Oh, any time she bumped into him he talked in the same friendly, teasing way he had always done. But one night she had been visiting her married sister and had come up the Whitburn Road into the Steel Yard when she saw him standing talking and laughing with the grieve from a farm over Torpichen way.

'Hello, Robert,' she said as she stopped beside him, mentally rubbing her hands in delight and determined to seize this heaven-sent opportunity and make the most of it.

'Ah, Polly,' he had smiled down at her, his eyes wickedly glinting. 'No boy-friend tonight?'

'Are you offering to fill the breach?' she asked, cheekily as you like.

She caught him winking at his companion. 'I might walk you home if you were extra nice to me.'

'You would be surprised how nice I can be,' she said and both men laughed.

'Come on, then,' she urged, taking his arm. 'It's late. Do you want to keep me up all night?'

'You never know your luck,' he said with another wink at his companion before bidding him good night.

Walking up the hills hanging on to Robert Kelso's arm, her heart was nearly bursting with excitement. She felt so proud that she prayed for someone, anyone, to see them together. She could hardly wait to boast about every moment of being with him. The other maids at Black-wood House or any other house would give their eye-teeth to have such a man to themselves like this. But it was her, always her and nobody else that Robert Kelso talked to and walked up the hills with.

Or at least, so she had thought.

By the time they reached the leafy entrance to Black-wood House, she had been almost hysterical with secret expectation. True, Robert had not spoken much on the way up the hills, but then he never did speak much; there was always that kind of absent-minded way about him and often she had to repeat what she said to him before getting any response. Still, all the time she was chattering she was having exciting visions of being kissed and fondled by him when they got to the gates of the house.

When the moment came, however, to her extreme chagrin all he did was put his hand at the nape of her neck and give her the kind of affectionate, playful push he would give to a child.

'Goodnight, Poll!'

The warmth of his big hand against her skin was too much of a torment to her. 'Aren't you even going to kiss me?'

'No!'

She felt angry. He could be an awkward bastard at times, but her need was greater than her anger. She managed a coquettish look. 'I'm willing to give whatever you want to take.'

'Why don't you marry Murdo McKay, Poll? He wants you.'

It was like a slap in the face. 'And you don't, you mean?'

'I have never given you any cause to think I did.'

'Oh, no?' she said, bitterness overflowing like bile. '*No?*'

'No!'

'You've found somebody else,' she accused, hardly able to credit it. 'Who is it? Anybody I know?'

'That's none of your business. Goodnight, Poll.' And he strolled away in a leisurely fashion as if he was just out enjoying the night air and she had never existed.

It was then Polly vowed she would find out who the dirty bitch was if it was the last thing she did. By the time she reached the side door fury was boiling inside her, giving her a raging headache. And her fury encompassed Robert Kelso.

Bastard! Bastard! she kept repeating to herself. Who did he think he was? And the slyness of him too. Nobody had seen him with any other woman except herself – nobody at Blackwood House, anyway. They would have taken the greatest delight in telling her so if they had, of that she was certain. Even if somebody from another house had seen him, the gossip would soon have reached her. Gossip travelled like a forest fire in the Bathgate hills. But she would ask, she'd ferret out the truth in some way, from someone.

Then, not long afterwards, a second blow came when Mrs Musgrove (may her black soul burn in hell!) dismissed her. No reason was given; there could be no reason, for she was one hundred per cent efficient – it was sheer evil spite that made the housekeeper do it. She hadn't the nerve to say so to Mrs Musgrove, of course, but she told everyone else. Mrs Musgrove gave the job to some orphan girl grom Glasgow, a pale scraggy creature who looked scared to death.

Polly had to go and stay with her sister in the village of Paulville, outside Bathgate, while she looked for another job. This was a terrible predicament to be in, because her sister Sadie's husband was a mean bastard and grudged every crumb she put in her mouth from his table.

Sadie always made excuses for him of course: he was a miner, he worked hard and needed peace and quiet when he came off his shift.

'Forgive me if I breathe,' she had told Sadie.

He hardly earned enough to feed Sadie and the children, her sister said. Was it Polly's fault if he was too stupid or too lazy to earn more money? She knew they thought there wasn't enough room for her in their house either.

'Do you think,' she said to them eventually, 'that I'd stay one minute longer in this place than I need to? This is not what I'm used to, you know.'

She meant it. The tiny terraced cottage in the Miners' Row was sheer purgatory for her and she just had to find another place or do something else to resolve her predicament. She could see herself being forced to go to Edinburgh or even further afield. The trouble was that Mrs Musgrove had written her a character which was almost more damning than not having a character at all:

Polly Gemmell, aged twenty-eight, height five feet, six and a half inches, belongs to the Church of Scotland, is an experienced dressmaker and hairdresser. She is also a good packer.

She has an air of impertinence about her, however, that makes her unacceptable in the establishment at the above address.

188

At the same time as she was searching for a place with growing bitterness and desperation, Polly continued to ferret around trying to find out what was going on with Robert Kelso. It seemed very strange that no one knew or had seen anything. Oh, he had been seen speaking to various girls at different times, but when she had followed up these leads they had come to nothing. None of the girls was walking out with him, although they made it obvious they would like to, given half a chance.

Yet she was still sure there must be someone. Then, quite out of the blue the most amazing, the most intriguing, the most incredible thing happened. Nothing she could be absolutely sure of, mind. But still . . .

She had been taking a walk up the hills for a breath of fresh air and to get away from the impossibly cramped condition of the Miners' Row for an hour or so, when she spied Robert Kelso riding down. Before she came near enough to speak to him she heard the rattle of a horse and carriage coming up the hill behind her and on looking round, saw that it was the mistress with Jacobs at the reins. She immediately drew back into the bushes, not wanting to be seen trailing up the stony road with her skirts dusty, her face bathed in sweat and her frizzy hair straggling down from her hat.

The gig stopped some way ahead of her and the master obviously wanted to talk to his grieve. Nothing unusual about that and of course Robert stopped to speak with his employer. But what did strike her as unusual was the expression on Mrs Blackwood's face. Surely she was not mistaking a look of absolute adoration? There was a hint of intimacy too in the glance Robert gave the mistress before spurring on his horse. Yet surely it was unthinkable? Of course she was some distance away and just getting a side view. And yet . . .

Polly had to go and sit down under a tree and try to sort out her confused thoughts and emotions. It would just be like that selfish, pampered bitch to want everything she could get and more. Well, if it *was* her, she

189

would soon put a spoke in that wheel: she would write and tell Mr Blackwood! That would soon sort out Robert Kelso as well, because without a doubt he would get the boot and quickly. He'd be out of that farmhouse and a job before he knew what had struck him – and serve him right!

It would be an anonymous letter of course, but even so when Polly later sat down in a corner of her sister's house, to actually write Lorianna Blackwood's name took more nerve than she possessed. It was such an out-rageous and shocking accusation. And after all, she could be wrong . . .

Eventually, gathering together all the courage and spite she could muster, Polly Gemmell put pen to paper. Whether she would have enough nerve to post the letter, she wasn't quite sure. She decided that first she would do well to put a few miles between herself, the Bathgate hills and Mrs Musgrove. Especially Mrs Musgrove.

CHAPTER TWENTY-TWO

Late summer was the season for the Highland Games and from early morning, through the mists from the hills and valleys, came the farmers and the grieves, the horsemen and the ploughmen, the shepherds and all the local people. They came on foot, on horseback, in farm carts and everything else including four-in-hand brakes.

The Games were held in the High Acres fields. As all the vehicles arrived they were parked in a circle round the roped enclosure, prices being charged on a basis of so much for a two-horse and so much for a four-horse machine.

Clementina was always allowed to come to the Games and it had been the highlight of her year, as it was for everyone else. Apart from the excitement of the parade of pipers and drummers in their beautiful tartan and the events that followed, there was also the novelty of spending almost a whole day with her mother and father – the only day in the entire year when this happened. Even then she was mostly with her nanny, but her mother and father were in the vicinity somewhere and would quite often wander up to her, when her mother would smile and bend down enclosing her in the perfumed shade of her parasol, and ask if she was enjoying herself. She was also given pennies to spend at the shows and stalls that the gipsies set up nearby.

This year, however, she anticipated the event with little interest; perhaps because Miss Viners was such a dampening influence. Nothing enthused or excited the governess so much as talk of the dead. She managed to harrow Clementina at the Games by telling her the story of the young man who, after the battle of Marathon where the Greeks had won against overwhelming odds, had run twenty-six miles to tell the Athenians the news as quickly as possible and had dropped dead with exhaustion on arrival.

Depressed though she was, however, on the actual day Clementina could not help being stirred by the magnificent parade of the pipers and drummers in their full Highland dress and plaids which reflected all the shades of the heather on the hills. Many of the onlookers were a stirring sight too, in their kilts and bonnets and adorned with Celtic jewellery set with Scottish pebbles, amethysts and cairngorms. She wished Miss Viners would go away and leave her to make what she could of the day on her own. Even the appearance of the woman had a crushing effect, with her prim hat and mouth, side braids and skinny flat-chested figure. Although when she was in the vicinity of Clementina's mother and father, she seemed to slip into a cloak of smiling and sugary charm which never failed to amaze the child.

Alone with her charge or out of earshot of her employers, the governess quickly reverted to her normal sharp-spoken, sharp-slapping self. Orders were rapped out in indignant tone as if Clementina's every movement was purposely aimed to insult her.

'Straighten your hat.'

'Shoulders back.'

'Don't scuff your shoes. Stop picking at your gloves. Ladies don't scratch. Don't wander.'

'Another look like that, miss, and I'll box your ears.' But Miss Viners' voice was muffled into insignificance, not only by the babble of other voices all around but by the sound of the bagpipes echoing across the fields and hills.

Clementina stood watching the dancers for a time. The girls looked very pretty in their velvet doublets in rich shades of green, blue, brown or maroon to tone in with the colours of their kilts. They also wore lace cuffs and jabot, and a broad leather belt with a silver buckle.

However, after a few minutes Miss Viners jerked her away. 'You want to go to the fair, don't ou?' she said impatiently.

'Yes.'

'Why are you dawdling about as if you were half dead then?'

It surprised Clementina that Miss Viners was not only going to allow her to go near the fair but actually intended to visit it herself; she had expected her to say that ladies did not go to fairs. Now here she was, not even strolling in a ladylike way, but hurrying towards the crush of stalls and tents and colourful caravans, her large eyes bulging with urgency. A great good-humoured jostle of people were enjoying the hoopla, the coconut shies, the swings and the side-shows.

'Roll up, roll up!' a thin swarthy-skinned man with black curly hair was shouting. 'See the smallest woman on earth . . .'

A tartan-shawled woman was selling ribbon-tied bunches of white heather. 'Buy my lucky heather!' she kept chanting. 'Buy my lucky heather!'

One man had a huge brown bear on a chain and was making it dance. Clementina caught glimpses of it between the crowd of bodies as she was pulled along by Miss Viners.

Somewhere someone was playing a barrel organ and everywhere a great deal of dust was being kicked up. At last Miss Viners stopped at a red- and gold-painted caravan which had a card propped outside saying: 'Gipsy Mally – fortunes told – cards, crystal and palm.'

Sitting with knees wide and skirts hitched up on the steps of the caravan was a wild-looking woman, brown eyes bright and cunning and hair a bushy tangle.

'Tell your future, missus?' she grinned at the governess, her white teeth predatory looking against her brown skin.

'You stay here,' Miss Viners instructed Clementina.

'Don't move until I come out.'

And with that she followed the wild-looking woman inside the caravan. The door shut behind them and after recovering from her initial surprise, Clementina gazed idly around. It was then that she heard someone call her name and noticed Johnny McPhail, the joiner's son from the village. Cheered a little by the sight of him, she waved. Then he was swallowed up by the crowd – but not for long. Suddenly there he was, standing in front of her with freckly face wreathed in smiles.

'What you doing?' he asked.

She shrugged. 'Nothing.'

He had a bag of very sticky toffee balls which he now pushed towards her. 'Take two.'

'Thanks.' It was quite a struggle to unstick two sweets from the gluey mess, especially hampered by gloves, but she managed it and stuffed both into her mouth. They bulged her cheeks and filled her with delicious comforting sweetness.

'Come on!' Johnny said.

'Where to?' she managed to get out, not without losing some saliva.

'I know how we can get into one of the shows for nothing. You just crawl under the tent.'

It sounded a great idea and, Miss Viners forgotten, Clementina followed Johnny away into the crowd.

★   ★   ★

Lorianna strolled along between Gavin and Malcolm. Gilbert was accompanying a young lady called Fenella Campbell, daughter of Colonel Hector and Mrs Amelia Campbell of Marjorybanks Street.

'Kelso should bring some kudos to the Blackwood estate, father. He's competing in a couple of events, isn't he?'

'It would please me better if, afterwards, he would refrain from strong drink,' responded Gavin. 'He brings

194

more disgrace on us than honour by his behaviour. I have seen him in the town.'

'Ah . . . yes . . .' Malcolm seemed to lose his nerve but managed to say, if somewhat feebly, 'He's a splendid athlete, though, don't you think?'

'Never let him hear you say that, Malcolm. He has a big enough conceit of himself as it is.'

'Ah . . . well . . .'

Lorianna had to bite her lip to restrain both a rush of loyalty to Robert Kelso and a bitter attack on Gavin. It gave her a headache merely to listen to his self-righteous hypocrisy.

'What are the events?' she asked Malcolm in an attempt to change the subject.

'In the athletics there is the 100-yards dash, the 200 yards, the mile and the high jump. The heavy events include the throwing of the hammer, putting the shot, tossing the caber, throwing a 56-pound weight over the bar and the distance – and of course, the wrestling.'

'What on earth is going on now?' Lorianna asked.

A noisy crowd had caught her eye and she could hear a pig squealing. Then she saw that everyone was trying to catch the pig and already half of its tail had been torn off.

'Oh, how cruel!' She turned away.

'Yes,' Malcolm agreed, 'that ought to be stopped. They grease the pig's tail and then the person who catches it . . . are you all right, Lorianna?'

She nodded and Gavin said, 'Are you sure, my dear? Do you wish to go back and sit in the carriage?'

'No, really, I'm fine.'

She had been looking forward to seeing Robert compete in the events and when she eventually saw him she could have wept with pride. He looked magnificent in his Highland outfit and when he looked across at her it was clear he more than approved of her own appearance. She was wearing a high-necked creamy-yellow dress that suited her dark brown hair and tawny eyes. Her hat was a wide-brimmed straw decorated with yellow roses and pale green satin ribbon, and the parasol she carried was of the same delicate green colour. Stationing herself at the edge of the roped-off enclosure, she watched Robert with soft, loving eyes as he stripped down to his kilt in readiness for the hammer-throwing event.

Eyeing up the heavy hammer with its long wooden handle, he rubbed his hands together to dry off any sweat, his powerful arm muscles rippling and dancing seemingly of their own accord. Then he strode purposefully to the throwing point and in one smooth sweep bent and grasped the shaft firmly in both hands, bands of muscle in shoulders and back bunching as they took the strain. He spun from the waist, his back arching to increase the spin; then, when he could go no faster, he let his body power off the right foot. With a bellow he released the imprisoned weight and, glad of its freedom, it hurtled up and out towards the sun. Like a tadpole in a stream it streaked, wooden tail wriggling as it flew until, tiring, it abruptly dropped earthwards, bouncing heavily across the sun-baked grass.

Heedless of Gavin, she applauded enthusiastically. Again Robert caught her eye, this time with that faintly amused but distant look he sometimes had.

None of the other competitors interested Lorianna in the slightest. All she was waiting for was Robert, when he took part in the weight-throwing. Then at last he was squinting up into the strong sunlight to study the flimsy wooden pole spanning the two tall uprights, fourteen feet high, which seemed to split the clear azure sky. Grunting with concentration, he hefted the solid square weight in a brown spade-like right hand and, tucking his kilt up over his left thigh, took up a broad straddle-stance. Then, gripping his thigh firmly, he began to swing the weight to and fro using his taut right arm as a pendulum. His back bent forward and then back to increase his momentum, the weight swinging in a ponderous arc through his widely-spread legs. Suddenly he thrust upwards and out, the veins on his forearms bulging like the gnarled roots of an oak. At the maximum sweep of the arc he released the weight and it soared ponderously upwards, teetering for an instant at the apex of its journey before crashing down on the far side of the bar.

What Lorianna would have given to have been able to go to him afterwards, to lay claim to him, put her arm through his and walk proudly away through the crowds with him. He belonged to her and she to him. In a surge of reckless desperation she almost went to him there and then in front of everyone, but suddenly she was diverted by Miss Viners hurrying towards her with staring eyes and trembling lips.

'Oh, madam, sir – what can I say? This is too terrible, but not my fault I do assure you. Miss Clementina has run away, disappeared! I have been frantically searching but to no avail, Oh, madam, I have the most dreadful premonition . . .'

★　　★　　★

Clementina had not enjoyed herself so much for a long time – in fact, she had not enjoyed herself at all for ages. Johnny McPhail was great fun and very generous with his toffee-balls. She had lost her hat in crawling under the tent, and later torn her dress in the hurry to get safely back out again as they were chased by a swarthy-faced man with a horse-whip. But Johnny had made her laugh and forget the catastrophe. She was actually skipping along hand in hand with him and squealing with laughter when she suddenly came face to face with her father.

She immediately stopped and stood frozen with fear, but Johnny flew away like the wind and disappeared into the crowd.

'Come with me,' her father said and silently, sick in her stomach, she did as she was told.

Soon her mother and Miss Viners were hastening towards them and her mother was saying, 'Thank God, she's all right! You are all right, aren't you, darling?'

197

'Yes, mother,' Clementina managed, but could not hear her own voice for the thunderous beating of her heart.

'Come with Miss Viners now,' said the governess in a smiling, wheedling tone. 'Like a good girl.'

'She is *not* good,' Gavin said, staring with cold reproof at Miss Viners over his pince-nez. 'Take her back to the house at once. See that she cleans herself up and send her down to my study as soon as I return home.'

'Oh Gavin,' her mother sighed. 'Must you punish her? The fair must have been a great temptation and . . .'

'She must be taught to *resist* temptation,' Gavin insisted.

For Clementina the fair no longer existed. The reality was the terrifying ordeal to be faced in the study. Each time it seemed to get worse – a change appeared to come over her father, a strange grunting, hand-groping wildness that she could not understand. It wasn't merely the beatings now – it was the rough fumbling, pushing and stretching between her legs that left her so bruised and tender afterwards she could hardly walk but shuffled slowly and painfully along like a stiff old woman.

'I hope he gives you something you won't forget for a long time,' Miss Viners hissed at her as soon as they were out of earshot. 'You'll be lucky if he doesn't kill you! Gypsy Mally said there was going to be a death.'

CHAPTER TWENTY-THREE

They had been very careful about never being seen together outside. But there had been times — wonderful times at night — when Lorianna had slipped out of the house to meet him in the woods. Sometimes the nights had been still and the sky full of the sound of redwings, a thin penetrating note that lingered in the air.

Robert would bring a warm plaid and wrap her in it and they would lie together until dawn brought the sweet song of the thrushes. Then they would watch the large-eyed robins feeding and the squirrels cheekily jerking and darting about as the early-morning sun made the fallen leaves shine like flames.

Everything was magic because of him.

One summer's night, daringly, she had swum naked with him in the river and he had made love to her in the water. Then afterwards on the bank she had stood stretching her arms heavenwards in ecstasy and shaking back her long, wet hair and he had come after her and made love to her again.

Once they had nearly been discovered by gipsies. The sound of a fiddle playing warned them at first and then they had seen through the bushes that a gipsy caravan had stopped in a grassy clearing. The fiddler was dressed in a shabby greatcoat, the goatskin wallet on his back containing the rough implements for compressing horns from which such men made spoons. In front of him wildly danced a dark-skinned woman with thick tangled hair, wearing a filthy ragged dress. The music quickened and her dance grew more and more frenzied. Lorianna watched in fascination until Robert put an arm around her and pulled her firmly away.

'Be careful she doesn't put a spell on you,' he said, smiling down at her. 'That's "Dancing Mally". She's supposed to be a witch! Everyone around here throws salt on the fire if she comes to their door — they say that counteracts her witchcraft.'

On another occasion they had had a very close shave with a strange-looking man wearing a long coat and a hat with a tall feather sticking up from it. Robert had pushed her out of sight just in time and bawled, 'Wattie, you fuckin' thief! I'll see you behind bars yet!' The man had immediately sped away like a hare and disappeared into the darkness of the countryside.

Lorianna had been badly shaken, not only because the man had nearly seen her, but because of Robert's roughness and his deep voice sounding so unexpectedly harsh.

Afterwards he had said, 'This has got to stop.'

'What do you mean?'

'You know what I mean. Someone is bound to see you eventually. It's one thing if you are seen walking about in the daylight. If people were to see us meeting and talking together then, even walking together, it would be all right; they would just think you were asking me something about the estate. But it's quite a different matter in the middle of the night.'

'I don't care. Why should I care?'

'Don't be foolish.'

'All right. So Gavin would throw me out — so I would be the talk of the Lothians, the scandal of the century — so I would be ostracised from society. I'm telling you I don't care, as long as I have you.'

Recklessly she raised her voice: 'Let them all know! Let them think what they like of me, do what they like to me . . .'

Suddenly his big hand slapped across her face. Shocked into silence she gazed at him broken-heartedly, helplessly.

'You will do as I say,' he said. 'And I say for your sake that this has got to stop.'

He walked away from her then and, sobbing quietly to herself, Lorianna trailed after him. She made no attempt to soften him with wheedling words or coquettish looks; she knew he was not a man to be moved by such shallowness. It was dark and cold and through the trees the gipsies' fire glowed, emphasising the darkness beyond. Occasionally a vixen barked or an owl hooted and once a deer crossed their path.

She never wanted to reach her secret gate and pass from his magic world into that of Blackwood House, but all too soon they had reached the wooden stile and beyond it the narrow footpath which led through the thick, damp, earth-smelling foliage to the gate. There she stood with her head bowed, glossy hip-length hair hanging loose over her cloak. After a moment or two he gathered her into his arms and buried his face in her hair so that she barely heard his words.

'Flower, flower . . .'

'Darling, I love you,' she sobbed. 'Don't stop me from being with you, please. Oh, please!'

'We're not going to meet again at night,' Robert insisted. And she had to be content with that.

Night after night she lay empty-armed and aching for his big hard body, sleepless as an owl and waiting only for the daytime when she could be with him once more.

Her life in Blackwood House became unreal and misty, something on which she could no longer concentrate. Even Gavin remarked on her far-away look and growing absent-mindedness. Oblivious of her surroundings, her passion became a constant flame inside her, burning only in the direction of the farmhouse and only assuaged there when she ran into Robert Kelso's arms. There it flared wildly until it burned itself out, leaving her exhausted as she returned home to the misty unreality once more. Then the flame would remorselessly begin to burn deep inside her once more and she would exist in an agony of abstraction, waiting for another day when she could be with him.

Oh, the ecstasy of mouth on mouth, tongue on tongue, skin on skin, groin on groin. She no longer wanted him to be gentle with her. The slow tender exploration of his lips over her mouth and face, neck and body at the beginning of every lovemaking had become a torment which drove her wild and made her claw at him in her efforts to force him harder against her. But he was too strong for her puny fingers and continued to love her at his own pace. Even when she groaned and wept and cried out to him in a sweet anguish of passion, he only hushed her and continued to take his own leisurely time. Until at last he would quicken, sharply thrusting, often rolling over and over with her on the hard floor of the kitchen until she was bruised and gasping for breath and hysterically happy. And then exhausted.

She had long since ceased to care what was happening in Blackwood House. It didn't matter that Mrs Musgrove's tall black-clad figure was always waiting for her at the top of the stairs, literally to force her into the bedroom and push her down on to the bed.

'You're like a madwoman,' the housekeeper said. 'No one must see you like this. Rest!'

And Lorianna would rest. Lying there listening to the monotonous click-click of Mrs Musgrove's knitting needles, she would become almost hypnotised until eventually the back of the housekeeper's head – the dark hair with the stark white line of its middle parting and the tight twisted knot at the nape of the neck – would become misty and fade. And then the rest of that day and the night and the next morning would have to be lived through before she could go to Robert again.

The only other time when Lorianna's emotions were stirred was when Clementina came down to the sitting-room. The child was becoming quite grown-up; she came by herself now – quiet, self-contained, a model of politeness. Her behaviour was so painstakingly correct in fact that Lorianna could not help feeling slightly uneasy. It hardly seemed quite natural for a child – after all, she still was only a child – to appear so anxious to be perfect. It was almost pathetic.

'Darling, are you all right?' she found herself asking one evening. 'Is Miss Viners a good teacher? I mean, she's not unkind to you or anything?'

'No, mother,' Clementina said politely.

'You are quite well, then?'

'Yes mother.'

Lorianna eyed the silver sweet dish and then glanced over to see if Gavin was looking. His eyes were fixed on his book, although she had the strange feeling that his attention was on Clementina. She decided not to risk offering the child the dish as she usually did when Gavin was not there. Clementina, she noticed, was also eyeing her father somewhat nervously. Instead of proffering the dish therefore, Lorianna surreptitiously took a sweet from it and on the pretext of kissing Clementina good night she slipped the sweet into the pocket of the child's pinafore.

'Good night, dear.'

'Good night, mother.'

'Say good night to father and then on you go upstairs.'

'Good night, father.'

'Good night,' Gavin called gruffly without raising his eyes.

After Clementina had gone, Lorianna said to Gavin, 'Are you sure that governess is all right?'

'Of course,' Gavin said. 'An excellent woman! And deeply religious. Her credentials are of the very highest – she's a clergyman's daughter; her father was a respected minister in Fife.'

'Clementina *seems* to be making good progress,' Lorianna said, as if trying to convince herself.

'There is not the slightest doubt about that.'

Gavin's attention settled back on his book and she was left to stitch absent-mindedly at her embroidery or wander through to the piano in the drawing-room and play sweet, sad tunes as the flame began to lick at her loins and burn up inside her, until she was nearly weeping with the ache of the hot emptiness that only Robert Kelso could fill.

Tossing and turning alone in bed, she tried desperate masturbation to assuage her torment, but the lonely degradation of it released all her tears and she wildly sobbed herself to sleep with Robert's name on her lips. And when she awoke each morning his name was still in her thoughts.

'Robert, Robert!'

'You're like a madwoman,' Mrs Musgrove said.

And that was how she felt.

CHAPTER TWENTY-FOUR

The letter came with the afternoon post. Lorianna saw it lying on the hall table, even picked it up and gazed at its odd childish printing. It was addressed to Gavin, so of course she did not open it. Later she was to wish she had done so — then she would have torn it to shreds and watched it burn on the sitting-room fire.

They were having guests to dinner, Mr and Mrs Forbes-Struthers and Jean Dalgleish and her husband. Gavin was rather late in coming home and did not open the letter straight away, but went directly to his dressing-room to bathe and change. When he eventually appeared in the sitting-room his red hair was slicked close to his skull and darkened with water and his beard clung flatly to his face. He looked correct and formal in his very stiff high collar and highly-buttoned dark suit. Lorianna was looking especially beautiful in a shimmering gown of silver with a daringly low neckline and a long train attached to the bodice. At her neck were high rows of pearls fastened with a silver clasp and from her ears hung pearl drops, all dazzling with the dress against her dark glossy hair.

Gavin brought the letter with him and sat down opposite her to read it. Right away she saw that there was something wrong. His face suffused with angry colour, his eyes glittered behind his pince-nez and his mouth trembled with emotion.

'What is it?' she asked.

'I knew he was a bad influence all along,' Gavin said. 'An impertinent, ungodly, intemperate man like that!'

'Who?'

'Kelso.'

She had to grasp the arms of the chair to steady herself. 'What about him? Is there something in that letter?'

Gavin flung it across to her and it landed on the floor at her feet. Trying not to reveal that her hand was shaking, she picked it up and read:

'You think you're a great Christian and family man and all. But under your very nose someone in your own house is acting the dirty bitch with Robert Kelso. He's got her eating out of his hands. Does what he likes with her. Has his own way any time. No decent girl would want to work in a place where there's such dirty, evil goings-on.'

Gavin said, 'How dare he corrupt one of our maids: How dare he come into my house and taint it with his evil ways?'

Lorianna hovered hysterically between laughter and fearful sobs. 'Anonymous letters should surely be burned and ignored, Gavin,' she managed finally. 'They are the product of a sick mind.'

'I could believe it of him. Had it been Jacobs or anyone else, I could perhaps have ignored it as you say, my dear. But not Kelso! This is exactly the kind of thing he is capable of.'

She could see that Gavin was trembling and she thought, how strange! How ironic! Here he was, the most evil person she had ever known – someone who had spent years sadistically hurting women – getting so outraged and indignant at the imagined seduction of a servant by his grieve. His dislike of Robert must be greater than she had thought. It amounted to positive hatred, she saw now, and suddenly she felt afraid for Robert more than herself.

'Try to be fair, Gavin. You have no reason to say that about him. He has been a good conscientious worker for years; you have said as much yourself. The farm's only a hobby with you; it is Kelso who runs it, keeps us supplied with all our food and . . .'

'I have never denied that he could run the farm efficiently. But I have never liked him as a man. *Never!* I have had cause to warn him several times about his behaviour and his attitude. That man has never known his place and has always thought he could get away with anything he chose. But this time he has gone too far. I shall put him in his place all right — in the gutter, that's where he belongs! Once I am finished with him, there will not be a gentleman in Scotland who will give him employment.'

Lorianna thought he was never going to stop talking about it. All through dinner he ranted and raved, mightily encouraged by Mrs Forbes-Struthers who thought all servants were a disgrace.

'You will dismiss him, of course?' she said.

'After I have told the scoundrel what I think of him,' Gavin replied.

'I wonder who the maid is?' Jean asked. 'Have you any idea?'

'No, but tomorrow I shall question the staff most thoroughly,' Gavin assured her.

'And dismiss her too, I hope,' said Mrs Forbes-Struthers.

'Of course! When I think,' Gavin sighed and shook his head, 'of the sinfulness being perpetrated under my very roof!'

Lorianna felt sick at his sanctimonious self-righteousness, but dared not say a word. She felt herself on a dangerous slippery slope, leading to heaven knew where. Knowing her husband as she did, she could see that he was going to enjoy questioning both Robert and the women servants about the secrets of their sex life, and that nauseated her too. Gavin was feverishly angry, but underneath the anger was an intense enjoyment, a mental rubbing of the hands, a fiendish glee. He was sexually excited.

This suspicion was later proved correct when he tried to come into her bed. In horror she endeavoured to fight him off, managing in the violent struggle to reach the bell-pull and give the three tugs signalling that she wished

207

Mrs Musgrove to come upstairs rather than any of the other servants. Within moments there was a sharp rap at the door and Gavin had barely time to scramble from the bed and into his robe before Mrs Musgrove entered the room carrying a candle. She was dressed in a dark maroon-coloured robe and her hair hung in a plait over the front of one shoulder, but she looked none the less formidable.

Gavin was almost speechless with fury. 'How dare you come barging in here like this!'

'Madam is not well, sir and it is my duty to look after her both day and night.'

'She is perfectly all right at the moment, so you can return downstairs where you belong.'

Ignoring him, Mrs Musgrove strode across the room, put down the candle on the bedside table and said, 'Madam is extremely distressed.'

Lorianna clutched at the maroon gown and began to weep. 'Don't leave me, Mrs Musgrove! I . . . I feel so faint and ill. I need your help.'

'And you shall have it, madam. I'm sure Mr Blackwood will see it as his Christian duty to ensure that you receive nothing but the best care and attention.'

Mrs Musgrove stayed with her until morning and then tugged the bell for Lizzie to come and take over. Lizzie had been instructed to give her mistress breakfast in bed and Lorianna was glad that she was spared seeing Gavin at breakfast, where apart from anything else she feared he might have broken the normal breakfast silence by talking to Gilbert about the letter. Gilbert had been out the previous evening and so did not yet know about it.

But after she heard Gavin and Gilbert ride away to Bathgate to the factory she was in an agitation to get up and fly to the farmhouse in order to warn Robert. Then it occurred to her that he would not be there. He was never at home in the mornings, but rose very early and rode around the estate attending to his various duties. He could be anywhere on the estate's many acres of rolling fields and hills and woodland. She could have wept with her frustration and growing alarm.

As if nothing unusual had occurred the night before, Mrs Musgrove arrived as usual for their morning discussion of menus and other domestic matters.

Lorianna shaded her eyes with one hand. 'For pity's sake, Mrs Musgrove, I cannot concentrate on all this today.'

'It would help if you could try, madam.'

'You don't know all that I have on my mind just now.'

'Baxter, the parlourmaid, has been talking about a letter Mr Blackwood received. Apparently he was discussing it while she was serving at table.

'My God!' Lorianna groaned.

'Don't worry, madam. Nothing will ever go further than the four walls of this house. They would not dare — they all know that it would be as much as their job is worth.'

'You have told them so, I suppose?'

'Certainly, madam. I don't hold with servants gossiping.'

'My God, what am I going to do?'

'You should keep calm and do nothing, madam.'

'But I must go and . . .'

'No madam, you must stay and allow other people to look to themselves. They are more able than you.'

Lorianna's lips trembled. 'What will happen?'

'I would think that Mr Blackwood will return early after lunch, send for Kelso to question him here and then perhaps dismiss him.'

'Perhaps? You think there might be hope that . . .'

'Mr Blackwood has threatened to dismiss Kelso before, madam, and in the end has not done so.'

Lorianna began to feel slightly calmer. 'Yes, I remember now. Yes, that's true.'

'Kelso is always very calm, very sure of himself. And he's a man. He can take very good care of himself, madam. Now, I believe you have a luncheon appointment today and that you and Mr Blackwood are going out for dinner this evening. So we shall not require either a luncheon or a dinner menu for today. But I thought for tomorrow . . .'

Lorianna made a conscious effort to concentrate. She was grateful to Mrs Musgrove for being so reassuring and also for reminding her of her luncheon appointment with Mrs Anderson. In her anxiety and distress she had completely forgotten about it. She resolved to see Robert at her usual time this afternoon, when they would discuss everything that had happened.

And yet, all the time, behind her polite concentration, behind the welcome reassurance, anxiety still lurked.

CHAPTER TWENTY-FIVE

Clementina had grown to fear every adult in her life. Even her mother was not to be trusted, because she was ruled by her father. Her whole existence now became a test of how to avoid getting smacks or reprimands or worse from one adult or another. Whatever she did was sure to be wrong in the eyes of at least one of the grown-ups. The best she could do was to try her very hardest not to annoy her father, because she feared him most of all.

For example, Miss Viners would send her down to the kitchen to fetch more milk for nursery tea. But the moment she put her head round the kitchen door a red-faced harassed Cook over at the stove, madly whisking some sauce or cream with a tiny sheaf of bleached birch twigs would shout at her to go away. At her busy times, Cook couldn't stand any distractions from anybody. It was then, as Henny used to say, that Cook was at her most volatile. But Clementina daren't think of Henny, in case the floodgates of her grief would burst open again. So, jug in hand, she would wander up and down the long, stone-floored passageway trying to decide what to do. She considered stealing some milk from the pantry but if one of the maids or – horror of horrors – Mrs Musgrove caught her she would either have her ears boxed, be given a punching or be marched upstairs to the sitting-room and reported to her father. If she dared go back to the kitchen, Cook would get really angry and perhaps throw something at her. If she went back upstairs to the nursery without any milk, Miss Viners would be furious and would punish her.

So she would just stand in the darkening passageway clutching the empty milk jug, paralysed with fear, not knowing what to do.

Her dream of escaping to Edinburgh became more and more desirable and urgent, until she felt she could not bear to wait until she had saved up any more money – she had to go *now*.

A perfect opportunity presented itself when Miss Viners said she would be going off early to attend some-one's funeral. Mother was always out in the afternoon and father would be at the factory. Miss Viners had also told her, 'You've not to go and visit your parents today, because your father and mother will be busy getting ready to go out to dinner.'

So it would be perfectly safe for her to set off early for Edinburgh. Nobody would know. She wondered what she should take with her and decided on a rag doll made from one of Alice's old stockings, a clean handkerchief and of course her pennies. The rag doll Alice had made had been christened Black Mammy because the stockings were black and Alice had sewn on brown crosses for eyes and a red cross for a mouth from scraps of darning wool. Clementina loved the doll very much.

There was a signpost on the Drumcross Road that pointed to the left towards Edinburgh and that was the direction Clementina took, clutching Black Mammy under her arm and with her pennies safely tucked away in the pocket of her pinafore. After a while she came, rather confusingly, to another signpost which pointed down to the right for Edinburgh; eventually she reach-ed a big main road where yet another sign pointed to the left.

Already she was getting tired and trailing Black Mammy by the arm alongside her. There was quite a lot of traffic on this road and she guessed it must be coming from Bathgate. Men on horseback cantered past. Open victorias – in which ladies sat, holding parasols high – swept along. Closed carriages rumbled noisily, whips cracking over horses with heads and tails held proudly. Carts and wagons of all shapes and sizes clattered behind heavy Clydesdales. Then suddenly the shadow of a victoria stopped beside her and she looked up to see the grim-faced figure of her father.

She stood perfectly still, clutching her doll, her mind completely blank. Then somehow she found herself in the carriage beside her father and he was turning the horses round and going back towards the house.

She realised that he too had been going to Edinburgh and the fact that she had diverted him from his journey and caused him the inconvenience of turning back would make her crime all the more serious . . . And therefore her punishment. Her heart was thumping so much she was sure it was making the whole carriage throb.

Into the drive they turned and still in terrifying silence. By the time they reached the house she was too weak to even try to climb down and had to be lifted. Up the stairs and into the reception hall. How quiet the house was! Into the study. Now nothing needed to be said. Tidily she laid down her doll. Then, bunching up her dress and pinafore, she unbuttoned her knickers and took them off.

The rough hands began rubbing and probing and she closed her eyes and bit her lip and tried to remember to be brave. But she could hear her father making strange noises now and they frightened her more than anything. She dared not open her eyes. The hands were quickening and soon their violence knocked her down and, as she lay on her back they spreadeagled her legs, making her terrifyingly vulnerable. Even her clenched teeth could not stop her moans and high-pitched squeals when she felt her father's weight come on top of her and something hard began bumping ferociously against her. She began to shriek with pain, forgetting about everything else, concentrating only on her agony.

Outside in the hall, Mrs Musgrove had come to stand at the top of the stairs as usual to greet Lorianna.

'Good afternoon, madam.'

'Good afternoon, Mrs Musgrove . . . What on earth is that noise?'

'I saw Mr Blackwood return earlier with Miss Clementina, madam. I believe he is in the study with her now.'

Lorianna screwed up her face. 'Poor little thing, I wonder what she's done now? She must be getting punished more severely than usual – she never cries out as a rule.'

Lorianna went over to hover anxiously outside the study door. Then, unable to stand the harrowing sounds any longer, she opened the door and looked in. Suddenly she was too horrified to cry out: beyond sound, beyond thought, hot bullets exploding in her head, she stumbled into the room, seized a heavy metal ornament and brought it crashing down on Gavin . . . His skull cracked like an eggshell. She heard it.

Clementina was still shrieking, but when Gavin slumped heavily down on top of her, his body obliterating even her face, the shrieking stopped.

Blood was oozing from his head and ear as Lorianna dropped the ornament.

Mrs Musgrove was in the room now. 'Keep quiet and just stand there until I come back,' she commanded. 'I will take the child upstairs.'

Lorianna couldn't move. She stood watching as Mrs Musgrove pushed Gavin's body aside, lifted the unconscious child and carried her from the room.

Gavin's eyes were open. He was staring at her in incredulity and reproach. Mrs Musgrove returned and shut the door behind her, saying, 'She's all right. I've put her to bed.'

Still Lorianna could neither move nor make a sound.

'And I have sent Lizzie for Kelso. Come through with me to the sitting-room and I'll pour some brandy.'

They were both sitting silently sipping brandy when Robert Kelso arrived with the maid. Lorianna rose, swaying to her feet, staring tragically at him.

'Oh, Robert!'

Mrs Musgrove rose, straight-backed and sharp-eyed. 'Get back downstairs, Lizzie, and don't dare to breathe a word of this to anyone.'

'What's happened?' Robert asked the housekeeper, at the same time crossing the room to take Lorianna into his arms and press her head against his chest.

Mrs Musgrove looked away, her mouth twisting.

'What the hell's going on?' he repeated.

'Mr Blackwood's dead. She's killed him. He was trying to rape the child.'

A sickened expression contorted his features for a moment and then they were calm again.

'Well?' said Mrs Musgrove.

'We shall have to send for the police.'

'Do you want her to hang?'

'I didn't mean to kill him,' Lorianna whimpered. 'I didn't mean it, Robert.'

He hushed her gently and then said to the housekeeper, 'They will have to know.'

Her mouth twisted again. 'So this is all you care about her? I might have known.'

'What are you talking about, woman? We have no choice.'

'Of course there is a choice; there has to be a choice. We must get rid of the body. You will have to take it away and bury it somewhere on the estate.'

'No.'

'They'll hang her!'

'Shut your mouth, woman!'

Lorianna was sobbing now, clinging to him and trembling violently.

'Hush, flower,' he soothed. 'I won't let anyone hurt you.'

'You're just like the rest, all talk,' Mrs Musgrove sneered. 'But when it comes to the point . . .'

'Be quiet, I said!'

'You've got to help her.'

'How did he die?'

215

'She hit him on the back of the head with a metal ornament.'

After a pause he said, 'It's got to look like an accident.'

'How can it?'

He paused again. 'Leave it to me. All you have to say is that he went out riding and didn't return.'

Lorianna clung tighter than ever, her voice rising in panic.

'Oh, Robert, I'm so afraid.'

'Remember,' he repeated to Mrs Musgrove. '*He went out riding*.' Then to Lorianna, 'Hush, my flower.' Rocking her back and forth in his arms like a child, he soothed her with soft whispers.

CHAPTER TWENTY-SIX

It had been hot and sultry all day and there was hardly a breath of air. The branches of the trees hung motionless, not a leaf stirred.

Wattie McLeod peered up at the sky. Earlier it had been copper-tinted; now dark clouds had rolled in one on top of the other.

Usually, if it was a really dark night and no moon, the wide open hills were safe. On a moonless night the woods had an impenetrable blackness and a poacher would need the eyes of a cat to see to do his work. But if it was bright and he could see his way he avoided the hills because a watcher could spy him miles off.

Tonight he felt in his bones that there was a summer storm brewing. A gust of wind would come and blow the cloud clear of the moon and there would be a flash or two of lightning. Then he would be able to make his way in the woods all right.

Sure enough the leaves were beginning to gently rustle. Might not be much of a wind – not a gale, at least, and that was good. He had to be able to hear when a rabbit was moving in its burrow and when it was likely to bolt, so that he could grab it the moment it was in the net. With the 'oak's mysterious roar' overhead, and the moan of the gale as it rushed through the hawthorn, it wasn't so easy to make out the low, thumping sound of a rabbit in its warren.

As Wattie reached the woods a peal of thunder rumbled and cracked high above and lightning sizzled over the tree-tops. Then came a few hesitant droplets of rain

217

that soon changed into a hurried pattering. He hunched into his long coat and sought temporary shelter in the hollow of a big oak tree. There he listened as the rain rose to a roar within the forest. He waited until it gradually diminished once more to a soft pattering on the leaves and was just about to step out and get on with his work when his sharp ears detected another alarming sound: someone was approaching on horseback. Quickly he shrank back into the tree again. And just in time. The horse passed too near for comfort and the rider was unmistakably Robert Kelso, the grieve.

Then something else caught Wattie's eye – there was a large bundle slung over the horse in front of Kelso, covered with a plaid. Hardly daring to breathe, he watched the grieve dismount and lift down what he could now see was a body. Still holding the body, Kelso looked around as if wondering where best to lay it down. Eventually, he chose a spot with the head resting back against a boulder. Then, leaving the horse beside the body, he walked away with the plaid slung over his shoulder.

Wattie waited for a long time before stealthily moving from his hiding place and going over to peer closer. The dead man, he discovered, was the master of Blackwood House.

No poaching tonight, he decided. Safer for him to be home tonight and as many folk knowing as possible. He wasn't going to be mixed up in this dirty business. The thought of going to the police never occurred to him. The less he had to do with the police and the further he kept from them the better – that had always been his policy.

He stayed at home the next night as well, because there were police all over the place and they had found the body. A riding accident, they were saying it was. Let them say what they liked, as long as they steered clear of him. He felt uneasy though and drank more than usual to steady his nerves. He didn't feel like talking to anyone and was standing alone in the Railway Tavern in Bathgate when one of the Blackwood horsemen came up to him.

'It's a bad day all round, eh?'

'Oh, aye? And how's that?'

'You know what I'm talking about – the accident! The place has been hotching with police these past few nights.'

'Police don't worry me,' maintained Wattie.

'A likely story!'

'Aye, I could tell them a story, right enough.'

'What do you mean?'

'A queer sort of accident,' Wattie said darkly. 'Aye, very queer.'

'What makes you say that?'

'I have my reasons.'

'Are you saying you know something the police don't?'

'Never you mind what I know. What I know and what I see is my own business.'

But of course people never did mind their own business and the man he had spoken to must have babbled to the police, because the next thing Wattie knew they had called at his cottage and taken him away for questioning.

★　　★　　★

Mourning didn't suit Lorianna. The high-necked black dress seemed to drain from her every last shade of colour and her face was a dead white mask in which her full red mouth paled into insignificance. Even her normally glossy hair, warm in colour as rich brown earth, looked dull. Only her eyes, large and luminous, still caught and riveted the attention.

She had been confined to bed; she didn't know for how long, since she had been dazed rather than calmed by Mrs Musgrove's regular administrations of laudanum. The housekeeper had moved into the dressing-room so that she could be near her during the night. Sometimes Lorianna cried out in her sleep and jerked awake, sweating and trembling from a nightmare. But there was something nightmarish about Mrs Musgrove herself. Her tall, black-clad figure seemed always to be hovering over Lorianna and she had discovered that the housekeeper not only had a powerful personality but also possessed the physical strength of a man. Dazed though she was, Lorianna had tried to get out of bed but Mrs Musgrove had physically restrained her, had actually held her down on the bed.

Now the housekeeper, by sheer force of will, was trying to keep the daily routine in operation as if nothing had happened. She was sitting opposite Lorianna at the window of the sitting-room, hard-covered notebook and pencil in hand.

'Madam,' she repeated, 'you're not concentrating.'

'I beg your pardon.'

'You must think only of each present moment. You must concentrate.'

'Yes.'

'Life has to go on.'

'Yes, of course.'

'As I was saying, we shall have to buy more dress material. Miss Clementina needs mourning clothes too.'

'I cannot bear this,' Lorianna said suddenly. 'I *must* see him.'

'Who, madam?'

'You know perfectly well.'

'If you mean Kelso, it's impossible.'

'Why?'

'He has been arrested.'

For a moment or two Lorianna stared at the older woman in bewilderment. 'Arrested?'

'He was seen. And they found blood on his clothes.'

Lorianna rose to her feet, swaying slightly.

'I must put things right immediately. Ask Jacobs to bring the carriage round.'

'What can you put right, madam?' said Mrs Musgrove, rising too.

'I must tell the police the truth so that they will release Robert.'

'They won't release him now, no matter what you say.'

'Of course they will. They *must*.'

'No, madam. Even if they believed you, he is still an accessory to murder. You would both hang.'

'*Hang?*' The word was an incredulous high-pitched whimper. 'Hang Robert?'

Her heart had begun to race wildly in her chest.

'If you leave well alone, he'll have a good chance with a good lawyer.'

'But I can't just . . . I can't just . . .' She began to sway like a drunk woman.

'It's all right,' said Mrs Musgrove. 'I have seen him, and he says to tell you just to keep quiet and do nothing. He will be all right; he knows what he's doing and his lawyer says they will never convict him.'

'But I . . . I . . .' Her mind was refusing to function. 'I . . .'

Mrs Musgrove gripped her arm. 'I think you should go back to bed.'

'No . . .' She tried to prise the hand away and was unexpectedly revolted by the slippery contact of silk mittens. 'No, leave me alone!'

'You are ill.'

'Send for a doctor, then.'

'The doctor has seen you and he told me to ensure that you had plenty of rest and quiet.'

'Send for him to come again, I want to speak to him . . . Or the minister . . . Send for the Reverend Marshall. I need to speak to somebody.'

'You can speak to me, madam.'

'No, somebody else. I need help and advice.'

'I can give you all the help and advice you need. And I am advising you that what you need just now is to keep quiet. You will do him no good by trying to tell what really happened. Once you do that, he has no

221

chance at all. Nor have you.'

Lorianna fought to quell her rising panic. 'All right,' she said. 'I shall say nothing to anybody. But one thing I must do, Mrs Musgrove and that is go to see Robert. Where is he?'

'In the Calton Jail in Edinburgh.'

She could not bear to think of Robert in jail. He needed the freedom of the hills and the woods, the rivers and the lochs.

'How can a visit be arranged? I must find out immediately.'

'Well, if you must go . . .'

'Yes, I must.'

'Then it will have to be done very discreetly.'

'That was why I suggested the doctor or the minister. Did the Reverend Marshall not have something to do with prisons at one time?'

'I believe so.'

'Then he will know and be able to advise me. Send for him at once, Mrs Musgrove.'

'Very well, madam.'

Within the hour the Reverend Marshall, a tall grey-bearded man, had arrived in the sitting-room and was offering his hand to her.

'How are you, my dear?'

Mrs Musgrove remained to hover beside Lorianna.

'Madam has been in a very shocked and overstrained condition, sir, especially since she heard that her grieve has been arrested for the crime. She cannot believe that he is guilty; he was always a good and trusted employee.'

'I wish to speak to him,' Lorianna said. 'Could you arrange it?'

'I have tried to advise madam against such a rash course of action, sir,' interposed the housekeeper, 'but she is so distressed by the whole affair.'

The Reverend Marshall patted Lorianna's hand. 'Don't worry, my dear. I know the prison chaplain and will speak to him straight away. I shall be through in Edinburgh tomorrow anyway. A terrible business! I must say I was shocked when I heard about Kelso. I find the charge hard to believe myself. Many a time I've had a chat with him, you know, when I have been doing my parish rounds. We used to stop and pass the time of day when we met on the road.

'I was watching him at the Highland Games recently and thinking what a fine figure of a man he was. Good at his job too, by all accounts. Many a gentleman farmer around these parts envied your husband for having such a good man to run things for him.'

'You will arrange for me to visit him?'

'He will be allowed visitors, there is no problem there. But I will see that your visit is a private one – for that I shall speak to the chaplain.'

Lorianna closed her eyes. 'Thank you.'

'Would you like me to say a prayer?'

She nodded. Dazed with the dregs of laudanum and with her suffering, she stood with eyes closed, the drone of his voice acting as a soporific.

Mrs Musgrove's hand tightened round her arm again, hard fingers bruising tender flesh.

'I ought to put her to bed, sir. All this has been too much for her.'

Lorianna was aware that she was being led away. ' I shall hear from you tomorrow?' she whispered. 'I am depending on you.'

'Yes, my dear,' the Reverend Marshall gazed at her pityingly. 'Try not to worry.'

Worry seemed such a mild and inappropriate word. She could think of no word adequately to describe her condition. She felt she was dangling on the edge of a black pit, unable to contend with what was at the bottom but without the strength to stop herself from slowly sliding in.

'Stay there until I come back,' Mrs Musgrove snapped. 'I must go and see him out.'

Suddenly Lorianna's anxiety tipped over into fear.

'Don't you say anything to him about me.'

'Say anything about you, madam?'

'There is nothing wrong with me; I am perfectly fit to travel to Edinburgh. But whether I am or not and whether he arranges anything or not, I intend to go. Nobody is going to stop me from seeing Robert, do you understand?'

'Yes, madam.'

And so it was arranged. Eventually she and Mrs Musgrove set out in the closed carriage with Jacobs up in front.

The word 'prison' to Lorianna had meant Robert being restrained, shut away and kept from his wide open hills and the countryside he loved. She had not been prepared for the sight that met her in Edinburgh.

Princes Street was the main street of the city and was dominated on one side at the west end by Edinburgh Castle, perched high above on a rock. But at the other end of the long street, directly facing the carriage as it progressed, was Calton Hill. High against the skyline monuments jutted; the Observatory, the Dugald Stewart Monument, the National Monument, the Nelson Monument in the shape of a giant telescope, the obelisk of the martyr's monument in the old Calton burying ground. And there, creeping up the side of the rocky hill like a black fungus, was the Calton Jail, more castellated than the castle with its crush of square and round turrets, towers and high walls.

'I did say you should not have come,' Mrs Musgrove said, as if sensing Lorianna's horror. 'This is no place for you.'

A nerve fluttered in Lorianna's cheek and her voice shook. 'This is no place for Robert.'

Lorianna kept her black veil over her face, but this did not protect her from the all-pervading smell of the place. She thought that as long as she lived that terrible prison smell would remain in her nostrils.

What was it? The musty dampness of the walls? The

rats, mice and beetles that scurried about inside them? Urine and faeces from innumerable chamber pots? The concentrated stench of human bodies? A combination of all of these things, but something more. Something indefinable and unique to the place – a sickness in the air.

It penetrated even to the chapel vestry where she waited and where eventually Robert was brought to her.

The door shut behind him leaving them alone, and she stood looking at him. The mean little room, his shabby prison rags, nothing could demean him or detract from what he was: her beautiful man.

Enfolded in his arms for a blissful minute, nothing mattered any more. It was all a bad dream and nothing had any reality. Everything that threatened them – the hangman, the prison, the warder, the police, the courts, the judge, the jury, the whole of society itself – was of a different world, a world of ignorance and lack of understanding and cruelty beyond all comprehension. Nothing was real and true and good except him, and their love for each other.

'My love,' she said, 'I must get you out of here. I must tell them the truth.' She put her fingers gently to his lips to stop him from interrupting. 'I don't care what happens to me. Truly I don't. All I care about is you!'

'It's no use, flower,' he said. 'My only chance is to depend on the lawyer. He's a good man who will do his best for me.'

'But darling, I cannot bear it. It's because of me that you are in this awful place and your life is in such danger. I cannot go on living in Blackwood House – a free woman, as if I have done nothing – when it was I who killed Gavin, not you.'

'Hush!' He lowered his voice. 'They are just outside the door and might hear you.'

'I can't bear it, Robert.'

'For my sake, you must!'

'But it's for your sake that I must tell them the truth.'

'It could only make things worse and it certainly

wouldn't make them release me from here. All it would do is involve you. That's the only thing I dread, flower. Don't do that to me.'

'Oh, Robert!'

'I want to think of you walking in the Bathgate Hills as free as a bird. I like to imagine you looking across the spread of fields and woods in all their warm colours and seeing the Forth glistening in the distance. In my mind and heart I'm always with you there.'

Oh, love that needs no words. The wordless journey through the eyes into the soul. Skin that knows skin, the familiarity of flesh and bone. Love beyond flesh.

'Don't come back here again for any reason,' he said. 'My flower must not wither in such a place.'

He kissed her gently, then put down her veil and before she could stop him he had called for the guards and they were leading him away.

She felt herself shrinking like an old woman. Mrs Musgrove had to support her, half-carrying her from the prison into the carriage.

Not a word passed between them during the whole journey back to the Bathgate hills and Blackwood House. Leaning back against the padded seat of the coach, eyes closed, Lorianna felt herself from time to time drift mercifully into unconsciousness.

Opening her eyes eventually as the coach rocked up the Drumcross Road, she saw the beautiful arch of trees and the sight of it and of the hills beyond brought a rush of tears to her eyes, a sudden panic of sobbing.

It was impossible that Robert should not be here in the countryside where he belonged.

'Control yoursefl!' Mrs Musgrove said coldly. 'We shall soon be at the house and the servants must not see you in this state.'

'I don't care about the servants. I don't care about anybody, except him.'

'Yes,' Mrs Musgrove mouth twisted. 'And look where it's got you!'

226

'What do you mean?' Lorianna sobbed in bewilderment. 'Nothing has been Robert's fault.'

'No?'

'No!'

'I warned you that men were nothing but trouble. They are not worth it.'

'Robert is worth anything!'

'Keep your voice down,' the housekeeper said. 'I knew it was unwise to go there. That man has you demented. You must lie down as soon as we get in and I will give you some medicine.'

Lorianna didn't want to take any more laudanum. It would be like leaving Robert and drifting away into a muzzy, pain-free world on her own. A sense of urgency made her want to be alert to follow his trial – to remain aware of every detail of what was happening to him. At the same time she didn't know how she could endure it. Again Mrs Musgrove had to support and half-carry her, for she hadn't enough strength to climb from the carriage and walk the few steps into the house.

Lizzie opened the door and ran to help Mrs Musgrove. One on each side, they half-carried, half-dragged her up the stairs and into the bedroom.

The sweet perfume of flowers drifted in through the open window from the leafy garden, but Lorianna still had the smell of the Calton Jail in her nostrils, thick, sour, all-pervading. She felt sick.

'I don't want any medicine,' she said, trying to push the black-mittened hand away.

'You must take it.'

'No! Leave me alone.'

She could hear keys jangling and the sound brought the prison back, the horror of it weakening her so much that Mrs Musgrove succeeded in forcing the laudanum into her mouth.

CHAPTER TWENTY-SEVEN

Miss Viners would not have missed the trial for anything. She was dressed in her good brown coat topped with a narrow fur at her throat, the furry face of the dead animal vying with her own in sharpness and bobbing about as she hurried along.

Parliament House had always fascinated her. Lying to the south of the ancient St Giles Cathedral in Parliament Square, the ground on which the building now stood had originally been the burial place attached to St Giles and had lain open to the south, descending in successive terraces down to the Cowgate. Typically of hilly Edinburgh, this meant that only one storey was seen from the north but from the south at least half a dozen.

Inside there were endless dark stone stairways to descend, leading to range after range of vaults and cellars which had to be explored by flickering match or lanthorn. Had they disinterred all the bodies which had been buried there when it was the graveyard of St Giles, she wondered. Or were the bones of the dead still rotting down there? One thing was certain in her mind: their spirits would be haunting the place. If only she could slip down and make contact with them! Once, when attending another murder trial, she had managed to go some way on the pretext of being lost. But before she was found and banished upstairs again, all she had managed to hear echoing through the gloom was the brisk but ghostly sound of legal feet overhead. Down there were the cells of the police office where Kelso was being held at this moment, waiting to be led up the trap-stair to the dock in the Justiciary Court.

Reaching the covered arcade off which led the entrances to the courts of law and justice, she went into the entrances and along the corridor to peep into the Great Hall where once the Parliament of Scotland had sat. It was crowded with counsel parading ritually back and forth. Under the dark, oak-beamed roof, attired in their billowing black gowns, they were like restless, sharp-faced crows. They were obviously intent on considering or discussing their briefs, and looking down on them with equal solemnity from the tiers of heavy pictures on the walls, or from the statues on their plinths, were the judges and law commentators of the past. Such as the sardonic-mouthed Braxfield, or Old Forbes of Culloden who stretched out a thin stone hand as if trying to still the waters of strife.

Miss Viners tried to pick out some of the actors who would be taking part in the drama of the Crown *versus* Robert Kelso, but failed and had to content herself with hurrying away to make sure she had a good seat in the court where she would be able to see everyone there and thoroughly enjoy herself.

John Stirling, counsel for the defence, was pacing alone. He was a tall, slender man with a slightly forward stoop and silvery fair hair under his short bar wig. Despite his usual air of quiet confidence appropriate to the dignity of his profession, a faint creasing of his eyes and a tightness at his mouth betrayed that he was worried. Over the years he had developed an instinct and this instinct now told him that Robert Kelso was innocent. The trouble was that the man was being uncooperative. He was hiding something, Stirling felt sure. With stubborn insistence Kelso had claimed he had not killed Gavin Blackwood and when first questioned by the police, he had been equally adamant that he had had nothing to do with Blackwood's death. The police had called him a liar and said they had a witness who had seen him in the woods where Blackwood's body had been found. Kelso denied that he had set foot out of his farmhouse all evening and then just clammed up. This denial would be used as corroborating evidence against him.

The witness the police spoke of would, of course, be the Lord Advocate's star performer and would be put in the witness box early this morning while the jury were wide awake and willing to listen.

Stirling sighed as he made his way out to the corridor, his legal papers clutched in one hand. 'Ah well, *unus testis, nullus testis**!'

In over a hundred years the sombre dark oak courtroom had seen most of the notable criminal trials of Scotland. Now, in the grim sunken dock facing the judge sat Robert Kelso, flanked by two policemen wearing white gloves and each armed with a baton. Not that the batons would be the slighest good if Kelso turned nasty, Stirling thought. The man looked as strong as the proverbial ox.

Stirling fussed absently with the papers on the table in front of him. Perhaps his unease, a feeling indeed that amounted almost to sadness, had something to do with the fact that Kelso was like himself a 'Bathgate bairn'. Not only that, he had often admired Kelso's performance at the Highland Games and shared in the pride of his achievements in bringing honour and credit to the town.

He stole a glance at Kelso now, dwarfing the two policemen in the dock. What a fine athlete he was, someone of unusual physical strength. The 'Iron Man', that was how he was known in the Bathgate Hills. He was gazing up at the golden coat of arms on the wall high above the judge. It was an imposing piece of metal sculpture, dominated by a lion and a unicorn and the words of the old French motto – *Honi soit qui mal y pense*. Eventually Kelso's head bowed slightly and his eyes acquired a blank, faraway expression.

---

*trans. 'one witness, no witness.'

'His Majesty's Advocate against Robert Kelso,' called the clerk of the court.

Automatically Stirling rose and said, 'I appear for the accused. He pleads not guilty.'

The clerk of the court asked him to be seated and then, with none of the preliminary speeches of English courts, the trial in the Supreme Criminal Court of Scotland began.

The bearded Lord Advocate rose like a black iceberg from a white sea of papers. 'Call Crown witness number one.'

All the time the formal witness was being given of identification of the body, Stirling was mentally bracing himself for the witness on whom he had no doubt the Crown's case must rest. This witness was called as number three.

The Lord Advocate's ample girth exuded authority and the voice emerging from the black-bearded face filled the court like the ringing of some giant bell.

'Your name is Walter McLeod?'

'Yes, it is, sir.'

Stirling thoughtfully tapped his fingers against his mouth as he appraised the man in the box. Wattie McLeod, the local poacher. Spruced up for the occasion, with hair plastered wetly to one side and shoulders screwed back as if on army pay parade.

'And you live at Oaktree Cottage in the Bathgate Hills.' The bell was majestically pealing out again.

'That's right, sir. I do.'

'What age are you?'

'I'm fifty-six years of age.'

'What is your occupation?'

'I'm a moudie catcher, sir.'

'For the benefit of those in the court who do not understand the vernacular, could you explain what that term means?'

'I catch moles which are causing trouble for farmers and ruining their land.'

231

Stirling allowed himself a mental smile. He would soon make short work of this philanthropic respectability in cross-examination. His main thrust in Kelso's defence, in fact, would have to lie in completely discrediting this witness. And then through witnesses of his own to establish the excellent character of Robert Kelso. Still pursuing the line of character, Stirling thought ruefully that it might have helped if the judge, the Lord Justice Clerk, had been a countryman like Kelso, or even if he had been a man of less bilious constitution. A lot could depend on his Lordship's liver.

'Now, let me get this quite clear,' the Lord Advocate was booming out. 'You are saying that you saw the accused, Robert Kelso, lift the body of Gavin Blackwood from his horse and lay it down on the ground with its head resting on a boulder.'

'Yes, sir. That's exactly what I saw. And he left Mr Blackwood's horse there, and when Mr Blackwood was found like that folks thought he'd had an accident and fallen off his horse.'

The Lord Justice Clerk, resplendent in his robes of scarlet red with white silk cape, and cuffs on which shone small cut-out diamonds, leaned forward on the bench and stuck out his sallow face to ask querulously, 'Can you be more specific about the distance you were from the accused when you say you saw him place the body on the ground?'

'Yes, my Lord. I was about two feet further away from Kelso than I am now and I could see him just as clearly.'

The judge sank back into his nest of scarlet silk again. The Lord Advocate, however, knowing the line of questioning Stirling was bound to take, quickly jumped back with, 'Although it was a dark and stormy night?'

'The moon was shining then, sir. And the storm had abated. I was just about to step out of my shelter in fact, when Kelso came along.'

'And you are perfectly convinced that the man you saw is the man in the dock. There is no doubt in your mind?'

'None at all, sir. It was him all right.'

Wattie's apparent self-confidence began to diminish as soon as he saw Stirling stand up. This was no Edinburgh birkie; this man knew him. This man belonged to Bathgate – and his father before him. As far back as Wattie could remember, there had always been an office in Engine Street with a brass plate you could see your face in and the words: 'Stirling and Dunlop, Solicitors and Notaries'.

'You say you are a mole-catcher,' Stirling asked.

Wattie's heart sank. 'Yes, sir.'

'Who employs you?'

'Eh?'

'I will repeat the question,' Stirling offered obligingly. 'Who employs you?'

'Eh . . . farmers.'

'Which farmers? Can you give us names and addresses of – say – two farmers who have given you employment recently?'

'Wel, eh . . . John Hunterson of the Mains was the last . . .'

'The last job you did as a mole-catcher was for a Mr John Hunterson?'

'Yes, sir.'

'When was that?'

Stirling was gratified to see that the witness was beginning to look distinctly shifty.

'I'm not sure.'

'Was it last week?'

'Eh, no.'

'Last month?'

'Maybe a wee bit longer than that.'

Stirling smiled encouragingly. 'Last year?'

'Aye, it could have been.'

His father had always said, 'Never cross-examine crossly', and Stirling asked with a quiet mildness of which his father would have been proud, 'What have you been living on since, then?'

'Och, eh, this and that. I manage not bad.'

'I put it to you, Mr McLeod, that you manage very well.'

Wattie shrugged uncomfortably. Then in the silence that followed as Stirling leaned towards the table and fingered some papers, his nerves strained so much that he was on the point of shouting out, 'You sly bastard, you're doing this on purpose!' when suddenly Stirling spoke.

'Is it true to say that you have been convicted on no fewer than nine occasions for poaching?'

'A man has to live,' Wattie countered resentfully.

'Am I supposed to infer from that remark that you make a living from poaching?'

Wattie hesitated and then thought— 'What's the use?' John Stirling knew perfectly well he was a poacher and had been all his days.

'I suppose you could say that.'

'I do say that. You are a poacher, Mr McLeod.'

'A man's got to make a living,' Wattie repeated with growing indignation. 'Some people would have me starve.'

Stirling raised an eyebrow. 'Some people? What people?'

'Him for a start!'

'Are you indicating the man in the dock, the accused, Robert Kelso?'

'I am.'

'He made it difficult for you to go about your business, did he?'

'He did, sir.'

'I see. So in fact, contrary to what you said when questioned by the Lord Advocate, you did have an axe to grind with the accused.'

'Well . . . I suppose if you put it like that. But I wasn't the only one. Many a man that worked under him hated his guts.'

Stirling was beginning to feel quite optimistic. There was no doubt in his mind that he was completely dis-

234

crediting the poacher's testimony. Yet still the unease persisted. It was not until witnesses four and five were called that he understood why – they, and not Wattie McLeod, were the Crown's trump cards.

Witness number four was Jessie Kirk, the dairymaid at the Blackwood home farm, and she testified that she had been out walking with her sweetheart on the night in question and had seen Kelso on horseback riding towards the Littlegate woods. She was a good witness for the prosecution, open-faced and clear-eyed and with a firm, sure voice. She was absolutely certain of what she had seen and looked straight at the jury when she said so.

Stirling rose to cross-examine her.

'Have you ever seen Mr Gavin Blackwood out riding at night?'

'No, sir.'

'Never?'

'Never, sir. Mr Blackwood never did much riding round the estate, but when he did it was always during the day.'

'Have you ever seen Robert Kelso out riding at night?'

'Apart from the night Mr Blackwood was found dead, you mean? Oh, yes, often. Kelso often rode at night.'

'Very well. Now let us come to the night in question. You say you saw Robert Kelso on horseback riding towards Littlegate woods?'

'Yes, sir.'

'You could see quite clearly?'

'Oh, yes, sir. Perfectly clearly. I'm quite sure it was him.'

'Very well, what colour of horse was he riding?'

'A black horse, sir.'

'You're quite sure of that, too?'

'Oh, yes, sir. Kelso always rode a black horse.'

Stirling smiled. 'But if what you say is true and it was Kelso riding towards the Littlegate woods, he must have been riding a tan-coloured horse with white face markings.'

235

For the first time Jessie Kirk looked uncertain. 'I don't understand. He always rides a black horse.'

'But it was Mr Blackwood's tan-coloured horse that was found in the woods that night.'

After a few worried seconds Jessie said, 'Maybe I was wrong about the colour of the horse. I mean, at the time I wasn't thinking of that exactly.'

'I understand,' Stirling said kindly. 'And of course you naturally took it for granted it was Kelso's horse?'

'That's right, sir,' Jessie agreed gratefully. 'I mean, it's what you'd expect, isn't it?'

'Exactly. Just as you would expect the rider to be Kelso.'

'That's right,' Jessie quickly agreed before a worried look clouded her face again.

Stirling continued, 'You didn't expect to see Mr Blackwood?'

'No, sir.' She was beginning to sound cautious.

'And that was why you didn't see him.'

'Objection!' The Lord Advocate boomed out. 'Counsel is leading the witness.'

The scarlet silk stirred slightly. 'Objection sustained.'

Whatever small success Stirling might have achieved by his questioning of witness number four was soon dispelled by witness number five. Andrew Scott was the ploughman who had been out walking with Jessie Kirk. He was a surly-looking fellow with an untidy moustache, suspicion in his eyes and rough square hands that gripped the edge of the box with aggression, not fear. He too was positive he had seen Kelso riding towards the wood.

'What colour was the horse?' Stirling asked eventually.

'I wasn't looking at the horse. I was looking at Kelso,' Scott growled. 'Anyway, it would have been difficult to tell what colour it was with such a big man as Kelso on it as well as what he had in front of him. I thought at the time it was the body of a young deer he had under that plaid . . .'

And so it went on, with witness after witness building

up damning evidence against his client. From the beginning, when it was established that the blow to the deceased was more likely to have been delivered by a left-handed person, and of course Kelso was left-handed. To the end, when it had been established by the prosecution that Kelso had a motive. Blackwood was not only proposing to dismiss him from his job and the farmhouse that the grieve had made his home, but had threatened to use his influence in preventing Kelso from being employed anywhere else. If Blackwood had been allowed to have his way Kelso's life would have been ruined.

Stirling decided that for the most part he would have to fall back on the evidence of Kelso being a man of unimpeachable character, and appeal in the strongest terms to the sympathy of the jury.

Only too well aware that he would do this, the Lord Advocate in his address to the jury, after giving all the reasons which indicated why they should find the accused guilty of murder, added, 'Do not allow sympathy to play any part in your deliberations. You must be impartial and dispassionate towards both the deceased and the accused. We are concerned with facts, not sympathies. The sentence is for the judge. You, members of the jury, must concern yourself only with the evidence, only with the facts, of which you are the masters.'

After the Lord Advocate sat down, Stirling rose.

'May it please the court?'

The judge nodded his assent and Stirling continued to speak carefully and sincerely. First of all he concentrated on working on the emotions of the jury.

'Look at the man in the dock. Would you send such a man to his death on the evidence of a poacher and two illiterate farm-workers, all of whom could have a grudge against Kelso because he was such a conscientious and strict taskmaster?'

Meticulously he explained the unique position of Scottish law.

'The onus of proof of guilt rests with the Crown and

237

the standard is not on a balance of probabilities but proof beyond reasonable doubt. Unlike England, indeed unlike any country in the world, we have a third verdict, a safe-guard against any miscarriage of justice — the verdict of "Not Proven" '

He concluded his speech by telling the jury, 'You must be really certain. We can all err. If error there might be, then err on the side of safety by acquitting, not the other way round.'

Stirling stood for a few seconds, staring at them as if quietly willing them to echo what had been ringing so strongly in his mind from the start — 'This man is not guilty.'

Then he sat down.

★   ★   ★

For Lorianna the sharp eyes of reality had softened and blurred. It was not true that Robert was in Calton jail — he was in the farmhouse kitchen. The fire glowed warmly through the mellow shadows and low-ceilinged room. They were both naked and he had his big arms wound round her, her cheek smooth like petals against his chest. They were in a dream of love. Her hair was unpinned and gently swaying and she could feel its silky caress against her hips.

Sometimes the dream faded and the sharpness returned like the shock of icy water. Then she cried out and strug-gled up in bed, only to be forced back again by cruel hands and the sound of keys and the feel of them, cold and hard and threatening.

But she wanted to know what was happening to Robert. She demanded to know and Mrs Musgrove said the trial was nearly over.

No more laudanum. Oh, no! She wanted to be alert and able to greet Robert when he came home. She would wear her most beautiful dress and together they would walk on the hills and look across the fields and woods.

Together they would gaze at the silver water of the Forth. Never again would they be separated from each other. She waited, hands tightly clasped, as eager-eyed as a child.

On the day of the verdict, Jacobs went to Bathgate for the paper. Mrs Musgrove met him at the door on his return and took it from him, but she no longer had it in her hands when she went back upstairs to the sitting-room.

'Where is the paper?' Lorianna rose from her chair. 'Give it to me at once.'

'It's better you should not dwell on such things.'

'What things? What are you talking about?'

'Just accept and then try to put it all out of your mind. It's the only way.'

'Give me the paper!'

'He has been found guilty and sentenced to death.'

Lorianna shook her head. A pulse had begun to leap and throb at her temple.

'Accept it? Put it out of my mind? You must be mad!'

'What else can you do?'

'Anything! Everything!' Lorianna said wildly.

'Calm yourself! Don't talk foolish.'

'Calm? *Calm?*' A huge, thunderous wave of horror was fast approaching her. 'I must go to him right away.'

Mrs Musgrove caught her before she reached the door. 'He doesn't want you there. He said so – he doesn't want you.'

Lorianna flailed about, struggling with the woman with all her strength.

'Robert! Robert!'

Then suddenly the black of Mrs Musgrove's dress completely engulfed her and she slithered into it, sick and suffocating. When she awakened she was lying in bed in her nightdress and the doctor was bending over her. She gazed at him from a dazed blank mind.

'Just rest, my dear,' he said. 'You're going to be all right. You took these little fainting fits when you were carrying Clementina, remember? You just need to be careful and ensure that you get plenty of rest.'

Lorianna continued to stare at him.

The doctor sighed. 'I know how you must be feeling, my dear . . . Your poor husband . . . But everything's mixed with mercy. Try to look at it this way . . . At least you will have something to remember him by. You will be very proud and comforted, I'm sure, if you have a son in his image.'

Mrs Murgrove showed the doctor out and when she returned Lorianna said, ' I'm pregnant?'

Mrs Musgrove gave one of her terrible travesties of a smile. 'Perhaps it will be a girl.'

Lorianna tried to keep calm.

'I shall get up and get dressed; then I shall go straight to the governor of that prison before it's too late and plead for Robert's life.'

'If you refuse to believe me, believe *him*. There is absolutely nothing you can do except make things worse.'

'You fool of a woman!' Lorianna said. 'How can they be any worse?'

'They would hang you.'

'Let them! I would rather die with him than live without him.'

'Don't be so foolish.'

'Can't you understand? Don't you know what loving someone means?'

'Oh, I know all right.'

'Well, if that is so, how can you speak to me like this? How can you try to stop me going to him? How can you imagine I could live without him? I can't do it; I won't do it!'

'You're pregnant.'

'I don't care. I don't care about anything except living with him or dying with him.'

'You're not leaving this house.'

'Oh no, Mrs Musgrove, you shall not do this to me.'

'*For* you.'

'No, nothing's for me except him. I mean to go.'

'It's no use. He dies first thing tomorrow morning.'

The wave hit her now, buffeting her in horror and panic, snatching her breath away. She felt herself physically struggling in it, clawing at it, gasping in it, trying to scream out. Praying to keep calm.

'Mrs Musgrove, for pity's sake, help me! There is still time to get there in a fast coach.'

'Madam, it's no use, believe me. I am acting for your own good and you will see that in the end.'

The end? The end?

'I'm going to Robert.'

'I must stop you, madam. It is my duty to do so.'

Dear Jesus! Robert's life was ticking away.

'Don't touch me, Mrs Musgrove. I'm not going to let you do this to me – it's wrong.'

The housekeeper's strength was like iron and Lorianna's struggles were like those of a butterfly against it – and like a butterfly she was pinned down.

'I shall call for Gilbert,' she sobbed. 'Or Malcolm. They will help me.'

'Master Gilbert is staying with his fiancée's family and Master Malcolm is back at university,' Mrs Musgrove said calmy. 'You and I are the only ones here, madam, and I'm going to look after you. It will be a long night, but it will pass.'

She thought of Robert in his cell. No, this night would never pass. They must be together just once more. Even to die together, only to be in his arms.

Did she struggle all the long night? Did she wail and sob and scream? Or did it all happen in the prison of her heart and mind? Heart of my heart. Love of my love. Life of my life.

Don't leave me . . .

★   ★   ★

A group of sightseers had assembled in the bright sunshine on the Calton Hill in the hope of getting at least a

241

glimpse of the procession to the scaffold. The merest glimpse was all they were afforded, and that only because Kelso was so much taller than any of those with him. The baillies, clergy, warders, prison governor, victim and hangman soon covered the fifty yards or so to an outhouse on the western side of the prison which had been selected as the place of execution.

It was soon over and everyone was impressed by his tranquillity. The chaplain began to recite the Lord's Prayer, but Robert Kelso didn't seem to be listening. He was thinking about Lorianna and when the bolt was drawn the last thing he saw in his mind's eye was the flower of her face.

Part 2

DISILLUSIONMENT

CHAPTER TWENTY-EIGHT

Alice Tait had gone to the Calton Hill to watch the procession. She remembered Kelso from her days in Blackwood House. Not that she had really known him except as one of her many persecutors. He had been a figure of authority – someone to be feared, someone you hid from or ran from when you had been stealing turnips or apples or keeping Eck McColl off his work by having a bit of houghmagandy in the corner of the hayfield. She had always flown like the wind at the sight of the grieve, but somehow she felt resentful and angry at the Edinburgh folk who had brought him here to destroy him. She felt a kinship with and a loyalty to the big countryman. He was of peasant stock like herself; they had shared the same fields and trees and hills above Bathgate. And as far as what Kelso was supposed to have done to Mr Blackwood was concerned, that was one cruel sod who deserved to die. Him and his holy ways! The devil, more like. She remembered the vicious way he used to beat Miss Clementina.

After Kelso had been hanged she felt sad, as if a part of herself had been destroyed, had disappeared forever along with him. She never got over it, although often she thought she had. Then she would be parading along at the eastern end of Princes Street, glance up at the Calton and remember him and feel homesick. It meant that she avoided the east end when she could and tried never to look up at the Calton. Not that this was easy, because it was one of the places that overlooked and dominated the city.

It was daft, Alice kept telling herself, to think about the man. Why should he, of all people, make her feel anything at all? There was no answer to that, except that he did. Two years after the hanging her eyes still wandered towards the prison rearing high on the Calton Rock like a brooding evil over the city. It had swallowed up the grieve and she imagined that if she allowed her feet to stray too near again, it would swallow her up too.

This became quite a superstition with her and when any of the girls she knew landed in the Calton, she greatly angered and embittered them by refusing to go anywhere near them at visiting times. In fact they never forgave her and she could not regard one of the girls as her friend. She developed great ingenuity, a gift of the gab, not to mention fleetness of foot in order to avoid ending up as a prisoner in the Calton herself. ·

When first she had come to Edinburgh, plump and rosy-cheeked from the country, she had been taken in and given shelter by an elegant lady – or what seemed to be an elegant lady – dressed in an elegant gown and a feather boa, with feathers in her hat and very pretty boots showing from beneath her skirts. Queenie Dunlop, she was called, and she had been parading along Princes Street when Alice bumped into her. Queenie had been very friendly, and professed to be extremely interested and concerned about Alice's predicament. She had taken her to a house in St James's Square and it soon became obvious that the place was a brothel. Not that Alice had known the meaning of the term at first and anyway the word was never mentioned.

Queenie always boasted that she ran a very high-class establishment and there could be no question that the steady stream of gentlemen who visited her house were high-class. There was an elder of one of the most popular churches in Edinburgh. There was even one, Queenie said, who 'trod the floor of Parliament House'. There were stockbrokers, merchants and doctors, all happily married men by all accounts, some arriving on foot, discreetly muffled up and with hats drawn down; some dashing out of cabs and in through the door that was waiting open for their convenience. Unmarried men, soldiers and commercial travellers were less sneaky and sly. They marched up the stairs boldly, sometimes in noisy groups out for a lark. Queenie, on that first day, had given her a few glasses of wine and something to eat; Alice hadn't enjoyed anything so much for years. She needed food more than most; it stoked her up and gave her round ball of a body the fuel needed to bounce it along at its usual pace, and to fire her equally energetic imagination.

Alice used to imagine that one of these jolly young soldiers would take a fancy to her and whisk her away to foreign parts. In her mind's eye, she had even seen herself being married and having a guard of honour of soldiers with swords making a silver roof under which she and her beloved walked from the church. She fancied being married and having children. But in her heart of hearts, it was the wife of a countryman she would like to be and live in a cottage like her Granny who was now dead and buried. Even her auntie Bella had gone, she had no idea where. The farmer's wife had chased Alice when she had once gone to see her at the farm. 'A wicked, lying hussy', the farmer's wife had called her; apparently Auntie Bella had become pregnant and blamed it on the farmer.

It had come as a terrible blow when eventually, after some months, Queenie had flung Alice out. Apparently the customers no longer admired her as a sonsy, rosy-cheeked lass from the country. Now she was just a pasty-faced, fat girl.

It was truly dreadful to be out wandering the windy Edinburgh streets with nowhere to go and nothing to eat. She had had to pawn her coat and hat and wear the shawl out of her box. She never managed to redeem that coat and hat, although in time she had managed to buy another hat, a real dashing one with purple ribbons and scarlet feathers. But even that hat had gone now.

She couldn't compete with the girls from Queenie's place. All the clothes there belonged to Queenie and they had to skud about the house half-naked or play cards or do whatever they could to kill time until dusk. Then Queenie got them all together, unlocked the rouge and hair-oil, the scent and silks and satins and they all dressed up and went out to parade along Princes Street. Except Queenie, who kept a check on the door and the girls as they returned with lovers. Queenie only took an airing in Princes Street during the day. After promenading for an hour or two she would do a little shopping in some of the best shops and eat a cake at a confectioner's counter.

The hours of darkness were the time when her girls had to go out no matter what the weather was like – as often as not shivering in their silks and getting soaked to the skin.

All the same Queenie's place, Alice realised now, had been a very genteel brothel and there was all the difference in the world between the prostitutes of Princes Street and those of the High Street of whom she was now one. She hated the Princes Street crowd now and she and the other High Street girls called them 'Flash Mauls'. She told herself that she was lucky to be away from there; St James's Square was much too near the Calton to her liking.

Of course, the 'Flash Mauls' in their long rustling silk gowns hated the High Street girls in return and contemptuously called them 'Petticoats', because of the short woollen petticoats they wore instead of gowns.

Not that the prostitutes of the New Town and the Old Town ever met. The gardens of Princes Street marked the line. The earthen Mound and the north bridge separated the two classes of prostitutes as completely as if they were the outward lines of two opposing armies.

Alice now had lodgings at Nelly Rudd's place in Covenant Close in the High Street. She didn't much care for Nelly Rudd either, but regarded her as an old harridan who, like the potato, seemed to thrive and grow fat buried in rottenness. There was nothing Nelly would not do for money. She would have murdered any of her girls and sold them to the body-snatchers if there had been any still going around, and Alice wasn't all that sure that there were not. The ghosts of Burke and Hare still haunted the place, that was for sure. Often, in dark closes and corners of the High Street, bare-headed and short-skirted, Alice shivered with more than the cold as she waited for customers. She needed quite a few customers to enable her to pay for her lodgings at Nelly's, over and above which she needed money to buy her own food which she cooked (if she was ever lucky enough to have a bit meat or tripe) in Nelly's kitchen. More often than not, she just had bread and dripping or a lump of cheese. Sometimes though she managed a hot pie or a fish supper. Her mouth always watered at the thought of that. Especially a fish supper, which was lovely and filling as well as delicious.

It was terrible to be hungry, as she often was now even though she spent all she earned — apart from what she had to pay to Nelly — on food and wine. She needed the wine to give her courage to face the dark closes and wynds of the High Street. It was a constant source of anguish and terror to loiter in them alone at night, something that never diminished no matter how tough an exterior she tried to assume in order to protect herself. There in some damp, stinking, echoing tunnel she would stand, never knowing if the shadowy apparition approaching was a ghost or another Jack the Ripper. And when the menacing shadow materialised close up as a fat-bellied, bushy-moustached man, she would cling to him in relief, welcoming him in a crazy futile way as some sort of a protector. And then she would take him back to Nelly's and become bawdy and jolly with relief over innumerable glasses of wine or spirits. There were a few shillings to be made out of buying wine and spirits wholesale by the bottle and doling it out in small, dearer, amounts to customers. Nelly bought the bottles and so she made most of the money but the girls got their share, albeit a small one. Nelly's favourites were those who could persuade customers to buy the most drink. This meant that the girls as well as the customers had to be heavy drinkers because naturally the customer paid for his girl's drinks as well as his own.

Alice always drank as much as she could because, apart from the money this earned, it made her temporarily feel cheerful. Sometimes it even made her feel warm and safe. But she could never manage to drink as much as the rest, especially Sadie McPhee who downed gallons of the stuff and then, after spewing up, was ready to start all over again. Afterwards, however, Alice just felt colder and more afraid than ever. Not that she ever showed it of course – that would have been only to invite the derisive laughter and tormenting tricks and taunts of Nelly Rudd and the girls.

To survive in the High Street you had to be tough and, outwardly at least, Alice was as tough as the rest and tougher than some. Like Cissie Urquhart, for instance. Cissie had tried to earn a respectable living as a shirt-maker to keep her and her bedridden mother. But she was paid so little for working such long hours that she had been forced to turn to prostitution so that she and her mother could survive. At the shirt-making she had worked from early dawn until the clock struck midnight, toiling until she had become gaunt-faced, half-starved and utterly exhausted with each racking week's ceaseless stitching. Cissie still looked nothing but skin and bone after she had taken to the streets and still she could not earn more than a pittance. She was so wretched and ashamed about what she was doing that often she burst into tears, putting the men off. And even worse, Cissie couldn't drink at all.

It was after her mother died that she had ended up at Nelly Rudd's and Alice had got to know her and immediately taken her under her wing.

'You'll be the death of me yet, so you will!' Alice was

always telling her. And often she would shout at the weeping Cissie, 'Bloody hell! Can you not learn just to open your legs and shut your eyes? Be like me. Think of what it means. A fish supper, for instance. Or a lovely hot juicy pie!'

Sometimes Alice had a right barney with Nelly Rudd in her efforts to protect Cissie and stop her from being flung out. Sometimes she had to fork up for Cissie's lodgings when she hadn't made enough to pay for them herself. That made Cissie even worse, since she was even more ashamed and upset about having to take money from Alice than having to earn it from customers.

'One of these days,' Alice kept warning her, 'I shall pulverise you, so help me God! If you would just relax and let the customers get on with it, you'd soon get used to it.'

But instead of soon 'getting used to it', Cissie soon just withered away and died. When that happened Alice managed to keep drunk all that day and all that night. The day after, she had felt as if she was about to die herself. Wandering agitatedly about the narrow grey streets, she had looked up at the Calton and remembered Robert Kelso and the green hills of Bathgate. Then, reaching the safety of the dark tunnel of a close, she had sobbed brokenheartedly into her petticoat.

CHAPTER TWENTY-NINE

'There's mother out walking,' Clementina said, peering out of the narrow school-room window. 'She must be feeling better.'

She could not bring herself to say that Mrs Musgrove was walking by her side and that Lorianna had her arm linked in that of the older woman and seemed to be leaning heavily against her. As a child Clementina had been afraid of the housekeeper. Now, at fourteen years and on the brink of womanhood, she detested her. As the daughter of the house, why wasn't *she* down there at her mother's side? She burned with indignation at the unfairness of the situation and blamed it, for the most part, on the housekeeper.

Mrs Musgrove guarded Lorianna like a jailer. It was almost as if she had some power over her. It was understandable certainly that her mother would need someone to lean on and to look after her following the terrible trauma of father's death. It must have been a dreadful time for her to live through. For Clementina, life had gone on much the same. She remembered Mrs Musgrove telling her that father had been found murdered and mother had collapsed with shock. Later she'd learned from one of the other servants that the grieve had been hanged. But none of it had ever seemed real. It was yet another nightmare. Previously she had not given her mother much thought — there never seemed any point. Her mother had shown little interest in her and indeed often appeared to actively dislike her and avoid her. There never had been any question of love. Now, although still certain that her mother did not care about her or even give her a thought, Clementina could not help feeling concerned for her. There was something so heart rendingly vulnerable about her appearance, even from this distance.

Lorianna was as elegant as ever, but had lost weight. There was in fact such a fragile look about her that it seemed as if one puff of wind might flutter her away beyond anyone's protective grasp. More and more Clementina worried about her mother and felt for her, until a need which she thought she had crushed long ago was reawakened: she longed to touch her mother and be close to her. She knew of course that such feelings were hopeless, since every ounce of love and affection her mother possessed was concentrated on baby Jamie. She had less time and inclination than ever to have anything to do with her daughter, even if Mrs Musgrove had been likely to allow it.

'You just upset her,' the housekeeper said, and secretly and in regretful bewilderment, she had to admit to herself that Mrs Musgrove was right. The mere sight of her seemed to plunge her mother into acute distress. So for her mother's sake, because she loved her truly, she tried to hide away and keep out of her sight as much as possible.

Miss Viners' sharp voice interrupted Clementina's thoughts. 'Return your attention to your history book at once.'

Clementina sighed and reluctantly went back to sit down at her desk.

'Ladies do not slouch.' Miss Viners was wearing her reading glasses and she stared accusingly over them. 'Especially small ladies.'

Miss Viners certainly didn't slouch. She was erect at all times, stiff and hard and flat as a tall plank of wood. Even her side-braids looked as hard as cart-wheels; they made her face look narrow and seemed clamped so tightly against her ears that it was a wonder she was able to hear a sound.

Clementina propped her elbows on the desk and thumped her chin rebelliously into her palms.

'History's so dull!'

'Dull? *Dull?*' Miss Viners echoed. 'How can history be dull?'

'All those boring old dates to learn.'

'These are important stepping stones in the background of us all.'

'They don't mean anything to me.'

'Perhaps it is you who are dull. Have you ever thought of that, young lady?'

Clementina's brows came down. 'I'm not dull. Quite the contrary. That's why I'm complaining about having to sit here learning lists of dates and then having to repeat them to you over and over again like a parrot.'

Miss Viners removed her spectacles and tapped them against the thin line of her mouth before observing, 'Yes, I have sometimes wondered about the value of teaching by rote myself.'

She often surprised Clementina like this and as a result Clementina had acquired some measure of respect for her.

'I know history shouldn't be dull,' she said now.

'No, indeed,' Miss Viners agreed. 'Especially that of our own country. Scotland has had a turbulent and fascinating history. One only needs to walk through the streets and wynds of Edinburgh to see proof of that.'

'The ancient buildings, you mean?'

'Yes.'

Clementina brightened, 'Can't we go through and see them, Miss Viners? Can I not learn the history that way? Go to the Castle, for instance? Just reading about these places isn't the same.'

Miss Viners fished up her sleeve for her handkerchief and dabbed daintily at her mouth.

'I don't know if such a project could be arranged.'

Clementina was beginning to feel quite excited. She

had always wanted to explore Edinburgh.

'There are trains. So we wouldn't need mother's carriage. And we could stay at Malcolm's house overnight and then you could go to one of the Edinburgh meetings.'

'There is a spiritualist convention on next week.' Miss Viners' dark eyes lit up, although she managed to retain her stiff composure.

'Well, then!' Clementina cried out triumphantly.

'Get on with your dates,' Miss Viners commanded.

Clementina dutifully lowered her head but she wasn't even seeing the history book. She knew Miss Viners' Achilles heel was anything to do with the occult or the spirit world and that an excuse to attend the spiritualist convention would prove too much to resist.

They would have their trip to Edinburgh all right. Miss Viners in her usual capable way would arrange it, even if this meant doing so through Mrs Musgrove. Miss Viners could be sickeningly obsequious and fawning when it came to getting her own way from superiors. She knew the way the land lay and, grossly unfair though she might think it, in Blackwood House Mrs Musgrove was everybody's superior. Clementina could have wept with the keenness of her pleasurable anticipation. She felt so much alone and cut off from the world in Blackwood House that she would have welcomed a trip anywhere with anyone. But to Edinburgh! To the capital city! The fascinating place that she had read so much about. What joy! And to think of all the interesting people there!

It was a great deprivation to Clementina to be alone. She didn't count Miss Viners as company. The governess existed in Blackwood House only because she had to, escaping down to Bathgate or elsewhere as often as she could. She did her job as conscientiously as she was able and earned her pittance of a salary and that was all. She had never shown the slightest affection towards Clementina and, apart from her education, never gave her a thought.

Sometimes during the past two years Clementina had been so lonely she had held long conversations with her doll. Or she had read to the doll some poem which had particularly moved her and she had wanted to share with someone.

Miss Viners seemed to have no interest in poetry. Or even in prose fiction. All she taught were facts. Clementina had often wondered how this apparently cold factual approach to learning coincided with Miss Viners' belief in the supernatural. Indeed she had once asked her and the governess had bristled with annoyance.

'But the spirit world *is* factual. There is no contradiction between my intellectual approach to teaching and to the study of the occult.'

Nevertheless, Miss Viners did not prevent Clementina from reading fiction or poetry. In fact she never stopped Clementina from reading anything. It was just that Clementina could see that the governess was incapable of *warming* to it; it was simply a waste of time hoping to share any pleasure in it with Miss Viners and so she had shared it with her doll.

This was the rag doll called Black Mammy that Alice Tait had made for her years ago from one of her black woollen stockings and scraps of coloured darning wool. The doll was still very precious to Clementina and even now, at fourteen years of age, she slept with it cuddled close to her under the blankets. Of course she was careful never to let it be seen or alluded to during the day when Miss Viners was around. Perhaps quite rightly, Miss Viners would regard her love of the doll as unhealthy at her age and do something terrible to it such as tossing it into the school-room fire. There was no sentiment about Miss Viners.

'This is a hard world for most women,' she had said more than once. 'The quicker you learn that the better.'

In preparation for her visit to the capital city, Clementina busied herself re-reading every book about Edinburgh she could lay her hands on. Never for one moment did she doubt Miss Viners' capability in making possible the miracle of the visit. Sure enough, within a few days the governess had announced that they were going to Edinburgh and even that they would stay at Mr Malcolm's house in Heriot Row.

Malcolm was now assistant to an Edinburgh minister and had recently married a lawyer's daughter called Mary Ann. The lawyer, a widower, had died and left them the house in Heriot Row.

Miss Viners said, 'As the colossal figure of Portsmouth is the seaman, so the lawyer bestrides Edinburgh and brings his legal atmosphere and habit of mind into all departments and aspects of the city's life and people.'

'The Edinburgh people,' Mary Ann said, 'are the most responsible of all God's creatures!'

'In every department of the city's life,' Malcolm agreed, 'you find the same system of deferred judgement and striving for exactitude in statement. Even a humble Edinburgh grocer advertises in his window "Eggs *as fresh as possible* for sale".'

Malcolm seemed very happy in Edinburgh and Clementina was glad. She had always liked him better than Gilbert and at least he always made a point of speaking to her when he visited Blackwood House. She wondered what his house was like. This would be her first visit to Malcolm's new home and Miss Viners said that no doubt it would be very grand. But what thrilled Clementina most was the fact that Robert Louis Stevenson had once lived in Heriot Row and was supposed to have got his inspiration for *Treasure Island* from a miniature island in the middle of a pond in Queen Street Gardens, which faced the houses in the Row.

To walk the exact same ground as the author of *Treasure Island:* what a thrill! And as well as the Castle and Holyrood Palace, Miss Viners was to take her to see Greyfriars Church and the grave of Greyfriars Bobby. Not to mention the beautiful paintings in the National

Gallery. It was all so exciting. Edinburgh, the beautiful Athens of the North. At last, at last she was going to see it!

CHAPTER THIRTY

Miss Viners said, 'It is situated between the Pentland Hills and the Firth of Forth.' They were making their first excursion from Malcolm's house and it was one of the happiest days of Clementina's life. Everything was beautiful and intensely interesting. Even Miss Viners looked more attractive. Instead of her usual school-room black, she was wearing a brown skirt and jacket and a brown lacquered hat. The brown was certainly the darkest shade possible and the cut of the clothes unfashionable, but the high-necked, stiffly-boned blouse was a soft shade of beige. For the first time Clementina noticed that Miss Viners' eyes were not dull black but glossy brown.

Clementina was unaware of her own expensively-cut shorter skirt flouncing with petticoats, her neat jacket and white fur hat and muff. Her attention was caught by too many new and riveting sights around her. At times in her excitement she skipped alongside Miss Viners, her long hair swinging and bouncing over her shoulders. Until Miss Viners quelled her with a sharp reminder that she was a lady and ought to behave like one.

Miss Viners had been impressed with Heriot Row, its quiet genteel houses at the bottom of wide gardens and its exceptionally wide pavement. Clementina admired the New Town – the rare beauty of Charlotte Square, the handsome St Andrews Square and Queen Street, but it was the unexpected vistas which fascinated her most: how other streets fell away towards the Firth, for instance, and the illusion this gave that Edinburgh was hanging on the edge of the world. Some of these streets had statues showing sharp against the clouds like gods descending; it was equally intriguing to see Edinburgh citizens appearing – first hat, then head, then bended body, as if advancing out of a hidden sea. Clementina could imagine that away down on the Firth people in boats were looking up at her and Miss Viners apparently walking in mid-air. It was a most exhilarating sensation.

'The New Town is made up of elegant parallelograms . . .' Miss Viners prodded Clementina along. 'Pay attention, Miss! You are here to learn, not to dream.'

A cold east wind was blowing, but brilliant gleams of sunshine every now and again highlighted the classical buildings as Clementina and her governess made their way towards the main thoroughfare of Princes Street. The street was on a ridge and Princes Street gardens fell away into a pleasant hollow which accentuated the colossal height of the Castle Rock. The sound of pipers in the gardens swirled up with the wind, adding to Clementina's enchantment. Soon the Highlanders came marching into view to the beat of the drums and the skirl of the pipes. Then round the corner, magnificently wheeling, they took the hill by storm, tartans swaying and white gaiters flashing.

'The Castle Rock,' Miss Viners rapped out, 'is an extinct volcano and an excellent place of defence for our ancestors. This rock would have run with blood more than once, I dare say.'

From the ramparts of the Castle the views were breathtaking. Clementina could see across to the Highland hills. When she peered down over the parapet, down cliff and precipice, the tops of the trees in the gardens below were like tiny pom-poms. The tall proud buildings of Princes Street were reduced to a clutter of matchstick chimneys and doll's house roof-tops. At street level the air had been noisy with the clip-clopping of horses' hooves and the banging and bells of the tramway cars. Here they were nothing more than gently jingling toys.

Clementina refused to allow Miss Viners' ghoulish

tales about murders and the Castle ghosts to spoil her enjoyment and eventually the governess, as if angry at her lack of success in frightening her charge, jerked her away.

'We are now in the Royal Mile,' she informed Clementina shortly afterwards, 'which stretches from the Castle to Holyrood Palace. The whole of Edinburgh life was concentrated on this thoroughfare before the building of the New Town.'

'The buildings all look so *ancient*,' Clementina said in wonderment.

'They *are* ancient,' Miss Viners snapped impatiently. 'The Royal Mile is composed of the Esplanade, Castle Hill, Lawnmarket, Parliament Square, High Street and Canongate. Are you listening, miss?'

Clementina nodded enthusiastically.

'At one time,' the governess continued, 'the whole area was in the grip of a hunchback cobbler nicknamed General Joe. He had unkempt hair and vicious eyes and the magistrates were terrified of him. He imagined he was some kind of Robin Hood and used to go about robbing and killing the rich – often by beating and burning – and giving to the poor. It is said that this so-called General Joe could summon thousands of people by just walking down the High Street beating a drum. People would flood out of all these closes and vennels like rats following the Pied Piper of Hamelin. When he died thousands attended his funeral. Sometimes one wonders if evil spirits like that of General Joe still cling around this place. The feeling of death and evil spirits is very strong in this part of town. You can almost see them flitting about these dark closes. Think of Burke and Hare, for instance . . .'

But Clementina was thinking of roistering gallants in velvet and lace clashing swords in every dark close entry. And she could see, between the long grey cobbled Mile of tall ancient houses, the figure of Bonnie Prince Charlie riding on his charger among the shouting crowds that crushed in on either side. She saw him looking up at hands waving to him from the high windows like the

261

white wings of thousands of birds.

Miss Viners' voice had acquired an anxious tinge. 'I doubt if we should venture any further.'

'Why not?' Clementina cried out in disappointment. 'Ghosts don't come out during the day. And we're not near the Palace yet and you *promised*, Miss Viners. You said we would go all the way from the Castle to the Palace.'

'That is correct. But there are too many ruffians and low-class people here for my liking.'

Indeed there was a growing crush of poor people milling about or standing at close-mouths or at corners. Barefooted, ragged children with gaunt, filthy faces and spindly legs jostled and scuttled about the cobbles like cockroaches. Shabbily dressed men lounged under an air of brooding hopelessness against grey walls. Women in shawls, some with babies wrapped in them, stood gossiping and blocking narrow pavements.

Then suddenly, astonishingly, Clementina heard someone yell out her name. She turned in bewilderment to see a fat, debauched looking woman in grubby white stockings and a short woollen petticoat flying in great delight towards her.

'Miss Clementina! Miss Clementina! It's me, Alice Tait!'

For a moment Clementina just stared in speechless disbelief. Alice had always been fat, but it had been a firm neat roundness like a tight little barrel. Even her cheeks had been round and firm and her hair, although a mass of unruly curls, had always been glossy and clean. Could this loose-fleshed, frowsy-haired, filthy-looking creature really be Alice?

'Alice!' she managed at last. 'Oh, Alice . . .'

'That settles it!' Miss Viners gasped. 'We're going back down to Princes Street.' Rage and horror raised her voice. 'Remove yourself from our path this instant, or I shall call for an officer of the law.'

'Where are you living, Alice? Where can I find you?'

Clementina called desperately over her shoulder as Miss Viners tugged her away.

Alice's eyes looked feverishly bright with eagerness. 'Covenant Close.'

'What do you mean,' Miss Viners asked breathlessly as she hurried Clementina along, 'where can you find her? You must never have anything – *anything*, do you hear, miss – to do with that dreadful creature. I always knew she was evil. She was sent by the devil and now she has returned to him.'

'Poor Alice!' Clementina was torn between gladness at seeing her friend again and horror at the state she was in. 'She looks as if she has suffered terrible deprivation.'

'In your reading,' Miss Viners said, 'have you never come across the word "prostitute"?'

Clementina hesitated. 'Someone who sells her body to men?'

'Exactly.'

'You mean Alice is a prostitute?'

'Precisely.'

'But how can you know?'

'It is quite obvious by looking at her.'

Clementina could think of nothing more to say. She felt more upset and confused than ever and was glad when Miss Viners decided that they should return immediately to Heriot Row.

'I think after lunch a quiet afternoon indoors is called for. You can take notes and make sketches from memory in your notebook. I will rest so that I may be able to go to my meeting tonight.' The governess plucked her handkerchief from her sleeve and dabbed it around her mouth. 'This unpleasant interlude has quite shaken me up.'

They had been given accommodation in the top attic flat of Malcolm's house and this is where they were served with lunch. Malcolm had explained that, much as Clementina was welcome in his home and indeed more than welcome to share their table downstairs, the latter would not be wise on this occasion because Mary Ann

263

was in a somewhat delicate condition. Great care had to be taken that she did not become over-excited.

Miss Viners, who at the time had smiled and nodded and almost curtseyed in agreement, had later told Clementina bluntly that what the stupid man meant was that his wife was going to have a baby.

Left alone after lunch in the small dormer-windowed room that served as a temporary sitting-room, Clementina tried to sort out her thoughts.

'Poor Alice!' The words kept returning to her mind with the picture of the ex-nursery-maid. But it was the eyes she remembered most – they were Alice's eyes all right – bright and eager and excited and so obviously glad to see her.

Surely there must be something she could do to help her friend. Surely things could not be as bad as Miss Viners had said. The governess always looked on the black side of everything.

Alice looked ill and neglected. Maybe she simply lacked sufficient strength to keep herself clean or enough money to buy proper clothes to decently cover her.

Something must be done.

All the old feelings of affection and camaraderie with Alice came rushing back to warm Clementina and fill her with longing. Alice Tait had given her more time and shown her more affection than Lorianna ever had or ever would. Alice had been like a sister. Indeed, Clementina doubted if a sister could ever have been so close.

Now Alice was ill and in need and she, Clementina, was well and strong and had money in her purse. Surely it was her duty to do what she could to help her?

Once she had tried to run away to Edinburgh to be with Alice, knowing that somehow, together, they would struggle through life and survive. They had struggled successfully through many vicissitudes before and they could do so again.

Suddenly it occurred to Clementina that this truth could still apply. And what could be better? Here she was, already in Edinburgh and even in possession of Alice's address. Covenant Close. She had read about that. It was in the Covenant Close that a copy of the National Covenant was placed, in order that anyone could add their signatures after the Covenant had been approved in Greyfriars Church in 1638. So at least Alice was fortunate enough to have found a respectable house for herself that was steeped in Scottish history. Clementina's mind was made up. Happiness surged through her veins. Tonight after Miss Viners left for her meeting, she would slip quietly from the house and away to the Old Town.

She was going to be with Alice again.

CHAPTER THIRTY-ONE

Alice was so feverish with excitement and so sure that Clementina would come that she didn't go looking for any customers. In fact she actually refused a couple and was roundly cursed as a result. For hours she hung about the High Street and the close-mouth, her thoughts dancing a jig of happiness and her feet itching to join in the dance of delight.

Lord's sake, what a pair they had been together, she and Clementina, and they would be again. Clementina would be glad of the chance to escape from that Miss Viners. Her and her spirits of the dead! Miss Viners didn't care a twopenny-toss for Clementina. And Clementina's mother cared even less. Nobody had ever cared about Clementina or looked after her like Alice.

Oh, Clementina would come all right and they would be like two peas in a pod. Just like they used to be. It was as much as Alice could do to prevent herself from jumping up and down and clapping her hands like a child.

Nothing would stop Clementina once she had made up her mind. Stubborn as a mule, that girl was, and as tough as old boots. If she could, she would have run out of the tower house after Alice when she left – young as she was at the time, Clementina would have come to Edinburgh to be with her then if that bloody Miss Viners hadn't stopped her by locking her in. That woman had a face as sharp as a pen-knife and a voice to match. She would cut the heart out of anybody. But not Clementina – that girl had spunk! Most folk would be afraid to come to the High Street by themselves in the dark. But not her. Not a bit of it! Alice could bet her life on it. It wouldn't matter if Clementina did feel afraid – sheer stubborn determination would make her come.

Honest to God, she was a character that one. Always had been. Emotion juddered so violently over Alice that she could have sobbed with it. Yet she had never felt so happy.

Everything was going to be all right now. She would have plenty to eat . . . new clothes . . . a nice place to live. Together they would work miracles. They always had before. They would get a cottage, just as soon as they had gathered together enough money. With that blonde hair and those eyes, Clementina would have customers queueing up for her; she could make a fortune in no time.

The lonely abyss of Alice's existence, in which there had been nothing but hopelessness, miraculously disappeared. In her imagination she saw Clementina and herself in their country cottage. It had flowers at the front and a vegetable patch at the back, and a couple of fruit trees. There were hen-houses a bit apart, and a pig-sty, and a cow in the meadow.

'Oh my God!' she kept chanting, sometimes to herself, sometimes out loud, 'what a bit of luck!'

Darkness had crept over the High Street, making ancient buildings look secretive. Nervousness began to shiver up and down Alice's spine despite her happy elation. The tower at Blackwood House had been nothing compared with the Royal Mile. There were so many ghosts in the Royal Mile, all crowding in from so many past generations – kings, queens, dukes, churchmen, soldiers, martyrs, thieves and murderers – that it was a place more nightmarish than a thousand nightmares. Giant black tenements, or *lands* as they were called in Edinburgh, made high walls on either side of the narrow High Street and blocked out the occasional glimmer of light from the moon as it floated faintly in and out of the clouds. Often Alice thought she could see Deacon Brodie in a black mask, peering out one of the windows. Or she would imagine the swirl of his cloak and the turn of his lantern as he sneaked away to go about his evil business.

She was sweating now and trembling – she wasn't sure with what. Sometimes she felt quite dizzy and faint, but she guessed it was the excitement. She wasn't used to being happy. Eventually she decided it would be just as well to wait for Clementina indoors. Clementina knew the address and she would come all right. She'd find her.

Even during a bright sunny day outside, inside the close was always total blackness and she had to feel her way up the stairs and into Nelly's place.

'Where's the customers the night?' Nelly wanted to know. 'If you're no' bringing anybody in, that's you! – out on your arse for good.'

'Don't worry, you'll get your money.'

'Oh aye, how? You gonna' rob a bank?'

'I've got friends, that's how.'

Nelly's big bloated face contorted into a laugh. 'Friends? You? There's no one here that wouldna' spit on your grave. That right, Dot?' She addressed a red-haired girl who had come to get more drink for herself and her lover in the next room.

'You don't know the meaning of the word,' Dot sneered at Alice. She had never forgiven Alice for failing to visit her in the Calton jail.

'I'm fussy about who I pick for friends,' Alice said, with newly acquired pride in her voice. 'My friend's a real lady. She's not dirt like you.'

'Why, you . .' Dot flew at Alice with nails at the ready to claw into Alice's hair. It wouldn't have been the first time that Alice had been set upon and tugged about by her hair, but on this occasion she was saved by Nelly Rudd grabbing Dot and with the strength of a gorilla tossing her aside.

'Don't waste time on her! Take the drink through before he gives up on ye.'

A group of men and women had begun to sing drunkenly in a corner of the kitchen and Nelly had to raise her voice to be heard above them.

'A lady, you say?'

Nelly had tiny piggy eyes and they had acquired a flinty, calculating gleam.

'But strong as a wee horse,' Alice boasted. 'And with hair and eyes the likes of which you've never seen.'

'And never likely to see, I dare say.'

'Are you calling me a liar?'

Nelly Rudd's smile was something most horrible to witness and not only because of her broken teeth, beer-brown with decay. It was the way her coarse, dirt-ingrained skin creased up, making her whole face assemble in an obscene leer.

'I just thought it might be one of your wee stories. You have told a few before, if you stop to think on it, Alice. You've always been a great one for getting carried away.'

'You'll see,' said Alice. 'She'll be here any minute.'

'Oh aye?'

'I'll just go and have another look down the stairs.'

'She'll enjoy a wee glass with us, no doubt?'

But Alice had hurried agitatedly away without hearing.

There were always rows on the stairs, always a violent jangle of sound. Sobbing appeals, threats, taunts, cursing, the scraping and stumbling of heavy boots in the blackness, the thump of blows and the panting of men in drunken fights. Alice had to descend by dead-reckoning and by sound. She could not imagine hell as being any blacker. Outside on the cobbled High Street again, a gas-lamp made a puny circle of light that only intensified the darkness in the narrow thoroughfare.

Had Clementina got lost? She would not know Edinburgh very well and probably had never been out alone in the city's streets without Miss Viners to guide her. Worry increased Alice's agitation. She tried to soothe herself by thinking of the cottage in the country and walking in the hills and tending the animals; and such was the fervour of her imagination that in the midst of the stench of beer and vomit in the High Street she could smell hayfields.

She was almost there, so strong was her longing.

'Bloody hell, Clementina!' she burst out loud eventually. 'Why don't you come, damn you? Come! Come!'

CHAPTER THIRTY-TWO

Heriot Row was deserted. Moonlight glimmered for a moment in the deep, dark sockets of windows and then retreated. The trees in Queen Street Gardens gently sighed. The gas-lamp Clementina paused under seemed to have a voice. She almost made sense of its hoarse, confidential whisper, but was too busy concentrating on which way to turn. Not that she was particularly worried about getting lost. For there, across the other side of the city, silhouetted against the night sky, were the craggy heights of the Old Town. A few square glimmers of light showed that there was someone in the Castle. Lights winked here and there lower down, then multiplied as they rose higher. Buildings in serried rows with crow-stepped gables like ladders climbed to the heavens. Towards the top the lights grew dimmer and rarer. The moon sliding out from behind some clouds pinpointed windows and closes like caves far up on a mountainside.

Somewhere, in one of those caves, was Alice. Covenant Close, she had said. With firm determined steps Clementina aimed for Princes Street and the valley of the Gardens. Then up the steep Mound on to the Lawnmarket. The Old Town fascinated her. In these ancient houses all the great people of Scotland had once lived. She had read that at one time 150 Lords, 160 Members of Parliament and their families and followers had crowded into the closes and courts when Parliament was sitting. Even in the last century there had been two Dukes, sixteen Earls, seven Lords and seven Lords of Session, thirteen

271

Baronets and three Commanders-in-Chief living in the Canongate.

As for Covenant Close, what an historic place that was! Clementina was looking forward to seeing it, especially the sacred apartment in which the Solemn League and Covenant had been signed. Wise and good men had taken part in this 'act of faith' and she would not be afraid of their ghosts.

There were other phantoms of former days, however, that did make her feel uneasy. Edinburgh had so many places in which ghosts lay in wait, unexpected archways and alleyways, and long almost perpendicular streets of stairs crushed between buildings so close together you could touch each side.

So many queer little graveyards with tombstones sloped over ravines as if, as Miss Viners said, even the dead in Edinburgh could not be shut out from her great views.

Clementina was surprised to see not ghosts in the Lawnmarket, but real flesh and blood people. It wasn't too late an hour, but certainly late enough for so many young children to be roaming about. As she made her way down on to the dark High Street the feeble light from the gas-lamps picked out more and more people – women with shawls over their heads and held tightly under their chins, other younger women in short woollen petticoats and bare heads, men reeling drunkenly about.

Clementina tried to quell her mounting apprehension. No harm would come to her once she found Alice. This thought bolstered her courage and when a foul-smelling man staggered in her path and tried to detain her, she haughtily ordered him out of her way. The man immediately mimicked her voice and other men and women nearby roared with laughter and joined in the sport. Like demented witches, women leered and sneered and pushed around. Men became all groping hands which exploded instant panic in Clementina and she had never felt such relief in her life as when Alice suddenly came crashing through the circle of her tormentors. The same Alice who had helped her fight off the tormenting village children. Only this time she was screaming obscenities as well as hitting out with fists and feet. It was a relief to get her courage back and to land almost as many punches as Alice; it didn't take long for the drunken crowd to melt away.

'Oh, Alice!' Clementina clung round her neck, half-laughing, half-crying. 'I knew I would be all right once you were here. I knew you wouldn't let anybody hurt me. Remember how you always used to look after me when I was wee?'

Alice had gone quiet and Clementina let go of her and stood back. It was difficult to see through the gloom, but even so she felt shocked anew at the change in her.

'What's wrong?' she asked anxiously. 'Are you ill? Don't worry, Alice, I will look after you. We'll look after each other.'

Alice looked as if she was searching for words and no longer knew which ones to choose. She looked bewildered, almost tragic.

'It's all right, Alice,' Clementina soothed. 'Take me to your house and then we can talk things over and plan what we're going to do. Everything is going to be all right. I am well and strong and I'm going to do whatever I can for you.'

She linked her arm through Alice's and held tightly on to her. Then, going up the dark stairs, they held hands.

'Remember going up and down the tower stairs?' Clementina asked. 'Remember how you always used to take me with you – even when you were off duty – rather than leave me alone when I was afraid? I have never forgotten you for that, Alice. In fact I . . .I . . .' – she was glad of the darkness and Alice's silence to cover her embarrassment– '. . . loved you more than my mother. You always meant more to me than any of my family.' She was glad she had said this because it was the truth, and she had always wanted to say it. Despite her embar-

273

rassment, it gave her a deep feeling of satisfaction and happiness.

Alice led her first of all into the kitchen and here Clementina's happiness evaporated with horror. A huge bloated woman whose fingers were thick with rings came leering towards them.

'Come away in and get a heat at the fire, lovely,' she invited. 'You'll be Alice's bonny wee friend. Och, and you are too.'

The fire blazed hot as hell, casting a fierce sulphurous glow through the place and, helped by a candle flaring in a beer bottle, lit up a bed-recess in which three working lads and some women were sitting drinking.

To the left of the kitchen, the sacred apartment where the Covenant had been signed was now a dingy cavernous hole filled with ramshackle beds, as were the other rooms. They were all crowded with drunken men and women and Nelly Rudd kept collecting entrance fees for the rooms as well as selling the occupants drink.

Clementina refused the drink the proprietress offered her but Alice downed hers thirstily.

'Alice,' Clementina whispered, 'we can't stay in this horrible place. We must get out of here.'

'Bloody hell!' Alice said. 'I need another drink.'

'Oh, Alice . . .'

Clementina felt panic rising again and had the sudden feeling of being caught in a nightmare. Even the smell of the place was overpowering.

'All right, all right,' said Alice.

'Where you goin', hen?' Nelly Rudd's big bulk blocked their path.

'Where do you think?' Alice replied cheekily.

'Maybe you should leave your nice wee friend here till you come back, eh?'

'Don't be bloody daft,' Alice scoffed. 'She'll bring them in like the bloody Pied Piper.'

'Aye, right enough,' Nelly agreed.

Out in the street Clementina breathed a sigh of relief.

'Oh Alice, I have never been so afraid in my life! Thank goodness we've escaped from there. Where are we going now?'

'Come on,' Alice said. 'Run!'

They ran without stopping until they had reached Princes Street. It was the dividing line and one that Alice knew she could no longer cross.

'Right,' she said. 'Now, get to hell out of here!'

Clementina gazed at her in bewilderment. 'What do you mean?'

'Are you stupid or something?' Alice made an ugly sneering face. 'I never want to set eyes on you again, that's what!'

'You can't mean that!'

'Why can't I?'

'But we wanted to be together?'

'Maybe that's what you wanted, but not me. I've got plenty of friends, Nelly Rudd included. I don't need you! You're just a bloody nuisance to me, always have been. Bloody stubborn little brat!'

'*Alice!*' Tears were filling Clementina's eyes. 'Please don't say that!'

'Why not? It's the honest-to-God truth. You were always hanging round my neck. I was glad to get away to be rid of you, and I'm bloody sure I'm not going to have you hanging round my neck now. So piss off!'

Clementina began to sob uncontrollably.

'Piss off!' Alice screamed. 'You horrible little brat! No wonder your father beat you and your mother hates you. If they never bloody well wanted you, why should I? Get out of my sight!' She gave the now hysterically weeping Clementina a push that sent her stumbling on to the road. 'I never want to see your face again, do you hear? Not ever again!'

With that she turned and disappeared into the darkness.

Clementina was sick with grief. She never knew how she got back to Heriot Row and into the house. In fact she became so ill that she had to remain in bed for the next few days. Then she had to be taken home in Malcolm's carriage which, although he said she was more than welcome to, nevertheless he had to point out was a great inconvenience for poor Mary Ann.

The doctor who came to Blackwood House pronounced that there was nothing physically wrong with her and that her 'little upset', as he called it, must have been caused by the excitement of visiting the City.

It would have been easy, Clementina sometimes thought, to just turn her face to the wall and die. She wanted to. Yet, at her lowest ebb, a stubborn tide rose up in her and she thought, 'To hell with them all, including Alice!' She didn't need any of them; she had survived before on her own and she would survive again.

Part 3

REBELLION

CHAPTER THIRTY-THREE

Clementina stared solemnly at her reflection in the long mirror. It was a most important occasion – the most auspicious day in her life.

'It is lovely, Miss Clementina.' Flora McGregor, the maid, stood back sighing with admiration at her own handiwork.

'It makes me look more mature,' Clementina agreed with satisfaction.

'Are you quite certain now that your mother said you could have it up?' Flora's soft Highland voice went on. 'Most young ladies have to wait until they are seventeen or eighteen.'

'It's *my* hair,' Clementina insisted stubbornly.

The maid's hands flew to her mouth. 'You have not asked!'

'I am sixteen. By Scottish law that means I am old enough to marry, so I'm surely capable of deciding how I should have my own hair dressed!'

'Och, now you have done it!' Flora's words escaped before her natural caution could prevent them. 'Mrs Musgrove, if not your mother, will be wanting to know on whose authority . . .'

'I don't take orders from Mrs Musgrove,' Clementina interrupted disdainfully, unable to resist a slight emphasis on the '*I*'. What she refrained from saying was that even if her mother noticed, she wouldn't care how her daughter's hair was dressed. All she cared about was little Jamie and it was quite embarrassing the way she doted on him. Indeed, it even seemed to embarrass Jamie, who often struggled angrily from her embraces. Only the other day Clementina had seen him stamp his foot in exasperation and shout, 'Leave me alone, Mamma! I'm not a baby any more.'

Already at the tender age of five, Jamie had the arrogance of all males. Clementina had noticed that even amongst the farm labourers' children she used to play with, males had lorded it over females. It was a characteristic she had come to resent bitterly. What made the male sex so superior? she would like to know.

Still, she could not help being quite fond of Jamie, who was such a robust, independent child – not at all thin and weedy like Gilbert and Malcolm must have been and still were. Jamie somehow never looked the part in the 'little Lord Fauntleroy' velvet suits and fancy lace collars that Lorianna liked his nanny to dress him in for his many outings with both nurse and mother. Jamie had jet-black straight hair that somehow made him look tougher than the blue-eyed, curly blond-headed sons of his mother's friends. Even the fact that he had inherited his mother's brown eyes did nothing to soften this effect. Normally he was a calm, self-absorbed child who was quite happy left to himself. Indeed he seemed to prefer this and became quickly bored with his nanny's or his mother's attempts to entertain him with nursery rhymes or games. He liked to spend hours on his own setting up battles with his toy soldiers. Or doing jigsaw puzzles of farmyard scenes. Or making trees or animals with modelling clay. It only annoyed him if somebody tried to join in. But he especially hated being dressed up and taken out.

'Of course,' said Flora, who always tried to keep in with the powers-that-be, even the junior ones, 'you have the nerve to stand up to Mrs Musgrove. She terrifies the wits out of *me!*' She caressed the nest of amber hair and then held it between her outstretched palms like a sacred offering, while admiring it this way and that in the glass. 'Yes, you have got the nerve all right, Miss Clementina. They are always saying that about you downstairs. "She has nerve enough for anything, that one", they say.'

Clementina glanced above her own reflection to study that of the maid. McGregor was a ruddy-cheeked woman whose eyes, although apparently wide and frank, could somehow give the impression at times of hiding rather than revealing the person inside. She had been trained as a housemaid under Ella Baxter, but had eventually been instructed to spend her time partly as Clementina's personal maid and partly in keeping clean the school-room and Clementina's and the governess's rooms.

This arrangement had come to pass when Jamie had been born and the whole of the top floor of the tower had been taken over for his needs. Now Jamie and Nanny Hawthorne slept in the night-nursery and Miller, the new nursery-maid slept in what had once been Alice Tait's room. Clementina had been given the room downstairs next to the school-room which up to that point had been used for storing schoolbooks – and other books discarded for various reasons from the downstairs library – slates, chalks, pointers and a miscellany of equipment gathered over a period of years dating from Gilbert's first school-days.

In converting the room from a general dumping ground to a bedroom for Clementina (the irony of the situation had not escaped her) the books had been left until either another place could be found for them or a decision made about throwing them out. As a result, Clementina had spent many an hour reading them by candle-light. Not that she needed to be furtive. Nanny Hawthorne's duties did not include any responsibility for her and to Miss Viners she ceased to exist after four o'clock when the governess finished lessons for the day. This state of affairs had its compensations, because it afforded Clementina much more freedom than most of her contemporaries and was something of which she took full advantage.

'Leave my hair now,' she told the maid. 'Tell me how I look in the skirt.' She rose from the stool, marched back and forth in the small room and then gave a couple of twirls of the first long skirt she had ever possessed.

Flora's eyes flickered ceilingwards. 'Beautiful! Beautiful! All at once you are a young lady instead of a young girl. You will be having all the young gentlemen after you.'

Clementina immediately rounded on the maid. 'I don't *want* all the young gentlemen after me.'

Flora saw that her compliment had somehow gone wrong, although she could not for the life of her think why it should have sparked off such anger.

'Of course not, and quite right you are, Miss Clementina. Quite right.'

'Nor do I need them.'

'No, miss.'

'Nor do you.'

'No, miss,' Flora repeated with somewhat less conviction.

'It's only a pretence that what every woman needs is a man. That's a lie perpetuated by men.'

'Yes, miss,' Flora murmured faintly. It was common knowledge that Miss Clementina had always been a strange rebellious child, never out of trouble and always saying odd things. Instead of getting better as she grew older, as everyone had hoped, she seemed to be getting worse. Cook blamed Mrs Musgrove, 'She's an evil influence on both the mother and the daughter, that one.'

But Flora thought Miss Viners had more to do with the way Clementina was growing up. After all, she was with her most of every day except Saturdays and Sundays when the governess's duties finished at one o'clock.

'All I want,' said Clementina earnestly, 'is to look adult and mature. Well? Do I?'

'Oh yes, miss. Oh yes, indeed.'

Clementina smoothed down the well-cut navy serge of the skirt, well pleased with herself.

'That will be all, McGregor.'

'Yes, miss.' Flora stopped at the door and added with a hint of slyness in her voice but only innocence in her eyes,

'Will you be dining downstairs this evening?'

Clementina was taken aback. It was the usual thing, once one graduated from childhood to maturity, to start having dinner in the dining-room with the other grown-ups instead of nursery tea. However, this would be a very daring thing for her to do, taking into consideration the fact that she had not been invited.

She managed to shrug in reply to the maid. 'I may. It depends.'

Flora gave a small smile before leaving.

Clementina stood rather uncertainly before the mirror now. She was far from sure if she really wanted to take such a step from the nursery into the world of downstairs. She seldom even went to the drawing-room or sitting-room to see her mother any more, preferring either to read in her room or, if it were summer, to take her book out to the garden. Quite often she visited her best friend, Millicent Price-Gordon, or one of her other friends. Millicent was eighteen, had put her hair up ages ago and was now dining with her parents every evening. But Millicent was different. Her parents wanted her.

Clementina tried as a rule never to think about her mother. To blank her father from her mind took little effort and for most of the time it was as if he had never existed. But her mother did exist and could sometimes appear unexpectedly in the garden or the reception hall or on the stairs. At these unplanned and unwanted meetings they greeted each other civilly enough and sometimes her mother forced herself to stand and chat for a few minutes, as if she were interested in finding out whatever she could about her daughter. Clementina knew it was a forced and artificial interest, a desperate attempt to appear dutiful. She saw it in the unnatural widening of her mother's eyes, dark eyes that so often had such a strange haunted look. She sensed it too in the tension that emanated from her mother's body, tension so real she could almost see and touch it.

Once, in a moment of weakness, she had actually

283

touched her mother. It was not long after Jamie had been born and she had been banished to the school-room quarters. It had been a wrench leaving the familiar night-nursery where she had once been so happy with Henny. The nursery quarters for better or worse had always been her domain, her home ground. And suddenly that ground had been snatched from beneath her. Suddenly everything had changed. Strangers had taken over – the new nanny, the new nursery-maid, the new baby.

Clementina had needed something or someone to hold on to then and had put out her hand and tentatively stroked her mother's arm. Ever since, she had been trying to forget the way her mother had involuntarily shrunk back, but she could never quite manage to heal the wound made by Lorianna's reaction. She could never completely erase the memory of the horror on her mother's face. For long days and nights, weeks, sometimes even months she would never think of it. Then at other times she would purposely dwell on the scene and would try in a sensible adult way to rationalise her mother's behaviour. But always the result was the same. In the end she simply shrivelled helplessly inside, grief-stricken, bewildered and unbearably ashamed. It had not been disinterest or dislike or even distaster she had seen on her mother's face, but *absolute horror*. It had only been a brief second before it had been brought under control and safely hidden behind a desperate smile and a rush of kindly words.

But Clementina had seen it, and just could not understand it. Even to this day.

Would her mother want to sit at the same table and eat with her? She very much doubted it. The problem was, should she insist on her rights by just going downstairs, taking her place and refusing to budge? After all, she was not a child any more. What could her mother do to her?

The question of 'rights' was much on her mind these days. Ever since, in fact, she had read *A Vindication of the Rights of Women* by Mary Wollstonecraft. Millicent

284

had read it too and been much excited by its contents which they discussed endlessly and with boundless enthusiasm. Now they had found Harriet Taylor Mill's *The Enfranchisement of Women* and John Stuart Mill's *The Subjection of Women* and all three publications had been passed around their other friends in Bathgate. It had become a regular habit that they all met together in each other's houses to discuss the startling and revolutionary ideas expressed in the writings and to explore how these could be applied to their own lives.

Clementina felt on the verge of an important phase in her existence, filled with many new, exciting and dangerous challenges.

Perhaps this auspicious day was presenting her with the very first one.

She decided to speak to her mother without further delay and with one last glance at her comforting grown-up image, she swished from the room.

CHAPTER THIRTY-FOUR

Mrs Musgrove adjusted the cushions behind Lorianna's back and while the shadow of the housekeeper lay over her and the silver chatelaine fingered a path across her lap, time was an agony to Lorianna. Like an animal in danger, she became absolutely still.

'Is that more comfortable, madam?'

Lorianna gazed up wide-eyed, 'Yes, thank you, Mrs Musgrove.'

The keys at the housekeeper's waist gently jingled as she straightened. She remained standing close to Lorianna, the heavy black material of her skirt forming a startling contrast against Lorianna's froth of pink sprigged chiffon.

'Don't work too long at that embroidery. Your eyes are beginning to look strained.'

Occasionally, when they were alone like this, Mrs Musgrove crossed the line that divided servant and mistress and they both knew there was nothing Lorianna could do about it. Not that she really wanted to. She needed someone to look after her, someone she could depend on, and there could be no doubt that the housekeeper was devoted to her and attended not only to the running of the house but to her every need and comfort. Lizzie, Lorianna's personal maid, seemed almost redundant; Mrs Musgrove was so often either hovering in the bedroom watching that the girl was attending to her mistress's toilette correctly, or else taking over from the maid herself. It was strange, Lorianna often thought, how despite all that Mrs Musgrove had done and continued to do for her, she could never feel comfortable in the house-keeper's presence – far less acquire any liking for the woman.

'I shall just finish the blue,' she said, lowering her gaze once more to her sewing.

Just then the sitting-room door opened and Lorianna looked up in surprise when Clementina entered. Her daughter seldom took advantage of their customary half-hour together before dinner and for this Lorianna was intensely grateful. The mere sight of Clementina never failed to plunge her back to the terrible night of Gavin's death; it was something immediate and involuntary, over which she had no control.

A thousand times of course she had tried to tell herself that Clementina was in no way responsible for the tragic sequence of events. Clementina had been wickedly sinned against and was completely innocent of sin herself. But still the girl continued to act as a catalyst and a passion of distress surged over Lorianna every time she saw her. Never had she felt towards anyone what she felt for Clementina, against which the emotion she had once nursed against Gavin paled into insignificance. At the same time she was appalled at herself and overcome with compassion for her daughter, yet her body nevertheless refused to allow her to make any loving advances. It was as much as she could bring herself to do to speak civilly; to speak kindly cost her so much effort that it drained her both emotionally and physically. More and more she longed to be at peace with herself and free of this exhaust-ing conflict. Sometimes, in the most secret and guilty place in her heart, she wished that Clementina would die. Immediately the wish was banished of course and a tide of love for her daughter would cleanse it away. She would remember Clementina as an infant in her arms; feel the tiny moist mouth enclosing her nipple and then sucking with an astonishing determination and strength that tugged down every nerve from breast to womb. It had been an ecstasy with which she had thought at the time that no man could compete.

'Yes, dear?' she asked.

'May I speak to you on an important matter, Mother?'

'Certainly, darling. Do sit down.'

Clementina stared defiantly, questioningly at the housekeeper and Lorianna hastily said, 'That will be all, Mrs Musgrove.' Then she indicated a seat over by the fireplace for Clementina, not beside her at the window. How prim and earnest and straight-backed the girl looked!

Lorianna returned her attention to the embroidery, helped by the light from the candelabra on the table at her side. Gavin had been prim and oh, so serious. All the years she had known him he'd . . .

'You never even noticed, Mother!'

'Noticed what, dear?' she murmured without looking up.

'My hair and my skirt!'

'You look very smart, darling.'

'I have had my hair put up and I am wearing a long skirt.'

'Yes, of course,' Lorianna smiled across at her. 'How nice.'

'Do you realise what this means, Mother?'

'That you are quite grown-up and I shall have to start introducing you to some eligible young men.'

'I don't want anything to *do* with men!'

'Nonsense, dear.'

'Mother, the reason I came downstairs was to ask your permission to have dinner with you from now on.'

'That's impossible!' The words rushed out before she could stop them and kept on echoing and re-echoing in her brain: 'Impossible, impossible.'

'Why is it impossible?'

'Don't be impertinent, Clementina.'

Conscious of her piled-up hair and the adult status it brought her, Clementina held herself with dignity. 'I'm sorry. I did not mean to sound impertinent, Mother. But I do feel it is only fair that I should be allowed to dine with you downstairs now that I am older. Millicent Price-Gordon has been eating downstairs for ages.'

'That girl is having far too much influence on you, Clementina. I am well aware of all the so-called progressive ideas she dabbles in.'

'We believe in justice for women. I can see nothing wrong in that.'

'You have never seen anything wrong in anything, Clementina. That has been your trouble. Right from when you were a small child you have caused nothing but problems. You were caught fighting with the boys — actually *fighting* . . .'

'The village children sometimes used to tease me, Mother. I had to stand up for myself. Being a girl didn't protect me, nor would I have wanted it to.'

'You should never have been near the village in the first place. Nor should you have indulged in any of the other disgraceful behaviour that was continually reported to me over the years.'

'It was just normal, childish . . .'

'It certainly was not normal, Clementina. Jamie is not causing me a moment's worry. He is such a good child. Why couldn't you have been like him?'

'Is it just because I am a girl, then?' Clementina said. 'Is that why you don't care about me?'

'Don't talk nonsense!' Lorianna pricked her finger and dropped her embroidery in her fluster. 'Now look what you have made me do! Go away! Get back upstairs to the nursery where you belong.'

'I have been in the school-room quarters for years now, Mother.'

Any guilty feelings that Lorianna suffered were crushed by the weight of her resentment. 'I meant the tower house – and you know perfectly well that I did.'

'If you cared about me, Mother, you would want me to be with you more often. Then I wouldn't *need* to ask!'

Lorianna's animosity began to lose ground as she stared at her daughter's pale stiff face. The girl's eyes were large and strained as if tears were being desperately held in check to remain a mere shimmering film of bright green misery. Lorianna sighed, her gaze retreating to the warm glow of the coal fire.

It was early evening and the heavy tasselled curtains had been drawn to keep out the cold March winds. The flames of the fire, the candles, the oil-lamps all pushed back the shadows. They reflected in the polished mirror of the furniture and tinted the air with a ruby glow. But for the moment the comfort of the room was lost on her. She longed for the help and support of her stepsons, Gilbert and Malcolm. Although what could they say on this issue? There was no obvious reason why Clementina should not eat at least one of her meals downstairs. They could and did advise against Clementina's interest in the Woman's Suffrage Movement and there were plenty of valid reasons to back up an argument against Clementina getting involved in that. But on this issue?

'It is not that I don't care about you, Clementina.' The words were squeezed out from a face contorted as if in pain. 'Merely that I value privacy at mealtimes whenever I can achieve it. One has to be civilised and retain a certain number of social contacts, but as you know, since your father's death and my nervous breakdown I have entertained hardly at all.'

'But this isn't a question of social contacts or entertaining. I'm supposed to be one of the family.'

'Yes, of course you are, dear.'

'Well?'

'Oh, here's Nanny and little Jamie!' Lorianna's face radiated relief as well as joy. 'Come and say "Good evening" to Mamma and Clementina, my precious.'

Nanny Hawthorne, her big square body firmly tied like

a parcel in a crackling white apron, beamed at her small charge.

'Who's been a good boy the whole long day, then?'

Jamie ignored the question. 'Mamma,' he said, 'when can I have a pony?'

Already Lorianna felt soothed. Jamie seemed to have such a still calm centre. Always she became more relaxed in his company and love washed over her like a benediction.

'A pony, darling?' she echoed smiling, indulgently. 'What made you suddenly think of a pony?'

Nanny Hawthorne said, 'Who's remembered that story his Mamma read to him the other day?' She winked knowingly at Lorianna. 'Mr Snowymane and his Farmyard Friends! Somebody never forgets a thing.'

Lorianna laughed. 'If Mamma gets a big hug and a kiss, she might be persuaded.'

The little boy marched across to her and climbed on to her knee and gratefully Lorianna kissed and caressed the child. Clementina could hardly bear to look as Jamie clung round Lorianna's neck. There was something almost indecent about the way that the beringed fingers eagerly explored his head and neck and spine, the way the tawny eyes closed in rapture.

Lorianna had never touched her in any way at all in her whole life, Clementina thought bitterly. She managed to retain a dignified and smiling expression but in her mind she was scowling.

No, to be perfectly accurate there had been one or perhaps two occasions when those slim fingers had fleetingly brushed her cheek. It had been in front of guests and she remembered her mother asking, 'Isn't she beautiful?' The gesture had been made with a hasty, guilty look in her husband's direction. Lorianna had always been dependent on male approval. She had taken it for granted that what the males in the family said must be right, and her husband had said that Clementina should not be petted.

Gavin had also said she was not to have a pony. He would have been different with Jamie though, thought Clementina.

'Can I have a pony, Mamma?' Jamie disentangled himself from his mother's embrace. 'I would very much like one.'

'Ahem!' Nanny Hawthorne meaningfully cleared her throat. 'I didn't quite hear you, dear.' This was Nanny's usual reminder that he hadn't said 'please'.

'Please?' Jamie responded.

'Give Mamma another little kiss and then I promise to ask Jacobs' advice first thing tomorrow.'

'About getting a pony?'

To see the child's face light up with such wonder and delight, Lorianna would have agreed to anything.

'Yes, my precious. I expect Jacobs will know how we can get a lovely little pony just for Mamma's good little boy.'

Clementina's mental scowl darkened. Oh, how she had once longed and prayed and begged for a pony. And all she had received was the dictum: 'Children should be seen and not heard', and eventually a beating. Girls especially, she had been led to understand, should know their place and keep quiet. They should learn to be modest, industrious and obedient, and busy themselves with their samplers. She had *hated* her samplers – her stitches had always turned out knotty and grubby and squint and sent her into fidgets of impatience. And she had hated every boy for miles around who trotted free and proud on a pony.

But she didn't hate Jamie and when he came skipping towards her delightedly, crying out, 'Clementina, Clementina, I'm going to get a pony. Aren't you pleased?' she kissed him and said 'Yes, of course', and wasn't he a lucky boy and think of all the fun he would have once he had learned to ride it. And it would be a good friend for him too, wouldn't it?

She was deeply wounded when Lorianna interrupted

292

with, 'Clementina, didn't you say you were going out somewhere?'

It was always the same. Her mother didn't want her to be one of the family and was always trying to shut her out. Even when she had tried to visit Jamie upstairs in the nursery, and on one occasion taken him out to play in the garden, her mother had been outraged that she had dared to interfere with Nanny Hawthorne and Jamie's routine and had forbidden her to set foot in the nursery again.

'Yes, Mother,' she said, adding with defiant determination, 'but you haven't answered my question.'

Her mother's eyes were melting over Jamie, her hands fondling him. 'What question?'

'Starting tomorrow, may I have dinner in the dining-room with you every evening?'

Lorianna turned impatiently towards her. 'I told you . . .'

'No, you didn't, Mother.'

'Well . . .' she flapped a hand vaguely in Clementina's direction ' . . . if you must, but only when I am dining alone. Not when I am having guests. Tomorrow my solicitor, Mr Stirling is coming to dinner. We have business to discuss.'

'The day after tomorrow, then?' Clementina persisted.

'Oh, very well.'

'Thank you. Good night, Mother. Good night, Jamie.'

For a few seconds the joy went out of Lorianna's eyes. Then she looked at her son and immediately forgot her unease. Here was Robert's flesh and blood as well as her own, the flower of their love and passion – her only reason for living.

'Come to Mamma, darling,' she said, 'and tell me all about the kind of pony you would like and what you're going to call it.'

And as the child came towards her with love in his eyes, she thought, 'Oh Robert, Robert . . .'

Later, while Nanny Hawthorne was having dinner

Clementina went up to the nursery to have a proper talk with Jamie. He always seemed far more natural and unrestrained when alone with her. Sometimes she wrestled with him until tears of hilarity came to his eyes. Sometimes they had a pillow fight with her bouncing up and down on the bed along with him. His strength and fierce energy always surprised. He was a real tough little tyke.

'Right,' Clementina said to him now, 'what's the pony to be called then?'

'If it's a white one I'll call it Snowball,' he announced. 'If it's a black one I'll call it Darky.'

Clementina made a face. 'Not very original.'

He frowned at her. 'That's what I want.'

'Yes, and you always know how to get what you want, don't you?' she teased. 'Yes, mamma. No, mamma. Kiss, kiss. Sook, sook.'

He lunged at her in mock fury, fists clenched and they tumbled about the bed giggling and breathless with their exertions. Until suddenly Nanny Hawthorne came bustling into the room and hauled Clementina away.

'This simply will not do, young lady. Although you're not fit to be graced with the title. I've never seen any young lady behave in such a wild and rough manner in my life. Master Jamie will never settle to sleep now. I shall have to report this to your mamma and you know what she said. Any more of your carry-on and you wouldn't be allowed to set foot in the nursery again.'

'We were only having fun,' Clementina protested. But as usual it didn't do any good. She was forced marched from the nursery and banished downstairs on her own again to the long silent night.

CHAPTER THIRTY-FIVE

'Excuse me, madam.'

Lorianna turned to face Ella Baxter, the head house-maid, stiff as a doll in long black dress and crisp white apron and cap.

'What is it?'

'Mr Stirling has arrived, madam.'

'Oh yes, show him in at once.' She had met John's mother and sisters socially but, because he was away so often in Edinburgh, she had only got to know John some time after Robert's trial. She had made sure that she was also invited when she heard that he was to be a guest at one of Jean Dalgliesh's many dinner parties.

She somehow felt that Robert made a secret bond between her and the man who had tried to defend him. She persuaded him to speak about the trial. She felt compelled to keep drawing assurance from him that everything humanly possible had been done in Robert's defence.

'John!' She stretched out her hands in greeting, trembling with relief and pleasure at the familiar sight of his tall figure, immaculately dressed in evening suit with white piqué shirt and white tie. 'I am so glad you have come.' She held up her cheek for his customary kiss, and still holding her hands he surveyed her.

'You look even more lovely than usual, Lorianna.'

His courteous smiling voice helped to soothe her troubled spirits.

'That colour suits you.'

He was referring to her tawny-coloured evening gown

which complemented the warm, dark tones of her hair and eyes and highlighted her creamy skin. The gown was daringly low cut and she wore a deep pearl choker. Pearls also decorated the train of the dress.

Baxter was retrieving Stirling's hat from where he had placed it on a chair and Lorianna lifted a hand to detain her as she asked her guest, 'You will have a pre-dinner refreshment, John?'

'A glass of whisky, thank you.'

Lorianna nodded to the maid, who immediately went over to the drinks cabinet. After she had poured the drink and left the room, Lorianna came to sit beside Stirling on the settee and he asked, 'How are you, my dear?'

'Rather worried, actually.'

Stirling frowned. 'About what?'

He had a habit of stooping forward when in conversation with anyone, as if always wanting to make quite certain he caught exactly what was being said. He leaned towards Lorianna now, the light of the oil-lamp glistening on the silver at his temples. Despite this sprinkling of silver, he had a smooth youthful skin and clear intelligent eyes. He had never married, although many women had looked at him invitingly and many a Bathgate mother still dreamed of having such a charming and elegant son-in-law.

Sighing, Lorianna rested her head against the cushions. 'Clementina has put up her hair and has appeared in her first long skirt. She has also asked to dine downstairs in future.'

Stirling relaxed. 'An excellent idea and surely nothing to worry about. You are alone far too much, Lorianna. You daughter's companionship at the dinner-table will take you out of yourself.'

Lorianna smiled vaguely in his direction. 'Clementina can be rather a trial at times.'

'You mean her interest in women's suffrage? That is probably only a phase. She's young and idealistic and I expect she sees the present female agitation as a great and beneficial movement for social reform.'

'I wonder if these friends of hers are being a bad influence? I realise Clementina is precocious; she always has been. Still, they are all older than she is.'

Stirling patted her hand and she felt an immediate heightened awareness of him. It was as much as she could do to control the urge to cling to his hand and hold it against her. She was not in love with him, but he was a man and she had such a hunger in her for loving.

'The fault doesn't lie in Clementina being easily influenced, my dear,' he was saying. 'That is a womanly virtue. What she needs is the influence of a good husband.'

Lorianna closed her eyes. 'Oh, what a load off my mind it would be if she were married and safely settled in a home of her own.'

Thoughts of loving had brought the memory of Robert to her mind. Even now, after six years, it still hurt to think of his name. For so long the anguish of his terrible death had been too much to bear and she had retreated into a kind of madness where she had tried to deny the cruel progress of time and keep him with her. By sheer wild force of will she refused to acknowledge his loss and continued to love him as passionately in death as she had loved him in life. He would come back, she kept telling herself. No one could prevent her strong, beautiful, loving Robert from gathering her into his arms once again.

Only Jamie had saved her sanity. Jamie with his black hair and his stubborn sense of independence, who was already so like his father.

And of course Mrs Musgrove, who acted as both nurse and jailer. For months, indeed until after Jamie was born, no friends – not even Gilbert and Malcolm – had been allowed to see her. Blackwood House had been a strange, cut-off secret place then, a world of its own, peopled only by women.

It still retained something of that intense atmosphere, and only her stepsons' insistence had eventually overruled Mrs Musgrove's ban on visitors. Now, sometimes Jean Dalgliesh came for lunch or afternoon tea and about once a fortnight Gilbert and Malcolm and their wives came to dinner. The only other regular guest – and the most hated, as far as Mrs Musgrove was concerned – was John Stirling.

'Men have caused you nothing but trouble,' Mrs Musgrove insisted. 'The less you have to do with them, the better.'

Trying to keep herself in the present, Lorianna said to Stirling now, 'I was thinking of calling a family conference to discuss what we should do about Clementina.'

'Why don't you start entertaining a little more? It would be good for you as well as Clementina. I have several clients who have sons – very personable young men – just the type that Clementina should meet. A couple of them even have titles. Perhaps you would like to add them to your guest list when you are arranging her first dance or whatever. I can give you their names and addresses.'

'What a good idea, John! It's time Clementina attended her first dance. She is quite right and I ought to be treating her more like a young lady now. She isn't a child any more.' A hint of anxiety returned to her eyes when she added, 'She doesn't mean any harm, you know, John. And I do love her.'

'Of course, my dear. She is a charming girl. And I'm sure that if she is guided and influenced in the right way she will soon settle down and forget these foolish ideas she has been harbouring.'

'Yes, you're quite right. She needs to meet someone who will love her and look after her.' Lorianna's expression had become dreamy. Across her mind's eye was drifting a delightful picture of Clementina in a fashionable wedding dress, looking blissfully happy. Gilbert was proudly giving her away and Malcolm was performing the wedding ceremony. Jamie, her beautiful Jamie, was an adorable little page-boy, in plum velvet with ecru lace collar and cuffs . . .

'There, you look better already.' John was smiling at her and she forced her attention back to him.

'I don't know how you do it, but I always feel better after talking to you,' she said.

'It's my job,' he reminded her.

'Oh, John!' She laughed and coyly lowered her eyes for a second to show to advantage the thick sweep of her lashes. 'Surely after all these years our relationship is more than just a cold business one?'

'Certainly not cold, my dear.' He lifted her hand and brushed the back of it with his lips.

'Friends, then?' She arched a brow, eyes coquettish and inviting.

'Good friends, I hope,' he said with one of his little courteous movements, the merest suggestion of a bow.

It was only recently that Lorianna had found herself beginning to adopt a consciously flirtatious role with John. She wondered if he had noticed her change of attitude towards him and if so, what he thought about it. She hardly knew what to make of it herself. For so long she had hardly been aware of his existence. She had lived for Robert and after Robert's death she had lived with his memory. And as her body had recovered its strength and her craving for physical fulfilment had increased, she had desperately held him in her mind and masturbated to a climax that only increased her agony of loneliness.

Memories were not enough.

'I hope so, too.' She lowered her eyes again, somehow managing to convey the sense of modesty and restraint that was proper for any respectable woman in the circumstances.

Suddenly the maid, Baxter, appeared in the doorway.

'Dinner is served, madam.'

Lorianna rose in a graceful, sensual movement that rustled her petticoats like a whisper of excitement. Her hand slid into the crook of John Stirling's arm and her brow arched provocatively again. 'Shall we?' she said.

CHAPTER THIRTY-SIX

'I must say I agreed with Gladstone,' Malcolm smiled, 'when he said that allowing women to become mixed up in politics would trespass upon their delicacy, their purity, their refinement, the elevation of their whole nature.'

The fine china tinkled as Lorianna poured the steaming brew from the silver teapot and handed each cup to Baxter, who passed to each person in turn.

Malcolm's wife Mary Ann, in a fluffy fur hat, was gazing at her husband in adoration and admiration and she was more startled than anyone when Clementina said, 'Rubbish!'

Malcolm clung to his smile but his mouth and eyes acquired a tinge of pain.

Half Clementina's attention was on the cake-stand. There had never been anything like this in the tower house – plum cake, iced buns, girdle scones and blackcurrant jelly and sugar biscuits. She was enjoying herself immensely.

'Don't argue,' said Gilbert.

'I wasn't arguing,' Clementina retorted. 'Just expressing an opinion. But what's *wrong* with arguing?'

Baxter, poker-faced, offered her the choice of the cake-stand and Clementina concentrated on the serious decision of whether to have a piece of plum cake or a sugar biscuit. This was important, because for all she knew she might not get the chance of the cake-stand a second time.

'It's not ladylike,' Gilbert said. His long side-boards and drooping moustache accentuated his lantern jaws and his bulbous eyes gave him a constantly indignant expression.

Having selected a piece of plum cake, Clementina chewed earnestly at it.

'That's a man-made rule, Gilbert, and one of man's most selfish. I don't care about being a lady.'

'What *does* she mean?' Hilda, Gilbert's wife, her sallow complexion not enhanced by her brown dress and yellow-trimmed hat, asked her husband. She had a habit of ignoring anyone or anything she felt unworthy of her direct attention.

'Dear Clementina,' Malcolm said gently, 'the rules we live by on earth *must* be man-made – with the help and guidance of God, of course.'

'Why must they?'

Malcolm's expression remained hanging in mid-air as if he had forgotten how to change it. Mary Ann came quickly to his rescue. 'You're just being silly, Clementina. You know perfectly well that you must try to behave like a lady. It's only right and proper.'

'Right and proper to be submissive and passive, you mean? Oh yes, that's very convenient for men, I must say. And of course, if a man puts forward a good argument different rules apply – *he's* considered forceful and intelli-gent.'

'You will not make much of an impression on men, Clementina,' Gilbert said, 'if you show yourself to be either forceful or intelligent.'

'That's disgraceful, Gilbert!'

'Not at all. Woman has always had a beneficent and charming influence over man. Never a forceful one. She has her intuition and is able to whisper in his ear that little word which in the past has sometimes shaped the destinies of nations.'

Clementina felt like knocking him to the floor with one forceful punch, but instead she brushed some crumbs off her new long skirt with brisk efficient movements and said, 'It's just as well, then, that I have no desire to make an impression on men. Nor, by the way, do I feel any need for their approval.'

'You see what I mean?' Lorianna enquired helplessly of the men.

'Yes, indeed I do, step-mamma,' said Gilbert, 'and of course you're perfectly right. Something will have to be done.'

'*Now* what are we talking about?' Clementina wanted to know.

Malcolm cleared his throat and eased his dog-collar away from his rather prominent Adam's apple. He was not as tall as his brother and his clean-shaven face had a milder and more open expression. But like Gilbert, he was one of Pharaoh's lean cattle.

'We think, my dear, that's it's time you were enjoying a little more varied social life.'

'I'm perfectly happy with my social life, thank you very much, Malcolm.'

Mary Ann coyly patted the back of her hair and fiddled with the mother-of-pearl comb that held it up underneath her furry hat. With a flutter of her eyelashes she said, 'We mean the social company of suitable young gentlemen.'

'How many times must I say it? I don't want anything to do with men! I don't need them.'

'Clementina!' Gilbert's impatience was starting to show. 'I am beginning to think you are not quite as grown-up as you seem to believe.'

'Are you saying, Gilbert, that a sense of independence is a sign of immaturity?'

'I am telling you that society has certain rules which have to be complied with.'

'Man-made rules.'

'Don't keep saying that as if it were something reprehensible.'

'But it *is* reprehensible,' maintained Clementina.

Lorianna sighed, 'Darling, I was married and mistress of this house at your age.'

'Well, that was fine if it was what you wanted, Mother. It's not what *I* want.'

'You'll do as you are told,' Gilbert said. 'Your mother and Hilda and Mary Ann are all planning to give dances and soirées and invite as many eligible young men as can be persuaded to come. You will come and you will behave yourself, do you hear?'

Clementina hesitated. Then she thought, oh to hell, why should I worry? The dances might provide her with an opportunity to meet lots of new women and so spread the suffragist message. She and her friends had been talking about holding public meetings, but so far they were not quite sure if they would have enough support. There was plenty of suffragist activity in Glasgow and the capital city of Edinburgh, they knew. But in a small market town like Bathgate? Not that they were afraid of opposition, but they did need a solid nucleus of women to organise such events. If they did arouse sufficient interest, perhaps they could establish a branch of one of the suffragist movements in Bathgate. It was all very exciting and worthwhile.

'You will enjoy it all,' Malcolm was saying kindly. 'There is no need to be anxious.'

'I am *not* anxious. And yes, I probably will enjoy a wider social scene. I am interested in people and like meeting them and discussing their ideas and points of view.'

Hilda said, 'I don't think this plan of ours is destined to have the success we are hoping for, Lorianna. Most young women with the prospect of a dance in view would immediately think of what whey would wear. *She* thinks of discussing ideas and points of view.'

Mary Ann giggled and her husband said, 'Oh I shouldn't worry too much. Dear Clementina, I'm sure, will soon be swept off her feet by some handsome young man and all her problems will be over.'

'I hardly think so,' Clementina said drily. 'My main problem at the moment is how to get the right to vote so that I can control my own destiny.'

'Oh, to hell with the right to vote!' Gilbert exploded irritably.

'You are perfectly at liberty to banish your rights, Gilbert, but not mine.'

'Can you imagine her,' Hilda enquired of her husband, 'charming any eligible young man into asking for her hand? I certainly can't.'

'I don't *want* to charm any young man. Nor do I intend to try.'

'And you have the cheek to accuse men of being selfish!' Gilbert said. 'It has obviously never occurred to you that this family will not only have to put up with you but support you for the rest of your life if you fail in your duty to marry.'

'If women like myself had the right to work – as I believe we should – that problem would not arise, Gilbert. Believe me, I have no wish to be dependent on you or any man.'

'A woman's work is in the home,' Gilbert said.

'You will change and see things differently once you are married and have a dear little family of your own,' Malcolm assured her. He and Mary Ann now had a daughter named Victoria on whom they both doted. 'I often think of the words of De Quincy: "The loveliest sight which a woman's eye opens upon in this world is her first-born child; and the holiest sight upon which the eyes of God settles in almighty sanction is the love which soon kindles between the mother and her infant".'

'May I have another cake, Mother?' asked Clementina.

The tawny flecks in Lorianna's eyes leapt like flames into life, but she answered with only the faintest betraying tremble in her voice, 'Yes, of course, dear. Do help yourself.'

'That's all settled, then,' said Gilbert.

'Yes,' Lorianna smiled. 'It will take me a few weeks to organise everything properly of course, but I will have the first social gathering. Then perhaps a month or so after that occasion, either Hilda or Mary Ann can take their turn.'

'Hilda can be next,' Gilbert said. 'And by the time Mary Ann does her turn of duty, let us hope that some man has taken the bait.'

Clementina decided she would just enjoy the tea and cakes and ignore them. They could do what they liked – no one was going to force *her* into marriage.

She had no desire even to contemplate such a death sentence, because that was what it would be. She felt she was at the beginning of her life and had so much to look forward to and achieve. She refused to accept what Miss Viners had said some years earlier. When she had asked, 'What am I going to do when I grow up, Miss Viners?', the governess had replied abruptly, 'Nothing. You're a lady.'

The prospect had shocked Clementina and filled her with fearful depression. But it was only a temporary panic. She was made of sterner stuff than that and she was not going to go through her whole life as a useless parasite with nothing better to fill her time than the futile accomplishments that every lady was supposed to acquire – embroidery, piano playing and perhaps a little French. Anything more serious or systematic in the way of education might scare away potential suitors, so they said. Medical experts even claimed that if a young girl overloaded her brain it could have dire consequences. Her brain would burst, for instance, or she would develop atrophy of the uterus. Opinion held that 'nice' girls had no business knowing too much and everyone, including Clementina, was familiar with the verse;

Oh pedants of these later days, who go on undiscerning,
To overload a woman's brain and cram our girls with learning,
You'll make a woman half a man, the souls of parents vexing,

To find that all the gentle sex this process is unsexing.
Leave one or two nice girls before the sex your system
smothers,
Or what on earth will poor men do for sweethearts,
wives and mothers?

Clementina didn't care what anybody thought. The enforced triviality and self-denying vacuity that middle-class girls endured at home was not for her.

To give Miss Viners her due the governess had, over and above the required 'accomplishments', conscientiously provided her with a good basic education. There had been the 'three r's' and also history and mythology; they even did some reading in philosophy.

Once her mother, on discovering that she was learning about the mythologies of Greece and Rome – the heroes and nymphs and stories like the Iliad and the Odyssey – had sweepingly condemned the learning of such heathen mythologies: 'Useless knowledge like that is not going to be any good to you at all, Clementina.'

But the next day at lessons Miss Viners had said, 'How would you know what a person meant if they spoke to you of someone having "Herculean" strength?'

Clementina had seen the point. Words were not only sounds. There was reason behind them.

Lessons had been dull at first, for there had never been the slightest sense of humour or fun about Miss Viners. But over the years they had developed a kind of hypnotic interest. Clementina had graduated from the horrible screech of slate pencil on slate as her hands slipped on a line or figure, to the splutter of real ink and a quill pen in her much blotched copy-book. Learning had gradually become a challenge that suited her stubborn, sturdy spirit. Over the years of determined plodding more and more flashes of insight rewarded her. Many hours of reading began to fall into place and consolidate and illuminate the formal part of her learning. It was also to Miss Viners' credit that she encouraged her pupil to read widely. It was the governess she had to thank for being introduced to *A Vindication of the Rights of Women* and the essays of John Stuart Mill and Harriet Taylor Mill.

Miss Viners, she discovered eventually, nursed some secret bitterness about the role of women in the scheme of things. Her clergyman father had always wanted a son to follow in his footsteps and had been acutely disappointed to be burdened with a daughter. A daughter could not take up the ministry or indeed do anything except become a governess after his death. It was then Miss Viners had found herself left penniless and without even a home to call her own.

'You will never be allowed to do anything you really want to do either, you know,' she told Clementina. 'There is no point in building up your hopes. You will not be allowed to go to University, but your young brother Jamie will. And he will get first class training for a career that will stand him in good stead and provide him with a good income for the rest of his life if he needs it.' She gave a humourless laugh. 'Which he won't, because when your mother dies he will inherit this house, the estate, everything. You will end up having to toady to some man in order to survive,' she said bitterly. 'Just as I have to do to rich people.'

It was enough to make anyone bitter, but what worried Clementina more than the property or the money was the denial of her individuality and the free development of her potential. She wanted to be independent, to travel and see things.

In other words, she wanted and was determined to have the same freedom and opportunities as men. Sometimes she dared not dwell on the unfairness that existed between men and women – it made her hate the male sex so much.

But there was something else too. In a mixed company she could argue with any man present and tell him a thing or two and no mistake. But if she ever found herself alone with a man, no matter how nice or mild or inoffensive he might be, sooner or later she experienced a surprising undercurrent of fear. It was only a tremor, which never came anywhere near the surface. She never allowed it to do so. Contemptuous and impatient with any kind of weakness in herself, she tossed her head in disdain at the image of the timorous, dependent and fundamentally weak female upon whom society smiled so indulgently. She was not timorous; she was not weak; she was afraid of nothing and no one. She kept bullying herself into believing this and for the most part she knew it to be true.

The tremor was always stilled and quickly forgotten. Only the bitterness and the sense of injustice was allowed to remain.

CHAPTER THIRTY-SEVEN

Clementina walked down the hill to Bathgate despite the wintry darkness. Her mother was out with the carriage to a family dinner at Gilbert's. The purpose of this particular dinner was to get down to some of the practical details – such as guest lists – of the coming season of dances and parties that the ladies of the family were concocting between them for Clementina's benefit.

'It's better that you should not be there, dear,' Lorianna had told her. 'You would just confuse the issue and annoy Gilbert with your foolish talk.' Then she had tried to impart some of the motherly advice that she apparently felt it was now her duty to administer. 'You really must try to be more circumspect in gentlemen's company, darling. Even with your own family. It never pays to upset any man; you only cause harm to yourself in the end.'

'Do at least try to be tactful,' Lorianna was always urging. 'Men don't like to be contradicted. Listen to them nicely, even if you don't agree with them. And if you don't agree with them, keep your opinions to yourself.'

When her mother spoke like this it made Clementina feel sick with anger. Of course men disliked being contradicted – the spoiled, selfish bores. Why should she listen to them nicely – or in any other way? What had they to commend them except their selfishness? And why should she pander to it?

Now as she walked to Bathgate, the night was alive with creepings, hootings, bleatings and rustlings. Nearby a stream tinkled through the heather, but Clementina heard nothing but the thudding of her own anger in her ears. She walked purposefully and fearlessly. The countryside at night had the familiarity of long years and the only thing over which she exercised some caution was the placing of her feet on the rough stones of the Drumcross Road. Now the road dipped steeply down and she could see the polka dots of light in the Bathgate streets below. Soon she began to discern the faint flutter of candles in house windows and the occasional winking of carriage lanterns like moving stars.

She was going to a meeting in the Co-op Hall in Jarvie Street and glad of the chance to hear a rousing talk that she had no doubt would take men down a peg or two. She had seen the advert a few days ago in the *Courier* and she and all her friends had been absolutely thrilled about it. Two quite famous suffragists who had been speaking in Glasgow were breaking their journey at Bathgate en route for Edinburgh. It would be most interesting to see what kind of audience attended – this would be a good indication of the extent of support for the suffragist movement in Bathgate and West Lothian. The notice had apparently been in the *Scotsman* as well, and so the news would be more widely read than by people in the Bathgate area only. She was meeting her friends Millicent, Betsy, Eva, Kitty and Agnes inside the Co-op Hall. Whoever got there first was supposed to keep seats for the other five.

Clementina was becoming more excited with every step, although she was not the type of person to indulge in much emotion and certainly not to allow it to get the upper hand. She strode out smartly, her feet making crisp cracking sounds on the loose stones and her skirts swishing. Her three-quarter coat was fastened with eight buttons that neatly nipped in the navy serge at the waist and smoothed it down over her hips. She would like to have worn one of the new style blouses with high round collars and tie like a man's, but her mother refused to allow the dressmaker to make her one. The way her mother was interfering with her freedom just now was most annoying. It was only because she wanted to get rid of her of course – Clementina knew that perfectly well.

The plans her mother was busying herself with all of a sudden were not for what she called 'your "Coming Out", dear.' It was for her 'getting out'. The unusual interest in her clothes and the long talks she was having with the dressmaker who regularly visited Blackwood House did not indicate any interest in Clementina, except as an object to attract some man who would take her away from Blackwood House forever.

The collar of the blouse she had been forced to wear was boned at the neck right up to just below her ears and edged with a frill that tickled her ear-lobes and chin. Similar frills protruded from under the sleeves of her coat and also annoyed her. She was not a 'frilly person'. The dressmaker was at the moment working on another blouse which, although having lace inserts and rows of pleats and tucks, at least did not have frills. Unfortunately it had not been ready for wearing tonight.

Clementina was having the same problem about hats, preferring the wind tugging at her hair and the freedom to concentrate on more important things. But her mother had become surprisingly emotional about hats; it was the nearest she had ever seen her mother to losing her temper and actually becoming violent. She had become so upset in fact that she had rung for Mrs Musgrove, which had annoyed Clementina as much as anything. For a long time after her father died, Mrs Musgrove had prevented her from seeing Lorianna. She had been only a child at the time and had not understood; it was strange, frightening time and she had wanted so desperately to be with her mother, even for only the occasional half-hour in the sitting-room. But Mrs Musgrove always seemed to be hovering about, ready to bar her way. Once, in desperation, she had actually struggled with the housekeeper and could never forget the iron grip of the mittened hands and the painful bruises they had left on her arms.

So far as wearing a hat was concerned, her mother had said, 'You will do as you are told or I will have you locked in your room until you see sense.' Her eyes looked wild, almost crazed and her wide mouth had such a venomous twist that Clementina was quite taken aback. 'No friends. No books. Nothing. You will just sit there and contemplate your disgraceful behaviour until you learn to be more obedient and respectful towards your mother.'

Then Mrs Musgrove had arrived and led Lorianna to a chair before ordering Clementina from the room. Her mother had sat there and never raised a murmur of protest when a servant spoke so harshly to the daughter of the house.

Clementina had been tempted to sulk but then thought better of it. She needed to get out and around and see her friends, for they had much to discuss and plan. So she capitulated about the hats and even apologised to her mother, because when she came to think about it, she had been arguing rather a lot with her lately. That was only because they had so little in common. Of course her mother was so terribly old-fashioned. And so weak! Much as she loved Lorianna, she couldn't help despising her a little too. It was bad enough allowing herself to be dominated by her husband – but by a servant!

Her mother had accepted her apology with good grace, but Clementina could see that when she turned away she was trembling and Mrs Musgrove had put a heavy hand on her shoulder and gripped it until the trembling stopped. It occurred to Clementina in surprise that her mother was in fact an extremely emotional woman under her normally crystal-cool and graceful exterior.

So, she was wearing a hat. It was the plainest she could lay her hands on – a wide-brimmed navy felt, decorated with a white ribbon and two white roses to match her blouse. She could admire large curling feathers, great clusters of fruit and flowers and yards of frothy veiling on the hats that her mother or her friends wore, but she somehow felt ridiculous wearing anything so fancy her-

313

self. As soon as her mother and the milliner turned their backs, she denuded the hats that had been made for her of all such extravagances. Once Lorianna, seeing her wearing a black felt with only a white grosgrain ribbon to relieve its plainness, had accused her of looking like a common working woman. But Clementina didn't care. As she tried to explain to her mother, she just wasn't a person for any kind of fuss or fol-de-rols. And that, as far as she was concerned, was that.

Now she crossed to the right side of the road, past Torpichen Street, then Marjorybanks Street, Gideon Street and round into the deeply shadowed Jarvie Street where gas-lamps skirted themselves with misty grey circles. The clock on the Parish Church tower opposite the Co-op gloomily struck seven times, the sound echoing sadly over the old gravestones. A group of women, some of them heavily veiled, were talking in low apprehensive voices outside the door as if trying to pluck up courage to go in. Nearby a few working men were gathered, all dressed in caps, mufflers and shapeless jackets and trousers. Clementina marched past them and then past the ladies in the door and straight up the stairs into the hall. As she mounted the stairs, she heard the door creak open again and then the nervous whispering of the ladies as they followed her up.

The hall, at the end of the dimly lit corridor past the Co-op offices, was full, mostly with women. Only a handful of men were present, one of them being the Reverend John Ainslic, a gentleman with a snowy white moustache and a thatch of hair parted in the middle who was acting as chairman.

Millicent and the other girls were already seated at the front and they waved to her to join them. Millicent was looking absolutely stunning in a soft-collared blouse, a broad grosgrain tie and a hat in the style of a man's exaggerated tweed cap.

'Not too bad a turn-out,' Clementina said once she was settled. 'Especially for a dark winter's night.'

'I'm just afraid there are going to be more,' Eva said grimly.

Clementina looked round at her in surprise. 'The bigger the audience the better, surely:'

'Not necessarily.' Eva was a tall, lanky girl with a fur tippet at her neck and fur bobbles on her hat. 'It was advertised in the *Scotsman*, you see, and my brother and all his friends saw it.'

'You mean they're going to turn up?'

'Maybe a lot more. But I'm hoping it was just a joke.'

'What was?'

'You know Aleck's at Edinburgh University?'

'Yes.'

'Well, a notice was being passed round. It said: "University Anti-Suffrage Society Unlimited. Supporters travel by 6 pm train to Bathgate. Bring your own hatchets and battle-axes." '

'Oh, for goodness sake,' Clementina rolled her eyes. 'Your brother and his undergraduate friends are really infantile. This is another example of their childish pranks . . .'

The Reverend Ainslie had risen, smiling, to his feet. He cleared his throat. 'Ladies and er . . . gentlemen, my appearance in the chair is not an affair of ornament or meaningless embellishment of the proceedings . . .'

Suddenly there was a noise like distant thunder from somewhere along the corridor. The hall reverberated discernibly under their feet and the ladies in the audience moved uneasily, stealing little glances over their shoulders.

The Chairman also looked worried as the noise grew louder and nearer and began to sound like the clatter of many boots. Nevertheless he continued '. . . I appear as an avowed advocate of women's rights. There is not, in my view, a single social, political or theological problem which can rightly be stated where woman is not the fundamental factor of it. To ignore her presence, to leave her out of the consideration is to present the play of *Hamlet*

315

without the Prince of Denmark . . .'

The hall door burst open at this point and a crowd of young men streamed in from the corridor in a gust of noise and hilarity.

The chairman raised his voice in an attempt to be heard above the racket as men clambered over the wooden forms and jostled each other for seats, yelling and shouting and singing: 'Vote for Edinburgh University!' 'Down with suffragette spinsters!' 'All the nice girls love a student . . .'! '. . . What we want in society is less caste, less convention, more freedom and more rationality of outlook . . .' 'All the nice girls love a spree . . .'

The Reverend Ainslie mopped his brow in obvious distress, but the two women speakers sitting on either side of him at the table betrayed only a look of boredom and disgust. Clementina felt absolutely furious. Already there must be about a hundred men in the hall and they were now singing 'Lead kindly light . . .' which was obviously meant as an insult to the minister.

When she turned round to glare at the intruders she noticed an elderly lady sitting behind her, trembling with a handkerchief pressed to her mouth and tears in her eyes.

'. . . So far as votes for women are concerned,' the chairman pressed on desperately, 'it is purely and simply a matter of logic . . .'

A dog chain flew through the air, narrowly missing both the old lady and Clementina.

'Do you need a chain, minister?' a male voice yelled.

There was shocked silence on the platform but, unable to contain herself any longer, Clementina stood up and, facing the riotous men, called out in a loud clear voice, 'No, he doesn't, but *you* need a rattle. Why don't you go back to the nursery where you belong and take your infantile friends with you?'

Eva tugged at her coat and forced her to sit down again. 'Don't provoke them,' she said. 'There's no telling what they might do.'

316

'Why shouldn't I provoke them? They're provoking me!'

She felt as she used to do when the village boys tormented her. Action dispelled fear and now, as then, she had the urge to dash in with fists flying, not giving herself time to feel afraid, refusing to be intimidated or defeated. Before she had the chance to do anything, however, someone sent a missile crashing through one of the windows and her friends cried out in alarm, Eva clinging to her all the more fiercely. The loud explosion was followed by another and another, accompanied by the light tinkling sound of glass. Then there was the thunder of benches being upturned. A gas-mantle was broken, then a second, creating dangerous pools of darkness.

'Let's teach them a lesson!' someone bawled.

The Reverend Ainslie immediately called out above the din, 'I declare the meeting closed!'

Then he hastily proceeded to shepherd the two speakers from the platform and out of the hall, not without considerable protest on their part. The men originally in the audience took their cue from the minister and, using themselves as shields, began helping the other ladies out of the dark shadowy hall amid much jeering and jostling. To her extreme annoyance Clementina found herself among those being, as far as she was concerned, forcibly ejected. Never before in her life had she felt so infuriated. It ought to be the students who were being forced to leave, not the speakers or those in the audience who had come to hear them.

'Votes for Women!' she yelled in a last burst of defiance as she was rushed bodily out of the door.

She had to clutch at her skirts to keep herself from tripping on them as the man who had a grip on her arm was propelling her at such a speed along the corridor and down the stairs. She could hear the stamp of angry feet close behind them, but her companion managed by dint of sheer agility and speed to get in front of the crush of

317

people who had escaped from the hall ahead of them.

Out in the street he asked, 'Where's your carriage?'

'Let go of me!' she demanded. 'I didn't come in a carriage.'

'You live nearby?'

'No, up the hills at Blackwood House.'

'Good God! Come on!'

'What are you doing?'

'At the moment I'm getting you out of a dangerous situation. What I should be doing is putting you over my knee and spanking you. Women's suffrage! What next!'

Before she knew what had happened he had hoisted her on to a gig and they were racing along Jarvie Street and up the pitch-black Drumcross Road. It was obvious from the arrogant tone of his voice what he thought and his all-too-male attitude made her speechless with anger.

'Does your mother know you walked this road alone in the dark tonight?'

'That's none of your business,' she snapped.

'I'm making it my business.'

She was glad of the pure, icy air fanning her cheeks. The man was only a bulky shadow sitting next to her on the wooden seat, but she could detect the resolution in his voice. Her most sensible course, she decided, was not to say any more. So she just sat very prim and straight-backed, white-gloved hands folded on lap, trying her very best to ignore him.

CHAPTER THIRTY-EIGHT

'It will mean a lot of extra work, won't it?' Lorianna said worriedly.

Mrs Musgrove sat opposite her like a column of darkness on the pink damask settee.

'I have always managed in the past, madam,' she said.

'You don't foresee any problems, then?'

Mrs Musgrove's mouth inclined to one side. 'Not with the staff.'

'Oh?' Lorianna enquired, suddenly cool. 'And what am I supposed to infer from that remark?'

'It has crossed my mind that you may find Miss Clementina will present a problem.'

'Miss Clementina,' Lorianna said, 'has always presented a problem.'

'Yes, madam.' Mrs Musgrove's eyes lowered to study the notebook on her lap, leaving Lorianna in a wake of unease.

'You mean a specific problem at the moment?'

'Yes, madam.'

'If you are referring to these suffragette meetings Clementina and her friends have been organising in Bathgate, I know all about them. Imagine having the temerity to even consider getting up and speaking in public, especially after what happened at that meeting when the English suffragettes were here. I don't understand young girls nowadays. Mrs Price-Gordon is dreadfully worried about Millicent getting insulted and abused if she gets up on the platform. I'm concerned about Clementina too, of course,' she added hastily, flushing in annoyance at the housekeeper's sharp-eyed, sardonic glance. 'And needless to say I have warned her against the dangers of this suffragist bee she has in her bonnet just now, and especially about speaking in public. I have told her that ladies just don't do that. But you know Clementina, Mrs Musgrove. There's an unladylike . . .' she hesitated in genuine bewilderment '. . . tenacity about her. Where she has it from, I simply cannot imagine. She is not at all like me — or her father, for that matter. I suspect she will revel in any trouble that might arise at her meetings. I can't help feeling sorry for the people who try to oppose her.'

Mrs Musgrove's ironic smile once more edged across her mouth and Lorianna said, 'You don't agree?'

'Oh yes, madam.'

'Well, then . . .'

'The specific problem I was thinking of was how Miss Clementina would conduct herself towards the men you have invited to your social gatherings.'

Lorianna shook her head perplexedly. 'I just don't know what to do about her.'

'Perhaps if you tried to give more thought to why Miss Clementina feels as she does towards the male sex . . .'

'Do you think Miss Viners has anything to do with the way Clementina is?' interrupted Lorianna. 'I have always thought she was filling the girl's head with far too much book learning and strange ideas. Do you think I should get rid of her? Now that I come to think of it,' she continued, not giving the housekeeper a chance to reply, 'why should I keep paying for a governess? Clementina is too old for the school-room now. And anyway, she doesn't need further education if she is going to get married.'

'I doubt if Miss Viners can be blamed for Miss Clementina's rebellious nature. I cannot say I blame her for rebelling on this occasion — why should she want anything to do with men? They will only mean trouble for her, just as they meant trouble for you. And they will mean trouble for you again if you're not careful.'

'If you are referring to Mr Stirling, Mrs Musgrove — although you have no right . . .'

Mrs Musgrove raised an eyebrow. 'You have a short memory.'

There was something in the sharp, straight stare that frightened Lorianna. The housekeeper's eyes reminded her of the quick black eyes of the crows which used to cause so much damage to her father's fields. Her father had waged ceaseless war against them, but could never defeat them or chase them away no matter how hard he tried.

'Mr Stirling is my friend, that's all.'

Lorianna turned away to gaze vaguely out of the sitting-room window, her yellow dress like a dazzle of sunshine against the dull backcloth of the cloudy day. She fingered the sparkling crystals looped across her neck and bosom.

'I still think it's time Miss Viners' term of employment ceased. She has been here a long time and I appreciate her good qualities, but she is no longer required. I shall speak to her today and give her notice. And an excellent character, of course.'

'What about your son?'

Lorianna whirled round, transformed into a beacon of enthusiasm. 'Oh, he's perfectly happy with Nanny Hawthorne. She looks after him so well, does she not? He won't require a tutor for years yet and then later he must go to one of the best schools we can find. I shall get Mr Stirling to advise me about that when the time comes. Eventually, of course, he will go to University. I am sure he's going to be terribly clever. Already he shows signs of an exceptional intelligence, don't you think? And such a strong independent spirit!'

Mrs Musgrove, mouth tip-tilted in the expression which Lorianna could never quite define as being a calm smile or a secret sarcasm, replied 'Yes, madam.'

Lorianna was relieved when the housekeeper left. And yet some dregs of uneasiness remained. Sometimes she thought the woman was inhuman; Mrs Musgrove's complete disregard and distaste for men didn't seem natural.

Seldom free of the terrible need for physical contact with a man, the madness of Lorianna's grief for Robert had exhausted itself. The wildness of her distress had petered out and she only suffered the occasional spasm of anguish on the rack of memory.

But her body still cried out, thirstily, hungrily, for loving. She had learned of course to keep such emotions decently hidden and in check within the conventional armour of ladylike behaviour and pursuits.

She was devoted to her son and savoured every moment she spent with him – touching him, holding him, kissing him, rubbing her cheek like a purring cat against him.

When she was not with Jamie, she threw all her energies into good works. She took posies of blooms and sweetmeats, home-made preserves or other little delicacies to any woman on the estate who was sick or in childbed. She kept a record of every child on the estate and every Christmas she travelled round in the carriage with a little gift for each. Many of these gifts, like miniature rag dolls, embroidered handkerchiefs or pincushions, she made herself, the work conscientiously filling the long winter hours.

Then of course there were the reciprocal visits of Gilbert and Hilda, and Malcolm and Mary Ann who had produced a sweet little girl. Not such a darling child as Jamie, of course, but a nice little girl nevertheless. One of the gifts Malcolm had given her for Christmas was a beautiful family photogreaph of himself, Mary Ann and little Victoria, taken at Townsend's at the corner of Whitburn Road and South Bridge Street. It was there she always bought her sheet music and had several times taken Jamie to be photographed.

Thinking of her son, she glanced lovingly at the ornate silver-framed photographs crowding the table near where she was sitting: Jamie as an infant in her arms; Jamie in his first short gown; Jamie standing like a little man in his sailor suit. She lifted up the most recent photograph to study it more closely. Even at five years of age there was a serious 'I'm my own man' kind of look in the child's eyes which reminded her of Robert. She kissed the cool glass before replacing the photograph on the table.

She decided she must take Jamie to Townsend's again very soon and have a picture taken of him in his new kilt and tartan tammy. Gilbert had made her laugh recently when she, Nanny Hawthorne and Jamie had visited his house for tea. Jamie had been wearing his kilt and bonnet but as Nanny had put it, '. . . very reluctantly, to say the least.'

Gilbert had said, 'Today he reminds me of a thistle . . .'

They had all laughed except Jamie, who stood looking more prickly than ever but to her, at least, absolutely adorable.

Gilbert and Hilda, who had twins – a girl and a boy – seemed very fond of Jamie. 'He will be a great help to his uncle Gilbert in the factory one day,' Gilbert liked to prophesy.

Lorianna was worriedly hesitant, having no idea what factory management entailed. She had never set foot in any factory in her life far less their own, and she didn't want Jamie to be pushed into work in which he might not feel happy.

'Do you think that's the sort of thing he should do, Gilbert? Would it be a congenial vocation for him?'

'The family business? Why not? You're surely not thinking, dear step-mamma, of trying to turn him into a namby-pamby creature like Malcolm? Putting Jamie into the cloth? No, never! Our Jamie will prosper best in the factory alongside me and my Gordon.'

'Oh well,' Lorianna smiled, 'there are quite a few years to go before he needs to do anything. Except acquire a good education, of course.'

Thinking of Jamie made her remember that she had promised to take him down to Bathgate today to give him a glimpse of the cattle market and the shows across the road from the ring in which the cattle and sheep were sold. The last time she had done this more by accident than intent. She had taken Jamie to Bathgate to be fitted for new shoes and when she had set out in the victoria with Jacobs at the reins she had forgotten that it was market day. At first, seeing a leisurely stir of cows being herded up the hills from the market, she felt annoyance at the delay they would cause to the victoria's progress. But on seeing the interest and delight they gave to Jamie her reaction quickly changed to one of pleasure. Anything that made Jamie happy gave happiness to her. How he had laughed and clapped his hands in excitement and actually tried to lean from the victoria and endeavour to touch the animals. He had not been at all afraid and she had felt so proud of him. She had explained about the market and cattle-ring where the animals were paraded and bought by the farmers and then herded up the hills — as often as not by some Bathgate boys to whom the farmer paid a few pennies.

Jamie had been fascinated and she was pleased and flattered by his rapt attention. Then he had pleaded to be taken to see the cattle-ring. She had eventually given in and ordered Jacobs to take the victoria as near to it as possible.

Now Lorianna was looking forward to today's outing and was just about to ring for her maid to discuss what she should wear when the sitting-room door opened and Clementina entered. The sight of her immediately dispelled any pleasurable emotion.

'Yes, dear?' Lorianna enquired in a carefully controlled voice.

When Clementina shut the door, came purposefully into the room and sat down, Lorianna groaned mentally. 'What now?' she thought, detecting a hint of desperation in Clementina's emerald eyes. But of course the girl was always so earnest it was difficult to be sure.

'Mother, it's not always possible for me to have the use of the victoria or the brougham and I am sure you don't want me to walk down to Bathgate. You have told me before how unladylike you believe it is to indulge in such long hikes, especially on public roads.'

'What have you been up to now?' Lorianna asked automatically.

'Nothing, Mother. But I do think that I ought to have a bicycle.'

'A bicycle?' Lorianna gasped, forgetting her self-control in the unexpected horror of the moment.

'There is absolutely nothing wrong in having a bicycle, Mother. It's the modern way for young ladies to get around nowadays. Everybody has one.'

'I'm sure every lady has *not* got a bicycle, Clementina.' Lorinna pressed one hand to her bosom in an effort to contain her palpitating fluster. 'I can just imagine you flying around on one of these dreadful contraptions, your ankles showing and your hat being blown off in the wind.' She closed her eyes in an effort to shut out the picture.

'It's not like that at all, Mother. It's very dignified,' Clementina persisted. 'And I can assure you that all my friends *do* have bicycles. Cycling clubs are now the rage.'

'Quite apart from any other consideration, Clementina, your friends are all older than you.'

'Surely, Mother, if I am old enough to get married – as you obviously believe I am – I am old enough to have a bicycle?'

Lorianna leaned back on the cushions, wishing with all her heart that Gilbert or Malcolm or John would suddenly appear to deal with Clementina and relieve her of the exhausting worry. 'It's not just a question of age,' she began.

'Well, what is it a question of, Mother?'

'I am doing my best, Clementina, to teach you how to

325

be ladylike, so that you will one day attract a gentleman who will wish to devote the rest of his life to protecting you and taking care of you. I don't want you to end up an old maid. You won't always have me, you know. Or even Gilbert or Malcolm.'

'Two points occur to me, Mother, apropos of what you have just said. That is, if we leave aside for the moment the whole question of the other, and to my mind more fulfilling, roles in life that a woman could and should have apart from marriage . . .'

Lorianna's gaze wandered helplessly around as if seeking some means of escape, but ignoring her mother's apparent lack of interest Clementina pressed on '. . . One, the opportunity to meet gentlemen and two, being attractive to them. Firstly, I must say, Mother, that you are somewhat out of touch with modern thoughts and habits. Being a member of a cycling club is an excellent way of meeting gentlemen. Two, being able to cycle is nowadays an attractive accomplishment much admired by modern young men. So, in effect, looking at the question from your point of view, the fact is that to own a bicycle would enhance my marriage prospects rather than diminish them.'

Lorianna had noticed the time – she was going to be late for her outing with Jamie. She rose in panic.

'You are making me late for an important engagement with all your silly talk.'

She had just reached the door when Clementina said doggedly, '*Can* I have a bicycle, Mother?'

Sparks began exploding in Lorianna's head and she had to close her eyes and cling to the door handle for support.

'We'll see,' she managed to say by some miracle of self-control before escaping from the room.

CHAPTER THIRTY-NINE

Later that evening Lorianna had barely swallowed her first spoonful of Cook's special orange and tomato soup and was just settling down to enjoy its fragrant bouquet and delicate flavour when Clementina said, 'I have seen a bicycle in Bathgate that would suit me perfectly, Mother.'

Lorianna went on spooning soup as if by merely ignoring Clementina she would cease to exist.

'I could show it to you tomorrow, Mother. We could go down together in the victoria. I would be very grateful to have your opinion.'

Lorianna dabbed at the corner of her mouth with a pristine white napkin. 'You know perfectly well, Clementina, that I know nothing about bicycles and so could give you no opinion at all. I would be genuinely interested to know, however, what their attraction is.'

'Well, in the first place,' Clementina warmed to the subject, happy and excited to be sitting alone with her mother in the dining-room for the very first time, 'I need one as a handy method of transportation . . .'

'All right,' Lorianna interrupted. 'Now this is what I will do. I will instruct Jacobs to purchase a nice little gig and he can press one of the riding horses into service, so that you can have it at your disposal as often as you want.'

'All I want is a bicycle, Mother.'

Lorianna gave up trying to concentrate on her soup. 'But why, darling? I honestly don't understand. A gig would be so much more comfortable. Perhaps we could even get one with a hood?'

'Comfort is not the only criterion in life. I enjoy new and challenging things and I believe in healthy exercise in the fresh air.'

'Why can't you just be content with walking for exercise? And you play tennis and have learned to ride now.'

'I have just told you, Mother, that I enjoy new and challenging things and all my friends have bicycles. Why won't you believe me?'

'Oh, I can believe that all your suffragette friends will have one.'

'Well, then . . .'

Lorianna signalled for the maid to remove her soup plate. 'It's all quite beyond me.'

Clementina finished every last drop of her soup with obvious relish before remarking, 'That's because you are getting old, Mother.'

Lorianna couldn't help laughing, 'Clementina, I am only thirty-three.'

'Thirty-three!' Clementina echoed in a mixture of sympathy and horror as if the number had been ninety-three.

'You will reach that age soon enough yourself, dear.'

Her daughter shrugged. 'All the more reason to enjoy life while I can, I suppose.' Adding as an afterthought, 'And that means getting a bicycle.'

Lorianna waited until the maid had served the rabbit in tarragon with creamed potatoes before saying, 'What about the challenge of marriage and motherhood?'

'That's not a challenge.'

Lorianna raised her eyebrows. 'Oh, don't you think so? I can assure you from the experience and wisdom of my great age that it most certainly is.'

'Well, it's not the kind of challenge I need. *I* need a bicycle, Mother, not a man.'

'Oh, Clementina!' she laughed helplessly this time. 'Really darling, I wish you wouldn't say such ridiculous things.'

Clementina stiffened indignantly. 'What's so ridiculous about it? It's a perfectly true statement of fact.'

'You have never had a gentleman friend and that's to be expected because up to now you have been too young. But now it's only natural that you should at least show some interest. Aren't you looking forward to meeting all the nice young men I am inviting to your first dance?'

'No.'

Lorianna stared at her daughter curiously. 'Don't you ever think of men at all?'

'Not really.'

Now it was Clementina's turn to be curious. 'You were married to father at my age, you said?'

'Yes.'

'Do you ever feel you have missed a lot in life, Mother? Your own freedom and individuality, for a start. I mean, you have never had the chance to develop the real you, have you? You have always lived through a man. And now you're so set in your ideas and ways that you're not able to change.'

A soft dreaminess drifted over Lorianna's face. 'If it's the right man, if you really love him, freedom has no meaning. If you love a person you want to become part of him, merge into him, become one with him in spirit, in mind, in body.'

'Is that how you felt about father?' Clementina asked with interest.

'Get on with your dinner,' Lorianna's words were suddenly as sharp as icicles. 'Your food is getting ruined. If you must sit at table with me, please keep quiet and at least try not to spoil my meal.'

Clementina lowered her head and pretended to be interested in the contents of her plate, but she was having to struggle to keep her breath even and not betray any sign of the unexpected distress she felt. She had been so happy for a few minutes, imagining she was getting close to her mother. Even when they had been arguing it had been a new and wonderful experience.

Lorianna was unable to prevent her eyes straying to the

329

bent head and heaving shoulders. It was unbearably pathetic to see how the girl loved her and could be so easily hurt by her. She longed to draw the still, silently struggling spirit close. Clementina was her own flesh and blood and at moments like this she knew without a doubt that she loved her daughter with more passion and tenderness than Clementina would ever be capable of. Yet even now she could not bring herself to touch her.

All she could manage to say was, 'I'm sorry, dear; I did not mean to sound harsh, it's just my nerves. I did warn you that I needed peace and quiet at mealtimes.'

'It's all right, Mother,' Clementina said, keeping her head down but starting to energetically cut up her food, 'I won't talk any more . . . except – *can* I have a bicycle?'

CHAPTER FORTY

The bicycle proved a great joy and the freedom it gave Clementina was most satisfying to say the least. Up and down and around the hills she pedalled with great concentration. She became a familiar figure busily whirring about the streets of Bathgate dressed in her pleated skirt, neat white blouse, long tailored jacket and no-nonsense hat perched on her cushion of glorious blonde hair.

At first she had thought that time might lie heavily on her once Miss Viners had left and no more hours had to be spent in the school-room. Now, on the contrary, she never seemed to have enough time for all she wanted to do and see – and of course, as she was still relegated to the tower house for most of the day, alone and unsupervised, she had more freedom than many of her friends.

She had known every corner of the countryside around Blackwood House since her childhood, but there was so much of West Lothian that she had not seen. It was an area, she soon discovered, of great diversity.

The Bathgate hills divided the north from the south; good low-lying agricultural land from high moorland rich in wildlife. Despite misty mornings, showery days and keen winds tugging at her skirts and hat, she and her friends explored the hills when they could, often with picnic lunches packed in baskets attached to their handlebars. Hills like the Cairnpapple, which commanded one of the most spectacular views in West Lothian. If the day was clear, the panoramic view stretched from sea to sea across Scotland, ranging from Goat Fell on the Island of Arran off the west coast, to May Island off the east coast.

Clementina and her friends enjoyed the scenery. Bumpy rides over rough roads elicited many a squeal of laughter from them. They relished the challenge of steep hill paths, and were captivated by the tranquillity and historic interest of villages like Torpichen. But their greatest joy, what they thrilled to most was their long discussions about *The Cause* and what they planned to do for it. At every opportunity — when they stopped to admire a view, or to have a breather, or to eat their picnic lunch or tea — they plunged into long and enthusiastic discussions and arguments.

Eva tended to view the militancy of Mrs Pankhurst and her Women's Social and Political Union with some trepidation. Eva was a bit anaemic and tired quickly. Even her eyes looked as if they were sinking with exhaustion into the shadowy hollows of her face. She also became out of breath sooner than the others when out cycling. It was hard for her to keep up with them for long and soon the cry would echo back to her on the wind, 'Come on, Eva! Put a spurt on! You can do it if you try!' Sometimes, if she got too far behind, they would say, 'Oh, let's stop for a bit and give poor old Eva a chance to catch up.'

About the Women's Social and Political Union, Eva said, 'It's definitely been organised on military lines, Clementina. She's calling for "volunteers for the front for danger work", and she talks about "the rank and file" and "raids" and other such army phraseology.'

'No one,' Clementina pointed out, 'has ever got the vote except at the risk of something like revolution.'

'What good is it doing?' Eva had countered. 'Just look at the awful publicity the Cause and everyone connected with it is getting in the papers. It always was sneering and belittling, but now they are accusing suffragettes of being lesbians and saying that we ought to be shot.'

'Some of the suffragettes are lesbians,' Betsy chipped in impatiently. 'So what? That's not the point.'

'The point is they are always trying to discredit us,' said Eva. 'I don't believe I have ever read a sympathetic word in any of the papers. Not ever! And just think of the amount that has been written about the suffragists and suffragettes during the past two or three years. Practically every day there has been some news item.'

'Exactly,' Clementina agreed. 'Before 1905 when Christabel Pankhurst and Annie Kenney got arrested for heckling Churchill at that meeting – and incidentally can you imagine a man being arrested just for shouting out 'Will the Liberal government give men the vote?' – before that meeting we got no publicity at all. The press completely ignored anything the suffragettes said or did and nobody knew anything about the cause, although lots of women had been working conscientiously for it for years. It is the Pankhursts who have brought it for the first time to the notice of the general public.'

Kitty, who tended to be very excitable, jumped up and down and clapped her hands. 'Now nothing can hold us back.'

'Anyway,' Betsy said, 'it has to be run like a military campaign because it's a war and all that dirty propaganda just goes to prove it.' The lively and intelligent daughter of a gloomy widower whom she seemed destined to look after for the rest of her life, Betsy welcomed a war or an earthquake or indeed anything that might alleviate the boredom and frustration of her life.

'That's right,' Clementina agreed. 'It's a war against men.'

Eva, however, could not be won over to sympathise with the Pankhursts' methods and leaned more towards the break-away Women's Freedom League led by Mrs Billington-Greig and Mrs Despard. She had been in agreement with Clementina and the others about organising meetings in Bathgate, but since the terrifying experience in the Co-op Hall she had lost some of her enthusiasm for the idea. In fact she had been having nightmares ever

333

since that evening and the pallor of her thin face and the hollows under her eyes looked more pronounced than usual as a result.

'You do still believe in the Cause?' Clementina always liked to establish the facts and know exactly where everyone stood.

'Oh yes,' Eva said with renewed fervour. She had once longed to study medicine, but it was her 'couldn't-care-less' brothers who had automatically been sent to Edinburgh University. She would never be allowed to follow any profession and for no other reason than that she was a woman. 'Definitely!'

'Well, that's all that matters,' said Clementina.

'I'm not so sure. I mean, I sometimes wonder if I have the right qualities.'

'Of course you have!' Clementina assured her. 'Anyway, we have agreed that we're not going to be a branch of the WSPU or the Freedom League. We're starting a West Lothian Justice for Women Group, and we need not advertise any of our meetings in the *Scotsman*. We'll just make hand-bills, and notices to stick up in local shop windows. That way we shall only attract local people. It was idiotic students from Edinburgh who caused all the trouble, don't forget!'

Agnes, who was very petite and ladylike and wore a protective veil over her hat and face, said, 'At our meetings we're aiming to speak to ladies of the area and make them see the truth and fairness of the Cause, so that they will join us in sisterhood . . .'

'Do you not think any local gentlemen will appear?' Eva asked.

Betsy replied for Agnes. 'Let's hope at least they will give us a fair hearing if they do. That's all we need. If we put forward a good sound argument, surely everybody with any intelligence will see reason eventually?'

Clementina agreed that it was certainly a case of persevering. Nothing, she had found, came easily in life. They had eventually managed to hire the Co-op Hall and to distribute the hand-bills and now she was on her way to Agnes's house in Bathgate for afternoon tea and a last-minute discussion with the rest of the girls prior to the public meeting scheduled for the following day.

Although she revelled in cycling out in the company of her friends, Clementina also savoured times like this when she pedalled along on her own and had time to think and plan and dream. She too believed in the rightness of 'the Cause' and was determined if necessary to devote her whole life to seeing justice done to members of her own sex and to improving their lot. People like Betsy, for instance, who had a quick intelligent mind but who, like so many others, had been denied the opportunity of using it to full advantage. Her duty, her father told her, was at home looking after him. And if she tried to argue with him or disobey him (which she often did), he punished her by stopping her allowance, refusing her the use of the carriage or any of the horses. On one occasion he had humiliated her by ordering her maid to lock all her clothes in the cellar and then give him the key. She had been unable to get dressed for weeks, and had been forced even to eat in her bedroom. And of course, he never allowed her to have any friends to the house. There was not the slightest chance of Betsy going to University or of doing anything that would be personally fulfilling. Betsy and the others were lucky if they managed to escape from their homes for their cycling runs, which like their occasional evening rendezvous could only be managed as a rule if their respective parents were out somewhere and unaware what they were up to.

Often Betsy groaned, 'So many long empty days, so many weary evenings that never seem to end. For years I have sat watching the drawing-room clock, thinking it would never reach the ten. And just imagine, I have another thirty or forty years of this to endure.'

Unless of course they managed to get the vote and have a say in changing the laws and the whole concept of women's role in society, thought Clementina.

335

Suddenly her bicycle swerved towards a ditch as the handlebars almost jerked from Clementina's hands. Then she heard a hissing noise from the front wheel. She dismounted to examine the bicycle and discovered that it had a puncture.

'Dash!' she spoke aloud in her annoyance. In her rush to get out she had omitted to bring her puncture outfit and book of instructions. Now she would have to either wheel the bicycle down to Bathgate or leave it here propped against the bushes until she returned from Agnes's house. Either way it meant a long walk and she would be late. Standing with arms akimbo and hat slightly askew, she didn't hear the gig approach until it was nearly upon her and then she started in surprise.

'Hello, in trouble again?' the man at the reins enquired. His words had a suble inflection of humorous incredulity which annoyed Clementina.

'What do you mean "again"?'

His face was very tanned and dominated by a cleft chin and eyes that jabbed darts of mockery down at her.

'Votes for women!'

She flushed with anger at the derision in his voice. 'Oh, it's *you*.'

'You don't sound very pleased to see me.'

Clementina straightened her hat and tidied herself as efficiently as she could. 'Should I be pleased to see you?'

He shrugged. 'Here I am, in a position to rescue you again.'

'As I told you before, I am perfectly capable of walking to and from Bathgate.'

'May I at least be allowed to mend your puncture?'

His quick smile was the most disturbing she had ever seen in her life. It wasn't merely a movement of lips but seemed to release, for a few dangerous seconds, a vital energy charge between them – a kind of suppressed lightning.

She looked quickly away. 'In my rush to keep my engagement I have forgotten my puncture-mending outfit. I shall have to leave the bicycle here and collect it later. Or have one of the servants pick it up for me.'

The bicycle was already perfectly well propped up against the bushes, but she fussed with it and pretended to adjust it into a more suitable position.

'I would deem it an honour,' he said, 'if you would allow me to drive you down to Bathgate – to save you from being late for your engagement.'

She had never before heard a voice so cultured or so forceful. There was not a trace of either a Bathgate lilt or a soft Scottish burr, so she thought he must be English. She hesitated, not wishing to appear unnecessarily rude, and he immediately held out a hand for her.

'I'm Douglas Monteith – and you?'

She accepted his help up on to the gig. 'Clementina Blackwood.'

'How do you do, Clementina?'

She was about to correct him and say 'Miss Blackwood' but before she got the chance he had sent the horse galloping away and was saying, 'I have a confession to make. I already knew your name.'

'Oh?' She looked round at him. 'I didn't know yours.'

He smiled without turning towards her. 'Ah, but I have been doing a little detective work.'

She bristled, not liking the thought of someone trying to obtain information about her behind her back. It seemed an infringement of her freedom and privacy.

'A pity you had nothing better to do,' she said.

'Oh, we are very independent, aren't we?'

'I am. I don't know about you.'

He flashed her a smile that seemed to tangle her nerves and melt her bones. The astonishing experience only lasted a moment before she pulled herself together again, but it disturbed her. 'I like a woman with spirit,' he said.

'No, you don't.'

His laughter rang out and echoed like a bell in the clear air. 'What an odd little creature you are!'

'I'm entitled to my opinions.'

'And what in your opinion, is the kind of woman I like?'

She shrugged. 'Most men like obedience, Mr Monteith. And not just simple obedience either.'

'Oh, call me Douglas, please.'

It would be terribly modern and daring to call a gentleman by his first name after such a short acquaintance, but wasn't that exactly what she wanted to be?

'Douglas,' she said firmly.

There was something about his eyes. They seemed to be continually glimmering. One way and another they made her feel most disconcerted. She tried to quell the levity in his manner by her earnest stare and the seriousness of her conversation.

'Men turn the whole force of education to effect their purpose of creating willing slaves.'

'Really?' he said, and still there was the infuriating cut of laughter in his voice.

'You can't deny it.'

'Perish the thought!'

'Women are taught that it's a virtue to submit, and to yield to the control of men.'

He glanced round at her and there was something not only suggestive but positively wicked in his eyes. She fixed her attention on the road ahead and a few minutes' silence followed as the horse spanked along, the spring sunshine flicking through the branches of the trees like the jerky pictures in the Picturedrome. Down the steep incline now towards the cosy huddle of houses in the valley, their red tiles shimmering after the recent rain.

Then the silence began to unnerve even her. 'You have to agree,' she blurted out eventually.

'I don't *have* to do anything,' he replied.

'Huh! That's so like a man.'

'I *am* a man.'

'You know perfectly well what I mean.'

'Where are you going, by the way?'

'To visit my friend Agnes.'

'It would help if I knew where friend Agnes lived.'

'Oh,' she flushed with annoyance at her own stupidity. 'It's only a few minutes along the Glasgow Road — a house called "The Elms".'

'Ah, yes.'

Clementina felt acutely self-conscious driving through Bathgate beside Douglas Monteith. He had such an arresting appearance that she imagined that everyone was bound to notice him and feel as upset and disturbed as herself. She kept trying to concentrate her thoughts on the agenda for discussion at Agnes's house. It was so important to plan the following day's suffragist meeting down to the last detail. Nothing must go wrong and they must make sure they took every advantage of the platform to put across their message in the clearest and most logical way. But sitting next to such a virile man, with his long legs taking up most of the space and, as the gig rattled along, one of those legs sometimes brushing against hers, she found it impossible to think clearly and logically.

Then, unexpectedly, he reined the horse to a standstill, 'Here we are!' he announced and jumping down came round to help her alight.

Before she could stop him, instead of taking her hand to assist her he had caught her by the waist and, despite her indignant cries of protest, whisked her playfully up in the air before depositing her on the ground. For the first time she realised how tall he was in comparison with herself. Her head barely reached his shoulder. She looked up at him, trying to appear calm and unflustered. 'That was quite unnecessary.'

'But nice!'

'Good afternoon,' she said, hastily escaping from the look in his eyes and marching briskly towards the gate of 'The Elms'.

CHAPTER FORTY-ONE

Rhona Lindsay read the notice with bitterness and derision. It urged everyone to come along to the first meeting of the newly formed West Lothian Justice for Women Group. The meeting was to be held in the Co-op Hall and the speakers were to be Miss Betsy Kyle-Ormiston and Miss Clementina Blackwood. Rhona turned away from the notice hugging her shawl tightly around her shoulders, eyes and mouth flint-hard. Justice for women as dished out by the double-barrelled Miss Betsy and the wealthy millowner's daughter, Miss Clementina – what a laugh! What did the likes of Miss Blackwood, of all people, know about justice or the lack of it?

'What justice was there in my mother's death?' Rhona thought in sudden anguish.

Her mother, like many other workers in the Blackwood Mill, had wasted away, coughing and spitting blood, poisoned by inhaling too much cotton fluff from the air. All her life her mother had slaved for the Blackwoods. Her father had toiled for them too and eventually been killed in one of the all-too-frequent and horrifying accidents in the mill. Both their lives had been sacrificed so that the Blackwoods could live in luxury in their grand house somewhere up in the Bathgate hills. But not content with that sacrifice, her mother was not cold in her grave when Mr Gilbert had tried to put Rhona out of the mill house which had been her home all the nineteen years of her life. This was despite the fact that she had worked in the mill since she was eleven, when she had started as a half-timer, doing school lessons as well as work. Most of the children had been so exhausted with working that when they got to school they just fell asleep. But not Rhona. She had had enough restless energy and determination, even at that age, to make the most of the few opportunities that came her way and she had paid alert attention to the teacher and learned all she could.

When, the day after her mother's funeral, the order had come via the foreman for her to quit the house, she had been incensed with bitterness and grief and kicked up hell at the injustice and inhumanity of it. All the other women at the mill had become infected by her anger. There had been dark murmurings among the men workers too and meetings began to be held around machines during meal breaks.

The foreman had eventually reported back to Mr Gilbert, who had then sent for her. She remembered his office with its dark wood-panelled walls and desk, buttoned leather chairs and sofa and turkey red carpet. There had been a big fire burning in the hearth and she had felt instinctively drawn to its luxurious warmth. She remembered too the way Mr Gilbert had looked her up and down and how she had thought to herself, 'He'll know me again, that's for sure.'

He was a tall, lean man with silky reddish hair like his late father and he sported a pearl tie-pin in his cravat. 'What is the meaning of all this trouble you're causing?' he asked.

She tossed him an impertinent look but said in a mild voice, 'Trouble, sir?'

'I've got a family for that house. I have promised it to them.'

'But it's my home. Such as it is,' she added, unable to keep the sarcasm from her voice.

'Why should I allow you to stay there by yourself when it could give three of my other workers – a man, wife and child – a roof over their heads?'

'Where would I go? . . . sir,' she added with only the hint of a pause.

He shrugged. 'You can find lodgings somewhere, surely.'

'In one of the other mill houses?'

'Why not? It's only fair.'

Fair? She had laughed in his face, a hard, derisory laugh. This was Blackwood justice. He hadn't even any idea of what his houses were like inside. There wasn't enough room for one person to live in a civilised manner, far less a family and even less a lodger.

'You call it fair,' she asked, 'to try to evict me the day after my mother's funeral?'

'Watch your tongue,' he warned. Then, as if to help control his temper and give himself time to think, he had lit a cigar and taken a few leisurely puffs at it before speaking again. This time he sounded quite reasonable and pleasant. 'Leave it for now. Get back to your work and I will see you later.'

He had seen her later all right. It had been dark; the streets were deserted and the village asleep when she had heard the tapping at the door. She had been sitting up in bed – a candle dancing in the draught at her side – trying not to think about the terrible ache she felt at the loss of her mother, the frightening aloneness. She thought it must be the Donaven children from next door and was immediately grateful at the prospect of their company. Their mother's time was near and it had been arranged that they would come to her house to be out of the way as soon as Mrs Donaven went into labour.

But to her astonishment it was the tall figure of Mr Gilbert standing in the shadow in the doorway.

'Well, let me in,' he said quietly.

She stepped back, suddenly conscious that she was wearing only a threadbare nightgown and that her hair, free of its usual inhibiting pins, was such a thick wild mass of curls that it looked as if she had never managed to force a comb through it.

Snatching up her shawl, she hugged it around herself. He came in, shut the door and glanced around. 'I thought I would have a look at the place.'

She stood very still and silent, not yet able to grasp that he was there, far less comprehend why.

She struggled to gather her wits together. 'Does that mean I can stay?'

'Not so fast,' he said in low tones. 'What can you do for me?'

If she had had a knife in her hand at that moment she would have killed him. But it was not only him her spirit railed so bitterly against – it was the whole unfairness of the world. The order of things that said people like her should have so little and people like him should have so much – and still want more. A weight of helplessness pressed down on her, although she still hid her true emotions behind a careless bravado.

Rhona had bought time with the only currency she had. And she needed time to come to terms with her grief not only at the loss of her mother but the thoughts of her mother's miserable, wasted life.

Later she had looked at herself in the cloudy, rusted mirror in the one-roomed hovel that was her home and could not blame herself for what she had done. Indeed, she knew she would do it again with any gentleman who could offer her escape from the Blackwood Mill and the Blackwood village. Perhaps set her up with beautiful clothes in a snug little cottage somewhere? She also knew that it was only a dream and dreams didn't come true. Only nightmares. While the world kept on turning in its usual unfair and unjust way.

The West Lothian Justice for Women Group! She laughed to herself every time she thought of it. To hear what Clementina Blackwood had to say about justice was a chance that could not be missed. Even to see the young lady in question would be an interesting experience. She had never of course clapped eyes on any of the Blackwood women. Needless to say they never came anywhere near the mill.

Rhona had been in Bathgate doing some shopping

when she had seen the notice and, rather than tramp the long walk to Blackwood village and then return to Bathgate later for the meeting, she decided to rest in the Steel Yard and eat a bit of bread and cheese until it was time to go up to Jarvie Street to the hall. Now she sat watching the world go by, a strangely compelling figure despite her shabby skirt and boots and tattered shawl. Her restless, watchful eyes were an unusual violet colour. There had always been a wildness about her – her mother used to say it was the gipsy in her blood. Her grandmother had been a gipsy before she married and had never really settled down; she had run away after giving birth to her father and was never seen again, so Rhona had never met her. Often though, when bands of the travelling folk with their colourful caravans moved along the country roads or stopped to light their fires and cook their meals, curiosity would overcome her. She would loiter near them, burning to know if her grandmother was still alive and one of their dark-stained number.

'All you need,' her mother used to say, 'is a pair of golden earrings to look the part.'

Often she used to think that she might not only have a gipsy grandmother still around, but gipsy uncles and aunts and cousins for all she knew.

Envy filled her at the sight of smartly dressed ladies passing in their elegant carriages. Every fur cape, every muff, every feather boa, every frilly parasol was unashamedly coveted by her. And oh, the gorgeous blouses and dresses and hats! Strong white teeth tugging greedily at the bread and cheese, she told herself that she could look as good as – better than – any of these grand ladies, if only she could wear clothes like that. She had no false modesty about herself; she knew she was not only beautiful, but possessed the extra almost mystic quality of the gipsies. Her mother, she had often suspected, had been ashamed and worried about this, but she wasn't – she was proud of how she looked and what she was.

Nothing could change that. She even hoped that, like

the gipsies, she had the power to bring bad luck when she cursed someone, because she cursed the Blackwoods each and every one of them, including Miss Clementina.

Rhona hoped this meeting would turn out to be one of the most violent suffragette meetings ever. She hoped Miss Blackwood and her double-barrelled friend would be heckled, set upon and if possible run out of town. Or, even better, arrested and flung into jail.

She still felt hungry after the bread and cheese was finished but there was nothing else. It had grown chilly too and a breeze had come to flap at her skirts. Getting up, she stamped her boots and rubbed her hands to try to get her circulation going again. Eventually she picked up her basket and made her way along Engine Street.

'The West Lothian Justice for Women Group,' she kept thinking. 'Blackwood justice. What a bloody laugh!'

CHAPTER FORTY-TWO

It was a humiliation to have had to ask Agnes's father if she could be taken home in his carriage and it went against Clementina's principles of self-sufficiency and independence. But it was either that or risk being accosted by Douglas Monteith on her way back home after her visit to Agnes. It was such an irritation altogether, because she felt a long energetic walk would have done her good. Anyway, Agnes's father was such a pompous bore – she had naturally hoped that he would simply order his coachman to drive her home. But oh no, he had to take full advantage of the situation and insist on coming too.

'Ah, you see!' he guffawed. 'This suffragist nonsense is all very well but what would all you helpless little creatures do without us, eh?' His hairy cheeks puffed out. 'You'll grow out of such silly notions of course and then you will be only too glad of the lifelong support and protection of a good husband.' He leaned back in the carriage, hands clasped contentedly on his huge corporation. 'But meantime my dear, take my advice and have a little thought and care for the future. You may spoil your chances of getting a man if you're not careful.'

Agnes had made an urgent whispered plea to Clementina before she had left 'The Elms': 'For pity's sake, don't let Papa provoke you, Clementina. It will only make everything more difficult for me and we don't want to risk anything going wrong before tomorrow's meeting. Just ignore him.'

Clementina was not used to bottling things up and it

was only with great difficulty that she refrained from saying anything. By the time she reached Blackwood House and had been subjected to a continuous lecture on how to please men and the rewards and joys of devoting her life to being a wife and mother, she was ready to explode with her frustration. He seemed to think that because she had no father it was his duty to give her appropriate fatherly advice. It was the same with Eva's father. It was also as if they sensed that, although she was the youngest of the group, she was the strongest and most dangerous and therefore the one most needing to be disciplined and taught a thing or two.

She was palpitating with repressed anger by the time Agnes's father bade her good-bye. Her irritation and frustration prevented her from getting a good night's sleep – something which all the girls had agreed was vital so that they would be as alert and clear-headed as possible for the meeting next day.

Clementina blamed Douglas Monteith. Had it not been for him, she would have walked back and the fresh air and exercise would have done her good. Then she would have slept well and everything would have been fine. She stiffened with tension every time she thought of the aggravation he had caused. All day before the meeting she had a splitting headache. But with sheer will-power and concentration on the importance of the Cause they had to put across, she managed to control both her headache and her nerves and reach the hall to all appearances a very calm and capable young woman. She also looked beautifully turned out in her navy hat with its emerald ribbons to match her eyes, her navy jacket and skirt and high-necked emerald blouse. It was, she had discovered, very important that she should take care to look her best in order to combat the dreadful and wickedly untrue image of suffragettes that all the papers and magazines were putting across to the public. Their favourite was a weird word picture of a gaunt female with a raucous voice and truculent demeanour, who

347

always wore elastic-sided boots and carried a big 'gampy' umbrella. Even the postcard manufacturers and toymakers were part of this conspiracy. The shops were full of toys such as the jack-in-the-box type she had seen, where instead of Jack popping up, there was an effigy of an ugly witch-like woman with pocked skin, wearing spectacles and frumpy clothes and holding a flag on which was written 'Votes for Women'.

In reality, any suffragettes she had seen were most elegant and attractive women. Indeed a large proportion of them were writers, artists and actresses who were not merely attractive but stunningly beautiful.

Her first surprise was to find the hall nearly full but mostly with working-class women. There was a fair sprinkling of ladies though, and a few gentlemen as well as some obviously working-class men.

Kitty was already fussing about on the platform setting out glasses and a water decanter. The rest of the girls were sitting in the first row as if they had been turned to stone. For a horrible moment Clementina thought they had completely frozen with nerves and the whole thing would fall through. She could understand how they felt. Apart from the occasional suffragettes who caused a sensation by travelling around the country speaking, it was really unheard of for a woman to speak in public.

'Are we ready?' she asked her friends, as if daring them to say anything but 'Yes'. 'We have still another five minutes, but as everyone's here so early . . .'

It had been agreed that they would all march up and sit in a row on the platform to give each other moral support and to represent the starting committee of the newly formed West Lothian Justice for Women Group. Only two of them, however, would speak and answer questions – Betsy and Clementina. Agnes was to act as chairman.

'I'm ready if you are,' said Betsy, getting immediately if somewhat stiffly to her feet. 'Come on, Agnes, you're chairman, don't forget.'

348

A quiet but resolute voice emerged from behind Agnes's veil. 'If we all keep together we shall be all right.'

'Of course,' Clementina said impatiently. 'Come on!'

They had barely assembled on the platform when a man roared out 'If you can't get a man of your own, away home and attend to your father!' This was greeted with some raucous male laughter and stamping of feet.

'Ignore them,' Clementina hissed at Agnes. 'If we are going to fight for what we believe to be right, we must have courage. Start the meeting.'

Agnes calmly stood up to face the audience and in her sweet, ladylike voice said, 'Good evening, ladies and gentlemen. I would like to welcome you to this first public meeting of the West Lothian Justice for Women Group. I hope we shall gain your support in the struggle for women's suffrage. Getting the vote is only the first step towards achieving true justice for women . . .'

'The support every woman needs and wants,' a man at the front interrupted in a loud, pompous voice, 'is a good husband and there's no use you trying to pretend that's not true.'

'. . . But a vitally important one,' Agnes continued, to all appearances serenely unaware of the interruption. 'And I would like to propose a resolution that this meeting calls upon the government to grant facilities . . .'

'Did you hear what I said, miss?' The man's voice had turned nasty, but Agnes refused to be ruffled.

'. . . to the Women's Enfranchisement Bill, so that it may become law during the present session of Parliament.'

This was met by a storm of male cat-calls, which did not however stop Betsy from jumping to her feet, hat feathers quivering, to second the motion and speak at some length.

'It's clear from the comments of the men tonight that a woman's interests are not taken care of through the votes of the man in her family. Women are not content with this,' she insisted. 'It denies us recognition as individuals

349

– human beings in our own right – and it's crucial that men should stop seeing us only in relation to themselves. It's time they took us seriously and realised we have minds and opinions of our own. Otherwise the suffragist movement will become an autonomous force completely outwith men's control . . .'

Her speech was constantly interrupted by heckling, but she seemed to gain strength as she went along and by the end of it she was shouting back at the hecklers.

Clementina spoke next on a theme dear to Betsy's heart, but one which it had been decided Betsy should not touch on in case her father found out and took revenge by becoming even more selfish and restrictive than he already was. Clementina cut through the man-made myth that women should be self-sacrificing and infuriated the men in the audience by mercilessly pulling to pieces the belief that women ought to sacrifice the development of their own personalities for the sake of men and children.

'This is a most convenient belief for men.' She spoke in clear, ringing tones, chin up and eyes bright with resolution. 'But it is a sin against women, because it's wrong for any human being to cease striving for self-development. By keeping women as slaves, men deny women this right. And they use the same arguments to support this slavery as men have always done to justify any slavery as far back as Aristotle. It has always been said that it was the natural order of things. It has a paternal quality. And, like a child, the slave is incapable of enjoying freedom. He is not educated enough or mature enough to cope with it. The dominant person in society and the slave, they claim, have different natures. Slaves should only try to be good slaves; that is where their happiness and self-fulfilment lies.'

Looking straight at the women in the audience now, she continued, 'Don't you believe it! It is not out of any consideration for women's interests that men want women to be womanly, to be pure and virtuous and to keep out of public life, to practise self-sacrifice, marriage and maternity. It is because this is in men's interests. Pure selfishness,' she said, 'is the motive of men's desire to oppress women. Men want women to specialise in virtue and sit at home, while they career around the world having sinful and enjoyable adventures. Men want women to be efficient only at massaging their egos so that they can appear twice their natural size. This is one of the ways in which the illusion of male mastery is kept intact.'

Her last words were almost drowned by the boos of the male section of the audience and cries of 'Get off!' and 'Beat it!', but Clementina kept forcing her words to surface. Her small but sturdy frame, far from beating a retreat, had such an aura of obstinacy that she looked as if she had nailed her shoes to the floor. Question time brought more angry abuse, but both Clementina and Betsy continued to face the challenge and refuse to be intimidated. Until, that is, one working-class girl wearing a coarse tartan shawl round her shoulders asked a question that took Clementina aback. The girl, whose name she later discovered was Rhona Lindsay, wanted to know if the West Lothian Justice for Women Group had thought about justice for working-class women.

'Does Miss Blackwood, for instance,' Rhona Lindsay asked, 'believe in improving the working conditions of women in the Blackwood Mill?'

This aspect of justice had never occurred to Clementina and she frowned, brows down, eyes thoughtful. Eventually she said, 'I don't know anything about the working conditions in the Mill.' She raised her voice above the jeering of the working men in the audience. 'But if you see me afterwards, I shall be interested to hear what you have to say on the subject.'

After the meeting she managed to have a brief few words with Rhona Lindsay and was impressed with the girl's intelligence and her strong sense of injustice. There was also something hypnotic about her violet eyes and the veiled impertinence in them that almost amounted to menace. Clementina was reminded of gipsies she had seen in the Littlegate woods. Although unlike the gipsies, Rhona's thick curly hair was bundled up on top of her head and at least partly secured there with hairpins.

'I take your point,' Clementina conceded, 'that the vote is not much use to working women unless it can be used to improve working conditions and general social and economic inequalities. But without the political power that the vote gives, surely no real pressure can be put on politicians to do anything?'

Just then Kitty flounced in and after giving Rhona a brief, uncomfortable glance, addressed Clementina. 'Your carriage is waiting in Jarvie Street, Clementina. The rest have all gone. Do hurry!'

'Very well.' Then to Rhona, 'We'll talk again.'

All in all it had proved a most exhilarating and challenging evening and once it was safely behind them, Clementina and her friends were able to discuss the meeting with enthusiasm and even enjoyment. There was also the wonderful sense of achievement, of at last doing something fulfilling and worthwhile. No fewer than twenty-nine ladies from Bathgate and the surrounding area had joined the Group and paid the agreed subscription. A group of ladies who had come from the nearby town of Linlithgow had suggested that if a meeting was held there, even more members would rally to the Cause. And so a meeting had been planned in that historic town which had played such a forceful role in Scotland's turbulent and bloody history.

On this occasion Clementina was interested to see, in the front row of the audience, the sullen-looking figure of Rhona Lindsay. Right from the start of the meeting until the very end, the violet eyes fixed on her with what to anyone with less spunk than Clementina would have been a totally intimidating stare. It was as if the girl hated her, Clementina thought. It was as if she was secretly sneering at every word she uttered. Curiosity had always been one of Clementina's strongest characteristics so, nothing

daunted, after the meeting she left the platform and stopped Rhona from leaving.

Rhona stared down in silence at Clementina's hand
resting on her arm as if it was a futile but repulsive kind
of bug.

'We didn't get the chance to finish our last conversation,' Clementina said.

The girl waited until Clementina had removed her
hand before shrugging, 'I hadn't anything else to say.'

'I'm sure that's not true. Have you time to step into the
ante-room? Just for a few minutes?'

Rhona shrugged again, but she followed Clementina
into the small room behind the platform. Once there,
Clementina immediately burst into the subject of politics
and social reform as if there had been no interruption to
their previous conversation. She had been giving the matter a great deal of thought and she now tried to explore
these thoughts about the policies of Mr Asquith and Mr
Lloyd George and other prominent and influential politicians. However, before she had got very far, Rhona dismissed her words with a scornful, 'What do the like of
them know about mill houses and working conditions in
the Blackwood mill? What do *you* know about them?'

'I'm willing to learn,' Clementina said.

Rhona gave a sarcastic laugh. 'How? By going to the
mill and seeing for yourself, you mean?'

'Yes, if necessary.'

'You won't do that.'

'Oh? And what makes you say so?'

Rhona's mouth twisted. 'I'm sure it's not the place for
you, you being such a fine lady!'

'If I say I will go to the mill to learn about what goes on
there, then I will. I always mean what I say.'

Despite herself, Rhona felt a glimmer of respect for
Clementina. There was something in those emerald eyes
that indicated a force to be reckoned with. She even
began to suspect that Clementina might have enough

nerve to carry out her threat and actually turn up at the mill. She smiled maliciously to herself at the picture this conjured up. That would give the fine lady food for thought all right.

Clementina's friends, on the other hand, were distressed and worried when they heard of the planned visit. There was no need to subject herself to such an ordeal, they insisted. Whatever the factory or conditions in it were like, it had no relevance to their aims. The Cause, after all, was to get a share in the franchise so that ladies could gain more control of their own destinies and have some opportunity to develop their potential as individuals.

Clementina's mind was made up, however, and she could — as her friends knew only too well — be exceedingly stubborn. So eventually, despite their pleas, she set out for the factory on her bicycle. It was a good few miles the other side of Bathgate, in the centre of a miserable huddle of two-storey houses and one-roomed hovels which had taken the name of the factory and become Blackwood village.

Her cycling expeditions had never taken her to this area before and she was immediately depressed by the sight of it. Over the other side of one of the hills and sunk in a small, claustrophobic valley, it looked dismal and cold as if no sunshine had ever reached there. The nearer she got to it, the more she became aware of the overpowering melancholy of the huge red-brick factory with its row upon row of bare windows and many turrets rearing up from the roof. As she dismounted from her cicycle and approached the entrance, she had a sudden shattering insight into what it must feel like to come here day after day, condemned to work in the place for the rest of one's life. It took all her will-power to prevent her feet from faltering and she only regained her strength of purpose from the challenge of a bowler-hatted and moustached foreman who dared to try to stop her from entering.

'I am Miss Blackwood,' she announced, brushing aside the horrified man. 'And I have come to inspect the factory and find out something about what goes on here.'

'Miss Blackwood!' The man hastened after her. 'This is no place for a lady. You are liable to get lost or faint or some such . . .'

'I have no intention of fainting,' Clementina told him. 'And to prevent me from getting lost, you may show me around. It would also help if you explained everything to me. Now, where do we start?'

He was a big iron-backed, barrel-chested man like a sergeant-major, but he hesitated, his mouth loose and weak and his eyes bewildered, in front of the small expensively dressed woman with the direct, determined stare as hard and glittering as emeralds.

'Well?' she demanded impatiently.

'Follow me, miss,' he capitulated.

For days afterwards Clementina could not rid herself of the nightmare of the next couple of hours. She became completely disorientated, knowing that she was safely at home in Blackwood House yet feeling she was still incarcerated in Blackwood Mill. Even weeks afterwards she would experience sudden rushes of noise in her head that would shake her whole body and for a few seconds would be completely smothered by the dense suffocating atmosphere of the spinning mill. Then she would have a spasm of coughing like the one after her visit, in a frantic effort to rid her nostrils, throat and chest of the fluffy pieces of cotton that had swirled around in the air like a thick cloud of poisonous snow.

★   ★   ★

Clementina had made sure by her serious and unwavering attention that she learned as much as possible. First there was the 'opening process'. She had been shown into the bale-breaking room where a man wielded a long-handled axe to break the metal band fastened round the tightly compressed bales of cotton brought from the cotton field. Then the bales were lifted through to the blow room – well-named because of so much blowing about in it. Afterwards they were tossed on to a spiked lattice feed that brought them up to a beater-roller in a rumbling chamber. The beater-roller kept knocking the cotton back so that it was rumbling about and getting opened, the heavy impurities being sucked out and taken away. A scrutcher lap machine called a double opener came next, the cotton falling on it in blanket form and being carried along another spiked lattice under beaters that continued to remove impurities. Then there was the carding engine, its noise battering at her head to such a degree that it was only with great concentration and determination that she heard the foreman's shouted explanation that the carding process converted the lap into a form of soft rope or silver. The lap of cotton was led in for several reasons, including the removal of finer impurities and the preparation of the fibre for parallelisation. The cotton fibres now became like a fine web. But there was still the 'licker-in' and the doffer cylinders and many other processes like combing and roving. Eventually the cotton or rove had the thickness of rather less than that of a pencil; for the first time it had a slight twist and as it was produced it was wound on to bobbins.

And all this rackety process that thickened the air with choking fluff was only the spinning *preparation*. The actual spinning, the deafening din, the overpowering crash of machinery, the madly whirling bobbins, the thick suffocating atmosphere, the rows of ghostly faced women remained with Clementina like a film that kept suddenly unfolding in a panic-stricken rush before her eyes.

She was overwhelmed by it all – the wit-shattering noise, the fluff, the nauseating smell of warm oily waste and the wretchedness in the women's eyes. She was so stunned to find that such a world existed and it was so different from anything that either she or her friends had ever experienced, that at first she could not even find a way to tell them about it. She just kept thinking about Rhona Lindsay and marvelled that the girl had survived her years of toil in the place. And not only survived, but had retained such a strong rebellious spirit.

CHAPTER FORTY-THREE

'Mrs Musgrove,' Lorianna said. 'I wish you would let Lizzie do my hair. She has lighter, nimbler fingers.'

'She can put it up as usual.' Mrs Musgrove's voice was strangely subdued and quiet. 'But brushing needs a heavier, stronger hand.'

The long strokes by brush and hand, tugging the head each time and more and more strongly, the electrical crackling of silk mittens, jerked Lorianna's heartbeats faster. She wanted the brushing to stop.

'I hope to goodness some nice young man acquires a special interest in Clementina tonight,' she said breathlessly.

'They will be after her like a pack of wolves.'

'I know she's beautiful with that gorgeous colour of hair and those stunning eyes. I know I shouldn't worry, but I sometimes think her cheeks are a little too rosy. There is an altogether too robust quality about her, in fact, which I am afraid gentlemen might not find very appealing.'

She gazed anxiously up at Mrs Musgrove like a lovely child. Her delicate complexion was paler than usual against the rich earthy gloss of her hair flowing free over her shoulders and the wide cherry softness of her mouth. 'Don't you think so?'

'She's not as beautiful as you, madam.'

Lorianna gave an embarrassed little laugh. 'I sometimes get the feeling that she's not my daughter at all and that she must be some kind of changeling. A milkmaid's daughter who has been passed off as mine! We are so different in so many ways.'

'Yes, she can look after herself. You cannot.'

'As if those suffragette meetings weren't enough,' continued Lorianna. 'Now there is all this business about the factory. She keeps going on and on about the working conditions there. I didn't believe she was serious when I heard her pestering Gilbert to show her around the place. I thought she was just being argumentative as usual and trying to shock and annoy everyone. But she actually went to the factory in spite of his refusal. She bullied one of the foremen to show her round . . . It doesn't bear thinking about, does it? Oh, for goodness sake, Mrs Musgrove, that's enough brushing. You surely have other more important things to attend to today?'

'Yes, madam.' Mrs Musgrove carefully placed the brush on the dressing-table, but even with that slow controlled movement there was the slight jangle of keys and the sound pricked at Lorianna's nerves.

'Send Lizzie to me at once.'

'Yes, madam.'

Lorianna could hardly contain her annoyance. She kept remembering that at an important occasion like a dance there ought to be menservants in attendance, a butler and a few footmen. She had said so to Mrs Musgrove, of course, but the icy response she had received told her, without the housekeeper putting it into words, that if she engaged menservants she would lose Mrs Musgrove's help and co-operation and dire consequences would result.

The sharp bird eyes had glittered with anger. 'Does madam feel she no longer has confidence in me . . .'

'No, no,' Lorianna had hastily assured her. 'I have every confidence in you, of course.'

And so it had been decided that additional maids would be taken on for the day. Lorianna and Mrs Musgrove discussed the menu for the supper and Lorianna did the floral decorations so that the house would look its best and most welcoming. She had worked for hours during the two days immediately prior to the event, until the house was a rainbow of colour and the heady perfume of shrubs and blooms now pervaded the whole place. It filled her with a sweet pain she no longer dared think about.

Another worry was over what Clementina would wear. She had ordered the dressmaker to fit her for several new dresses for both day and evening wear and a very special one for this evening. Clementina had not caused too much trouble over the numerous fitting sessions and the discussion about clothes, but on the other hand she had not shown much enthusiasm either. As Hilda and Mary Ann said, it didn't seem natural. They had been hysterically excited about their first dance and had chattered endlessly about clothes for months beforehand.

Even up to the last moment, Lorianna was haunted by vague fears and insecurities to the point of asking Flora McGregor, Clementina's personal maid, to keep a special eye on Clementina and make sure that nothing went wrong. She had a horror of Clementina deciding not to turn up and just disappearing; because of that she invited her daughter to have lunch with her in the dining-room, so that she could keep an eye on her for at least part of the time herself.

It was typical of Clementina that she was more pleased and excited about the simple meal shared between the two of them than she was at the prospect of the splendid and important occasion with so many prominent guests later in the evening.

'You look really lovely in that tea-gown, Mother,' she'd enthused.

'Thank you, darling.'

'I wish I was tall and regal like you. And I wish I had your pale complexion. And look at your lovely slim hands! Long fingers are supposed to be artistic. You could have been a writer or a painter or a . . .'

'Eat your soup, dear.'

'Didn't you ever want to be something?'

'Eat it slowly and calmly, Clementina. A lady should have self-control and dignity at all times, but especially at mealtimes.'

'Didn't you, Mother?'

'Didn't I what?'

'Ever want to *be* something?'

'I hope I have been a good wife and mother.'

'But I mean *do* something.'

Lorianna gasped with exasperation. 'Clementina, I had hoped that you would grow out of this irritating habit of yours.'

'What habit?'

'Continuously asking questions.'

'Miss Viners said it was a sign of intelligence.'

'It would have fitted Miss Viners better if she had instructed you in proper ladylike behaviour. I was always suspicious of that woman.'

'If that was how you felt, Mother, why didn't you *do* something about it? Why didn't you sack her the moment you felt she wasn't the right person to be teaching me?'

'She was your father's choice and presumably was giving you the kind of instruction that he wished you to have. It was not my place to interfere or go against his wishes.'

Clementina groaned and rolled her eyes upwards. 'Bloody hell!'

'Clementina!' Lorianna had turned sickly white with shock. 'How dare you use such language!'

'I'm sorry, Mother.' Clementina was genuinely upset to see the distress she had caused Lorianna. 'Please forgive me. I'll never do it again.'

'I should think not.' The slender fingers, weighed down it seemed by a large ruby and diamond ring, a diamond cluster and a broad gold band, fell trembling on to the gauzy lap of her tea-gown. 'Now you have completely spoiled what little appetite I had.'

361

'Honestly, Mother, I promise.'

'I dare not think of you behaving in such a shocking manner tonight, especially when I am so anxious that everything goes well for you.'

'Everything will be fine, don't worry.'

'I can't help worrying about you, Clementina.'

She could not eat another mouthful of anything, despite Clementina's desperate pleadings. In the background she could hear the frenzied activity of what seemed like the army of local women that Mrs Musgrove had engaged. There were loud bumps and scrapings as carpets were lifted and furniture in the sitting-room and drawing-room was dragged back against the walls to make room for the dancing. There was the sound of running feet and the excited babble of strange voices. Lorianna began to feel so agitated that in the end she was forced to retreat to her bedroom and lie down for an hour to try to calm herself. Lizzie shut the heavy velvet curtains to darken the room and left her to lie on top of the bed-covers in her loose ecru lace tea-gown. A big fire flamed silently in the hearth, creating a deep ruby glow and dark quivering shadows.

From distant parts of the house sounds of excited voices and hurrying feet continued to float towards her; sometimes the chinking of china and glass, sometimes the clatter of cutlery and silver trays agitated the air.

The dark room seemed haunted. Even when she closed her eyes she could still sense the shadows moving and feel the room's withdrawal from the rest of the house. She kept slipping back in time. Or was she dipping into sleep, where ghosts could come unbidden to torment her, make her cry out and claw up to awakeness wide-eyed, bathed in sweat?

'Did you say something, madam?'

Lizzie was lighting the candles with a taper. Once a highly nervous girl, she had been firmly trained by Mrs Musgrove. Now, although still thin and frizzy-haired, tending to be somewhat apprehensive at times, she was for the most part well-controlled and smoothly efficient. She came over and lit the oil-lamp by the bedside, tainting the air with the night-time smell of paraffin.

'Is it so late?' Lorianna jerked into a sitting position. Still disorientated with nightmares, she thought she saw Mrs Musgrove melt into the shadows. For a frightening moment she had the feeling that she had lost some time, that the dance was over and everybody had gone.

'Why wasn't I awakened?'

'Mrs Musgrove said the sleep would do you good, madam,' Lizzie told her. 'And you have still plenty of time to get ready. Mrs Musgrove says you are not to worry – Flora's seeing to Miss Clementina and everything else has been taken care of.'

Lorianna relaxed with relief, but was so shaken she was unable to leave the bed and stand up for a few minutes. When she fully recovered and could think normally, she decided on a gown of cream silk edged with gold embroidery. The gown emphasised her shapely figure by being draped in spirals round her body into a flounced train. The off-the-shoulder gold-edged bodice flattered her fair skin and the gold and diamond chain and matching earrings added a sparkle to it.

'My embroidered fan,' she told the maid.

'Oh, madam!' Lizzie looked quite flushed with pleasure. 'You do look beautiful.'

Lorianna smiled kindly at the girl, 'Thank you. Now I ought to have a look round to check that the preparations have all been completed and everything is perfect. Before you clear up here, run up to the tower stairs and make sure that Miss Clementina's ready. Then come straight back and tell me.'

'Yes, madam.'

Obediently the maid hurried away and after another glance at her reflection in the mirror Lorianna swirled her train aside and, petticoats rustling, moved elegantly from the room.

The reception hall, like the rest of the house, was filled

with fragrance. The floral arrangements were works of art in unusual shapes, and in colours that melted magically into one another.

The drawing-room looked twice its normal size now that the chairs and sofas and small tables had been moved back against the wall and the piano was over in the far corner. A three-piece band – a lady pianist, a male accordionist and a fiddle player – had been booked from Bathgate and they were already in place and tuning-up. The sitting-room had dancing space too and together the rooms provided what looked to her a very large floor area indeed, which she noticed had been suitably prepared with sprinklings of French chalk.

'Miss Clementina will be down in a minute, madam,' Lizzie interrupted her thoughts.

Lorianna relaxed with relief . . . But only for a moment.

'Does she look all right?'

'Oh yes, madam.'

'Good! You can go and clear up the bedroom now.'

The clock in the hall struck the hour. Only thirty minutes now before the guests would start arriving, although she expected the family and possibly John too to come earlier. She inspected the dining-room and found that Cook had surpassed herself in culinary artistry. She had decorated the sweets with spun sugar and created beautiful sugar baskets in all kinds of designs for the petit-fours. There were beehives and bird's nests and rose baskets and crowns.

Lorianna made a mental note to congratulate Cook; tomorrow she would tell Mrs Musgrove to send Mrs Prowse up to the sitting-room so that she could speak to her personally. Although the housekeeper might not like that. Anxiety about Mrs Musgrove was nibbling at her nerve-ends. She never dared to clear her mind enough to be able to think out her anxieties logically; they just remained a fearful suspicion. At the same time she was ashamed of her feelings.

When she returned to the reception hall Lorianna was met by the housekeeper, who looked very imposing in a black dress with a row of tiny buttons on the bodice and a stiff rustling skirt. As usual she wore silk mittens, but unusually she had a jet brooch at her throat and jet drop earrings dangled against her sallow jowls.

Lorianna managed to smile at her. 'You are looking extremely smart, Mrs Musgrove.'

The housekeeper's mouth tilted very slightly. 'Thank you, madam. And is everything else to your liking?'

Before she could reply, her attention was diverted by the sudden appearance of Clementina from the tower stair.

'Oh darling, how beautiful!'

'I'm glad you like it, Mother. It was your choice.'

Clementina gave the dress a careless swirl. It was a pale apple green satin with diaphanous chiffon sleeves and ruched chiffon over the satin bodice. A single strand of pearls lay at her throat and a pearl-topped comb nestled in one side of her hair like captured sunshine.

However, it was not the dress which had arrested Lorianna's immediate attention but the tilt of Clementina's head and the green sparkle of her eyes. For a shattering moment all other emotions were banished by a surge of pride in her daughter that was so unexpectedly powerful it almost reduced Lorianna to tears. Then other emotions, including apprehension, returned to battle with each other for supremacy and tighten her voice.

'Yes, it's very pretty, dear. Now come with me into the sitting-room and we will wait for our guests to be announced.'

The sitting-room, usually shadowy in the evenings, was ablaze with candles as well as oil-lamps, and the adjoining drawing-room was equally bright and gay looking.

Soon Baxter had announced the arrival of Gilbert and Hilda and Malcolm and Mary Ann. Not long after them John Stirling appeared, tall and elegant in his black tail-coat, stiff white shirt-front and black tie. Then the other guests began to arrive, a bevy of maids in the reception hall divesting the ladies of their wraps and the men of their top hats and gloves. The band was playing and the two rooms were a glorious riot of coloured gowns and sparkling jewellery. Everything seemed to be going splendidly. There was laughter and gaiety and chivalry and Lorianna was beginning to feel quite happy and light-headed. Several personable young gentlemen had seemed extremely interested in Clementina and she had danced with them very nicely and politely.

Lorianna was disappointed that the two titled gentlemen she had expected had not put in an appearance. One, had sent his valet with his apologies; apparently he had fallen from his horse only a few hours previously and broken his ankle. The other, had sent no word but to Lorianna's relief he did eventually arrive. She supposed it was a lord's prerogative to turn up whenever it suited him. Anyway, better late than early. Important guests like this often called in at various dances or balls that were being held on the same evening and left the one they judged to be the best until last.

She detected a glint of steel behind his apparently easy, relaxed manner and charming smile. Instinctively she knew he was a man with whom one would be allowed to go so far and no further – the very type of man Clementina needed. She understood too that the Dumbreggan estate was very large and wealthy. Her heart soared and sang; she was delirious with secret hope and excitement for Clementina's future.

She smiled at the man. 'Allow me to introduce you to my daughter, Clementina.'

'Lord Monteith . . .' Lorianna began.

'We have met,' Clementina interrupted in such an abrupt and rude manner that Lorianna was first shocked and then furious. Only by some miracle did she manage to remain outwardly cool and dignified.

'But not danced,' Lord Monteith said, cupping

Clementina's elbow as she was about to turn dismissively away from him and leading her, stiff and protesting, on to the floor.

★   ★   ★

On each occasion when they met after the dance, there always seemed to be not only a verbal and personality battle for supremacy between them but a physical one as well.

At the dance Clementina had struggled with all her might, yet always with outward dignity, to break free of his hold on her but without the slightest success. This surprised her, because she was much stronger than any woman she knew and had always regarded herself as a match for any man.

It was infuriating! Her face grimaced and reddened with the intensity of her concentration in fighting to push him away and break free of the grip he had on her wrist as he forced her round the floor. It was all to no avail and his show of strength seemed so calm and effortless. Even when she vigorously stamped on his foot he betrayed only a narrowing of his eyes and a brief murderous look.

Despite the injury she must have inflicted on him, indeed as if hell-bent on suffering or in the grip of some teeth-gritting obsession for revenge, he repeated the dance-battle over and over again during the evening.

Clementina could hardly believe her ears when, bidding goodnight to her mother and herself, he asked if he might call at Blackwood House next day. It was her turn to flash a murderous look. But Lorianna of course was delighted.

'I am warning you, Mother,' Clementina said later. 'I shall make a point of being out.'

'Don't be silly, dear. Why should you not want to meet such a charming gentleman again?'

'He's neither charming nor a gentleman, Mother.

367

He's . . . he's a stubborn, ungentlemanly bully . . .'

Lorianna shrugged slightly and glanced away. 'Oh well, dear — if you feel he's too much for you to cope with . . .'

'Too much for me to cope with?' Clementina echoed incredulously. '*Him?* Douglas Monteith?'

'Now that I come to think of it, he was very stubborn,' Lorianna said. 'Aggressively so. Yes, you are quite right, dear. It would be far safer to try to avoid him tomorrow.'

Bloody hell! thought Clementina. 'It's not a question of safety, Mother. I'm not in the slightest bit afraid of Lord Monteith.'

'Yes, dear.'

'I might see him tomorrow, I might not. It depends on how I feel — if I've nothing better to do.'

'Yes, dear.'

Next day she had thought, to hell with him, and gone up to see Jamie instead. Then, despite Nanny Hawthorne's protest, she had taken Jamie out to play in the garden. They had very quickly discarded his royal blue velvet jacket and matching beret and had a great time playing chases across the croquet lawn. Then they had a noisy and hilarious fencing match with the croquet mallets. Jamie eventually knocked the croquet mallet out of her hand, flung his own aside and lunged at her for a violent wrestle that knocked her on to her back, legs and petticoats flying.

'Clementina!' Lorianna's voice was a high-pitched wail of horror. 'Get up at once! And how dare you teach Jamie to copy your rough undisciplined behaviour.'

When Clementina scrambled to her feet, her horror matched her mother's as she caught sight of Douglas Monteith.

Lorianna, visibly shaking, seized Jamie's hand. 'Come, darling, Mamma will take you safely back to Nanny Hawthorne.'

In her agitation Lorianna forgot about Lord Monteith. He remained staring at Clementina and she could not imagine what he might be thinking. There was only dark forcefulness tinged with cool speculation in his eyes.

'Undisciplined is the right word,' he said at last.

'And you, I suppose,' Clementina said mockingly, 'are going to discipline me?'

'That is correct.'

She laughed. 'What conceit! For your information, Lord Monteith . . .'

'Douglas.'

'Douglas. You are not going to do anything with me.'

'Oh yes I am.'

'Get out of my way.'

'Not until you agree to take a walk with me.'

'I doubt if my mother would think that very proper.'

'I have your mother's permission.'

'Well, you do not have mine.'

'Why don't you relax?' he said, with the first glimmerings of a smile. 'You might enjoy it.'

'Look,' Clementina said, 'I am not one for beating about the bush.'

He laughed then, a quick burst of sound from a thrown-back head. Ignoring his laughter, although it secretly disturbed her, Clementina went on, 'I believe in being honest and coming straight to the point. You want to start courting me, don't you? I mean, this is the usual conventional procedure. The invitations, the calling, the walking out?'

He was obviously having difficulty in looking serious. 'That's correct.'

'Well, now that we have that straight, I can save you a lot of time and energy by just refusing you now rather than later. I have better and more important things to do with my life than be courted by you or anyone else.'

'How can you make any comparisons?' He took a firm grip of her arm and began propelling her towards the gate that was barely visible between the rhododendron bushes and trees and which led out to a country lane.

'Take your hand off me!'

369

'We can talk as we walk.'

'I don't want to walk with you. Why will you not take "no" for an answer?'

'Because I am even more stubborn than you, Clementina.'

They were going through the gate now and it was a strange red-gold place full of earthy smells and heady perfumes. Clementina felt strangely affected – she was unsure whether it was by the lush tangle of the place or by the closeness of the man at her side.

As if he too was affected, he stopped and turned her towards him, saying, 'I shall only take one kiss today. There will be plenty of time for others during our courtship.'

'I have already told you . . .' Clementina began, then stopped as Douglas bent down to kiss her. It was an unexpectedly gentle kiss and she had to admit to herself that she did enjoy it. She had in fact, never felt anything like it in her life. It gave her pause for thought and after a few minutes she found herself walking quietly by his side without realising it. Then she happened to glance up at him and caught the glimmer of amusement in his eyes. Bloody hell! He was laughing at her!

'I hate you,' she announced.

'Really?'

'I mean it. You are so typical of all I detest in the male sex – self-assured and arrogant and safe. You know that the whole of society, the economy, the law and the government, everything is geared to your convenience, weighted in your favour. You think you're entitled to have everything your own way. You're the favoured race, made in God's image. Instead, of course, the other way around.'

The amusement had disappeared now. 'That sounds like blasphemy.'

'What? That man made God in his image? It's just a statement of fact.'

'It's nothing of the kind.'

'If there is a God,' she said, 'why shouldn't it be a woman?'

He was losing his self-control now. Temper whipped across his face, tightening his muscles and coming to boiling point in his eyes.

'Don't be bloody ridiculous!'

'I shall be bloody ridiculous if I like!'

He grabbed hold of her shoulder and jerked her round at such speed she thought he had broken her neck.

'Never let me hear you curse again. You will remember that you're a lady!'

'Isn't that just typical,' she managed to say after she had recovered her breath. '*You* can swear because you're a man, but I cannot swear because I'm a woman?'

'That's correct.'

Her neck hurt abominably and, to prevent herself from weeping with the pain more than anything else, she stamped on his foot as hard as she could, then flew away to disappear in hiding places that were familiar to her from her childhood and of which he knew nothing.

'Just wait until I get my hands on you, you little devil,' he shouted in fury to the empty countryside. 'Just wait!'

CHAPTER FORTY-FOUR

'That's the mill bell,' Rhona Lindsay said. 'I shall have to run.'

'Can't you take the afternoon off?' Clementina asked. 'There's so much more I want to talk to you about.'

Rhona's dark eyes surveyed her pityingly. 'I would get my books, nothing surer. Then what would I do — starve?'

'Oh, surely not . . .'

'Miss Blackwood, I'd not only be without money for food, I'd be without a roof over my head. This house, like all the other houses around here belongs to the mill. It's been hard enough trying to keep it up until now.'

'I'm sorry. When is the most suitable time, then?'

Rhona shrugged, already at the door and tossing her shawl around her shoulders. 'Sunday, I suppose. Look, I'll have to run.'

'Why don't you come and have afternoon tea with me on Sunday?'

Rhona flashed her a sarcastic look as Clementina followed her from the dark interior of the hovel. 'At Blackwood House? You can't be serious.'

'I told you before that I always mean what I say. I will meet you at the gates at the foot of the drive at three o'clock. Don't be late.'

But Rhona was already flying away towards the mill, her shabby boots showing beneath her skirts, and Clementina could not be certain that she had heard.

The dismal tolling of the bell had stopped now and the rabbit warren of pitted, muddy streets around the towering prison-like factory were silent and empty, except for an ancient woman sitting on the step of an open doorway smoking a clay pipe and a little girl of no more than nine or ten, burdened with a sleeping baby tied to her back with a shawl.

Clementina felt weighed down by the whole place. It had taken all her courage to return to Blackwood village after her first visit to the mill, but she had felt she must speak to Rhona Lindsay again. There were so many questions she wanted to ask, so much she needed to learn. She had been used to the cottages of poor people like Alice Tait's Granny in Littlegate. Now, in comparison with Rhona's one-roomed hovel, Granny's cottage seemed quite a desirable place. The window in Rhona's house was tiny and set in a stone wall about three feet thick. Above it hung a paraffin lamp and beneath it was propped a cloudy, rusty-looking mirror. No fire burned in the narrow, black-barred grate, and it seemed colder inside the house than outside. A frousty, earthy smell invaded the nostrils and dampness crept over the skin and could be seen in dank patches and fungi on walls. On the stone mantelshelf, instead of ornaments, there were two flat-irons and an iron stand. A pair of brass-studded leather bellows hung on a worm-eaten door that looked as if it had been knocked together by a child with planks of wood of different lengths and widths. Two wooden spar-backed chairs and a table were the only furniture, except for the set-in-the-wall bed which looked like a dark oak coffin. Clementina had never seen any place so comfortless and the idea of living so close – literally in the shadow of the mill – and being summoned to toil in it by the mournful bell first thing in the morning and again in the middle of the day, depressed her beyond words.

Yet Rhona apparently was one of the lucky ones because she had the house to herself and no other mouths to feed but her own. She had found out after she had come to know the girl better that her father had been killed in an accident in the mill and her mother had not long since died of cardiac asthma. The poor woman was already worn down by several miscarriages of course. This was quite commonplace, according to Rhona. All around, all the time, women were being exhausted and ground down by continuous pregnancies. In that case, how could they ever develop as individuals or have any freedom from man's domination, Clementina said, as long as this state of affairs continued? They would have to learn about birth control. Rhona had given a humourless laugh and told how she'd heard tell of a nurse who had lost her job for explaining to a woman about that.

'The powers that be want us to multiply as much as possible so that they'll have plenty of cheap labour,' Rhona said. 'It pays them to keep us in ignorance. That's why nobody knows anything about how to stop babies coming; they just keep breeding more mouths to feed and worry about.'

'Do you,' Clementina asked, 'know anything about it?'

Rhona shrugged. 'I'm better educated than most. I get books out of the Co-op library.'

'But do you know about birth control?'

Rhona looked sullen. 'How'm I supposed to know about such things?'

'There are books about that too,' Clementina persisted.

'I've never seen any.'

'There are only a few. Dr Charles Knowlton wrote *The Fruits of Philosophy or The Private Companion of Young Married People*. I've got his book at home; I'll let you read it. My governess got it for me.'

Rhona raised a surprised brow. 'You were allowed to read that sort of thing?'

'Well, I was by my governess. My mother would have fainted with horror if she had known.'

It was to occur to Clementina eventually that here was an area where she might be of practical help to women. And not only working-class women. She was aware too that none of her friends knew anything about 'such things'. Yet surely all women should have control of their own bodies and be able to decide when they were going to be pregnant and how many children they wanted?

It seemed incredible that information on contraception had met with such active opposition from almost every religious body and government in Europe and America. Until only a few years ago, birth control advocates were still being prosecuted and at least one had been imprisoned with hard labour. People might still be imprisoned for telling people about this, for all she knew. Anything was possible. She believed it was yet another example of the terrible subjection of women by men. It was men who were making the rules about childbearing – men who did no child-bearing themselves. She had read in the newspapers that men were making great efforts to stop scandalous practices in the mines and were trying to make them safer. Why then did they oppose so vehemently anything to make life safer and better for women? According to statistics mining was man's most dangerous trade, yet it was four times as dangerous to bear a child as to work in a mine.

The entire situation was completely illogical and could only be explained in terms of men not regarding women as human beings like themselves, with feelings and equal rights to freedom and justice. What Rhona had said was true enough – men politicians were no use. So far as the male politicians were concerned it was 'Freedom for everyone – except women'. 'Justice for all – except women.' It made her so angry.

In the month that followed her first visit to Rhona Lindsay, the more she thought of the idea of giving women information about contraception the more convinced she became that this would be a more telling and practicable blow for freedom than anything else. She determined to increase her own knowledge on the subject first of all and to track down every source of information. This was not easy and it was especially difficult to actually get her hands on any contraceptives. There were none on display in any chemist's shop and the few chemists that supplied them only circulated their price lists and catalogues privately. To get these you had to write especially for them and this she did to an Edinburgh chemist, signing herself *Mr C. Blackwood* to ensure that she would not be discriminated against.

Kitty and the rest of the girls were absolutely shattered when she told them and even Betsy was rocked on her heels. But they had seen the sense and rightness of it while still struggling to gather the kind of courage to take action themselves, courage that seemed to come naturally to Clementina and which never ceased to amaze them.

Before Clementina had even mentioned her plans to her friends, however, she had discussed the subject with Rhona Lindsay on the Sunday of the mill-girl's first visit to Blackwood House. Clementina had gone to the big iron gates promptly at three o'clock and found her already there, standing shivering in a collarless shirt blouse with rolled-up sleeves and a thin black skirt. She was neat and clean and her thick hair had been well brushed and pinned up. Although it was a summer's day, there was a keen blustery wind and she looked blue with the cold.

'Good grief!' Clementina said. 'This wind is enough to give you pneumonia. It must be cutting right through you. Why didn't you wear something warmer?'

The girl tipped up her chin, eyes flashing. 'I wasn't coming up here wearing an old shawl for folks to look down their noses at me!'

'There's only me in the tower. Everyone's out for tea – even Jamie and his nanny. Come on, you're needing a hot drink right away. Then afterwards we will look out one of my coats for you to wear going back home.'

She'd also given Rhona a long black jacket, a frilly blouse, a skirt and a pair of shoes. 'You look marvellous in that blouse,' Clementina enthused. 'I've never liked it on myself; I never felt comfortable in it.'

The girl's curly hair had tumbled loose from the pins that secured it and despite the fact that she tried to appear

376

nonchalant, her face was flushed with pleasure and excitement as she tried on the garments.

Rhona was a little taller than Clementina and so the skirt hem needed taking down and while they sat talking after tea Rhona unpicked the hem, pulling and biting at the threads with her strong white teeth as if, in her excitement, she could not wait until she returned home.

She seemed to alternate between extremes of mood. Sometimes her eyes lowered and she spoke dully with a sullen droop to her mouth. At other times there seemed a wildness about her and she was like one of the animals that darted about bright-eyed in the grounds outside.

Clementina marvelled at the wild free spirit she detected. She couldn't fathom how it had blossomed and become so vibrant and strong in the repressive squalid conditions she had witnessed. She had expected Rhona to feel uncomfortable on that first visit to Blackwood House and made the mistake of saying so, because she was surprised how Rhona seemed to be enjoying herself. The first half-hour was rather tense, until after they reached the tower house and she had ordered McGregor to bring up afternoon tea. Once they were alone again and settled down to drink their tea and eat the bread and butter, Sunday jam and cake Flora had brought, Rhona seemed to be in her element.

When Clementina remarked on this the eyes had sparked with anger. 'Why should I feel uncomfortable? I would be perfectly happy staying the rest of my days in a luxurious place like this.'

Clementina had never thought of the tower house as being luxurious. Indeed with its lack of curtains, bare walls, echoing wood floors and spartan furnishings it was not luxurious, except of course in comparison with Rhona's damp comfortless room in Blackwood village.

She was glad Rhona had enjoyed herself so intensely and made sure her new friend paid further visits. On each occasion she gave her a blouse, a hat, a petticoat, a pair of stockings or even just a handkerchief — and on each occasion Rhona accepted the articles with a kind of furtive pleasure like a jackdaw collecting stolen treasure.

By mutual agreement and understanding the visits were kept secret. It was not that either girl was lacking in the courage to stand up to the disapproval and wrath of Clementina's mother, but facts had to be faced. Clementina had no right to insist on bringing people into her mother's house of whom her mother would disapprove and whom she would forbid to enter.

'If you were married and it was your own place, it would be different,' Rhona said. 'Although then you'd have a bloody husband to contend with!'

If her habit of dropping the occasional swear-word into her conversation was meant to shock Clementina, it failed. It did shock Clementina's friends however, especially Agnes. And Eva had more than once told Rhona that using such words only proved that the speaker had a limited vocabulary or a limited self-control or both. But Rhona just flashed them a smile as if she found keen enjoyment in shocking them and rousing their criticism.

'I've no intention of getting married,' Clementina informed her and Rhona had hooted sarcastically.

'Oh no, you don't care a fig for him who keeps chasing after you. A bloody lord, no less!'

Clementina had flushed with anger. 'No, I do not. His title may impress you, as it certainly seems to impress everyone else, but it doesn't impress me in the slightest – any more than does the man himself. It's not my fault that he keeps turning up at any social function I attend. And you have no idea of the pressure I am under from my mother. Everybody in the family – even the family solicitor, would you believe – is trying to persuade me to succumb to the infuriating man's advances.'

'Well, I've seen his lordship a couple of times when he's been going through Bathgate in his carriage and . . .'

'Oh, he has a certain magnetism,' Clementina conceded. 'I'm not denying that. That's no reason, however, for throwing myself into his arms.'

Rhona laughed, tossing back her head in the careless uninhibited way she sometimes had.

'I don't see anything to laugh at,' Clementina protested.

Rhona shrugged. 'You always get so hot under the collar when you speak about him.'

'The reason for that is quite simple. He makes me angry!'

'It strikes me,' Rhona said, 'that you're more angry at yourself than him.'

There was some truth in this. Clementina would never admit it to Rhona or any of her friends, but Douglas Monteith disturbed her in a way that was sometimes quite frightening. And she was angry at herself for feeling frightened, of being prey to emotions over which she seemed to have so little control. She never failed to muster some self-discipline when she found herself in his company, but even these efforts had been undermined by him.

'Relax,' he commanded. 'I'm not going to eat you.'

'Are you suggesting I am afraid of you, Lord Monteith?' She tried to intimidate him with her formal address and her unblinking jewel-hard stare. 'Because I'm not.'

'Of course not,' he said. 'Perish the thought!'

And still there was the mockery in his eyes and voice that refused to be intimidated away. Indeed, the stronger line she took with him, the stronger and more forceful his attitude became. It was like a test of strength of which he was determined beyond all doubt to win. Even when he turned on the charm, and could when he liked, he infuriated her.

He had spoiled the soirée at Agnes's house as far as Clementina was concerned. Normally this was a very enjoyable and relaxed affair. Agnes looked quite angelic playing the harp and was usually teased good-humouredly about this. Millicent had a marvellous memory for recitations. Clementina always contributed to the evening by singing a couple of songs and accompanying herself on the piano. On the last occasion however, she had been quite distracted by Douglas standing close beside her, supposedly to turn over the pages of her music. The nearness of him, especially when he bent across her, made her voice tremble as she sang and she became quite tense – indeed she was so furious at her own weakness that she could think of nothing else the whole night.

To bring relief to her pent-up feelings, she told Rhona how Lord Monteith kept forcing his attentions on her. But Rhona had been no comfort at all, had seemed quite bitter in fact.

'Poor little you!' she had sneered. 'Being courted by a wealthy aristocrat! My heart bleeds for you.'

Rhona wasn't a very likeable person at times, yet Clementina was becoming more and more aware of a bond between them. Trying to analyse her feelings, she had wondered if it was because she had always been looked after by poor people when she was a child – even Miss Viners had been as poor as a church mouse – and that was what gave her the strange affinity with the working-class girl. She had not the deep affection for Rhona that she felt for her other friends. Apart from anything else, she had known Millicent and the rest for years and years, whereas she hardly knew Rhona at all. She was beginning to see, however, that despite resentment, sneers and at times, Clementina suspected, even hatred, Rhona had acquired a grudging respect for her.

In many ways, Clementina returned that respect.

But of course Rhona didn't understand about Douglas. Even if he had no title, she would have still regarded him as an enviable catch simply because he was wealthy. Clementina was fast coming to the conclusion that at rock bottom Rhona was only capable of thinking in terms of money. Those who had money and those who had not. Rhona spoke about money and material things a great deal and with such a hunger in her eyes that Clementina had once said, 'Sometimes I think you would sell your best friend if you were offered enough.'

And she had not been surprised when Rhona had given one of her mysterious, wicked smiles and said, 'Of course!'

CHAPTER FORTY-FIVE

Lorianna, John Stirling, Gilbert, Malcolm, Hilda, Mary Ann and Clementina had been invited to stay at Dumbreggan for a few days as part of a house party. Everyone except Clementina was feverishly excited about the prospect. There was to be a ball and Clementina and Lorianna had spent much time being fitted for suitable gowns – something that Clementina considered a terrible waste of time, but she managed to control her impatience and her tongue for her mother's sake.

Douglas lived in the house with his widowed father – an eccentric and violent kind of man as it turned out. But it was the house that had an intimidating effect on Clementina at first. It had been visible from a distance and the carriage had travelled some way through parkland and wood before suddenly – as they entered the gates and progressed along a straight drive-way flanked by lawns that seemed to stretch for miles – the vista of the house and gardens opened up to them.

On one side of the enormous building, beyond more expansive lawns and a lake, there rose up a huge bank of rhododendrons and azaleas which when in bloom must have been a stunning mountain of colour.

Later they were to discover that on the opposite side of the building and beyond it, past lawns and woodland gardens and easier seen from the upper windows, was the Firth of Forth spanned by the engineering wonder of the Forth Bridge.

Clementina was impressed despite herself and her heart began to play tricks. Her first fleeting moments of intimidation soon vanished, however. She was so angry and embarrassed at the way her family showed how impressed they were by behaving at times almost obsequiously. Even her mother, who at least retained her cool dignity, was affected. This showed during private moments when she was alone with Clementina; then emotion would flare up and she would show by her desperation that it was vitally important to her that Clementina made the most of what she kept calling 'a marvellous opportunity' and even 'this honour'.

There was more in her mother's attitude than her usual longing to get rid of Clementina. Now there was the added intensity and hope that they might acquire an aristocrat in the family. And not merely an aristocrat, but a titled man who owned Dumbreggan!

Even the pillared hall was magnificent, its floor of inlaid marble typical of the rich materials used throughout the whole of the house. The drawing-room with its white silk curtains bordered with turquoise, the silk brocade on the walls and the exquisite embroidery of the chairs – all this made both Mary Ann and Hilda go into breathless eulogies of praise and admiration.

The sumptuous ballroom with panelled ceiling of different painted scenes, walls hung with embossed velvet, curtains woven with gold and silver thread and Louis XVI furniture sent them into more twittering raptures and made Clementina perversely critical of everything.

The intensity of the secret glances her mother flashed at her grew murderous. But Clementina became angry with herself too. She managed to refrain from being critical in Douglas Monteith's presence, for after all, she and her family were in his home as his guests and enjoying his hospitality. Her irritation with her family, however, kept spilling over to some degree when she was in Douglas's company. And on each occasion she upbraided herself afterwards for showing herself in such a bad light. Especially in comparison with Lady Alice Cunningham, who was such a sweet and agreeable creature. There was no inner or outer conflict there – at least, none was visible in the serene features. Her mother, the Marchioness of Annonford, was a plump, talkative woman with diamonds and feathers in her hair. Her voice dominated the conversation after the ladies had withdrawn from the dining-room in order to allow the men to enjoy their after-dinner brandy and cigars. Her talk unravelled loudly and carelessly, entangling Clementina in it despite herself. The subject had turned to another house party that the Marchioness and Douglas's Aunt Elizabeth had attended recently and Lady Elizabeth remarked that house parties were not what they used to be. The Marchioness, with a supercilious glance in Clementina's direction, said, 'That's because they are not so select now. One even finds oneself having to mix with people in trade!'

Clementina, who believed her time would have been far more usefully and interestingly spent in the company of Millicent and her other suffragette friends, including Rhona Lindsay, said in a matter-of-fact voice, 'The country would be a very poor place without trade. Indeed, it would grind to a complete halt. People in trade fulfil a practical and valuable role in the economy.'

The Marchioness's indifferent stare wafted away. 'I don't know about such things,' she replied carelessly.

'I believe you,' Clementina said. 'I'm sure there are a great many subjects about which you know nothing.'

She groaned to herself the moment the words were uttered. It was quite unforgivable to speak to an older woman in such a manner. She felt sick, especially when Lady Alice intervened immediately and loyally, saying,

'Oh, on the contrary, Mamma is exceptionally well-informed.'

Mary Ann made a frantic attempt to change the subject with simpering praise of the Marchioness's mauve silk dress, praise which that lady chose to ignore.

Lady Elizabeth stared disapprovingly down her lorg-

384

nette at Clementina, who stared back at her in wide-eyed regret and embarrassment which Lady Elizabeth mistakenly took for defiance.

'What did you say your name was?'

'Clementina Blackwood.'

'Ah, so you're the one!'

'What do you mean, Lady Elizabeth?' The words arose from spontaneous curiosity, but only served to increase her apparent air of impertinence.

Lorianna's smouldering dark eyes tried to annihilate her daughter, but she was saved from further explosive emotions by the return of the men and a change in the conversation.

Clementina could not help noticing how different from the rest the Monteith men looked. It was not just the fact that Douglas and his father were resplendent in full Highland dress; they both had an air of self-confidence and authority which made Gilbert and Malcolm seem like mere lackeys. John Stirling had more presence with his cool courteous manner. He was listening intently to the conversation of a small, portly man with steely grey hair and a beard like that of King Edward.

Douglas announced, 'We have been discussing photography and how it has developed in recent years. Everyone's albums used to be filled with nothing but stiffly-posed unsmiling figures, bushy-whiskered papas, stern matriarchs, or yeomanry officers posing with their helmets on plaster columns.'

Douglas's father, a bearded giant of a man, boomed out, 'Not enough formality around nowadays.'

As if waiting the signal of his voice, two long-legged grey wolf-hounds almost as tall as ponies came padding into the room and flopped down at the Earl's feet.

'Well, like it or not, Father,' Douglas grinned, 'I intend to take a great many informal photographs of these beautiful ladies during the weekend.'

The ladies laughed behind their fans in delight and anticipation. Except Clementina, who was always genuinely interested in anything new.

'I suppose recent progress in photography,' she said, 'has greatly extended the camera's possibilities?'

A suspicion of a smile clung on in Douglas's eyes, but his voice became serious. 'Yes, we are not only able to record each other's appearance now, but also architecture and scenery.'

'It could be used as a record of our time. Something useful to pass down to our children.'

Clementina had meant the words in a strictly general sense, but she felt an immediate shock of intimacy at their utterance. The words 'our children' seemed to reflect back to her from Douglas Monteith's eyes as a passionate caress.

'Fit you better to get in a sight more hunting and shooting,' his father growled. 'You'll be turning soft!'

Lady Alice hastened to bring reassurance. 'Oh, I don't think you need worry about Douglas on that score.'

Unlike her mother she was of willowy proportions and gentle-voiced and she had a habit of lowering her eyes when she spoke. She looked, Clementina thought with a bitterness that surprised herself, very biddable, a most properly behaved and obedient young lady.

'When are you two getting married?' the Earl suddenly demanded. 'You have been playing the field for far too long. I want to see a grandson before I die.'

'And so you shall, father,' Douglas said. 'But you don't look as if you're going to die for some time yet.'

'Well, at least get her to play a tune for us. If there's not going to be any entertainment, I'm going to bed.'

'Alice!' her mother commanded and Alice immediately rose and glided away to the grand piano at the far end of the room.

Clementina knew in her bones that the dark-haired beauty would be a wonderfully accomplished pianist and, of course, so she was. Sitting listening to the immaculate rendering of Mendelssohn's 'Songs Without Words' and gazing in despair at Lady Alice's erect and graceful figure ethereally clad in white chiffon, Clementina struggled not to hate her. After all, the girl had not done her any harm and had in actual fact been unfailingly charming to everyone. The piece completed to perfection and duly applauded, Lady Alice made a little curtsey before returning to her place beside her mother on one of the exquisitely embroidered chairs that lined both walls of the salon.

'Miss Blackson . . . Blackstock or whatever you call yourself . . .' The lorgnette was aimed at Clementina again and her heart sank. 'What can you do?' The additional unsaid words – 'Apart from being shockingly impertinent' – hung accusingly in the air for everyone to see.

Before she could steel herself to reply, Douglas said, 'Clementina has a charming singing voice. I was most impressed with it at the Andersons' soirée.'

'Anderson? Anderson?' his aunt repeated. 'Who are they? Really Douglas, you ought to be more careful about the company you keep.'

'Time he was married,' his father boomed. 'He has sown enough wild oats for ten men his age.'

Ignoring the older man, Douglas said, 'Will you accompany yourself, Clementina, or would you prefer Alice to . . .'

Obediently Alice rose. 'I should be most pleased to oblige Miss Blackwood.'

'That will not be necessary, thank you,' Clementina said firmly. 'I will not sing, but if you wish I will recite some verses by our national bard, Robert Burns.'

Lorianna closed her eyes as her daughter rose and walked purposefully into the centre of the room. Surely the dreadful girl was not going to repeat that poem she had recited to the family the other day after they had angrily reproached her for her lack of encouragement of Lord Monteith's advances. 'You see thon birkie ca'd a

Lord,' she had said, 'what struts and stares and a' that. Though hundreds worship at his word, He's but a coof for a' that.' Clementina, she remembered, had tossed her head in much the same defiant manner as she was doing now and continued. 'For a' that and a' that, his ribband, star and a' that, the man (and woman, Mother, she had added) of independent mind, He looks and laughs at a' that.'

'If she comes out with that poem now,' Lorianna thought, 'I shall die. And if God is not merciful enough to let me die – then I will live to kill Clementina.'

But she was spared 'For a' that and a' that' because Clementina in a loud determined voice recited:

My heart's in the Highlands, my heart is not here;
My heart's in the Highlands a-chasing the deer;
Chasing the wild deer and following the roe,
My heart's in the Highlands, wherever I go.

This was bad enough, as it did nothing to portray any delicate or ladylike sentiments. However, it seemed to appeal to Douglas's father who, after Clementina had gone through all the verses, applauded with such embarrassing loudness that it disturbed the dogs. They scrambled to their feet barking excitedly and were only quietened by the Earl snarling at them and cuffing them so roughly that Lorianna had to turn away in distress.

Later she accused Clementina of spoiling the evening and letting down not only herself but the whole family. Clementina thought this was only too true, but stubbornly refused to admit it either to her mother or to the rest of the family who also bitterly upbraided her. Alone in the big, four-poster bed with its crimson and gold canopy and hangings, Clementina squirmed with embarrassment and regret as she relived every moment over and over again. She had been so gauche in comparison with Lady Alice. What must Douglas think of her? Yet what did it matter what Douglas thought of her? She had to be honest with herself; she had to be sensible and face facts. It mattered very painfully what Douglas Monteith thought of her.

CHAPTER FORTY-SIX

The next day Clementina dressed with care in a beige silk blouse with a high, stiff neck and front fashionably pouched over the waist of her black skirt. She felt self-conscious in the hands of an aloof and silent maid and although she longed to ask if it would be proper and becoming to wear jewellery at this early hour, she decided it would be unwise. After anxious debating with herself she pinned a cameo brooch at her throat. She thought she looked rather nice and that her mother would be pleased with her. But on the contrary Lorianna, meeting her just outside the dining-room, hissed, 'You could at least have worn a gown. I can't even trust you to dress attractively.'

Of course, Lady Alice was wearing a gown. The vision of the tall slender figure in the stunning robe of all-over embroidery immediately and profoundly depressed Clementina. Next to Lady Alice, she felt like a prim 'schoolmam' or a sturdy working woman in her plain blouse and skirt. It was a truly terrible start to a disastrous day.

Later, Douglas had suggested riding around part of the estate and, still trying her best to be agreeable and pleasing Clementina readily concurred, despite the fact that she had only learned to ride since her father died. Before that she had never been allowed to do so. Lady Alice had owned and ridden a pony since infancy, it seemed. Clementina had never known anyone to sit so gracefully side-saddle; it always felt very awkward to her. She would have long ago ridden astride, had she not known how it would have shocked and distressed her mother.

Lady Alice had even managed to follow Douglas over a high hedge with smooth and effortless ease. Whereas when Clementina had tried to do the same (she groaned inwardly every time she thought of it) she had parted company with her horse and landed in a most unsmooth, undignified fashion in a ditch. Once Douglas had made sure she was all right and no bones broken, he had laughed and shaken his head at her muddy and dishevelled appearance and said, 'Oh, Clementina!'

'We should have been more thoughtful, Douglas,' Lady Alice said. 'Poor Clementina is not used to the way we live.'

Clementina vowed she would never forgive Douglas for laughing at her, especially in front of Lady Alice. He had even laughingly drawn attention to mud on her face and tried to wipe it off with his handkerchief. She had brushed his hand aside, remounted her horse, cantered back and made another gallop at the hedge, this time successfully clearing it. Douglas clapped and shouted, 'Bravo!'

But that didn't help and she was bruised and aching all over. Even her heart ached and all she wanted was to be back with her real friends doing things that really mattered. But there was still the ball to get through before she and her family returned to Blackwood House the next day. She dreaded it now; she imagined having to watch Douglas spending most of the evening with Lady Alice in his arms and the prospect acutely distressed her. She kept wishing she could somehow avoid the ordeal by taking ill or by fainting and having to be rushed home early. But apart from being disgustingly healthy she was just not the fainting kind. No doubt Douglas would only laugh at her if she tried.

As it turned out the ball was even worse than she had feared. Sitting beside her mother, energetically fanning herself, Clementina watched Douglas in merry conversation with a stunning red-head in a shockingly low-cut green satin dress. The girl's long diamond earrings swung about and flashed as she laughed and chattered and tossed up coquettish, inviting glances at him. Soon they were dancing so close together that they looked as if they had merged into one body.

'Clementina.' Lorianna ventured gentle restraining fingertips on Clementina's arm. 'There is surely no need to use your fan with quite so much fury and desperation. You can't be feeling all that warm. It looks neither dignified nor ladylike. Try to be a little more restrained in everything you do.'

Clementina hardly listened, never even turned round.

Now he was being cornered by another proud mamma, literally cornered, while the matron with the large pearl-buttoned bosom eagerly pushed her daughter towards him. The way the daughter – a shapely girl in coffee-coloured lace and amber choker – almost purred and rubbed herself like a cat against him was too disgraceful for words. It made Clementina feel ashamed of her own sex. But, of course, she realised that this kind of eager desperation was only the result of the moral and social code created by men. Women *had* to get a husband. According to this code, it was their proper goal in life. If they did not succeed in getting a husband they were condemned as failures. They had no resources and it was looked on as a disgrace, as if they had failed in business.

Lady Alice would not fail, Clementina felt sure. She danced like a dream in Douglas's arms and she too kept gazing up at him coyly, invitingly. Clementina's fan flapped more furiously than ever.

The dazzling ballroom with its crystal and gold chandeliers, its gold and silver walls, swirled with colourful gowns like a garden in full bloom. When Clementina, in daffodil yellow satin, danced with Douglas she told him that with so many females chasing after him, it was no wonder he was so conceited and sure of himself. But, she said, he must not make the mistake of thinking that she was in *that* category of female, because she certainly was not. She had more important things to do with her life than chase after any man. She meant this most sincerely and it was most provoking and infuriating the way his eyes kept showering darts of mockery and amusement down at her. He spoke very little, while at times she lectured him at great length. It was disquieting to sense a purposeful presence about him that seemed to dominate her without resorting to words. Sometimes they danced in complete silence.

There was a full moon that illuminated the countryside with silvery brilliance and she was eventually persuaded to take a walk with him outside to look at the formal gardens. He explained that some distance from the other side of the house there was a lake and, across a footbridge beyond the bank of rhododendrons, a woodland garden. He would show her all that during daylight hours next day, but meantime he thought she would find that the formal garden looked very pretty by moonlight. The walled garden with its central fountain, gleaming white statues and heady perfume was an enchanted spot. Trees towered high all around creating another wall, dark green above ghostly grey, making the place secluded, secretive. For a time as they walked only the whispering and creak-ing of the trees broke the silence. It was cold and she was wearing a sable evening cloak loaned to her by her mother. She was glad of its coverage of the daring décoletée of her yellow gown with the figure-flattering draped bodice and skirt on which her mother had insisted. The skirt was caught at the sides with pearl embroidery motifs and tassels which bounced and swung about in a most titillating manner when she danced or walked.

'Wait!' His unexpected command surprised her on her way to examine one of the statues at closer range.

She turned with eyebrow raised and was about to ques-tion his tone of voice when to her astonishment and dis-may she found herself suddenly swept into his arms. His mouth came down over hers and the surprise and the delicious tremors awakened by it chased away any thoughts of resistance. Then his arms slid inside her cape and she felt the heat of his body pressed against hers. In sudden panic she struggled from him and brought her palm stinging across his face.

For a frightening moment she thought he was about to strike her back. His expression hardened and his eyes narrowed and flashed with temper. But the moment passed and coolly he moved away from her, saying, 'I'm sorry. I should not have done that. Shall we go back inside?'

As they strolled along together towards the ballroom he glanced down at her and asked, 'Am I forgiven?'

'Yes,' she replied, feeling inexplicably miserable. Somehow everything had gone wrong again. With other gentlemen at the ball she was extremely popular and in much demand for dances as soon as Douglas had taken her back to her mother and politely excused himself to go and partner Lady Alice. But she didn't care about any other man in the room.

'What have you done now?' Lorianna wanted to know and Clementina was grateful to a handsome young Guards officer who whisked her away in a polka and saved her from having to answer. She managed to smile at the officer and appear interested in what he was saying, but her attention kept straying in desperate attempts to keep track of Douglas. He seemed to be enjoying himself immensely with Lady Alice who, with her dark crown of hair and rose-pink confection of a ball-gown, looked not only startlingly beautiful but absolutely delicious.

Douglas did not ask Clementina to dance again, although sometimes while they were dancing with other people their eyes would meet and he would smile at her. She would smile in return and then smile just as brightly at her partner. The more deeply she suffered, in fact, the more she appeared not to care a fig.

CHAPTER FORTY-SEVEN

Coldness seeped into Blackwood House. Clementina was no longer invited down from the tower to share afternoon tea or any other meal when Gilbert and Malcolm and their wives came to visit. Nor was she included in any invitations to their homes. She had spoiled her big chance, the family bitterly accused. She ought to have captured Lord Monteith once and for all during that weekend at Dumbreggan. Lady Alice and her mother were lifelong friends of the Monteiths; they probably visited Dumbreggan every other day, but she would never get such an opportunity again.

Even the fact that Douglas included her in several invitations to tea-parties, tennis matches and picnics with his friends, and to go riding with them, did nothing to comfort and cheer her family. He was only behaving like the gentleman that he was, they said. As far as any romantic inclinations were concerned, he couldn't possibly retain any for a girl who had no idea how to behave like a lady.

'Lord Monteith has eyes only for Lady Alice now,' wailed Mary Ann. 'And to think we could have had such an important and influential man in the family.'

'She's never going to do *anything* right *anywhere* with *anybody!*' Hilda told Lorianna in front of Clementina.

Lorianna had leaned back against the cushions of her chair, shaded her eyes with her hand and said, 'Yes, it's not just Lord Monteith. She has spurned every man who has shown the slightest interest in her, and she will go on doing it – I know she will.'

Clementina was more upset than she cared to admit, especially about disappointing her mother. Alone at the dinner-table with Lorianna, she had tried to explain that she had not meant to spoil everything. She even managed a miserable apology and was rewarded by a visible struggle on Lorianna's part to be patient and kind.

It was perfectly true what Clementina had said – she had not meant to spurn Douglas. Her attack on him had been so sudden and spontaneous she hardly knew why she had acted in the way she did. Sometimes, trying to think back and relive the scene, her mind would go blank and she would experience spasms of fear. Eventually she managed to face the fear and to some degree even analyse why she suffered it. Her father had sexually attacked her. Sometimes the awful truth threatened to destroy her, undermine her whole existence. She had to take herself very firmly in hand and tell herself – 'It is in the dim and distant past. It is not happening now!' Still she was glad to retreat into the safety of other pursuits like her suffrage interests with her women friends and not to complicate her life with any man. She couldn't stand Mrs Musgrove, indeed had hated her since childhood, but it was true what the housekeeper said about men. They caused nothing but trouble. Another part of her still hopefully, trustfully clung to Douglas. When she entered a crowded room she found herself looking around, eager that he should be there and if he was not, then the crowded room seemed empty and without interest. Yet if he was, she quite often made a point of concentrating on someone else. Sometimes when their eyes met he smiled and came over to talk to her. She always meant to be pleasant and friendly – surely it wasn't always her fault when the conversation turned to controversial matters and he became angry with her. He had, she discovered, a temper that could flash like lightning across his face. She had never seen anyone whose expression could change so quickly and violently.

Secretly she dreaded his finding out about her latest activities. She and the girls had got themselves better organised now and had held quite a number of successful suffragette meetings. But, and this was the cause of her secret dread, they had also established a pattern of regular visits to the homes of working-class women in Blackwood village during which they passed on information they had gathered about contraception.

It was an ordeal having to go to the village every few weeks. The oppressive shadow of the mill, the claustrophobic crush of houses with their tiny, damp and overcrowded rooms, and the ragged and emaciated state of the people they were trying to help – all this depressed the girls. But they had decided that if improving the lot of women was their basic aim, then it was their duty to help these poor wretches because they needed help more than most.

Sometimes Rhona turned up at the houses and would sit by the fire nonchalantly warming herself, like a cat whose only interest is in its own comfort. But in many ways, subtle and otherwise, she laid proud claim to Clementina's friendship. Where the other working-class women would be grateful to the point of obsequiousness, Rhona would address her in an impudent way. While Clementina was talking to the women Rhona would interrupt with things like 'Good for you, Clemmy!' And when the meeting was finished and they were leaving, Rhona would grab Clementina's arm and say, 'Come on, Clemmy.' This was something she never did when they were alone. On the contrary, when they were alone Rhona behaved for the most part as if Clementina were contagious. Nevertheless, Clementina had come to the conclusion that Rhona secretly admired her for her participation in the birth control activities.

The trouble was what Douglas would think of her participation in such 'goings-on'. Even some of the village women's husbands had been shocked at their wives getting to know about 'such things'. To speak about contraception was ten times worse than committing murder, it seemed.

She wanted Douglas to think well of her and gradually they were building up some kind of a relationship despite their fiery arguments. There was no use pinning her hopes on anything permanent though. She seemed destined never to remain close to anyone for long. Her family were like cold strangers; her mother, despite her struggles, barely managed to be polite. The people who had looked after her when she had been a child had come and gone. Even the girls, although dear friends, had close family circles of which she was not a part. And eventually, despite their enthusiastic suffragette beliefs and activities, they would settle down, get married and have homes and families of their own. Already all sorts of little flirtations were starting up at dances, where amid much hilarity they raced up and down shiny parquet floors to 'Strip the Willow', 'The Dashing White Sergeant', eightsome reels, 'The Duke of Perth' and 'Petronella'. Soirées were more dignified, but much fun and camaraderie was found at cycling clubs, and skating on the pond in the garden of Blackwood House by moonlight had nearly caused them all to lose their hearts.

Agnes and Clementina had worn fur hats and muffs on that occasion. Betsy had sported a very chic green jacket with black buttons and black braiding on the skirt which daringly revealed not only her ankles but the tops of her boots. Eva's peaky face was barely visible between a wide-brimmed hat and a blue muffler. Millicent and Kitty were like twins in brown costumes with yellow mufflers and gloves. A crowd of young men from the surrounding area had come to share the fun and help the ladies fix on their skates and were soon gliding along the ice with arms around the ladies' waists.

Douglas had held Clementina close to him all evening and it had seemed to her as she swooped and swirled around with him in the moonlight that she had never been so blissfully happy in her life. Safely held in Douglas's strong arm and with the frosty air tingling their cheeks as they flew round the ice in perfect unison, she wished they could always be in such harmony and smooth accord. In her heart of hearts, though, she knew this was impossible. Her suffragette beliefs and activities were a sufficiently large bone of contention between them, but she shuddered to think how he would react when he discovered about her interests in birth control and contraception. She suspected that it would be too much for him to put up with; he would lose his temper with her completely and that would be the end – at least of any closeness between them.

On that magic night on the pond, however, she had forgotten about such dangers and they had continued to glide around together in a dream long after all the others had gone home. Then at last when she had been sitting on the seat and he had been kneeling at her feet removing her skates, she had been overcome with such tenderness for him that she put her hand out and wistfully caressed his cheek.

'Oh, Clementina,' he had whispered and kissed deeply into her palm. Then he sat on the bench beside her and gathered her into his arms. He kissed her gently at first and then more and more urgently, his mouth hardening against hers and forcing her lips open. She was gladly surrendering when suddenly the panic returned and with fast fluttering pulse she tried to push the weight of him away from her. Her body seemed to have taken over of its own accord and was violently trembling.

'Darling, darling,' Douglas soothed. 'Don't! It's all right.'

She was sobbing now because it wasn't all right. It wasn't all right at all.

CHAPTER FORTY-EIGHT

Clementina was lying pinioned on the floor, unable to breathe for the weight on top of her. Her legs were torn apart and the Cannibal Man was coming howling towards her, bringing terror beyond all terrors and pain thumping and stabbing into her most vulnerable parts.

She jerked awake to the sound of her own screams. Sweat was pouring from her and making the sheets clammy. She clutched them up against her mouth, wide-eyed in the dark. A creaking sound from outside on the landing squeezed high-pitched moans into the sheet; she dug her heels into the mattress and slid stiffly up against the pillows. The creaking was repeated every now and again, a ghostly echo in the silence of the tower. Never before had Clementina felt so isolated and alone. A heavy door on the nursery landing upstairs cut off the top floor; two doors and the spiral stairs separated the school-room quarters from the main part of the house.

The emptiness of the school-room and the adjoining apartments echoed back to her. She could be alone in the universe. As she became more wide-awake she realised that the creaking was probably the landing door – maybe she had not shut it properly when she came in. The wind was howling outside and the door was moving spasmodically in the draught. She ought to get up and shut it. Forcing herself to release the bunched-up sheets, she tentatively fumbled on the bedside table for a candle and the matches. The puny flame made the darkness crowd menacingly in on her, but she told herself not to be foolish. Everyone had nightmares at some time or other. But she didn't get up, telling herself that she would get so cold that she would be unable to get back to sleep. Then it occurred to her that she was too afraid to go back to sleep in case she would be at the mercy of the nightmare again. And somehow, lying with eyes straining to fight the weight of sleep, she became prey to all the frightening memories of her childhood. The awful desolation of losing Henny. The horror after Alice had been dismissed when she had been absolutely alone for the first time in the nursery quarters, knowing that Miss Viners was downstairs talking to the spirits of the dead.

Then memories of punishments came rushing at her from the dark tunnel of the past – the sharp pain of beatings, the agony of invading hands and, more than anything else, the anguish of love betrayed. She had loved her father and taken it for granted that he had loved her. But how could there ever have been love when he had behaved in such a bestial way towards her? When she'd heard about his death, she'd been glad to be free of her ordeal of pain and humiliation. Yet she'd felt guilty and heartbroken too.

She tried to be firm with herself. Everything always seemed worse in the middle of the night. She must be sensible; she was a woman now, not a child. 'It's in the dim and distant past,' she kept repeating with growing desperation. 'It is *not* happening now.'

Douglas loved her. Last night he had assured her over and over again that he did. And he said that he wanted to marry her. Nevertheless she had been unable to contain her panic. All she wanted to do was to rush away from him and escape into the house.

'I don't want to marry you, do you hear?' she had cried out eventually. 'I don't want to marry anybody. We can be friends if you like, but that's all.'

The nightmare still clung around her like a shroud and she had to give herself a cold sponge-down and take a determined trudge around the crisp white garden before she could face the day.

By the time she cycled to meet Millicent, Kitty, Agnes and Eva she had her unruly emotions firmly under control. They met just outside Littlegate village on the edge of the woods and, after parking their bicycles against a tree, they ate their lunch sandwiches while they stood chatting to one another. Betsy couldn't come because her father insisted that it was her duty to keep him company at mealtimes and to see to his needs. This was despite the fact, as Betsy said, that he never addressed one word to her at table, never even answered her when she spoke to him and of course had a houseful of servants to see to his needs.

'Well, what have we decided?' Clementina wanted to know. 'We have only a couple of weeks to go.'

She was referring to the big suffragette march and meeting in Edinburgh that they planned to attend.

'I think we should all just go on the train,' Millicent said. 'By travelling by rail we shall each have a return ticket and if we lose touch with each other it won't matter. We can make our own way home.'

Agnes said, 'I should prefer to go by carriage and you would be welcome to share with me. Mamma said I could have it. Papa doesn't use the brougham during the day and we would be back before he got home.'

'It would be a bit of a crush with six of us in a carriage,' Clementina said. 'Anyway, all the others are going by train as far as we know. And it's much faster and more convenient.'

It was decided eventually that the train it would be. Then they discussed for a while what they would wear on the big day. And they eulogised about their banner; they had taken much trouble in making it and were proud of its design of gold scales of justice and the colourful green lettering which proclaimed the name of their group.

The West Lothian Justice for Women Group had now no fewer than 170 paid-up members and there would be other banners carried by some of that number. Rhona and other women from Blackwood village, for instance, had a banner with 'A Good Cause Makes a Strong Arm' emblazoned on it.

'I do hope Betsy manages to join us.' Agnes sounded worried. 'It would break her heart if we had to go without her.'

'She will be all right, ' Clementina said. 'Her father's to be away in Glasgow that day, so she'll be free until evening.'

'Will you be all right, Clementina?' Agnes asked.

'Oh yes, nobody at home cares about me,' Clementina answered matter-of-factly.

Eventually, all their plans completed, the girls cycled away, leaving Clementina behind because she wanted to have a stroll round Littlegate before returning to Blackwood House. After her friends had left she remained resting against a tree for a few minutes, vowing that tonight she must make sure she had a better sleep. It was unlike her to feel so drained and exhausted. She breathed in the pungent smell of greenery and listened to sounds in the distance – the barking of a dog, the bleating of sheep and the measured clip-clop of horses' hooves. She could have slept there in the shelter of the tree with the autumn leaves rustling and gathering around her. Then suddenly she shivered. Wasn't it in this very wood that her father had been found murdered? She had been warned by Mrs Musgrove never under any circumstances to talk of the tragedy to anyone, but especially never *ever* to mention the subject to her mother. Apparently Lorianna had suffered a severe nervous breakdown afterwards and couldn't bear even yet to think about that terrible time.

And so the shadows of it were never dispelled. All she had ever been able to find out was that the grieve, Robert Kelso, had been hanged for the murder.

She had only a vague recollection of him: a big, powerful-looking man with broad shoulders and longish raven-black hair, darker even than Douglas Monteith's.

Pushing her bicycle, she started towards the village and as she did so a roe deer fled away, its white scut bobbing like a rabbit's tail, down one of the fern-edged, moss-carpeted paths and through the brown shadows of woods so thick that the paths had been protected from the recent early fall of snow. She passed along by the busy, tumbling river and then across to a stile which had to be climbed to reach the path to the village. With some difficulty she managed to get her cycle across, then she climbed nimbly over herself.

The village was a disappointment. Granny's house was like a haunted place with gaping windows revealing an empty black interior. She had gone, no one knew where. This saddened Clementina, although she knew it was silly to feel like this. After all, the old woman hadn't been her Granny but Alice Tait's. It was just – she had felt so in need of someone. For a few minutes she lingered outside the village shop as she had once done with Alice, as if hoping that by some miracle Alice would suddenly appear, plump-cheeked, mob-capped and ready for anything. But there was no sight nor sound of Alice – only the echoing tink-tink of the blacksmith's forge nearby.

With a heavy heart, Clementina mounted her bicycle and pedalled laboriously in the direction of the Drumcross Road.

Tonight she would ask Flora to bring her a glass of warm milk to make sure she could get a good restful sleep. This lethargy and depression would not do. No useful purpose could be served by it and she must be refreshed and fit for all she wanted to accomplish. At the moment, apart from her secretarial work for the West Lothian Group and her regular meetings about contraception in the homes of women in Blackwood village, she was writing a pamphlet about contraception with some diagrams drawn by Agnes, who was very artistic. It was planned to give these pamphlets out at the next meeting, which for the first time was to be held in a hall.

There were so many women whose health, strength and freedom had been eroded or destroyed by yearly pregnancies – not to mention horrific abortions and miscarriages – and who were anxious for enlightenment and help, that house meetings could not cope with them all. Women from other villages and even from Bathgate had come to hear about them and were pleading to be allowed to attend. A public meeting in a hall had hence become an urgent necessity. They had booked the Co-op Hall for an evening a couple of weeks after the Edinburgh suffragette demonstration and now the pamphlets were almost ready. Clementina had worked hard at them and Agnes had put much care and artistry into the diagrams and drawings.

Millicent, Betsy, Kitty and Eva had also been very busy. They had put together a box containing a layette to help the Blackwood village women when they did have babies. The idea was to cut down in whatever way possible the grinding worry to which the women were subjected. The box contained all the basic necessities for a confinement and was loaned out to the women as it was needed, each woman being allowed to keep the box until the baby was shortened. Among the contents were little bootees and a beautiful shawl knitted by Kitty, her fingers never at peace, her knitting needles flying at top speed. Long flannelette gowns had been produced by Betsy and Millicent. Eva had made vests and supplied nappies and little odds and ends like safety pins, soap and vaseline.

The box had proved such a godsend that they had determined to make up another one as soon as they could. In return, apart from their gratitude, they had the women's enthusiastic support for the West Lothian Justice for Women Group and quite a number of them were determined to march under the West Lothian banner in Edinburgh.

A strong sense of sisterhood was growing between not only Clementina and her immediate friends but also with the many other women with whom she now came in contact. She had been much comforted and strengthened by this, as they all had. Yet on this day, feeling over-strained, with nerve ends exposed after her nightmare night, she longed for another deeper kind of comfort, she was unsure of what nature. She wondered if she dare approach her mother, really try to get close to her. Perhaps she was much to blame for her mother's attitude. She *had* been a terrible disappointment. She *was* argumentative and it must be quite a trial for her mother, who was obviously very conventional, to have to struggle with someone in the family with such modern ideas. Especially after her mother had had to cope with a terrible tragedy in her life and then suffer such a debilitating illness.

The more Clementina allowed herself to think of her mother, the more loving and compassionate she felt until, by the time she was cycling through the iron gateway of Blackwood House, she wanted nothing more than to run into the sitting-room and into her mother's arms. When she saw the horse tethered at the door of the house she could have wept foolish tears of disappointment. It looked as if her mother had a visitor and so there would be no chance to have a confidential talk with her. In the reception hall, however, Mrs Musgrove met her and told her she must go straight into the drawing-room. Her mother wished to speak to her.

The moment she stepped into the room she was nonplussed by the sight of Douglas Monteith's tall figure in a dark suit and light waistcoat, standing with his back to the fire, smoking a cigar. The spicy aroma pervading the room added to her feelings of discomposure.

'You wished to see me, Mother?' Clementina said.

Her mother looked even more beautiful than usual in a cream silk dress with a high frilled neck and hair like polished mahogany. But her eyes seemed to burn unnaturally bright.

'Are you not going to say "Good afternoon" to Lord Monteith, Clementina? What will he think of your manners?'

'Good afternoon, Lord Monteith.'

'Lord Monteith,' Lorianna said, 'has honoured us by asking for your hand in marriage.'

'How dare you!' Clementina found herself trembling with emotion. 'I made my feelings perfectly clear to you.'

'That's why I'm here, Clementina.'

'But I have refused you!'

Her mother intervened. 'Clementina, I implore you not to be so perverse. You have no reason to refuse Lord Monteith. Apart from the fact that he can provide you with everything any woman could ever want or need, he loves you and is more than capable I am sure of dealing with . . .' she hesitated delicately, 'any little problems that may arise.'

Surely he had not betrayed her intimate moments of confusion and distress? She was speechless with fury for a moment, knowing that her rage was illogical because she had been longing to confide in her mother about this very subject herself, but not caring. How dare he! she thought.

'I shall never forgive you for this, Douglas!'

'Clementina, don't be ridiculous,' her mother said. 'Lord Monteith has behaved with absolute correctness and propriety in coming to me. There is nothing for you to forgive'.

'I have a right to say "No", Mother, and I have said "No" to Lord Monteith. We are not suited. Our temperaments, the way we live and our philosophies are completely at odds.'

Monteith sighed. 'Clementina, if it is your suffragette meetings you are worried about, I promise you I will allow you to attend them within reason. Obviously I wouldn't want to see you get hurt, and so taking part in anything illegal or militant would be out of the question, but otherwise . . .'

'You would be pleased to indulge the little woman,' Clementina interrupted with heavy sarcasm, 'so long as she asked your permission very humbly, and you happened to be in a good mood – and of course, she would have to be careful and show that she was suitably grateful if you felt beneficent enough to give your permission.'

'Oh, Lord Monteith,' Lorianna said, 'I do apologise. I

don't know why my daughter behaves like this.'

'Clementina!' She recognised the warning note in his voice, but had gone too far to change course. Recklessly, defiantly she said, 'Well, I'm not your little woman and never will be, thank God!'

The thunder of an approaching storm darkened Douglas's face, narrowing his eyes and hardening his jaw.

'You are not dealing with your mother or your brothers now, Clementina. You will do as I say.'

'Huh!' Clementina scoffed. 'You are *ordering* me to marry you, are you? Well, let me tell you, I am not your obedient slave, nor shall I ever be to any man.'

'God!' Douglas exploded, tossing his cigar into the fire. 'If you start on your bloody women's rights again, Clementina, I won't be responsible for my actions. I apologise, Mrs Blackwood,' he added, remembering the delicate sensibilities of the older woman who was shrinking back into the cushions of the settee, her hand shading her eyes in obvious distress.

'I know exactly how you feel, Lord Monteith,' Lorianna murmured.

'I have no wish to "start" anything,' Clementina said. 'In fact I'm going. I have another, more important engagement.' With a dismissive swish of her skirts she made to leave.

'No, you don't!' Douglas's long legs crossed the room with a rapidity that startled her and his voice contained such violence she didn't stop to think or feel any more – she just lifted her skirts and ran.

He caught up with her half-way up the tower stairs and knocked her up against the wall, making her immediately retaliate with a punch that sank her knuckles into his eye and nearly sent him reeling back down the narrow spiral stairs.

'Christ!'

'Lord Monteith!' her mother wailed behind him, 'it's no use. She is absolutely beyond the pale. Oh, please, just come away and leave her alone!'

408

Taking advantage of the few seconds while Douglas nursed his eye, Clementina raced up to the school-room quarters and shut and locked the landing door. And not a moment too soon.

'Clementina!' Douglas shouted. 'I am warning you. If you don't open this bloody door, I shall kick it in.'

She flew into her bedroom and locked that door as well. The landing door exploded with a thunderous noise that echoed not only in every corner of the tower but right down to the servants' quarters and brought them all running to the foot of the stairs.

'You will be terrifying my little boy!' Lorianna was sobbing hysterically now. 'Remember you are a gentleman. For pity's sake, have some consideration even if Clementina has not!'

Gradually the sobbing faded away and there was silence. Clementina could imagine Mrs Musgrove helping Lorianna on to the settee and sending servants scurrying for brandy and smelling salts, while Douglas made stiff apologies before striding from the house, mounting his horse and riding the long road through fields and hills back to Dumbreggan.

Clementina leaned against the bedroom door. She was safe. She was free. She was so miserable she didn't know how she would be able to endure it.

CHAPTER FORTY-NINE

'John!' Lorianna turned in surprise as Stirling entered the room without being announced. 'Where is the maid? I am so sorry about this. I will ring for her to take your hat and cane.'

Stirling regarded her enquiringly. 'Have I done something to offend your housekeeper? I seemed to get an even more frosty look from her than usual. I thought I wasn't going to get past her.'

'Oh dear!' Lorianna's brow creased with concern. 'I am sorry, John. She is a strange woman, but very efficient at her job.'

Just then Baxter entered, 'You rang, madam?'

'Yes. Please take Mr Stirling's hat and gloves and cane – and why didn't you announce him?'

The maid did not reply.

'Baxter,' Lorianna said in exasperation. 'I expect you to answer me when I ask you a question.'

After another awkward pause the maid said in a low voice, 'Mrs Musgrove said that Mr Stirling was not welcome, madam, and sent me back downstairs to the servants' hall.'

Lorianna gasped and had to sit down before she was able to speak.

'Mrs Musgrove is mistaken. I shall speak to her about this later. That is all, Baxter, you may go now.'

'Don't get upset on my behalf, Lorianna,' Stirling said when they were alone. 'As you said yourself, your housekeeper is a very strange woman. Sometimes a little eccentricity is the price one has to pay for an efficient servant.'

'She has always had a hatred of men, but recently this has become worse. It's Clementina's fault, of course. It was Clementina who drove Lord Monteith to act as he did. But Mrs Musgrove refuses to see it like that.' Lorianna helplessly shook her head. 'She will be refusing Gilbert and Malcolm entry next.'

'What on earth was Clementina thinking about?'

'Oh, I don't know, John. Her behaviour makes no sense. I have tried and tried to understand it, but I just can't. They seemed to me so well-suited.'

Stirling looked down at her and noticed how pale she was. The sweep of dark lashes was quite startling against the pallor of her cheeks.

'Allow me to pour you a little brandy, Lorianna.'

'Thank you.' She smiled gratefully at him.

When he bent over her and offered her the drink she noticed that his hands were slim and carefully manicured. The rim of the glass felt cool and hard against her lips, but the brandy warmed and strengthened her.

'I don't know what I would do without you, John.' She touched his arm and experienced through the smooth feel of expensive cloth, through the warm flesh, the long, hard bone.

He took the glass from her and put it aside before sitting down.

'Your daughter is still very young, Lorianna. She may yet see sense.'

'I doubt it, it's just how she is. Anyway, to put it mildly, Lord Monteith's patience is exhausted. He is turning to other prospects now and I cannot blame him, can you?'

'No, I'm afraid she has gone too far this time.' Stirling tapped his fingers absently on the arm of his chair. 'To have behaved in such an incredibly unladylike manner to such a man . . . His family goes back to the sixteenth century.'

'Mrs Anstruther-Brown was boasting about how he was paying attention to her daughter, Effie. She had invited him to attend her hunt ball and apparently Lord

411

Monteith never took his eyes off Effie the whole evening. I thought the awful woman was never going to stop chattering on about it.'

'Ah, well,' Stirling said. 'If a match between Clementina and Lord Monteith is not to be, it's not to be. Sometimes it is better not to struggle against fate, but just accept the inevitable and try to make the best of it.'

Lorianna's eyes widened. 'You mean I ought merely to accept the fact that Clementina's going to be an old maid, a failure, a subject for ridicule?' She flushed in sudden embarrassment. 'Oh, John, how tactless of me! I forgot about your sisters. I am so sorry.'

He shrugged. 'My sisters' failure to get husbands is an example of the cruel fate I referred to just now. They never had Clementina's beauty of course. She will meet someone else, you'll see. Someone she will want to marry. Try to have patience, my dear.'

It was true that she was impatient – irritatingly, agonisingly so. Guilt and shame, love and hatred jostled continuously inside her, giving her no peace. Clementina had behaved in an absolutely unforgiveable way, yet there was something so pathetic about the strained, eager-to-please look in her eyes that it brought love to pain Lorianna with its intensity.

Clementina had come to the sitting-room the other day and abruptly presented her with a birthday present. The girl was so graceless! It was a handkerchief sachet she had made and embroidered herself and her pride in it was obvious in her shining eyes and her air of excited expectancy. It had been clumsily and inexpertly sewn (Clementina had never excelled in any ladylike accomplishments) and more deserving of shame than pride. However, she later bitterly regretted her gasp of impatience.

'Clementina, how many times have I shown you how to do these stitches? And surely you could have kept your work in a sewing bag to keep it decently clean? It looks like something a five-year-old has done.'

'It is just that I worry about her so much.' Lorianna smiled at John as calmly as she was able, in an attempt to disguise the feelings about her daughter that he had detected. 'All I want is that Clementina should be happy and properly looked after.'

'Of course,' Stirling said.

'And how is your family?' Lorianna asked. 'Your mother and sisters are well, I hope?'

'Mother is getting very frail and hasn't been able to take her usual drive to see the shops. Something she sadly misses. But Abbie and Susan are in excellent health. I worry about them, of course. Which is why, although as I said I don't believe you need be too concerned about Clementina – she is still young – I can understand your anxiety. My poor sisters lead such empty lives. They walk miles, day after day, week after week just to pass the time. Or they play bridge with the same set of people – all spinsters like themselves. I see them all growing old together at that bridge table. It's very sad. One is forced to ask oneself "what use are they in the world?" '

For a moment they were silent with their thoughts. The clock on the mantelshelf whirred and struck seven with delicate tinkling strokes. The fire's glow occasionally flamed up and ruby light leapt into the amber pools of the oil-lamps. It enriched the gold of Lorianna's dress and danced spasmodically across the pink damask of the settee and red wall-hangings.

Then the companionable silence was broken by Baxter, who opened the door and announced that Gilbert and Malcolm and their wives had arrived.

Lorianna went forward to greet them warmly and bring them from the shadows of the doorway to the brightness of the fireside and the oil-lamps. The women preceded the men on a waft of perfume and with much rustling of petticoats.

'Hilda, you are wearing your new gown. How lovely! And Mary Ann, you're looking sweet and pretty as usual, my dear.'

413

Lorianna always found comfort in these family gatherings. They had a strengthening and stabilising influence on her life; she could cope with them. She knew where she stood with Gilbert, Malcolm, Hilda and Mary Ann. It was the same with John. With such loving and understanding company for dinner she would be able to forget, for a short time at least, the cuckoo in the nest upstairs.

As it happened, Clementina was not upstairs in the tower house at that moment – she was cycling over the hills to Blackwood village. It was a blustery night and trees on the horizon were like candle flames in a draught, blown so often by the wind that they had become fixed in that shape. Clementina too had become used to this high and exposed part of the countryside and was wearing a long scarf over her hat, tied firmly in a bow under her chin. It was hard going and her leg muscles were screaming for her to stop and rest. With stubborn determination, however, she pedalled on – skirts flapping noisily, loose coat ballooning out at her back and hundreds of leaves whirling down from the trees and dancing along the road all around her.

She was trying not to think of birthdays which wasn't easy because, apart from anything else, it was Rhona Lindsay's birthday and she had invited Clementina to have supper with her. Clementina could imagine what an effort this meant to Rhona in both financial and energy terms. After working a long day in the factory what the girl needed was a rest, not to start preparing a meal for a visitor. The little money she earned was barely enough to feed herself.

However, Rhona had her pride and Clementina knew it would be considered an insult if she refused or, worse still, invited her to a birthday meal at Blackwood House instead. And so the invitation had been accepted.

The wind was battering at her, retreating with a rush only to return, howling, to buffet her again. She was glad of the temporary shelter of a wooded area, where she dismounted for a time to recover her breath. The wild red

414

deer rutted at this time of year and the old stags guarded their groups of hinds against the attacks of the young stags. She could hear their roars, hoarse and deep, ringing through the woods.

She walked for a time on a carpet of orange and yellow, and fine coffee coloured leaves. The ground was also strewn with twigs broken in the wind and they cracked under her feet.

Over the hill now she cycled and down towards the village with its empty street lit by dismal gas-mantles puttering feebly within their glass lamps.

As soon as Rhona opened the door, Clementina saw that she, and indeed all the neighbours, had gone to a great deal of trouble to make the very best they could of the occasion. Obviously everyone had contributed something that they treasured. There was a green plush chair with a circular wood back of darkly polished mahogany which Rhona proudly invited her to sit on after she had helped her off with her coat. There were brightly coloured rag rugs, obviously newly washed, on the floor, and one in front of the fireplace. The fire was lit and sparked and crackled cheerily, its rosy glow reflecting in Rhona's cheeks. She was quite out of breath – either with excitement or the rush to get everything ready, or both. Her thick curly hair was escaping from its pins and tumbling down and her violet eyes were wide and wild-looking as she dragged a small table, ready set, in front of the fire.

'Shall I help you?' Clementina asked, half-rising.

'No,' Rhona said sharply. 'Sit down. I can manage.'

'Everything looks lovely,' Clementina said, peering at the table when it was placed in front of her, resplendent with a fawn-coloured crocheted cloth and odd pieces of china cups, saucers and plates. 'And I'm so glad of this warm fire! It was really cold coming over the hills; the wind was cutting right through me.'

'I've got soup!' Rhona announced breathlessly. 'That'll heat you up as well.'

She squeezed around the other side of the table to stir a

415

black iron pot that was balanced precariously on top of the coals and Clementina could see a pulse racing in her neck. Sweat glistened on her face, making her blouse cling damply to her body and revealing full thrusting breasts and pointed nipples.

'I have a present for you,' Clementina said, placing the package she had brought at Rhona's side of the table. 'Happy birthday!' She paused. 'Aren't you going to open it?'

Rhona attempted, not very successfully, to look cool, calm and collected. 'After I dish the soup.' It splashed over the rim as she was handing Clementina's plate across. 'Damn!'

'It's all right,' Clementina assured her. 'It just went on the tea plate, not on the cloth or my dress.'

She noticed that there was a matching tea plate propped up on the mantelshelf as an ornament and a green tin tea-caddy with gilt lettering, also one brass candlestick well-polished and topped with a newly-lit candle. The flat-irons that had previously sat on the mantelshelf had obviously been hidden away somewhere. Another candle guttered on the window-sill and there was an unlit one on the table. Before she sat down opposite Clementina, Rhona lit the table candle and its flame was reflected in her eyes.

Clementina said, 'This soup smells delicious. Hurry up and open your present, Rhona, so that we can start.'

With eager fingers Rhona tore the package open. Inside was a dark purple box and when she opened it and saw the earrings it contained, she gave a squeal of joy so intense that Clementina felt uncomfortable. Rhona could be emotional almost to the point of madness at times. Once at one of their house meetings in the village, one of the women's husbands had burst in – drunk – to drag his wife off, and to hurl filthy abuse at Clementina and Kitty who were conducting the meeting. Rhona had flung herself at the man like a crazed animal, spitting and scratching and nearly blinding him.

It was said of Rhona that despite the fact that she was a fine figure of a woman, she would never get a husband because no man would ever have the nerve to take her on.

'Oh, my God!' She skipped from the table and across to the cracked mirror on the window-sill. Fumbling impatiently, she put the earrings on and then held up the mirror to admire herself and shake her head about to make them swing and sparkle and her hair tumble down.

Clementina said, 'They're not real amethysts, but they look beautiful on you.'

'Beautiful!' Rhona echoed. 'Beautiful! I'll wear them tomorrow to Edinburgh.'

She came back to the table and began greedily supping her soup. Clementina had never seen her look so elated and happy. Between sups and without looking up she said, 'Thanks.'

'We must all look our best tomorrow,' Clementina said. 'There will be crowds lining the streets to watch the march and photographers from all the papers.'

'I'm going to wear that mauve hat you gave me last month and my black coat.'

'I do hope it doesn't rain.'

'It won't! It mustn't!' Rhona said passionately. 'It's going to be a great day. A day we'll remember all our lives. I just know it!'

CHAPTER FIFTY

'The Athens of the North', Edinburgh was called. Clementina remembered from her visit with Miss Viners years before how it was a city that seemed to be hanging on the edge of the world, a city of unexpected heights and chasms, a crush of buildings in a wild place of hills and yawning ravines. The main thoroughfare, Princes Street, stretched from west to east, cutting the city in half. At the west end and on the south side of the street beyond the statues and gardens, rose a high rocky cliff on top of which towered the 'Castle in the sky'. Behind and beyond it, clinging to the steep hill, was the Gothic Old Town, gaunt and perpendicular, a labyrinth of a place, a stony forest of ancient tenements and dark closes, giving the effect of one vast castle.

On the north side of Princes Street, behind the line of shops, stretched the elegant squares and Georgian terraces of the New Town, with streets that dipped steeply down to the silvery Forth.

But it was the formidable mass of the Old Town that meant Edinburgh to Clementina. Peaked, gabled and spired, its thousand windows, reeking chimneys, and the dark Castle solitary on its shadowy rock, fired her imagination and hurled her back to the heightened sensitivities of her childhood. Days of danger and adventure into the unexpected. Nights of ghosts and ghoulies and the strange unknown.

The turnpike stairs and narrow wynds where gloom hung all the year round reminded her of the tower in Blackwood House. Even on the sunniest day she had only to turn off the High Street, or the Canongate, to see people walking in shadow and disappearing into entries of impenetrable darkness to live in rooms where it was always night.

But it was not only the gloom that gave the Old Town its ghostly atmosphere. Because of the peculiarities of its architecture, much of the time it was shrouded in *haar*. Clementina had once asked Alice Tait what a ghost was like and she had replied, 'It's like a man made of *haar*.'

Haar was white and clammy and continually moving. It filtered down between buildings and through windows with small panes and heavy wooden frames. It drifted into dark closes and stairs. It appeared in houses. It came, wraithlike, towards you.

The only thing that could dispel the *haar* was Edinburgh's east wind. It had been said that Edinburgh was an 'east-windy, west-endy city' and certainly there could be no denying the 'east-windy' part.

On one visit to the city Clementina had seen a four-wheeled cab blown upside down. People walked with a forward tilt, faces tensely set and teeth gritted against the cutting edge of the wind – and a bitterly cold wind it was when Clementina and her friends arrived at Waverley Station. Hanging frantically on to their hats and skirts, they made their way up the Waverley Steps on to Princes Street.

Because of Agnes's fragile build and Eva's delicate constitution, it had been decided that they would not carry the banner that awaited them at the gathering place. That task fell to Clementina and Betsy. Agnes earnestly assured them that she was perfectly willing and able to take her turn, but Clementina and Betsy wouldn't hear of it. Agnes had never been lacking in courage and spirit and they respected and loved her for it, but there was no getting away from the fact that she was as petite and fragile as a china doll and would be liable to sink under the weight of a banner pole, no matter how hard she struggled to keep it up.

'But it's not fair, Clementina,' Agnes said worriedly. 'You and Betsy will get tired. I am especially concerned about you, Clementina. You're the youngest, dear — I think we all tend to forget that and expect too much of you at times.'

'She's as strong as a horse,' Betsy laughed. 'And as tough as old nails!'

Clementina laughed too, but she said, 'Not very complimentary, is it? I hope I don't *look* like that. I went to a lot of trouble with my appearance today.'

'If Betsy and Clementina get too tired,' Kitty burst out excitedly, 'Milly and I will take over, won't we, Milly?'

'Yes, of course. There's no need for you to worry, Agnes.'

'Oh, isn't it absolutely thrilling?' Kitty gazed around, flushed and saucer-eyed. 'Look at the height of that monument over there. I'd love to run all the way up to the top. What a fantastic view you must get over the whole of Edinburgh, right over the hill at the back to the Old Town and down over the New Town at the front and straight out to sea.'

Agnes put a gentle restraining hand on Kitty's wildly gesticulating arm and whispered close to her, 'Don't point and wave your arms about, dear. It's not very lady-like.'

Eva said, 'If you ran up all the steps to the top of the Scott Monument, Kitty, you wouldn't just be breathless, you'd be gasping with a heart attack. I know I would, anyway. I'd just die!'

'It is a fascinating place though,' Millicent agreed. 'All those monuments and ancient pillared buildings on one side of the street, not to mention the Castle perched up above them, and on this side such modern shops.'

The wind had dropped and it was not nearly so cold by the time they reached the gathering point. In fact it was unusually pleasant for the time of year.

'And to think,' Kitty gave a rapturous sigh, 'that we've the best part of the day still to come!'

Already both sides of Princes Street were lined with people waiting to get a good view of the suffrage demonstration and more people were adding to their numbers every minute. By the time the girls were nearing the west end they could only crush forward with great difficulty. Clementina, who was not much taller than the gentle little Agnes, pushed a path ahead for her friend with strength born of sheer stubbornness and determination.

'Don't worry,' she assured the uncomplaining Agnes, 'we're nearly there. Look, there are some Bathgate women! And yes, I can see the Blackwood village crowd now.' She waved enthusiastically. 'There's Rhona Lindsay. Doesn't she look smart?'

'My word!' Millicent said. 'Look at that fur hat and cape Effie Struthers-Brown is wearing.'

'Yes, it is rather smart,' Agnes agreed. 'And she looks very pretty in it. But have you seen the hat and cape that Lady Alice Cunningham wears? I have never seen anything so chic.'

'Or expensive,' said Betsy. 'You'd better watch out, Clementina! Lady Alice has been seen rather a lot recently with your friend Lord Monteith.

Clementina shrugged. 'It's no concern of mine who Lord Monteith keeps company with.'

'Oh? I thought you were madly in love with him!'

Agnes's soft voice came to Clementina's rescue with a gentle reprimand. 'Betsy, you can be tactless at times, dear. What Clementina feels or does not feel for Lord Monteith is her own private business. It's not for us to make pronouncements about it, especially in a public place like this.'

'Sorry!' said Betsy cheerfully.

'Are you all right, Eva?' Agnes turned her attention to her other friend, who was beginning to sound slightly breathless.

'Yes, I'm fine. At least, I will be when I get out of this crush.'

Eva was wearing a long chiffon scarf in a pretty shade

of pale blue; it was swathed over her wide-brimmed hat and down over her cheeks to tie in a big bow under her chin. Unfortunately, however, it seemed to accentuate the lack of colour in her pinched features and she looked as if she was positively shrinking with cold. But she insisted she felt fine.

Clementina caught up with Rhona. 'You look really beautiful in those earrings, Rhona.'

Rhona's face was ablaze with pride and excitement. 'Thanks! You're looking great yourself. A right smart turn-out altogether, eh? How do you like the Blackwood village banner? Bloody marvellous, eh?'

The various groups were beginning to organise themselves into lines behind their local banners, but it was a national demonstration and people had come from every section of the suffrage movement from one end of the country to the other. There was a buzz of eager voices and brave cheers as banners were heaved high. For miles back it seemed as if the streets had exploded into glorious life – a sea of rippling, dancing colour.

Kitty was almost skipping in a frenzy of excitement. Agnes tried to calm her by laying a hand on her arm. 'Sh! Sh! Kitty. You'll get so overwrought, dear.'

The pipe band, made up of members of the Men for Women's Suffrage League, burst into sound. The march began to move forward in closely packed sections spaced out with some yards in between. Eventually it came the turn of the West Lothian Justice for Women's Group to move and they went forward with Clementina and Betsy holding the Bathgate banner high, with Kitty, Agnes, Eva, and Millicent walking alongside them.

Clementina felt proud. It was true what Rhona had said; it was a smart turn-out altogether, but none smarter than the members of their own WLJWG, including the Blackwood Village branch which although made up of some of the poorest people in the county was neat and tidy and respectable looking. By this time the whole length of Princes Street was ten or twelve deep with spectators on either side and heads were bobbing up and down to make sure of a good view of the procession.

Everything went well until they reached the High Street and Parliament Square. A crowd of rough-looking men was waiting there, obviously eager to start making trouble. But there was also a group of police and Clementina hoped the presence of the blue uniforms would deter any troublemakers. However, when members of the Women's Social and Political Union began getting ready the carts on which they climbed to address the marchers, some of the men began shouting at them to come down or they would drag them down. Other men began pushing women roughly aside to get nearer to the carts. Because of the way the march had snaked into the Square, Clementina and her friends found themselves at the back of the vehicles and quite near to them. There was a tight crush in the square and surrounding area now and suddenly the commotion became worse instead of better when a policeman ordered the women to climb down. They indignantly refused, saying it was a perfectly peaceful and legal demonstration and not only had they every right to address the marchers, but they were entitled to police protection to enable them to do so.

Then suddenly, to Clementina's astonishment, the policeman and some of his companions dragged down the women and flung them roughly on to the cobbles. No sooner had they done so than several other women climbed up. Again the police hurled them to the ground and this time some rowdies gave them a kicking as they lay screaming and helpless on the ground.

Still more women struggled forward. Then the rowdies, seeing that no opposition was forthcoming from the police, became even rougher and began manhandling every woman within reach. Terrified women were punched and had their clothes ripped from their bodies and their arms twisted behind their backs.

Before Clementina's horrified eyes she saw Agnes suddenly grabbed not by a ruffian, but by a policeman who pinioned her round the waist with one arm while with his other hand he clutched at her breast — nipping and squeezing and twisting at it until she was crying out and sobbing not only with the excruciating pain but the terrible humiliation of it.

Without thinking, Clementina rushed at the man to punch and tear at his face with such vehemence that he let go of Agnes in surprise and pain. But quickly recovering he grabbed Clementina, only to let go of her again immediately and double up in agony when her knee stabbed into his groin.

Chaos now reigned. Injured women who had been punched and kicked were moaning and sobbing. Frightened women were screaming. Another policeman got hold of Clementina and, before she could bring her knee up again, he had twisted her round; immediately he did so, yet another punched her face, making blood spurt from it and soak down her green jacket. She felt sick and faint. Only the sight of men tugging Agnes's and Eva's skirts high in the air to reveal their underwear made her struggle and spit and bite and kick in a desperate effort to free herself and go to their assistance. Then suddenly Rhona came flying towards her, eyes and teeth flashing like a wild animal, to tear her free. Rhona flung herself at the man who had held Clementina until he was yelping and cursing with the pain of the long scratches on his face from her fingers. Clementina was dazedly aware of the Square filling with more policemen, who were drawing their batons to disperse the crowd. Now they were arresting women and throwing them into police vans.

'Bastards!' she heard Rhona say. Rhona had her arm around her, supporting her. They had been flung roughly into one of the vans and it was now shaking and jerking them as it raced away over the cobbles. Clementina's eyes throbbed with pain and she couldn't see very well. Her mouth felt swollen and she couldn't speak. Rhona was trying to mop her mouth with a handkerchief already soaked in blood.

'You're not going to faint or anything, are you?' Rhona was asking now.

Clementina eased her head a little from side to side and was frightened by the pain it contained.

'I think I took the eye out of one of the bastards that did this to you,' Rhona said with satisfaction. 'I hope so, anyway.'

With difficulty Clementina managed to move her mouth. 'Poor Agnes and Eva. How are they?'

Rhona looked around the crush of women. 'They're not among this lot.'

'Where are the police taking us?'

'Dunno. But wherever it is, we're here. The van's stopped.'

CHAPTER FIFTY-ONE

Often strangers had mistaken it for the Castle. Viewed on a gloomy evening, its blind bulk gripping the hillside, the medieval jail on Calton Hill did look like an ancient castle.

The Calton Rock jutted through the pavement and seemed to shoulder stairs this way and that; the very essence of Edinburgh hung around the endless steps and twisting stairs.

Near the Jail, another building perched up against the rock, a strange place with rows of dormer windows and an apron of hanging gardens at the front and a queer arrangement of stone gangways and steep stairs. It was said that prison warders and lamplighters lived in this isolated, fortified house.

But it was the Jail that hypnotised Clementina, rising into the sky like a dark personification of evil. It was evening now and rain misted the air. The lamplighters were lifting their long, brass-ended torches to light the iron lamps, making a long vista of little stars from the Edinburgh sky, down all its steep rainy streets to the sea.

Rhona kept a tight supporting arm around Clementina as she and the other women were hustled through the gloom and into the Jail. But soon, as in a nightmare, her friend was prised from her. Then she was shivering in coarse prison clothing; she was alone in a dark cell. Blood was hardening on her and it jagged like knives when she moved her mouth or tried to screw up her eyes. She tried to sit closer and closer into the corner, as if somehow she would be able to shrink right through the walls and disappear.

Far away, echoing through the *haar*, she could hear the clip-clop of horses' hooves on the cobbles. Nearer at hand was the soft scuttling of rats. Closing her eyes, she balled her hands tightly on her lap and prepared for the terror of the long night. And it was a terror with which even the ghosts of the tower could not compete. A night of strange sounds rising and falling like the groans and sighs of all the men and women who had been hanged there and buried in the unconsecrated graves in the prison yard outside. Here it was that the man who had killed her father had been incarcerated, perhaps in this very cell. The place smelled of the dead. She felt it thick and foul and icy cold in the air around her and could do nothing to protect herself against it as it gradually crept through her clothes and seeped into her nostrils and mouth. It was as if she was dying herself, slowly, minute by minute, hour by hour.

She longed for her mother, knowing at the same time this was like wishing for the sun or the moon. And the emptiness this knowledge brought was more painful than any physical pain she was enduring. It made her feel vulnerable, more helpless than she had ever felt in her life, even as a child. By morning she seemed to have become smaller too, like a child. The prison frock hung loosely on her and she walked with a stumbling, halting gait, hands seeking the walls for support as she made her way across the cell to a bowl of cold water there. With shaking, inefficient hands she washed the blood from her face. She tried to think sensibly. She tried to be brave. Surely she couldn't be kept here for much longer? She was not a criminal. If not her mother, then Gilbert or Malcolm would come and take her away. No matter how much they hated her, she was still part of the family and one of the family would get her out of the Calton Jail and take her back to the safety of home.

She thought that was what had happened when she was eventually allowed to dress in her own clothes, but she was shaken and as helpless as a child again when she was handed over into the custody of Lord Monteith.

Without a word he helped her outside and into his carriage. After he had whipped the horses into a gallop he rapped out, 'You're in no fit state for the drive to Bathgate. I shall take you to my town house.'

Free of the horrors and the crushing atmosphere of the Calton Jail, she began to feel a little more like herself despite her physical pain. She stopped slumping in the corner of the carriage and sat erect, fighting during every inch of the journey through the Edinburgh streets to rediscover her pride and courage. She could see they were making for the classical New Town, where monuments and public buildings all resembled those of Greece and Rome. One wide, stately street after another opened out with Doric and Ionic doorways and many columns and pilasters and tall windows relieved by classic lace-like ironwork. Along the airy width of George Street they drove now, the cool charm of its houses like well-kept, half-deserted libraries.

Eventually the horses galloped into Charlotte Square, desecrating the dignified quietness where nothing more violent occurred than the east wind ruffling the small trees and the patch of lawn in the central gardens. The terraced houses on the side of the Square along which they were travelling were made of honey-coloured stone and had a façade like some great palace. Each front door was topped by a semi-circular fanlight and the houses were fronted by fine wrought-iron railings with elegant lamps and torch snuffers.

Monteith stopped the carriage in front of one of these houses and helped her out. The door was opened by a tall woman with a neat waist, a large bosom and grey hair swept up in a top-knot. Her mouth sagged in shock at the sight of Clementina and Monteith pushed impatiently past her and guided Clementina through a marble-floored

428

entrance hall. She had sensed anger about him from the moment she had been able to gather her wits together in the carriage and now it was even more obvious in the rapid aggressive way he moved, in the hard set of his features and the dark glitter of his eyes.

As he passed through the glass doors to the inner hall and then up the winding stairs, he called sharply to the woman, 'Mrs Harper, send someone to fetch a doctor. Get one of the bedrooms ready and bring a pot of tea up to the sitting-room.'

'Yes, your lordship.'

Clementina was disorientated by the speed of events and she allowed him to seat her on a comfortable chair by an unlit fire which, instead of pulling the bell for a servant to attend to, he put a light to himself, using a pair of bellows to hasten it into a roaring blaze.

'You will feel better after a cup of hot tea,' he said.

She spoke carefully because of the pain of the wound at the side of her mouth. 'Why didn't one of my step-brothers come for me?'

'Gilbert is down in England on business. Malcolm is up North.'

'Oh, yes,' she murmured. 'I believe I did hear . . . Yes, I remember now.'

'Your mother didn't even know until this morning when I arrived at Blackwood House. I had read the report in the papers and went straight to see if there was anything I could do. Don't you have your meals with her?'

Clementina flushed, but managed to assume some dignity. 'When I am at home, of course.'

'Your mother was terribly shocked.'

'I'm sorry if she was upset.'

'I told her not to worry, of course, and that I would see to everything.'

'I am indebted to you. This is more than one should expect of ordinary friendship.'

'I know,' he said grimly and she lowered her eyes in silence, hurt beyond words. She struggled for strength, so

429

that she could get back to normal and not need to be dependent on anyone, especially on Douglas Monteith. The tea brought in by the housekeeper helped, although she had to sip the hot liquid very slowly and carefully because of the physical as well as the emotional pain she was suffering.

'I really don't need a doctor,' she managed to say eventually. 'If I could impose on your generosity for one more thing? If you would just take me home?'

'You will go home when I decide it's time for you to go home!'

Her breath jerked in her chest, but she couldn't voice her protest – she was not yet strong enough. Still in a state of shock from the violence she had suffered and the terrors of the Calton, she was afraid that somehow he could change his mind and take her back to the Jail and leave her there.

In wide-eyed petrified silence she watched him go over to the bell-pull. He had an angry, arrogant walk. Now that he no longer loved her, there was no telling what he might do.

When the housekeeper arrived he said, 'Mrs Harper, please take Miss Blackwood and put her to bed. No doubt there are some of my mother's things still lying about somewhere?'

'I have already some garments airing, your lordship.'

'Good.' Then to Clementina, 'I will see you later.'

To sink into the warm, luxurious bed was sheer heaven and lulled by the silence and the heat from the bedroom fire she fell asleep almost immediately. When she wakened the room was shadowy, but a candle flickered on the mantelshelf and another on the table beside the bed. The housekeeper was standing nearby holding another.

'She's awake, doctor,' Mrs Harper said.

'Ah, good evening, young lady.' A man with bushy white whiskers leaned over her. 'Now, you're going to be all right. I shall bathe your cuts and bruises and apply

430

something that will heal them in no time. Then I shall give you something to make you sleep until morning.'

'I just want to go home,' Clementina said.

'Ah well, all in good time, my dear. We'll see how you are tomorrow. Mrs Harper can bathe your face again first thing in the morning and apply more of the medication. I shall call in to see you again before lunch.'

She supposed there was nothing she could do but accept his advice. It was very comfortable in the big four-poster bed and no doubt after a good night's sleep she would be more able to cope with her situation. She could travel back by train if necessary and walk from Bathgate station up the hills to Blackwood House. Common sense told her she was not fit to do that at the moment, so she allowed the doctor to attend to her and dutifully she swallowed the sleeping potion.

The next thing she knew, she was opening her eyes to daylight. The fire was still burning merrily but the curtains had been drawn and the candles snuffed. A maid in a pale blue dress was hovering, smiling, at the foot of the bed.

'I'll tell Mrs Harper you're awake, miss. But first I'll help you up so that you can drink your tea and eat your bread and butter.'

It was then that Clementina noticed the tray on the bedside table. The tea refreshed her and, encouraged by the maid, she managed to eat a little bread.

Afterwards when Mrs Harper had attended to her face she asked the housekeeper, 'Where are my clothes? I should like to get up now.'

'The laundry-woman has been attending to them, miss.'

'Have them brought to me now, please.'

'Don't you think you should rest in bed until Dr Fraser sees you again, miss?'

'No, I should prefer to get up now.'

'Very well, miss.'

The clothes were all beautifully washed and pressed

and even the bloodstains on the green jacket had been successfully removed. Her face shocked her when she saw it in the mirror: one side of her mouth was swollen and discoloured and the skin around one of her eyes was quite purple looking. However, once she was smartly dressed and the maid had dressed her hair neatly, she looked quite presentable. She felt secretly nervous about going downstairs and facing Douglas Monteith, though. She would have preferred to slip quietly out of the house and make her own way to the Bathgate train. But it would have been shockingly rude to leave without at least bidding a civil goodbye to him after all he had done for her.

He was sitting in the parlour smoking a cigar and reading a newspaper when she entered. He immediately rose, folding the newspaper, the cigar gripped between clenched teeth.

'Good morning.' She greeted him in her normal businesslike way. 'I just called in to thank you once again for all you have done for me. As I'm quite recovered now, there is no need to inconvenience you further. I will make my own way home in the train.'

'You certainly will not.'

'I beg your pardon?'

'Clementina,' his voice lapsed into tenderness. 'Do you really think I'd allow you to leave here like this?'

'What do you mean? You can't keep me here against my will.'

'Have you looked at your face in the mirror this morning?'

She flushed. 'Now you are being cruel.'

'On the contrary, if you had completely recovered your normal practical self, Clementina, you would appreciate the foolishness of subjecting yourself to public scrutiny and probably more abuse by travelling alone looking like that.'

She realised he was perfectly right and after a moment of swallowing her pride, she said, 'Yes, of course. I have no choice then but to wait for your convenience, but I should be most grateful if you would take me home as soon as possible. I am very anxious for news of my friends. Have you any idea what has happened to them?'

Thoughtfully he pursed his lips. 'Yes, I thought I recognised some Bathgate faces among the people at the jail yesterday. No doubt they were the families of your friends who had come to collect them.'

'Was everyone freed, then?'

'As far as I know.'

'Thank God!'

She stared across at Douglas, his tall broad-shouldered figure elegantly clad in a grey lounge suit that looked particularly attractive against his dark hair. He stared back at her, his eyes becoming angry.

'I should like to get my hands on whoever did this to you!'

'Gentlemen did this to me, Douglas.'

'Men, perhaps. Certainly not gentlemen.'

'You believe in chivalry?'

'Of course. Women are, whether they like it or not, the weaker sex and must be respected and protected.'

'That's the philosophy of the dominant male in society and it has been institutionalised through the political, legal, educational, economic and family system, and sanctified by the teachings of the Church . . .'

'Yes, and why not? It's a correct philosophy.'

'It's not a correct philolsophy. It's an unequal power relationship.'

Douglas smacked his brow, 'Oh God!'

'And as for all this respect and care for the weaker sex,' Clementina continued sadly, 'it's just a façade. Whenever male power is threatened – as the suffragettes have threatened it – all the tenderness and respect goes by the board. Women are at first met with derision and then when men realise that their position of privilege is under serious and sustained attack, they hit out with real physical violence.'

Douglas tossed his cigar into the fire and was silent for

a few seconds before saying, 'Men who behave in such an ungentlemanly way are not fit to enjoy either power or privilege.'

'I wholeheartedly agree with you!'

A flash of amusement made his eyes narrow. 'What was that you said?'

'I wholeheartedly agree with you,' she repeated.

'I heard you the first time, but the words were such sweet music to my ears.'

'You're laughing at me.' She was appalled to feel weak tears filling her eyes.

'No!' Quickly he came towards her. 'Darling, you're still in a state of shock. There is no need to get upset. Just relax. Sit down here beside me on the settee and we can talk quietly together. Or I can hold you like this in silence and you can just rest against me. That's right, put your head down on my shoulder.'

It was comforting as well as comfortable sitting there cocooned in his arms with his lips gently brushing across her hair. She would have loved to stay like that indefinitely, eyes closed, body moulding into his in complete submission. But a sigh escaped eventually and Douglas titled up her face.

'Why the sad sigh? You're going to be all right. I shall look after you from now on.'

'If only it were as simple as that!'

'It can be as simple as that, if you will just allow it to be.'

She sighed again. 'What about my suffragette beliefs? They are part of me, Douglas.'

For a moment he closed his eyes. Then he said firmly, 'Very well, I will make a genuine effort to understand your point of view, but you must give me the same undertaking.'

'You have already made your point of view perfectly clear.'

'Clementina!' A warning ring of steel came into his voice, but was almost immediately brought under control. 'I am trying, really trying not to be dismissive about your opinions. The least you can do is afford me the same courtesy.'

She looked down like a contrite child. 'Yes, you're quite right.'

He couldn't stop a smile from twitching at the corners of his mouth.

'That's the second time you have agreed with me. We're really making progress! And I will tell you something else. We would make even more progress in another direction if it was not for your bruises.'

Clementina shrank away from him in embarrassment. 'I must look awful.'

'I wasn't thinking of how you looked – only how you must feel. I don't want to risk hurting you, that's all. You look like a miniature pugilist with that black eye and bruised lip, but it only makes me love you all the more.'

'I wish you wouldn't talk like this.'

'You would rather talk about women's suffrage than love?'

'I just want to get matters straight between us.'

'To be perfectly truthful, Clementina, I have never really given the question of women's suffrage much serious thought until now. I'm not a very political person.'

'Well, you should be!'

'Now, don't tell me what I should or should not be.'

Clementina opened her mouth to speak again, but Douglas quickly covered it with his hand. 'Let us stop and think, Clementina. Do we honestly want to explore our individual feelings? Or do we just want an argument?'

'All right,' she agreed. 'But I am afraid that's another part of me, Douglas . . .'

'Yes, I know. You enjoy an argument. But if we're going to get anywhere at all, this is not the moment to indulge in verbal fisticuffs.'

'I suppose not.'

'Good. As far as women's suffrage is concerned, I suppose — when I think about it — I feel that women are neither qualified nor capable of making any decision that would affect local or central government.'

'What basis can you have for believing that?'

'My experience of women, for a start.'

'Are you saying that I would be incapable of knowing how to use a vote if I had one?'

'No, not you.'

'Well, then . . .'

'But you are a most unusual woman, Clementina.'

'Nonsense! There are plenty of well-informed, capable women in the country.'

'Informed about what? Embroidery? The local gossip? The vapours? The latest fashion?'

'You know what I mean.'

'And you know what *I* mean.'

Clementina shook her head. 'What I always find so hard to understand, Douglas, is why men cannot see the justice in our cause.'

He raised a dark brow. 'Which is?'

'That men and women are equals and should be treated as equals.'

'But Clementina, men and women are not equal and never can be.'

'Not as long as men fight so viciously and unfairly to prevent women having equality perhaps.'

'No, it has nothing to do with that. Women are just different. And I do not intend that to be demeaning in any way. I think the differences in the sexes complement one another and are necessary to the happiness of both men and women — and certainly to their offspring.'

'You mean that the man should be the strong one who goes out in the world to earn a living and so on, and the woman should stay at home and look after the children.'

'Clementina, you cannot escape the fact that women are the child-bearers and because of that they must acquire different kinds of knowledge and skills and be different people, mentally, physically, and emotionally . . .'

'It does not need to be like that.'

'Now what do you mean?'

'With proper education . . .'

'You can educate a woman as much as you like, but you still won't change her role of child-bearer.'

'If she became educated on equal terms with men, she could compete with men in the outside world – providing she also had equal opportunities.'

'The point I'm trying to make, Clementina, is that there are basic biological . . .'

'I know. I know! But education can overcome that too. Women need to be more knowledgeable and in control of their own bodies. They have to be taught about birth control, for a start.'

Douglas thoughtfully pursed his lips. 'Oh, I don't know about that, Clementina. You are getting into very deep water there.'

'Yes, I know, but that's not going to stop me.'

His expression alerted. 'Stop you?'

It took all her courage to keep staring him straight in the eye. 'For some time I have been holding private meetings in the houses of the Blackwood mill-workers. I have been teaching them about contraception.'

'Clementina!'

'That's not all,' she continued in a lemming-like rush. 'There is going to be a public meeting on the subject. There were so many women, you see . . .'

'This has gone far enough,' he interrupted. 'For your own good, Clementina, I must forbid you to have anything to do with such a meeting.'

'You have no right to forbid me to do anything, Douglas.'

'Haven't I?' He kissed her gently yet passionately on the lips and she responded to him, but afterwards said sadly, 'I told you it wasn't as simple as you thought. You cannot change the way I am.'

'I don't want to change you, only to look after you. I'm quite serious about this, Clementina. You must forget all this contraception business. Enough is enough. You are going too far!'

'I don't think so. I feel very strongly about this particular issue and I couldn't forget about it even if I wanted to.'

In a sudden jerky movement Douglas pushed his hands back over his hair. 'Clementina, has it ever occurred to you how you make me suffer by getting yourself mixed up in God-knows-all-what?'

She rose and moved away from him so that he would not be aware of her distress.

'Yes,' she said with apparent calm, 'it has and I am deeply sorry. That's why I don't want to think in terms of anything more than a friendly relationship with you. And I'm serious about that, Douglas. Now, if you don't mind, I think I ought to go back upstairs.'

CHAPTER FIFTY-TWO

'You don't need him,' Mrs Musgrove repeated. 'I have looked after you before and I can look after you again.'

Panic fluttered like butterfly wings in Lorianna's head along with the words 'Clementina's in the Calton Jail.' The words awakened flashes of memory and she shook her head from side to side as if to prevent the memories from coming into focus. She wanted to banish the picture of Mrs Musgrove too. The black-clad figure of the house-keeper, big mittened hands clasped determinedly in front of her, eyes glittering like jet beads, was making her feel she had gone back in time. She was going to have to live through the terrible nightmare again.

'Please send for Mr Stirling.' The butterflies carried her words out shakily.

Still Mrs Musgrove didn't move. 'What good has any man ever done you?'

The memories were focusing despite her frantic efforts. She could see the misty evening creeping over the Calton Hill, hear the creaking and clanging of iron gates echoing against damp stone walls, smell the all-pervading stench of the place. She couldn't bear it. She began pacing the floor, her gossamer tea-gown floating and eddying around her.

'I need his advice about Clementina.'

She had to keep clutching at John. He was the only straw she had.

The housekeeper's mouth tilted down at one side. 'Oh yes? I thought Lord Monteith was looking after Miss Clementina.'

'Yes, but . . .'

John, John! She struggled to keep his face in her mind – to blot out Robert's. To keep at bay the avalanche of emotion that was threatening to sweep her away.

'That's what you have always wanted,' Mrs Musgrove was saying, 'to force them to get together.'

'Not in the Calton Jail! Oh, my God!' She began to shiver violently and the shadow of Mrs Musgrove lengthened across her.

'You are overwrought. Let me help you into bed and then I'll give you something to calm you.'

Lorianna covered her face with her hands. 'Oh my God,' she kept thinking. 'Oh my God!'

Just then there was a knock at the bedroom door and Mrs Musgrove snapped 'Enter'.

Baxter opened the door and said, 'Mr Stirling is here and . . .'

'John!' Lorianna immediately called out and Stirling, hovering anxiously outside in the reception hall, heard her and came striding into the room. She almost fainted with relief.

'That will be all, Mrs Musgrove,' she heard herself say. She didn't dare to look at the older woman.

The door clicked shut and Stirling said, 'I've only just seen the papers and came as quickly as I could.'

'Lord Monteith was here earlier. He said he would take care of everything.'

She was shivering violently and her calm words didn't seem to belong to her. She was hugging herself now, fiercely concentrating on trying to contain the avalanche.

'Lorianna, my dear,' he came towards her with arms outstretched. 'This is a terrible shock for you . . .'

Suddenly she flung herself against him and clung round his neck. 'Hold me, hold me. I'm frightened.'

'My dear . . .'

For a wild moment, clinging to him, feeling his body hard against hers, a wave of unexpected and uncontrollable passion took possession of her and somehow their mouths came together. She drank hungrily from him and when after a few moments he firmly disentangled himself from her, he was taken aback to detect in the eyes that stared up at him a sensual, indecent soul that shocked him profoundly. But he told himself that Lorianna had been completely unbalanced by her daughter's dreadful behaviour and subsequent arrest. As if the poor woman had not suffered enough violent shocks in the past.

'My dear,' he said gently. 'Try to keep calm. I'm here now and I will look after you.'

'Don't leave me,' she pleaded.

'Lorianna.' He hesitated. 'This may not be the most appropriate moment. I'm not sure. But I want you to know, if you have not realised it before, that I love you and would consider it a great honour if I could be with you always.'

He could see she was struggling with herself to assume a controlled and dignified manner.

'Is this a proposal of marriage, John?'

'Yes, my dear. I would have spoken to you in this vein before, but I knew the depth of your feelings for your late husband and how even yet you still grieve for him.'

'Life has to go on.'

'Yes, that's very true. Does that mean you could return my respect?'

'I have a very high regard for you, John.'

'Then we must be married as soon as possible.'

'Yes, dear,' she said dutifully. John would look after her. Everything would be all right now. Yet she felt sad, oh so sad. 'Robert,' she kept thinking. 'Oh, Robert'.

Stirling contemplated her beautiful face with its full mouth and large eyes and wondered if he should increase their pain by mentioning Clementina.

'My dear, are you quite certain that Lord Monteith was willing to attend to everything?'

'I can't go there.' Panic rampaged into her eyes. 'Not to the Calton Jail. Don't make me go there!'

'Of course not, dear,' he assured her. 'There's no question of such a thing.'

Her expression relaxed a little. 'Lord Monteith assured me that there was no need to worry. He said he would do everything that was necessary.'

'Well, try to look at it this way, my dear – that it's an ill wind, as they say. Let us hope this terrible business will draw them closer together and that Clementina will be more willing to accept him.'

'I no longer nurse any hope of Clementina, John.'

'You mustn't feel like that, Lorianna.'

'I can't help it. I somehow feel now that she is doomed.' Her eyes had acquired the strange haunted look he had so often observed about them in the past. 'Maybe she has been doomed from the very beginning.'

'That's nonsense, Lorianna. You're just overwrought and need rest and quiet. It would be best if I leave you now. I shall try to find out exactly what the position is with Clementina. Then I'll return again tomorrow and we can discuss our plans for the future in more detail. Now lie down on your bed and try to rest.'

'All right, dear.'

Obediently she went over to the bed and lay stiffly on top of the covers. Staring at the ceiling, she listened to his feet in the hall outside and then to the distant sounds of doors opening and shutting. Her mind was whirring round and round like some mad merry-go-round at the fair. She tried to slow it down and sort out her feelings of confusion. How could she marry any man except Robert? How could she allow another man to possess her body and soul? Was she being unfaithful to her dearest and only love by even thinking of any kind of union with another man? It was too terrible to contemplate. 'Oh Robert, Robert.' Grief and exhaustion dragged at her thoughts, but her loving and longing increased and winged free. She saw his face in her mind's eye, saw his big, strong, slow-moving body, felt his gentle touch. It was Robert's hands and not her own which tangled

442

through her hair and unloosed it from its pins, stroked it and spread it across the pillow. It was his warm hands which explored her face and body, cupped her breasts, caressed her abdomen and stroked her in secret places. She whimpered with need of him, shivering to a climax that immediately left her heartbroken and ashamed.

A sudden sharp rap at the bedroom door made Lorianna clutch her tea-gown around her and struggle flushed and breathless to a sitting position, her hair tumbling down in rich profusion over her shoulders. Mrs Musgrove had entered the room and was staring at her with an expression that shocked and frightened Lorianna.

'I knew it!' the housekeeper said. 'It's not safe for you to be left alone with any man.'

'I don't know what you are talking about.'

'It's all going to happen again.'

'Happen again?'

'The madness!'

'If you're talking about my relationship with Mr Stirling, there is nothing mad about it. We have a very high regard for each other and we are going to be married.'

'You can't marry him.'

'Don't be ridiculous! Of course I can marry him. I have been widowed for eight years and I'm still a young woman.'

'Have you forgotten what you suffered with your husband?'

'No. But Mr Stirling is different. He is a perfect gentleman.'

'You once thought your husband was a perfect gentleman – a perfect Christian gentleman.'

'John couldn't be like him!'

Mrs Musgrove's mouth twisted. 'I have told you, men are all the same.'

'No, Robert was different.'

'Yes, he took full advantage of your weakness and drove you to distraction.'

443

'It wasn't like that, Mrs Musgrove. You don't understand . . .'

'I understand that he had you so crazed that you committed murder!'

Lorianna cringed back against the pillows. 'How can you say such a terrible thing??'

'It's true.'

'That wasn't Robert's fault. It was Clementina's.'

Mrs Musgrove raised a thin brow. 'You blame the child?'

'You know what I mean.' Lorianna wrinkled her forehead and put a hand up to shade her eyes as if Mrs Musgrove's stare was giving her a headache.

'No, I don't know what you mean, madam. What *can* you mean? Clementina was also a victim of a man's evil ways; she too was taken advantage of. There is no limit to what men will do. Any man. That perfect Christian gentleman was the child's father!'

Lorianna began to cry. 'I was only trying to help her.'

'All that was needed was for him to see you there. To be discovered would have been enough to stop him. You were distracted, but you had been distracted long before that day. Every day when you came from Robert Kelso, you were half-crazed. You were flushed and dishevelled and you had the memory of a man's body on you, just as you have now.'

Lorianna hid her face in her hands. 'No, you're wrong. Just go away and leave me alone. You have no right to talk to me like this.'

'Haven't I? You wouldn't be alive now if it had not been for me.'

'I appreciate all you have done for me, but I can't go on like this. I *need* to be married.'

'You just think you do. What you really need is to be protected against yourself so that men won't take advantage of you and exploit your weakness.'

'Mrs Musgrove, I cannot help the way I am. Please believe me, I have tried.'

444

'I know you have. And you would have been all right if it hadn't been for . . . *that man*.' She spat out the last two words as if repelled by the obnoxious taste of them. 'Never a week has passed, hardly a day, but he has come here pestering you.'

Lorianna turned up a tear-stained face to the housekeeper. 'Can't you understand? He is a decent, respectable man who wants to marry me.'

'Just like Mr Blackwood?'

'I am not going to listen to you any more. You have an obsession about men; it colours everything. Mr Stirling and I are going to be married and that's all there is to it.'

'Oh no, madam.'

Lorianna gazed helplessly this way and that, as if seeking some means of escape.

'Mrs Musgrove, please get out of here. I have had more than enough worry for one day without you adding to it. My daughter has been arrested and taken to the Calton Jail.'

'Does Mr Stirling know?'

'About Clementina? Of course. That's why he came today. Immediately he . . .'

'About you.'

'About *me*.'

'Have you told him?'

Lorianna began to fiddle distractedly with a lock of her hair. 'Why should I tell him how unhappy I was with Gavin? What good would it do?'

'Oh, madam!'

'Why are you looking at me like that? Just go away!' Her voice had become plaintive and tinged with apprehension, like that of a frightened child.

'Hiding from the truth won't help you now.'

'Go away, do you hear?'

'You not only committed murder, but you allowed someone else to die for your crime. That's how the law would look at it and Mr Stirling is a lawyer.'

'Are you threatening me?'

'I am trying to help you.'

'John loves me.'

Mrs Musgrove's travesty of a smile chilled Lorianna. 'Oh, you mean he would stand by you no matter what you had done. I wonder! But of course, Mr Stirling is not the only member of the male sex you would have to consider. There is also your son.'

Lorianna suddenly withered back and was silent.

'One thing you can be sure of,' Mrs Musgrove said. 'You will always have me.'

CHAPTER FIFTY-THREE

The new family were in the house by the time Rhona got back to the village. The lock on the door had been changed and she was unable to force her way in, although she tried with all the strength and wildness that was in her. Shouting broken-hearted obscenities, she battered at it with her fists, kicked it and tugged at the handle.

Round the back in the coal-shed she found her few sticks of furniture. Her personal things, mostly articles which Clementina had given her, were in a tin box. She took this with her when she eventually left the house and ran towards the mill, fuelled by various emotions not the least of which was shame at being flung out on the streets. She made straight for the counting house where Mr Gilbert's office was situated, but was forcibly prevented from getting near the office door by one, two and then three clerks who had to use all their strength to drag her away. As she fought with them, cutting one on the mouth with the corner of her tin box, she shouted, 'That dirty bastard can't do this to me.' Her voice raised to a scream: 'I'll get you for this, do you hear?'

The cashier came hurrying towards the knot of men struggling with Rhona; she reminded him of a wildcat he had once seen near Loch Lomond when he had been staying at his brother's cottage. She had the same narrow, evil-gleaming eyes.

'Stop this dreadful behaviour at once!' he commanded. 'What do you expect Mr Gilbert to do when an employee is absent from her machine? And as if that's not bad enough, you have been in prison. We don't want your sort here – just take your cards and get out. If I see you anywhere near here again I'll send for the police.' Then to the men who were struggling, grey-faced and breathless, to hold her, 'See that you put her right out on the street where she belongs.'

This time she was literally flung on to the road, landing with a jolt on her right hip and elbow that sent pain stabbing up her arm and across her abdomen. Her tin box clattered on to the cobbles at her side. As she struggled to her feet, such a conflagration of hatred blazed within her that it cauterized the pain. She cursed the Blackwood mill, every dirty red brick of it, and everyone in it – and Gilbert Blackwood in particular. She hoped he would have nothing but bad luck and tragedies in his life from that moment on. She concentrated all her venom on him, wishing with all the passion in her that he would suffer the torments of hell. She cursed him and spat on the gates before tearing herself reluctantly away, feeling she had not done nearly enough but comforting herself with assurances that she wasn't finished with him yet. Her chance would come and he'd live to regret bitterly how he'd treated her. She'd find a way!

Her passion was so strong that it carried her along the street in her usual proud, head-tossing, hip-swinging swagger. But then, a lack of direction began to creep over her, allowing the pain to return. She had nowhere to go. The sudden knowledge brought an eruption of fear which she immediately quelled. She even laughed at herself. Of course she had somewhere to go. Wasn't she a good friend of Mr Gilbert's sister? Oh, what a bloody laugh! How about that, Mr High and Mighty Gilbert? Stepping out with a swing again and enough impudent bravado to cock a snoot at the pain, she took the road over the hills to Blackwood House.

Clementina would surely be there by now. They had said at the Jail that Lord Monteith had called for her several days ago. Wasn't it just like life that the ladies got out first and poor sods like herself with no lords to collect them were kept in longer?

She had become quite a regular visitor to the tower house to see Clementina and although the mistress of the house was still unaware of her existence, the staff knew her by sight and would cause no problems if they saw her coming in at the side door and sauntering up the servants' stairs.

Even the big gorgon of a housekeeper would be unlikely to stop her, unless of course to command her to wipe her feet and ask if Miss Clementina was expecting her. There might be some suspicion and questions about the tin box though, so just to be on the safe side she hid it under some bushes in the lane before reaching the tall wrought-iron gates of Blackwood House. She would collect it later, perhaps when it was dark. She felt excited now. Exhilaration was laced with fear, but not of a negative kind. It was more a hysteria that peppered her emotions, sparkled her eyes and brought a strange smile to her lips.

She was glad she was wearing her good black coat and mauve hat, and her beautiful amethyst earrings. Clementina had said they were not real amethysts, but who was to know that? She looked as much a bloody lady as anyone she would be likely to meet here. The thought bolstered her courage as she went through the gates and up the long carriage drive. It was then that hatred and bitterness entered her soul. Why should some people enjoy living in a beautiful place like this when others were condemned to spend their lives in ugliness and squalor? Why should people like Clementina Blackwood have so many material possessions that she could give away expensive clothes without as much as a thought? What made her one of the chosen few?

When the house loomed into view her feelings of resentment intensified. Here was space to breathe and stretch and live life to the full and here only two women lived: Clementina and her mother – neither of whom, she had not the slightest doubt, appreciated in the least how incredibly lucky they were. She went round to the yard and in through the side door. The corridor was shadowy and had a line of filled coal-scuttles along one side. She banged her leg against the sharp edge of one of them as she passed and cursed it under her breath. Through the closed door of the kitchen she could hear a woman's voice echoing angrily.

Rhona concentrated on moving smoothly and silently, although she couldn't help the slight scuffling sound her boots made on the flagstones. Up the stairs . . . Now the tricky part . . . The library corridor and the reception hall. Here she could quite easily be seen by Mrs Blackwood or any member of the family who happened to be visiting. But an empty hush lay over the place and she was able to glide across the luxurious carpet to open the tower door and slip safely up the tower stair. When she reached the school-room she didn't knock but just opened the door and walked in.

Clementina was sitting by the fire reading a book. She didn't look round at first, obviously expecting it to be her maid – someone she thought unworthy of any attention, no doubt. At that moment, staring at Clementina comfortably ensconced by the big warm fire in her good quality hand-stitched skirt and blouse, at the neck of which hung the art nouveau pendant of enamelled blue-birds' wings with a mother-of-pearl drop that Lord Monteith had given her for Christmas, Rhona hated her.

'Rhona!' Clementina gasped in astonishment. 'What are you doing here? I thought I would see you at the hall tonight.'

'Still friends, are we?' Somehow she managed to make the word sound like an insult.

'Of course. Why shouldn't we be? Come over here by the fire and get a heat. You look awful.'

'So would you look bloody awful if you had been

450

thrown out of your home and lost the only means of livelihood you had.'

'Bloody hell!' Clementina said. 'Now what are you going to do?'

'That's up to you. You got me into this mess — you, with all your meetings and talk about freedom and women's rights. What rights have I got now, eh? And what freedom — except the freedom to freeze to death or starve!'

'I'll see that doesn't happen, don't worry.'

Rhona crouched down in front of the fire, palms caressing the heat radiating from it. ' "Don't worry," she says,' she echoed sarcastically. Then a spasm of pain twisted her face as she hitched herself nearer the warmth.

'What's wrong?' Clementina's voice sharpened. 'Have you been hurt?'

'I told you. Your precious brother had me thrown out.'

'You mean, literally . . .'

'What else? I still feel as if the cobbles are digging into me. I must be black and blue.'

Clementina's eyes and mouth hardened. 'How dreadful! I shall have a word or two to say to him about this. And he's my half-brother, by the way, not my brother.'

Rhona shrugged. 'What difference does that make?'

Clementina glanced up at the clock. 'McGregor will be here any minute with my lunch tray. Were you seen coming up?'

'No.'

'Very well. I'll hide you here until we can work something out. You can sleep in Miss Viners' old room and during the day you can be in here. If you hear McGregor coming, just hide in that cupboard. There's plenty of space inside. I think I heard the landing door creak just now.'

Clementina put out a hand to help Rhona up, but it was brushed aside as the girl sprang to her feet like a

451

young gazelle and was across the room and into the cupboard in a matter of seconds.

Later, after McGregor had gone, leaving a tray on which sat a bowl of soup, bread and butter and a plate of apple pudding, Rhona emerged to immediately wolf down the lot. There was not even a crumb of bread left for Clementina.

'There are plenty of books to read to pass the time,' Clementina said. 'I have to go out. I've to see the girls and discuss some last-minute details about the meeting.'

Rhona suddenly remembered. 'You mean the one about contraception?'

'Yes.'

'I've got to hand it to you,' Rhona said grudgingly. 'You've certainly got a nerve.'

'We had no choice, as you well know. So many women are clamouring for information that a public meeting's the only way.'

'Well, I've had enough. I'm not going to any more of your bloody meetings – public or private.'

'I quite understand.'

'You understand nothing,' Rhona sneered.

Clementina rose and briskly smoothed down her skirt. 'I shall be back before dinner. I dine downstairs, but I'll try to slip some food up to you.'

'I can hardly wait!' said Rhona sarcastically.

Clementina's green eyes gave her a sharp appraisal. 'Are you sure you're all right?'

'What do you care?'

'Don't be silly, of course I care. You're my friend. You stood by me when I was hurt and needing help.'

'I'm all right.'

She barely gave Clementina a scowling glance as she left the room, but later she took up a stance at one of the narrow windows to watch the small trim figure in neat short coat and black straw boater mount her bicycle and ride off down the drive.

No sooner had the figure disappeared then she felt unbearably lonely and eaten up with regret. Going over to the fire, she flung herself on to the floor in front of it and began to weep broken-heartedly.

CHAPTER FIFTY-FOUR

'It's just that it's so soon after what we all had to come through at the Edinburgh demonstration,' Eva said. 'We have hardly had time to recover.'

'I can't see how we can back out now, even if we wanted to,' Millicent told her.

Betsy tossed her head. 'I'm still game, anyway.'

Agnes's eyes were strained and unhappy but she said, 'Yes, we've gone this far. We can't let people down at the last minute, it wouldn't be right.'

'I can understand how Eva feels, though,' Clementina said. 'The establishment is going to get to know about this and throw up its hands in horror. A lot of people are going to be not just shocked but outraged.'

Betsy laughed. 'That's putting it mildly. Wait until they hear what I have to say about venereal disease.'

'Do you really think you should, Betsy?' Agnes asked. 'I mean, don't you think that's going a bit too far? I admire your courage and your candour of course. But to men it's unthinkable that a proper woman should broach the subject of male sexuality – and venereal disease.'

'I know, I know,' said Betsy cheerfully. 'That will shatter their romantic conception of women, their rules about what makes a "proper woman", better than anything else ever could. I shall broach the subject all right, Agnes, and in clear and ringing tones, and in the worst possible taste!'

Millicent giggled. 'Betsy!'

'I mean it,' Betsy said. 'It's the only way. It stands to reason – they can't keep telling us what the rules of "woman's true nature" are if we keep smashing them and proving to them that these rules are only figments of their wishful imaginations.'

'The problem is,' Clementina said, 'that men are not logical. That they are creatures of reason is only another of the myths they have created. Women are only asking for a share in the political franchise and look how men are reacting – with absolute irrationality and ungovernable frenzy. Reason is just the name they use for their own emotions.'

A sigh lifted Eva's flat chest. 'I wish I could feel as brave as you and Betsy, Clementina. I agree with everything you say of course, but . . .'

Agnes gently squeezed Eva's arm. 'We all feel as you do at times, dear. It's nothing to be ashamed of.'

'It will be different from being out in the street, you'll see,' Kitty said. 'All that crowd milling about and those awful rowdies . . .'

'The boys in blue you mean?' Betsy asked sarcastically.

'Oh, but surely the police will have to maintain order and keep the peace and protect us at a public meeting?'

'They should have maintained order, kept the peace and protected us in Parliament Square.'

'Anyway,' Kitty said recklessly, 'I don't care. I'm going tonight. We owe it to our sisters who are being kept in bondage through ignorance and the dangers of continuous childbirth.'

'Hear! Hear!' said Millicent.

'You don't need to go, Eva,' Clementina said. 'Or you, Agnes. The rest of us would quite understand. You suffered more than any of us in Edinburgh – you had to endure terrible humiliation as well as physical pain.'

'All the more reason,' Agnes said quietly but firmly, 'why I should be loyal to the cause of justice for women. My mind's made up and I'm coming. I'm partly responsible for the production of the pamphlets anyway, so I ought to be there to help with their distribution.' She sighed. 'And none of us have suffered as much as

455

poor Rhona. She has lost her job and been flung out of her home on top of everything else.'

'Talk about nerve!' Betsy said. 'I always prided myself on being pretty spunky, but I would never have had the nerve to do what you're doing, Clementina. To hide that girl under your mother's roof is absolutely stunning!'

Clementina shrugged. 'I have to do something. It was because of me that Rhona got arrested and imprisoned. And what makes things even worse is the fact that it's one of my family who has sacked her and put her out of her house. I'm really worried about her. She won't admit it, you know what she's like, but she doesn't look at all well.'

'What are you going to do with her?' Millicent asked. 'You can't keep her there forever.'

'I have no idea. I'm just going to take one thing at a time. The first item to worry about is the meeting.'

'That's right,' Eva suddenly burst out. 'And I'm coming too. I know you would forgive me if I stayed away, but I'd never forgive myself.'

'It's all settled, then,' said Clementina. 'We meet at the hall tonight.'

Cycling up Hopeton Street, she tried not to think any more about the coming meeting in the Co-op Hall. It was something that had to be faced, that was all, and she would face it head on.

It was a cold day and by the time she had reached the Drumcross Road and dismounted because in parts it was too steep to cycle up, it had become still colder. The wind was hard and the air light. It was going to be a frosty evening. Before she had reached the top of the road she could hear hounds baying in full chorus and then the thud, thud of horses' hooves and the crash of bushes as the field took the jump. She breasted the hill and stopped to watch the hunt streaming along in their bright pink coats and yellowish-cream buckskins. Suddenly she recognised one of the riders on a big dock-tailed horse. Instead of yellowish buckskins like most of the others, Douglas Monteith was wearing very white and well-made leathers and looked extremely smart. She noted with some exasperation that her heart quickened at the sight of him. She found difficulty in breathing and warm colour began to creep up from her neck and suffuse her face.

Seeing her, he gave her a friendly wave in passing and she waved back energetically and with a spontaneous eagerness that embarrassed her afterwards. Especially when she noticed that the calm and aristocratic Lady Alice Cunningham was also one of the riders. Clementina became prey to extremes of emotion every time she was in Monteith's presence, it seemed, even for such a fleeting moment. It was both foolish and regrettable.

Without a glance at the pheasant, hare and rabbit that had been sent helter-skelter everywhere in the wake of the hunt, she got on her cycle and pedalled fiercely along the stony road, trying to ignore the illogical pangs of hurt she was feeling at being reminded that Douglas had a life of his own that was continuing happily quite separate from her. Why shouldn't he have a life of his own? She did. And she had chosen that it should be this way, so it was quite ridiculous to feel as she did now. She must be sensible. It was far better and wiser that they should keep their relationship on this friendly but subtly distant basis. He was always polite and charming to her at parties, but no longer forced any amorous attentions upon her. He would smile at her across a crowded room, but never rush towards her. She kept telling herself that this was wiser and better – they had nothing in common and every time they got closer they argued and he became angry. No, no, far better to keep their relationship cool like this. But how annoying it was that the cooler he kept it, the more foolishly emotional she became. In secret, of course; she would rather die now than let him know how she felt. Her mother had always said she was wickedly perverse and she was forced to admit to herself that it looked as if

457

her mother was right. This realisation made her feel ashamed and she determined more than ever to take herself in hand.

As soon as she reached the house she asked Mrs Musgrove how Lorianna was. The housekeeper, who seemed to have become one of the permanent shadows in the reception hall, assured her that she was being well taken care of but was still confined to bed and could see no one. Clementina had heard her saying the same to Mr Stirling who had become quite angry and insisted that he *must* see her. But then Mrs Musgrove, still barring his path, had informed him smoothly, 'Madam says she does not wish to see you, sir, and it is my duty to see that madam's wishes are respected.'

Clementina felt both guilty and sad that her mother's health had broken down again. As far as she understood from Mrs Musgrove, it was the same trouble with her nerves that she had suffered before. Clementina had no doubt that all the upset, scandal and worry she had caused by the violent scene with Douglas, and then getting herself arrested and flung into jail, was to blame for the relapse. She wished there was something she could do to be of help and comfort, but suspected that even the sight of her would do more to upset her mother than anything.

However, while she was at dinner she heard a commotion in the hall and Gilbert shouting, 'To hell with you! I don't care what you say. Hilda and I have come all this way to see her and see her we will.'

Then there was a banging of doors, so Clementina went out into the corridor and looked along to the hall. Mrs Musgrove was standing outside Lorianna's bedroom door, her sallow face contorted with hatred. Immediately her quick, sharp eyes saw Clementina she said, 'He will only upset her; he doesn't know her as I do.'

Clementina approached her. 'Yes,' she agreed, remembering how Rhona had been treated, the angry words spilling out before she could stop them. 'He's an ignorant insensitive lout.'

'Yes, you're learning what men are like the hard way. You're taunting them with your new ideas and ways and making them drop their masks and show themselves to be what they really are.'

'Not all men are the same,' Clementina's voice became frostier.

'Ah!' Mrs Musgrove's mouth twisted slightly. 'Of course! Every woman thinks she's found the exception – you believe yours is Lord Monteith.'

Clementina flushed. 'Lord Monteith isn't my anything.'

'Better for you that it should remain so. You have work to do – important work. He will only try to stop you.'

'Nobody stops me,' Clementina said. 'Or tells me what to do, or what not to do.'

'You're strong now,' the housekeeper said as she leaned closer to her and Clementina suddenly felt uncomfortable. All her distaste of the woman came rushing back.

'You're strong like a tree, Miss Clementina. He's just a rotten branch that has to be ruthlessly cut away. That's the only way any woman can keep what strength she has and survive.'

'I ought to go in and make sure Gilbert and Hilda aren't tiring Mother.'

The housekeeper said nothing more but Clementina felt the glittering eyes following her as she walked towards the bedroom door.

'You have the nerve to show your face in here?' Gilbert hissed immediately she set foot in the room. 'After all you've done to upset your mother and disgrace the whole family! You will be the death of her yet.'

Indeed Lorianna did have the look of death on her and Clementina was shocked by the sight of the still figure on

459

the bed. The beautiful face was so pale, the eyes so large and tragically haunted.

'Oh, Mother,' she said, ignoring Gilbert. 'I am so sorry.'

Hilda sniffed and addressed her husband, 'Sorry, she says. A lot of good that does anybody. A good whipping is what she needs.'

Clementina stood by the bed, hardly daring to breathe because she was in such danger of breaking down and weeping at the sight of her mother. She had never loved her so intensely as now – never ached so much to touch her and hold her.

'It's all right, dear,' Lorianna managed to whisper. 'It's not your fault.'

'If it's not her fault,' Hilda said, 'I don't know whose fault it is.'

'You have been far too good to her, Lorianna,' Gilbert said. 'And patient. Sometimes I think you have the patience of a saint.'

Clementina would have given anything to be able to assure her mother that in future she would be different. She would be quiet and modest, sweet and obedient and everything that Lady Alice was – with no thoughts of anything other than perfecting her embroidery and capturing a husband. But she couldn't. She wanted to say things like: 'I know we're different, Mother, and we don't understand one another. And I know you don't love me, but it doesn't matter. If you would just let me love you . . .' But she couldn't. All she managed was. 'I believe . . . we all believe that what we're doing is right, Mother. It's a matter of conscience.'

'Would you listen to that?' Hilda appealed to Gilbert. 'Conscience, she says. She doesn't know the meaning of the word.'

Tears welled up in Lorianna's eyes and Gilbert cried out indignantly, 'Look what you're doing to her. If you had a grain of conscience you would get out of here and leave her alone.'

Still gazing helplessly up at Clementina, Lorianna said, 'Tell Mrs Musgrove that I need her.'

Clementina nodded, not trusting herself to speak. Outside in the hall there was no sign of the woman and in an agitation of anxiety about her mother, she hurried along the library corridor and down the shadowy servants' stairs, lit only at intervals by candles in sconces. Impatiently she rapped at the housekeeper's door.

'Enter,' Mrs Musgrove's voice called.

She was sitting like a queen on a throne on a high-backed leather chair by the fire. On the table in the centre of the room, an oil-lamp spread a yellow pool of light that didn't quite reach her.

Rising as Clementina entered the room, Mrs Musgrove said, 'Has he gone?'

'No, not yet. Oh, Mrs Musgrove, are you sure that it's just mother's nerves? She looks so pale . . . and . . . I don't know . . . I feel terribly worried.'

'She'll be all right again in time. She just needs plenty of rest and quiet, the same as she did before.'

'She asked me to tell you she needs you.'

'I'll go to her now.'

As she passed Clementina, the housekeeper put a hand on her shoulder. 'Rest here if you want. And don't worry – I'll get rid of master Gilbert.'

Clementina remembered then that she had very much wanted to have a private talk with Gilbert and tell him in no uncertain terms what she thought of him. But unnerved by the few minutes with her mother and now by the oppressive atmosphere of Mrs Musgrove's room, she decided to postpone any confrontation with Gilbert until another day. There just wasn't time now – it would be enough of a rush to get to the meeting.

She managed to slip some food up to Rhona and while she was eating it in the school-room, Clementina went into the bedroom and changed into her navy-blue tailor-mades and her navy hat with the emerald green ribbons. This outfit, she always felt, looked both smart and business-like. Rhona was sitting soaking up the heat of the fire when she returned to the school-room.

'Would you look at that,' Clementina tutted with annoyance as she went over to stare out the window. 'It's lashing with rain. And listen to the wind! This will probably mean a smaller attendance.' It would be difficult enough for her to get down the hills on her bicycle to Bathgate tonight, but for most women from the outlying villages it would mean trudging for miles on foot and with nothing but a shawl to cover their heads and shoulders.

'Your hat will be ruined,' Rhona said, peering over Clementina's shoulder.

'Oh, never mind about hats!' Clementina said. 'It's the attendance that's important.'

Rhona's eyes flashed. 'Oh yes, I forgot! It's easy for you to say "Never mind about hats!" You've got so many of them.'

'Yes, I have. And you're welcome to your pick of them – I have told you before.'

Rhona looked sullen. 'Feels good to act Lady Bountiful, does it?'

'Look, Rhona, I know how you must feel. But try to be patient. I will work something out, I promise.'

'All right, all right.' Rhona began sauntering around the room, touching this and that and absently opening books and flicking over pages.

'Well, I'd better get away,' Clementina said. 'Aren't you going to wish me luck?'

'Oh, sure,' Rhona said without looking round at her.

Clementina hesitated at the door, staring worriedly at her friend for a minute before hurrying away.

She would be late if she didn't put a spurt on and outside, after tying a scarf over her hat and securing it firmly under her chin, she mounted her bicycle and raced down the drive and into the lane. It was sheltered there, but soon she had swooped out on to the Drumcross

Road and was battling against the wind and rain once more.

She was shivering and out of breath by the time she had reached Marjorybanks Street, her skirts were slapping wetly around her ankles and calves and her cheeks were bright pink and tingling. She forgot the trials of the journey however, the moment she turned into Jarvie Street. A large crowd had gathered, mostly well-dressed men of all ages but there were a fair number of ladies too. The ladies were middle-aged and elderly and well-protected from the elements in high-collared fur coats, capes, hats and enormous muffs.

'There's Clementina Blackwood!' one man's voice rang out. 'She's another of the ringleaders.'

Then the cry rose: 'Shame! Shame!'

'Filthy slut!' a man shouted. Another, eyes ablaze with hate, bawled into her face, 'You're a disgrace to the community and a danger to our wives and daughters.'

'A danger to you, you mean,' Clementina hurled the words contemptuously at the enraged bewhiskered man as she pushed past him and parked her bicycle against the wall of the building.

'What you need is a good thrashing,' a voice twisted with venom rasped out. 'A pity your father isn't alive right now to give you one.'

'That's her trouble,' another top-hatted man shouted. 'Her father spared the rod and spoiled the child.'

Somehow she managed to thrust her way through the jostling, hostile crowd and in through the door of the Co-op building.

She climbed the stairs, then strode purposefully along the corridor. The hall was packed to overflowing and she could see her five friends sitting with straight backs and stiff expressionless faces on the row of wooden seats on the platform. They had all dressed with great care and looked smartly turned out. Eva was wearing her fur tippet and her hat with the fur bobbles.

'Right!' Betsy said as soon as Clementina reached them. 'Here goes!'

CHAPTER FIFTY-FIVE

Betsy had hardly started to speak when several policemen filed into the hall and up on to the platform to confiscate the piles of pamphlets lying ready for distribution. The pamphlets were declared obscene and seized, but not before Clementina, Betsy and Kitty had each grabbed a bundle and started tossing them with all their might into the audience. For a few wild minutes the air was thick with flying paper and a forest of hands was shooting up, catching pieces and hiding them away under shawls and coats.

After the police left, Betsy told the audience, 'This proves my point. There is a way to prevent conception, but the mere idea of it frightens men so much that they will not permit women to know about it. It turns their world upside-down, you see. They have always believed that woman's only function is to be pregnant. Our duty, they have always told us, is to go forth and multiply in penance and pain. Oh yes, there has to be the pain. When Sir James Young Simpson, a Bathgate-born doctor, discovered the anaesthetic property of chloroform and tried to use it to help women in childbirth, was he hailed as a public benefactor?' She leaned forward, eyes flashing as bright as the glossy blue feathers curling down from her hat. 'Not a bit of it! He was publicly attacked, just as we are being publicly attacked. Men said he was flying in the face of Providence – that it was the judgement of God on sin that women should suffer the pain of childbirth. Men surgeons insisted the pain was good for their character. It took a woman, Queen Victoria, to put the seal of approval on chloroform by using it at the birth of one of her children.'

Right from the start there had been a rumble of unrest among the top-hatted men in the audience. Now one of them jumped to his feet and shook his fist at her, 'How dare you soil the late Queen's name by allowing it to pass your lips? Her Majesty had nothing in common with women like you. She said women's rights, with its attendant horrors, was a mad wicked folly and women like you ought to get a good whipping.'

'Aye and that's exactly what we should give them,' someone else shouted.

Betsy held her ground. 'Her Majesty was quick enough to accept chloroform as I have said, sir, because she needed it and so other women benefited. She didn't need power – she was the only woman in the country who had any. A pity she was like men in that respect and guarded it so selfishly.'

This caused an uproar but Kitty, who was chairwoman, excitedly appealed for the speaker to be allowed to finish her address and loudly banged the gavel on the table until she restored some semblance of order. Betsy then launched into the main theme of her talk, in which she accused men of not being able to accept the idea that women should have anything other than a *dutiful* attitude towards sexual intercourse. It worried them . . . It made them feel afraid . . . If women were not dutiful, men might lose some of their power over them.

'One of the classic male responses to women's greater freedom has always been to accuse woman of emasculating them. Well,' said Betsy cheekily, 'I believe they should never have had the power in the first place, so I am all for emasculating them.'

The men in the audience, although in the minority, created a furore of noise again, but Betsy shouted defiantly over it.

'They are afraid their masculine pride and privilege is being taken away at the mere suggestion of birth control.

466

I say, give them the fright of their lives. *Use* birth control! Use it all the time and start right now!'

Suddenly a man's cane came hurtling through the air and smashed against Betsy's shoulder, making her stagger back clutching at herself, her face twisted in agony.

Immediately Clementina jumped forward to take her place.

'Birth control means freedom for women. Don't let them tell you it's a *private matter*. That's what they say about everything that relates to women. The truth is that this is a question of women's politics versus men's politics. We have a right to campaign for birth control as we are doing tonight and we shall continue to do tomorrow and the next day and the next. We will not be silenced or intimidated . . .'

She then launched into a brief history of contraception, starting with the linen condom evolved by a sixteenth-century anatomist Gabriel Fallopian after whom the fallopian tubes were named. This was invented originally as a protection against infections like syphilis, and it was not until afterwards that it was found to reduce the risk of pregnancy.

'It was not all that successful though,' Clementina said, 'because a Parisian woman, Madame de Sévigné, described it as "an armour against enjoyment and a spider's web against danger".'

There was a titter of laughter at this from some of the women in the audience, but the men roared out indignantly, 'Shame! Shame!'

In the background Agnes tried to make herself heard: 'Clementina, Betsy's shoulder is paining her so badly I'm afraid she's going to faint. I ought to take her home.'

'Yes, of course,' said Clementina, without turning round. 'Don't worry, Betsy. I will tell them all you wanted to say.'

Agnes helped a white-faced Betsy down from the platform and the two women began squeezing through the crowds of jeering men who were now standing in the aisles. Clementina lost sight of her friends as the men closed around them. Raising her voice, she continued, 'Eventually the linen condom was replaced by the sheath made from the blind gut of a sheep, treated with chemicals and softened and dried. This became very popular in the eighteenth century, but it was not until the end of the nineteenth century that the chemical contraceptive pessary first came into vogue.'

'This filth must be stopped,' someone shouted. 'I'm calling in the police!'

Clementina ignored the interruption.

'In 1800 W. J. Rendall, a chemist in Clerkenwell, made the first commercial spermicidal pessary. It was a mixture of quinine and cocoa-butter made to melt at just above body temperature.'

'Filth! Filth!'

A feverish and perverted kind of excitement was mounting. She could hear it in the voices.

'There were various other means of avoiding conception of course, mainly with the use of chemical solutions by douching or by syringe. But most women were too afraid to use methods like these that would be apparent to their husbands. One would think,' Clementina shook her head, 'that husbands who had promised to love, honour and cherish their wives would have been seriously concerned about their terrible health problems, and the way in which their constitutions were being weakened by constant pregnancies and miscarriages. One would think,' she insisted over the heat of the rabble, 'that they would welcome contraception. But no. Oh no! They fight tooth and nail, as they are doing tonight, to prevent women from even hearing about such things. And they say it is unnatural, when they know perfectly well that the whole of civilisation is a never-ending battle with the effects of uncontrolled natural processes . . .'

Suddenly a crimson-faced, crimson-necked man rushed from the body of the hall and leapt up on to the platform, roaring, 'If no one else is going to stop this and give her the thrashing she deserves, I will!'

He made a grab at Clementina, hauled her – struggling ferociously – round to the front of the table and, to ringing cheers and gales of laughter and stamping of feet from the rest of the men in the audience, he sat on the table and made to force Clementina across his knee and pull up her skirt.

Suddenly she was panic-stricken. She was back in her father's study; only now his gloating eyes were multiplied a hundred-fold. As she struggled, little animal noises escaped from a throat almost paralysed with terror. She was saved by Eva who suddenly rushed forward, grabbed the jug of water from the table and poured it over the man's head. Now it was the women in the audience who laughed, and they did so in a wave of delighted relief.

Clementina quickly found her feet and, determinedly banishing childish fears from her mind, stood four-square in front of her dripping-wet and spluttering attacker. 'Leave the platform at once!' From the corner of her eye she could see policemen streaming into the hall again. 'This man is causing a disturbance and trying to break up . . .'

'It's you that's causing the disturbance,' the man shouted. Then to the approaching policemen, 'These women are causing a disturbance of the peace, officers. Indeed, they are inciting a riot and are a danger to our respectable and peaceful community.'

'Come on, miss.' Policemen were up on the platform now. 'You've gone far enough. It's time to stop now.'

'You mean bring the meeting to a close? Why?'

'Because of what the man's just said.'

'That man came up on to this platform and attacked me. Now, what are you going to do because of what *I've* just said?'

'Come on.' The policeman took hold of Clementina's arm and started dragging her away. Other policemen took hold of Eva, Millicent and Kitty, and Millicent shouted at the top of her voice, 'This is a perfect illustration of what we're always saying — there's no justice for women!'

Kitty, while struggling breathlessly with a burly policeman who had seized her round the waist and lifted her off her feet, managed to cry out, 'We're helping our sisters in need and will continue to do so in every way we can.'

'Votes for Women!' Eva had the temerity to yell before being jerked roughly away, fur tippet and fur bobbles bobbing.

All four girls were furious at the turn of events and, feeling that if they were to be arrested for attacking men they might as well be hung for a sheep as a lamb, they punched and kicked as many as they could en route from the hall.

At the Bathgate police station they were still protesting vehemently about the unfairness of their arrest. But soon events were to take an even more unfair and indeed sinister turn when they were roughly bundled into a police van once more. With lanterns swinging it galloped away through the gas-lit streets, then into the pitch darkness of the countryside beyond and suddenly it dawned on Clementina what was happening. 'They're taking us to the Calton Jail,' she said.

Automatically they moved closer together, linking arms and holding on to one another for comfort. They were silent for a time until Millicent said, 'It's so unjust!'

Clementina's brows went down and her jaw set. 'I'm not going to let them get away with it. I shall go on a hunger strike.'

'Clementina!' Eva whispered. 'You *can't!*'

'Better women than I have done it. Anyway, how else can I protest?'

'I'll do it too,' Millicent said.

'And me,' Kitty added.

Eva bit her lip. 'Well, if you really think . . .'

'Not you,' Clementina said as she put her arm around Eva's thin shoulders. 'You're very brave, Eva.' Her friend's eyes immediately and gratefully lit up, but the light was doused again when Clementina went on, 'But you're not physically strong. You need all the nourishment you can get.'

'But it's not right that you and the others should suffer and I should get off scot-free.'

'You're not getting off scot-free,' Millicent reminded her. 'You're getting stuck in the Calton Jail!'

'Yes, but . . .'

'No, please, Eva,' Clementina pleaded. 'If you starved yourself and became seriously ill, I should just feel it was my fault and never forgive myself.'

'Well,' Eva said, 'we'll see. But I don't want you to feel like that, Clementina. Anything I do, I will have thought out for myself.'

'I don't suppose we shall have time to do anything, anyway.' With one hand Kitty straightened her hat and tidied up wisps of hair. 'They can't keep us — it will only be for overnight. I mean, how can they? What have we done?'

'I know,' agreed Millicent bitterly. 'Fancy accusing us of incitement and abusing us as they've been doing, yet the militant men of Ulster who are opposing the Home Rule Bill are allowed to carry on their campaign totally unmolested.'

Eva sighed again. 'Sometimes I can't help feeling that even if we did get the vote, nothing would change. Men aren't going to alter their attitudes and beliefs overnight — they're too deep rooted and they've had them too long.'

'No, not overnight,' Clementina agreed. 'It will probably take years and years. That's because their attitude is such a deep-seated emotional one. It's obvious at all the meetings, isn't it? We don't get arguments. We get noise and derision and hatred and the smell of fear.'

'Don't forget the insults,' Millicent said. 'I'm so sick of being told that it's not "feminine" or "womanly" to speak out as we do. It's men who have made the rules about this ideal of "femininity" or "womanliness' that we're supposed to aspire to just to gain their approval.'

Kitty laughed uncomfortably. 'I suppose some people would say it makes life easier. I don't mind admitting that I find it the most difficult thing – not to care about getting men's approval, I mean.'

'Do you?' Clementina asked in surprise. 'It never bothers me.'

'Surely you are unusual in that, Clementina. I mean, it is *nice* to be approved of.'

'I don't think anyone has ever really approved of me,' Clementina said earnestly. 'Certainly not anyone at home, so maybe I just don't know what it feels like. A case of ignorance being bliss.'

Thinking of home suddenly made her remember Rhona. 'My God!' she cried out.

'What's wrong?' the others asked in alarm.

'Rhona! What's she going to do? Where can she go?'

'Hasn't she any friends in Blackwood village she could go to?' Kitty asked.

'If anyone there could have taken her in, she would have gone there in the first place. You've seen yourself how shockingly overcrowded these houses are and how poor everybody is. They can't feed themselves, never mind an extra mouth.'

'Anyway,' Millicent said, 'I had the feeling that she got rather too much approval from the male sex. I can't see any of those wives taking the risk of letting Rhona sleep under the same roof as their men.'

Clementina shook her head. 'That wasn't approval. They were just lusting after her body. Oh dear, I'm worried about her now. I feel so responsible for all this trouble she's got into.'

'Well, there's nothing you or any of us can do about it at the moment,' Millicent said. 'If we're heading for the Calton Jail, we'd be better to worry about ourselves.'

Clementina had no wish to contemplate this prospect and was only too glad to divert her attention to Rhona's plight. She would be lucky to get out of the tower house without being seen and even if she did – what then?

'I must get word to Betsy and Agnes,' she said at last. 'Perhaps they will be able to find her and help her.'

'That's if Betsy and Agnes are all right,' Eva said. 'They had to run the gauntlet of that crowd, remember. Not just outside but inside the hall. I just managed to get a glimpse of them, but I'm sure they were being knocked about and poor Betsy was already in agony . . .'

'Oh dear!' Clementina said.

A horrible foreboding had begun to creep over her and seep through her like cold *haar*.

CHAPTER FIFTY-SIX

The clock on the school-room mantelpiece struck midnight. The tower was eerily quiet and the chimes had a tinkling echo. The candles had guttered out and the fire had died; the room was in darkness now except for the faint glow of the moon slanting through the narrow window. As clouds scudded across the sky fingers of moonlight flitted about the room like ghosts. The tick of the clock seemed to be whispering in the darkness now, and from somewhere outside came the mournful hooting of an owl.

Crouched on the floor in a corner, Rhona tried to keep panic at bay.

'What the hell has happened to Clementina?' she kept thinking. Had she fallen off her bloody bicycle in the storm and broken a leg or something – or had she got herself arrested again?

She wondered if she should venture out and go looking for her, but at the same time knew she was too terrified to move. This place was haunted, she knew it in her bones. She could hear strange moaning sounds coming from the tower stair and she remembered what Clementina had once told her about the ghosts which were supposed to come out at night in the tower. Never in her life had she experienced such terror. She was stiffening with it, going icy cold with it, despite the fact that she had put on her coat and hat. Her throat had seized up so much that she couldn't have screamed even if she had believed that screaming would do any good. As time dragged slowly past she began to feel quite ill. She prayed for daylight to come so that she could escape from the place, despite the fact that she had no idea where she would go or what she would do. She decided to worry about that once she got out. Getting safely away was the main thing.

Exhausted, she dozed off occasionally, only to jerk awake more panic-stricken than ever. Each time she seemed more alone and the ghostly sounds had grown louder and nearer.

Eventually she woke with a start, feeling stiff with cold, but was relieved to see the first grey streaks of dawn lighten the sky. It gave her courage enough to struggle up and go over to the window. Although it was still dark down below, daylight was not far away. She must try to sneak out before the maids started moving about and the house came to life. She listened: the wind had stopped and no sounds came from the tower stair. She went over and opened the school-room door, cautiously peered out into the landing and listened again, just to make sure. Everything was still and silent so, reassured and yet still fearful, she crossed the landing towards the door that led to the tower stair. Taking a deep breath she opened it and made a rush into the narrow spiral stairway, its oil-lamps flickering low, its stone walls clammy under her trembling hands. She half-ran, half-fell down to the bottom until she was gasping tearfully against the door that led into the reception hall. It creaked open and she held her breath before slipping out and across the hall, then straight down the main stairway and out of the front entrance of the house.

It was not until she was outside and had run across a patch of lawn and then a path leading between rhododendron bushes that she realised exactly how she felt. Her stiffness had become concentrated on her lower abdomen; it was as if an iron fist had gripped her and was refusing to let go. She began to stumble awkwardly along and when she came to a five-bar gate she had to lean against it for a while to rest and try and breathe easily and keep telling herself that she had nothing to worry about —

she was going to be all right. She had to keep assuring herself of this, so that she could stifle the new fear which had begun to flicker at the back of her mind. She went through the gate eventually, remembering that this was one of the ways to the home farm. Clementina had taken her on a walk along this path during one of her Sunday afternoon visits. A part of her mind told her that she should be going in the other direction, down the hill to Bathgate, to try to find out what had happened to Clementina. But another part of her knew that she would never get there. Instinctively she was seeking rest and shelter, and she knew she would find it in one of the farm outbuildings that housed the animals. The iron fist kept tightening and slowing her down, until sometimes she gasped out loud with the pain of it and stumbled down on to her knees. It took her a long time to reach the home farm and by then daylight was bathing the countryside in shimmering colour. Or so it seemed through the moistness that hazed over her eyes. She could hear a cock crowing, cows lowing, and the trilling and chirping of a myriad of birds in the high trees. The first building was quite near now and she willed herself to reach it.

Entering through the wide stone doorway into the musky dimness, the cloying scents of horsesweat and manure filled Rhona's nostrils and permeated the whole lower floor. Midway along the back wall she could see, hugging the rough-hewn stone, a wide timber staircase to the hayloft. Sweating with the pain now, she tried to reach it, edging along inches at a time, every now and again sinking down on to her knees helplessly whimpering. Cramped windows stared emptily back on to the cobbled yard. Their beams of winter sunlight filtered through the cobwebs that festooned the tiny glass panes and played wanly across the heavy stone slabs where she crouched. As if in a dream she heard the gentle whinnying of the horses, the sounds blending with the creaking of wood and leather as the beasts shuffled and stamped contentedly in their stalls. For a time, the sounds soothed her and she was able to reach the staircase. Its ancient wood was silver-grey with age. The corners of the steps were thick with dust, leaves and mice droppings and she climbed very slowly and carefully.

Upstairs she gazed around to see where the best place would be for her to lie. The timbers of the roof swooped down steeply on either side, the central beams liberally striped with bird droppings. Hay was stacked steeply on all sides and the strange, sweet smell of hay-dust tickled the back of her throat.

A single pure beam of light speared the darkness like the voice of God, from a gap in the hayloft doors. She decided to lie there so that she could best see what she was doing. Because she knew what she had to do now . . . There could be no more evading the fact that she was having a miscarriage. She had seen her mother suffer too many in the past not to know all the signs. The first thing she would have to do was to take off her good hat, coat, skirt and blouse, so that they wouldn't be ruined or stained with blood. Then once they were safely laid aside, she would need to tear up her petticoats for cloths to help clean herself afterwards and to make pads.

As the pain increased into piercing torture and she was crying out with it, she cursed Gilbert Blackwood with all the strength that was in her. To shout obscenities at him or to mumble how she was going to get her revenge on him helped her through her agony.

Until at last it was all over and she lay exhausted, a piece of flotsam in the river of her own blood. She didn't stir for a long time . . . She just watched the motes of dust floating aimlessly in the beam of light like moths hypnotised by its brightness.

CHAPTER FIFTY-SEVEN

'Stand aside at once, woman!' Stirling's normally calm voice was strained with anger. 'It's a matter of urgency. I must see her, whether she wants to see me or not.'

'May I ask what this matter of urgency is, sir?' Mrs Musgrove's voice was now smoothly polite, yet with its usual cold, sarcastic twist.

'No, you may not!'

Lorianna heard the voices as if they were drifting towards her bed through the mist that so often veiled the hills in winter. They had an echo that reminded her of the hills too. It gave the voices an unreal quality and she thought she must be dreaming them. She had been having very strange dreams recently.

Then there was a crashing sound of a door opening and suddenly a real flesh-and-blood John was standing close enough for her to touch at the side of her bed. But the dark column of Mrs Musgrove was behind him, chilling the air. Lorianna gazed across at her in bewildered uncertainty.

Stirling, immediately following her gaze, said, 'That will be all, Mrs Musgrove.'

'I don't think madam wishes me to leave her, sir.'

'This is disgraceful!' His voice acquired the cutting edge of an icicle. 'You are exceeding your authority as a servant. If you value your position, do as I tell you at once.'

Mrs Musgrove stared at him with hatred for a moment. Then, as silent as a shadow, she withdrew.

As soon as the door clicked shut, Stirling sat down on

the edge of the bed and gathered Lorianna's hands in his. 'My dear, how are you? I have been so worried!'

The feel of his hands confirmed that he was real. 'Oh John,' she whispered. 'Hold me. Please! Hold me tightly, I'm so afraid!'

'Afraid of what, my love?' Gently he slipped one arm behind her shoulders and eased her up from her pillows.

'Don't leave me,' she begged.

'I won't, my dear. Just tell me what's wrong.'

She looked dazed.

'Maybe it's all just a dream. Maybe none of it ever happened.'

'What exactly are you talking about, Lorianna?'

'Only a dream.'

'My dear, the sooner we are married, the better. Then I can be here all the time to see that you are properly looked after. I don't trust that Musgrove woman; there's something about her . . .'

'I can't marry you, John.'

'Of course you can and you will. I shall have a minister come and perform the ceremony in this bedroom if necessary.'

'It's no use, I can't marry you.'

'But why not? What has made you change your mind? Is it something I have said or done?'

Tears welled up in her eyes. 'No, it's something *I* have done.'

'Tell me,' he said with quiet persistence. 'There must be no secrets between us.'

'Oh, John!'

'Tell me what it is that's worrying you so much. Then I can help and advise you.'

She began to tremble violently and he had to grip her with both arms in an effort to quieten her.

'You are all right, I'm holding you. You have nothing to be afraid of.'

'But you will leave me when you find out. You won't want to have anything to do with me any more.'

'Lorianna, what nonsense! I love you! But apart from that, I am an honourable man and not in the habit of breaking my word. I have said we are going to be married and we will be married.'

He waited as she visibly struggled to find courage. 'Gavin . . .'

'Your late husband, yes?'

'Gavin was not what everyone thought. He was not an honourable man, John. He was . . . He was dreadful. For years he made my life a misery. Then one day . . .'

'Go on,' Stirling encouraged quietly.

'I came in and found him . . .' She closed her eyes, trying unsuccessfully to blot out the scene. She even remembered the colour of the ornament: it was a large fat vase made of Indian brass with a pattern of dark reds, greens and blues round its golden centre. She felt its stiff coldness in her hands once again and smelled its metallic bitterness as she swung it high. She heard it echo and crack against Gavin's skull when she brought it down. His blood made new patterns, quick and vivid against the glittering brass.

'Lorianna?' Stirling said.

She took a long quivering breath. 'I found him trying to rape Clementina.'

'Good God!'

'She was screaming and screaming, I heard her all the way up the stairs and when I went into the study and saw . . . and saw what he was doing to her . . . I lifted an ornament and smashed it down on his head.'

There was silence for a long minute. Then Stirling slid his arms away from her and stood up.

'Oh, John,' Lorianna wept. 'I told you, you would want nothing more to do with me.'

'Hush!' he said, beginning to slowly pace the room. 'I am trying to think, to get everything straight in my mind. You killed him – is that what you are saying?'

'Yes. But I didn't mean to do it. It was such a shock and it all happened so quickly.'

'I can understand that. But how could you allow that man – what was his mane – Kelso? Robert Kelso, wasn't it? How could you allow him to be executed for a crime he didn't commit?'

'Oh Robert, Robert,' she thought. 'How could I?' Aloud she said. 'Mrs Musgrove sent for him and persuaded him to get rid of the body and he eventually agreed to make it look like an accident. She said they would hang me if he didn't. Then afterwards she said there was nothing I could do to save him. I tried, John. I swear I tried, but she had given me so much laudanum that I was in a daze and hardly knew what I was doing or what was happening. She kept assuring me that everything was going to be all right. They would never hang him, she said.' Lorianna moaned with the pain of the memory. 'And by the time I found out, it was too late!'

'How dreadful!' Stirling said. 'My poor Lorianna, to have lived with this terrible secret and this terrible burden of guilt all those years!'

Lorianna raised a tragic, tear-stained face to him. 'You don't hate me?'

'No, I don't hate you, but I certainly understand a lot more now. About that woman, for instance.'

'Mrs Musgrove?'

'She has been administering drugs to you again.'

'It's to keep me calm and to give me some peace from myself, John. You don't understand.'

'I think I am beginning to. Has she been blackmailing you, Lorianna?'

'I could still hang, couldn't I, John? If she told anyone?'

'She won't tell anyone.'

'Sometimes I think I don't care any more. Sometimes I feel it would be a blessed release to die. But it's Jamie, you see. He mustn't suffer. He loves me and I couldn't bear it for him to know.'

'He is not going to know. No one is going to know.'

'But John, how can you be so sure of that. Mrs Musgrove . . .'

481

'My dear, Mrs Musgrove is, to say the least, an accessory after the fact. Indeed, it seems to me that she is the one who bears the most responsibility, certainly for Kelso's death. She is in no position to say anything to anyone and I shall point this out to her in no uncertain terms.'

'I don't know . . .' Lorianna's eyes strayed vaguely away from him. 'I still feel uncertain, afraid . . .'

'Lorianna, trust me. I will deal with this woman. She will leave Blackwood House immediately and you'll have no more trouble with her.'

'Oh, but John.' Lorianna turned back to him in distress. She was wide-eyed and trembling uncontrollably. 'She has done so much for me. I can't dismiss her after all those years. This house and my needs have been her whole life. She has been absolutely devoted to me and I've depended on her so much. She has to be strong, you see, because I'm so weak . . .'

'Hush, Lorianna, you're becoming over-excited. From now on you will have me to depend on. I'll arrange for a quiet ceremony by special licence to be held here immediately. I'm making the decisions now and you must abide by them, do you understand?'

Gradually, helplessly, she relaxed back against the pillows. 'Yes, dear,' she said, but her nerves remained keyed-up, apprehensive.

'Good!' He stretched over for the bell-pull. 'What is it for your maid? I don't want the housekeeper to come – I'll deal with her in another room.'

'One.'

He gave the cord one pull and in a few moments there was a knock at the bedroom door and Lizzie entered.

'Stay here with your mistress. Don't leave until I return,' he told her and then to Lorianna, 'I'll speak to Mrs Musgrove. Then I shall have to go and attend to other business. There are the wedding arrangements and also the business about Clementina to straighten out.'

A startled expression leapt into Lorianna's eyes.

'Now, don't worry,' Stirling said quickly. 'She got herself into a bit of trouble again and they're detaining her in Edinburgh, in case you're wondering where she has got to. But I'll soon have her home again. Everything's going to be all right, I promise.'

She managed a tremulous smile.

After he had left she lay listening intently but could hear nothing but the spasmodic sparking of the fire and the rapid tic-tic-tic of the little jewelled clock on the bedside table.

'Is there anything I can do for you, madam?' Lizzie asked.

Lorianna impatiently shook her head. 'Sit down, Lizzie!'

'Yes, madam.'

Quietness again, her heart racing the clock. Then, at last the door opened and Mrs Musgrove came in.

'You can go now, Lizzie.' The voice was like cold water trickling down Lorianna's spine. She couldn't move, didn't have the strength to draw up any sound to her throat.

Lizzie's thin face strained with anxiety and she hesitated. 'Mr Stirling said . . .'

'Get out!'

Without another word, the maid hurried quickly away.

Another silence, like the silence in the room after she had committed the murder. A silence full of terror and horror and utter helplessness. A silence in which she knew her life would never be the same again.

She began to weep, quietly at first and then in loud abandoned sobs.

'Well may you weep,' Mrs Musgrove said.

'I am grateful for all you've done for me – truly I am, Mrs Musgrove.' Her voice sounded high and childish, not like her own at all. 'Please try to understand.'

'Oh, I understand all right.'

'He's going to look after me. I shall be all right.'

'He will cause you trouble and unhappiness, just like the last one.'

'No, no. You're wrong. He's different.'

'But you're the same!'

'I don't understand you.'

'Time will tell.'

'You're just trying to frighten me.'

Mrs Musgrove's mouth tilted into a ghost of a smile.

'Oh no, madam. You frighten yourself.'

Lorianna shrank further into the pillows as the older woman bent over her. The glittering eyes seemed to hypnotise her as the big black mittened hands cupped her face.

'I shall always be ready to return when you need me. And you will. Then everything will be as it has been before.'

To Lorianna's horror the sallow face came closer. Hard lips pressed down on her brow and the coldness of the kiss seemed to move through her veins until it reached her very soul.

CHAPTER FIFTY-EIGHT

After she had managed to clean herself up and struggle into her clothes, Rhona crawled over to a dry part of the loft, collapsed again and eventually drifted into an exhausted sleep. It was dark when she awakened and the smells of horse-sweat, manure and hay-dust were hot and sticky in her nostrils. From somewhere she heard the squeaking of rats. She still felt too weak to get up and make her way out of the place. Anyway, there was nowhere she could go, especially in the middle of the night. She lay stiff and silent, praying that the rats wouldn't come any nearer and at the same time straining to gather all her strength to overcome the horror of what she had been through the previous day.

She had had no idea that she was pregnant. Having always been irregular, she had thought nothing of it when she had missed a couple of months. She supposed it was lucky that she had had the miscarriage; she ought at least to feel thankful for that. She might have been burdened by an unwanted child that she could not have afforded to keep. Wealthy Mr Blackwood would have helped her neither financially nor in any other way, of that she could be sure. Hatred brought steel into her soul. She didn't need his help. She'd get over this. But she'd never forget, by God, she wouldn't!

Her mind concentrated on Blackwood. She imagined him sleeping peacefully beside his wife at this very moment in a luxurious bed in their mansion house. In the nursery quarters his children, Gordon and Giselle, would have been safely tucked in bed by their nanny. She wished ill to each and every one of them, drawing on every drop of her gipsy blood to come to her aid and concentrate her curses on them. She didn't want them to die through illness or an accident – their destruction must be much more complicated and long drawn-out. And it must be brought about by herself alone. She jealously embraced the right to this pleasure, hugged it to herself, looked forward to it, drew strength and purpose from it until, satisfied and almost happy, she fell asleep.

Rhona was awakened eventually by the clatter and scrape of metalshod boots floating up through the oppressive blackness as the farm labourers went about their early morning chores. She waited listlessly for silence to return to the bleak windswept yard before crawling painfully and with great care towards the stairway. Then, struggling to her feet, she stumbled down the stairs. It was still dark, but the moon lit up the tack and tools that hung at random, breaking up the solid shape of the massive oak beams that loomed sombrely overhead. Rain wept quietly down the windows, echoing the emptiness inside her as she lurched through the deserted stable to where the heavy timber door lay slightly ajar.

Gagging at the brackish, metallic taste in her mouth, her first thoughts turned to the immediate task of finding something to drink. She dragged her unwilling feet step by painful step through the scum-rimmed puddles of the yard to the old stone drinking trough where she sank down gratefully, her hands clutching at its slimy, lichen covered sides. Then she lowered her parched lips to its dark surface and took masochistic delight at the cold knifing into her cheeks and numbing her teeth.

Her main thought now was survival. She had to get help from someone, somewhere. It was then that her mind turned to Clementina again. She still had no idea what had happened to her, but surely she would be back home by now? She splashed some of the icy water over her face, then dried it on her skirts before tidying herself down, straightening her hat and making her way cautiously, gingerly from the farmyard.

The rain had stopped, but wind was still maliciously gusting across the countryside as if intent on searching her out to knock her off-balance and make her progress as difficult as possible. Her coat and skirts kept flapping violently to one side, dragging her with them so that she wove a jerky, zig-zag path. Determined not to lose her much-treasured mauve hat, she stopped several times to make sure it was safely secured by pins and all the time kept a firm hold of its brim – until eventually the wind sighed away to nothing and she was able to relax a little.

It took her a long time and it was daylight before she reached the five-bar gate that led into the garden of Blackwood House. Only sheer determination and will-power got her there and she kept the picture of the gate firmly in her mind as she moved slowly along. She had no eyes for the mounds on which rabbits were creeping and nibbling the grasses, the flock of wood-pigeons which had settled in an oak across the ploughed field, or the chaffinches and larks that rose up from the furrows and floated in the cold, clear air.

Sometimes she stumbled and fell on the deep grooves and waggon tracks and had to carefully clean her hands and skirt before going on. Sometimes she wept. Sometimes she felt utterly exhausted and defeated, but she never failed to milk a reserve of strength from her hatred of Blackwood. Occasionally, incongruously, she thought of her mother and father. She remembered as a child being dangled on her father's knee and being told what a beautiful little girl she was and her mother saying, 'Aye, and more's the pity that one day she'll be ground down and ruined by the mill the same as the rest of us.'

Rhona wanted to reassure her mother and father, to tell them that this wasn't going to happen to her – she would not allow it. Her life was going to be different from theirs, and from everyone else's in Blackwood village. She was different, and one day she would prove it. Prove it in a big way, moreover. One day she would be better off than Gilbert Blackwood or any of the Blackwood clan. She would see to that. Nothing and no one would stand in her way.

One day . . . one day . . . The words helped to push her on.

The five-bar gate creaked open, juddering against the lumpy earth at its base. Only a few yards to the house now and the side door.

Maids hastened along the corridor and up the stairs, some lugging coal-scuttles, some brooms, some piles of linen so high they could barely be seen peering over the top. Rhona made her way slowly along towards the stairs, but was suddenly stopped by Clementina's personal maid, McGregor, who appeared from the kitchen and said, 'Oh, it's you! Have you not heard? Miss Clementina is not here.'

Cook called from the kitchen, 'Who's that, Flora? A friend of Miss Clementina's?'

Rhona went into the kitchen, nearly swooning at its warmth and pungent smells of food. She did in fact stagger a little and Mima, the kitchen-maid who happened to be hurrying past, caught her with a squeal of panic.

Cook said, 'Well, don't just stand there squealing like a stuck pig. Bring her over here by the fire and sit her down. My God, you look as if you've seen a ghost. Didn't you know about Miss Clementina? How about a nice cup of tea?'

Rhona nodded gratefully and Cook rattled on. 'Well, pour her a cup then, Mima. See that girl? She's no use to either man or beast, far less a cook. Could you go a piece of this buttered toast? I was just enjoying a bit myself.'

Rhona accepted the toast and tea and ate and drank greedily.

'You needed that, didn't you? The colour's coming back to your cheeks already. Mima, don't just stand there gawping. Take these dirty dishes through to Janet. Aye, Miss Clementina's back in the Calton Jail. Did you ever hear the likes of it? God knows when they'll let her out this time.'

Bitter tears of disappointment pricked Rhona's eyes. She had been depending on being allowed upstairs to rest and recover properly on Miss Viners' bed.

'Och, don't worry too much about Miss Clementina,' Cook said. 'She'll survive all right, she's a right tough wee character. Always has been. I used to call her "wee ruffian". Always getting into trouble, she was. I've never seen anyone like that child for getting into trouble. We all thought she'd grow out of it, but not a bit of it!'

Rhona sat by the fire as long as she could, but Cook sent her packing eventually because she had lunch to start and no more time to spare. Leaving the house, she made her way slowly down the drive and then along the lane and out on to the Drumcross Road. Automatically her feet took her in the direction of Bathgate, although she had no idea what she would do there or where she could find shelter.

She felt bitter at Clementina for not being there when she needed her. Her and her bloody useless Cause! She felt bitter at Bathgate when she saw the smug snug cluster of it down in the valley. There was not one person there who cared whether she lived or died – not one person who would give her a second glance as she wandered the streets with nowhere to go.

But she would show them. She would make them look at her all right, she'd shake them out of their smug self-righteousness. They had no right to have so much when she had so little. It was so bloody unfair. But she'd soon make them sit up and take notice.

CHAPTER FIFTY-NINE

Clementina thought he would come. Sitting in the corner with hair tucked in the coarse cap, hands clasped primly on the lap of the apron that tied round the waist of the cold prison frock, she realised that she had been depending on him to come. But there had been no one these past nightmare nights and days except the lawyer Mr Stirling. He had seemed so out of place in the dark stagnant prison with his silvery fair hair and his elegant light blue morning suit and fresh pink flower in his buttonhole. He had been coldly angry and wanted to know if she was determined to worry her poor mother to death. Things were going to be different from now on, he warned her. He and her mother had been quietly married by special licence and now, as the head of Blackwood House, he would stand no nonsense from his step-daughter.

'When you get home, you will behave like a civilised and law-abiding member of the family,' he told her. 'You will eat all your meals with us in the dining-room, where I can keep my eye on you, and you will remain with us in the sitting-room in the evenings so that we know where you are and can see at all times exactly what you are doing.'

She had asked him for news of all her friends, including Rhona. Millicent, Kitty and Eva were apparently still in solitary confinement like herself. Both Betsy and Agnes had had to be taken to hospital with injuries they had received on the night of the meeting. No, he had no details of what the injuries were or how they were progressing. But he had no doubt they would survive to

490

cause trouble another day. As for Rhona, he categorically forbade her to have anything more to do with the ex-mill girl.

'She made a shocking exhibition of herself a few days after that notorious and disgraceful meeting of yours,' he said.

'Oh?' Clementina tried to appear calm and business-like. 'What did she do?'

Stirling looked genuinely shocked as he recalled the event. He had been in his office at the time and heard the dreadful commotion. 'She stole a hammer out of Gordon's and then rampaged down Engine Street like a wild animal smashing windows.'

'So she's here in the Jail, too?'

'Yes, and she'll be in a deal longer than you, I can tell you.'

'Can't you do anything to help her?'

He looked at her aghast, as if she had asked him to touch something revolting. 'Certainly not.' He had risen to go, then, 'I shall send Jacobs in the carriage to collect you as soon as I know when you are to be released.'

She had felt more depressed than ever after he had gone. It would seem that now, when she left the Jail, it would only be to go to another kind of imprisonment.

She didn't like Stirling. He gave every outward appearance of being a gentleman of refinement and taste, but she felt no warmth about him. Unlike Douglas Monteith, whose eyes when they crinkled up and smiled down at her radiated affection as well as good humour. Except when he was angry with her, that is. Then they hardened with a fury born of passion, not of coldness.

She longed for him to come and, surprised by the strength of her longing she mentally examined it, trying to make sense of it. She didn't *need* him to come and rescue her – Mr Stirling was going to help in every way he could in that respect. And at least she had no doubts about his conscientiousness and efficiency.

Was it Douglas's company, his physical presence, his

491

conversation? But in many ways his physical presence frightened her and in conversation they did nothing but argue and infuriate one another. It was not that she believed he meant to frighten her by the passion of his embrace. This fear, she realised, stemmed from something already within herself. She tried to probe and dissect and examine this flaw in her make-up, but was shocked at the unexpected surge of emotion that stopped her. Doors flew shut in her mind and every prop of courage crumbled and left her weak and trembling. Broken-heartedly she wept into the coarse sacking material of her apron. How ironic, she thought, all the torments of these past days had not made her weep. The doctor who had force-fed her, the wardresses who had cruelly held her down could not make her weep. Even when she was being punished by her father she had never wept. Now, sitting alone in the damp-floored cell, she could not control her heart-rending sobs. She wept until she was exhausted and could weep no more.

Clementina wondered what time it was. She had no means of telling the time. Her life had become punctuated only by the twice-daily torture of being force-fed by the same method used on lunatics. A doctor and five wardresses strapped her legs and arms to a chair and held her down as a steel gag was forced into her mouth to keep it open so that they could push a rubber tube down her throat. The pain was excruciating and the feeling when the tube reached her stomach, nauseated her. It made her choke and retch and violently struggle.

Now she heard them approaching again, their feet clanging in the corridor. Hastily she made sure her eyes were dry and she was sitting straight-backed and with chin defiantly raised. Doors loudly creaked open. Then the cries of other victims. Kitty? Millicent? Surely not Eva? Such pitiful groans, and such terrible spasms of choking and gagging and retching.

Nearer and nearer. Louder and louder. She tried to be brave, to face the horrific ordeal with dignity, but when the door opened and she saw her tormentors crush in, she immediately tried to dart past them out into the passage. When they seized her and dragged her back into the cell, she struggled with furious determination, but her body was held as if in a vice and she was bound to the chair. The tube seemed far too big; it wrinkled up and had to be shoved down again and again. She felt as if she was suffocating, dying a slow agonising death. Afterwards she was flung, teeth chattering and body trembling, on to the bed. And at once the door was locked.

She was alone again, sitting in the corner, fingers entwined on her lap.

She had thought he would come, she had been sure that he would come. And yet, what right had she to expect him to do so? She had no part in his life, nor he in hers. The path she had elected to tread was an independent one. She did not need any man. For the moment, ill-treatment and lack of food had weakened her. She was not herself, but a foolish child-woman longing for strong arms around her and the sweet, swooning effect of a kiss.

Time and time again Clementina struggled to discipline her mind and her unruly emotions. She thought of the Cause and the long fight still to come. She thought of her sisters in distress who were committed to suffer on until they gained their objective and saw justice done. She thought of freedom. She thought of Edinburgh with the sea at its feet and so many of its streets rushing headlong downhill like rivers in spate. And others wide and calm and others again snaking narrowly about towering tenements and furtive closes, as if seeking protection from the bitter east wind. A place of history redolent of old deeds and great days where so many causes had been fought and won.

She thought of Bathgate with its quiet streets and two-storey houses or one-storey cottages — clean and country-fresh. Except along the Edinburgh Road by the railway on a Sunday night, when the engines were fired up and the houses there got black with smoke. But the quiet was not disturbed by the ricochet of buffers, the crash of couplings and the piercing hiss of steam. People were accustomed to the railway – its swinging oil-lamps and shooting sparks were part of the Bathgate night.

Often when walking or cycling home, Clementina had stopped on the Drumcross Road to look down on Bathgate and seen the turbulent scarlet glow creeping up the sky from the railway, heard its far-off clanking and echoing whistle and felt comforted by it.

Oh, she had been so certain he would come. And now she chided herself for being foolish and illogical. After all, what would be the point of his coming?

She pondered bitterly at the cruel tricks God had played on woman. It was He who had made her weak in flesh and a prey to such conflicting emotions. It was He who had given her a brain that saw the weakness and illogicality and conflict and despised them. It was He who gave her the secret wish to be dominated and at the same time the free spirit to make her fight tooth and nail against domination.

Somehow, somewhere there must be an answer, but no matter how long she strained and strained her mind to think about it, she could not find one that made any sense.

Once she was well and strong again and free, she would discuss this with her friends. But thinking of her friends made her brow crease and her eyes strain with worry.

Gentle ladylike Agnes trying to protect the injured Betsy and men closing in on them at the back of the Co-op Hall and surging with them outside – that didn't bear thinking about. Rhona and Millicent in the other cells along the prison passage would survive their agonies. Perhaps the excitable Kitty might. But poor Eva?

Clementina closed her eyes and tried to blot out thought, to wait on her release and reunion with her friends with patience and fortitude.

As far as Rhona was concerned, she would have to find

some way of helping her and finding her a home and employment. But who did she know who would even consider for a moment . . .

It was then that Douglas Monteith returned with a rush to her thoughts. He was a wealthy man with a large estate and, if nothing else, at least he was her friend.

If she asked him, pleaded with him if necessary to do whatever he could to help Rhona, surely he wouldn't refuse her request?

She suffered the ordeal of the next few days until her release dry-eyed and by sheer stubborn will, and when at last she was set free and went to check on her friends at visiting time she found they had been taken home earlier that day. Only Rhona remained and when Clementina visited her she was unexpectedly shocked at her appearance. The violet eyes still fiercely glittered with emotion, but the dark shadows underneath them and the bitter twist to her mouth gave her a drawn look of suffering. The sight of her made Clementina all the more determined to swallow her pride and ask for Douglas's help.

'My mother has married again and by the sound of things it's going to be impossible for me to get you back into Blackwood House.'

Rhona shrugged. 'It was obvious I couldn't stay there for ever. Anyway, I wouldn't want to.'

'But there's no need to worry,' Clementina assured her. 'I have had a marvellous idea. I'm going straight from here to see Lord Monteith. He must provide employment for hundreds of people and on an estate the size of his there is bound to be some place he could give you to live in.'

Rhona surveyed her with narrowed eyes for a few moments. Then suddenly she threw back her head and laughed. But it was a hard sound, completely lacking in humour.

Clementina was indignant. 'It seemed to me to be eminently sensible and practical.'

'Oh yes?'

'Well? What's wrong with the idea?'

Rhona shrugged, her face expressionless. 'Nothing.'

'Very well, then, I'll go now.'

She was slightly irritated by Rhona's reaction. In many ways, Rhona was a strange girl. One never could be quite certain how to take her. Soon, however, her irritation was forgotten in the blessed relief of escaping from the Calton. Never had Edinburgh's east wind felt so fresh and invigorating. She imagined she detected a tang of salt blowing up from the Firth and it gave spice to her sense of freedom.

Jacobs politely saluted her and then helped her into the carriage.

But first she had told him where she wanted to go. A faint flicker of surprise had crossed his normally wooden features but only for a second. He was too well-trained a servant to risk revealing any emotion to his employers or any member of their family.

Oh, the excitement of galloping along Edinburgh's Princes Street with its windswept gardens and tramway cars and buses — cabs drawn by glossy black and brown horses, workmen on carts sitting heads-down and hands between their knees, resigned to the wind, and crowds of tilted-forward people pushing against it as it blustered along the pavement.

From the rocky Calton Hill it hastened Clementina to the Castle Rock at the other end of the busy street and away beyond it past elegant terraces towards the distant woods of Corstorphine.

Once out in the empty countryside, she relaxed back in her seat suddenly exhausted. The Calton Jail had taken its toll and she had lost a good deal of weight and with it much of her energy. The rhythmic clip-clop of the horses' hooves began to have a soporific effect and she must have dozed off to sleep occasionally, because in no time at all it seemed the carriage was swinging into the driveway of Dumbreggan.

It was only then that, suddenly alert and alarmed, she

realised the enormity of what she was doing. Even her mother would be horrified. It was one thing to call on Lord Monteith when invited and with the intention approved by her mother of responding favourably to his advances. But to suddenly arrive like this uninvited, unannounced, straight from Edinburgh's notorious prison, to ask him to give of his time, trouble and whatever resources necessary to help one of its inmates, was an incredible cheek. Even for her!

The carriage sped on and she was powerless to stop it. Soon it had drawn up in front of the house and with heart thudding and legs so weak they were hardly able to support her, she climbed out.

CHAPTER SIXTY

It was sunny but frosty and Lorianna was wearing a large fur hat. Her gloved hands were comfortably tucked inside a luxurious fur muff.

As she strolled down the lane between the high bushes and trees, she noticed that every twig on every tree and bush was sparkling in silver tracery.

There was a feel of spring about the air, despite the frost, and the signs of it were everywhere too. Butterflies were venturing tentatively out of hibernation and seeking with the honey bees the early flowers. More and more birds were bursting into happy sound. There were rapid twitterings and rich trillings, and how sweetly the larks were singing. Blackbirds warbled softly to themselves on the ground.

Lorianna felt wistful and sad, thinking of other springtimes which she had spent with Robert. Reaching the crossroads, she gazed across the fields in the direction of the farm and imagined she saw, on the ridge of the hill, his big figure on horseback silhouetted against the sky. She saw him working joyously in the fields . . . striding along the road . . . swimming naked in the river. Her beautiful man! He was all around her and her heart cried out in anguish to him. And as if in answer, she heard his voice echo back to her from the past, 'I don't want you to suffer, flower. That's the whole point.'

The words sadly soothed her. Gradually her anguish faded. Robert knew that she loved him and that love, come what may, would never die.

'I want to think of you walking in the Bathgate Hills

as free as a bird,' she heard him say. 'I like to imagine you looking across the spread of fields and woods in all their warm colours and seeing the Forth glistening in the distance. In my mind and heart I'm always with you there.'

Lorianna shaded her eyes with a gloved hand and gazed along the Drumcross Road. She could hear the distant echo of horses' hooves now and as she stood, the cool breeze ruffling the fur of her hat and high coat collar, she saw her husband come riding into view. Blinking away the moisture in her eyes, she waved a welcome to him.

★　　★　　★

At first a liveried footman left Clementina sitting on a golden throne-like chair in the marble hallway. Then, when he returned, he requested her to follow him into the morning-room. It was a delightful place with fringed ivory silk covers on a comfortable looking settee and chairs. Pink satin cushions added to the appearance of comfort. There were three tall French windows with mirrored alcoves in between, in which fitted specially-shaped tables and beautiful floral arrangements. But Clementina was so nervous she could not appreciate the delights of the room. In complete distraction she wandered over to the windows and gazed out at the stunning view over lake and woodland garden without really seeing it.

She couldn't think what on earth had possessed her to come. Her stay in the Calton Jail must have made her take temporary leave of her senses. She had absolutely no right to expect this man to do her any favours. She had been nothing but an aggravation to him and more than once she had thrown his proposal of marriage in his face and treated him not only with complete disdain, but with physical violence.

For all she knew, he was by now happily married to Lady Alice Cunningham and quite rightly had forgotten

499

all about the infuriating Clementina Blackwood. And here she was to infuriate him again!

She wished she could die. Anything rather than face him. For a shameful moment, she was tempted to escape through one of the French windows and take to her heels. But stubborn courage and the memory of the suffering in Rhona's face prevented her. Now that she was here she would just have to face the consequences of her rash decision to come. It never did any good to run away. And even if he refused point-blank to lift a finger to help Rhona, at least she could feel that she had tried her best for her friend. And so it was that when she heard Douglas Monteith enter the room she was able to turn towards him with what she believed to be perfect composure.

But despite the proud, brave tilt to her head, he saw the strain and apprehension in her eyes and he winced with tenderness. She had lost weight and there was a fragile quality about her that had never been there before. Her skin had the delicacy of fine porcelain and her beautiful candid eyes seemed to have grown too large for her face. However, there was still plenty of her usual decisiveness about the way she stood facing him in her sensible navy-blue coat, matching hat perched on top of her nest of blonde hair.

'I have come to ask a favour.'

'How like you, Clementina,' he said, 'to tackle things head-on, without the usual preliminaries.'

'What preliminaries?'

He indicated a chair. 'Won't you sit down? Can I offer you some refreshment? A pot of tea, perhaps? Or a glass of sherry?'

'No, I prefer to get to the point right away.'

He raised a brow. 'Which is?'

'I have a friend, Rhona Lindsay, who is still in the Calton Jail. I feel very guilty about her predicament and all the trouble she has got into since she has known me. She used to work for the Blackwood Mill and live in one of the mill houses. Now she has lost her job and her home. She has no references and who would give a job to someone who has been in prison? Except . . . perhaps . . . I thought . . .' She hesitated, but he didn't help her and she was forced to struggle on. 'As a favour to me, perhaps you would do what you could for her?'

He took a long time before answering and she had to stand suffering acutely under his amused yet thoughtful stare. Eventually he said, 'You're asking me to look after this . . . mill-girl friend of yours?'

'Yes. That's correct.' She tried to sound brisk and business-like.

'You have the cheek of the devil, Clementina and I ought to run you out of here by the back of your beautiful neck. But I will make a bargain with you.'

She gazed up at him and looked him straight in the eye, determined to ignore the thudding of her heart and be sensible.

'Very well. What are the terms of the bargain?'

'I will look after your friend, if you will allow me to look after you.'

She was completely nonplussed. 'I . . . I'm not sure I understand . . . What do you mean?'

'I am asking you to marry me.'

She hesitated uncertainly, the strain of her recent sufferings putting her at a distinct disadvantage.

'I don't think you're being very fair, Douglas.'

'Don't you?' he said in a tone of mild surprise.

She tried to think, to weigh up the situation calmly and sensibly. In doing so, it occurred to her that as Lady Monteith she would be in an excellent position not only to help Rhona but to have much more power and influence to wield on behalf of the Cause and justice for women in general. However, she had to be fair to Douglas; she had to be honest with him.

'I won't change,' she said.

'Never mind that just now.' Impatiently he brushed her words aside. 'Let us deal with one thing at a time. All I want you to do at the moment is answer my question.'

He watched her earnest face struggle with the proposition and eventually come to a decision. Suddenly she stepped forward and resolutely stuck out her hand. 'I accept the bargain,' she said. He took the small hand in his and then with a groan gently pulled her into his arms.

'Oh, Clementina!'

'I think I will have that pot of tea now,' she said briskly.

For a second, temper flared in his eyes. Then, just as suddenly, he laughed. He couldn't help it. She was the oddest, the most infuriating, the most impossible female he had ever come across in his life. But there had been eccentric members of the Monteith family before, so one more wouldn't do any harm. Anyway, for better or for worse he adored her.

'I will ring for some tea,' he said, his eyes glimmering down at her. 'Do sit down and let us discuss how best I can help Rhona Lindsay.'

THE END

OPAL
by Elvi Rhodes

Edgar Carson has returned from the trenches to find that the land fit for heroes didn't exist. The only nice thing that happened to him was OPAL, the small, tough, Yorkshire beauty who married him. But by the time the 20's came, Edgar was on the dole, and Opal was pregnant for the second time. Bitterness began to corrode Edgar's spirit.

But Opal was a fighter – she wasn't going to let the times, the drudgery, the poverty destroy her, or her family. They started with a 'house shop', just sweets and cotton reels sold from the top of her sideboard, and from then on she didn't stop – for Opal's dream was her own department store and a grand life for all of them . . .

0 552 12367 6   £1.75

THE DAFFODILS OF NEWENT
by Susan Sallis

They were called the Daffodil Girls, spirited and bright, enduring, loving and dancing their way through the gay and desperate twenties.

APRIL   who married the tortured and sexually suspect David Daker, convinced she could blot out his memories of the trenches.

MAY   pregnant by her handsome music hall star husband who didn't want to settle down.

MARCH loved and betrayed by the man who had fathered her child, and who still wanted her.

The Daffodils of Newent – three wonderful girls whose story began in A SCATTERING OF DAISIES.

0 552 12579 2   £1.75

THE SUMMER OF THE BARSHINSKEYS
by Diane Pearson

'Engrossing saga . . . characters who compell . . . vividly alive'
Barbara Taylor Bradford

'Although the story of the Barshinskeys, which became our story too, stretched over many summers and winters, that golden time of 1902 was when our strange involved relationship began, when our youthful longing for the exotic took a solid and restless hold upon us . . .'

It is at this enchanted moment that THE SUMMER OF THE BARSHINSKEYS begins. A beautifully told, compelling story that moves from a small Kentish village to London, and from war-torn St. Petersburg to a Quaker relief unit in the Volga provinces. It is the unforgettable story of two families, one English, the other Russian, who form a lifetime pattern of friendship, passion, hatred and love.

'A lovely, rich plum of a novel. Read it and enjoy'
Jacqueline Briskin

'The Russian section is reminiscent of Pasternak's DOCTOR ZHIVAGO, horrifying yet hauntingly beautiful'
New York Tribune

Something about the beginning of this book caught at me and I read it, then had to read it through more or less in one fell gulp. It comes across with the genuiness of a Lark Rise to Candleford . . . a compelling story and a splendid read'
Mary Stewart

0 552 126411   £2.95

CSARDAS
by Diane Pearson

'A story you won't easily forget, done on the scale of GONE WITH THE WIND'
Mark Kahn, *Sunday Mirror*

'Only half a century separates today's totalitarian state of Hungary from the glittering world of coming-out balls and feudal estates, elegance and culture, of which the Ferenc sisters – the *enchanting* Ferenc sisters – are the pampered darlings in the opening chapters of Diane Pearson's dramatic epic CSARDAS. Their world has now gone with the wind as surely as that of Scarlett O'Hara (which it much resembled): handsome, over-bred young men danced attendance on lovely, frivolous belles, and life was one long dream of parties and picnics, until the shot that killed Franz Ferdinand in 1914 burst the beautiful bubble. The dashing gallants galloped off to war and, as they returned, maimed and broken in spirit, the new Hungary began to emerge like an ugly grub from its chrysalis. Poverty, hardship, and growing anti-semitism threatened and scattered the half-Jewish Ferenc family as Nazi influence gripped the country from one side and Communism spread underground from the other like the tentacles of ground elder.

Only the shattered remnants of a once-powerful family lived through the 1939–45 holocaust, but with phoenix-like vitality the new generation began to adapt and bend, don camouflage and survive . . .'
Phyllida Hart-Davis, *Sunday Telegraph*

0 552 10375 6   £2.95

A WOMAN OF TWO CONTINENTS
by Pixie Burger

From the elegance of the London Season, to the plains and mountains of Argentina . . . from a luxurious villa on the Riviera, to an Estancia in South America . . .

She was an Anglo-Argentine – clinging fiercely to the old life-style – to a world of Edwardian garden parties and formal elegance, a woman in a land dominated by men . . .

First Edie, then her impetuous daughter Yvonne, and finally her granddaughter, fought for their identity in the cruel, beautiful, mysterious world of Argentina, searching for happiness and an answer to their passionate need for love . . .

0 552 12142 8   £2.50

COPPER KINGDOM
by Iris Gower

The Llewelyns lived in Copperman's Row — a small back-street where the women fought a constant battle against the copper dust from the smelting works. When Mali's mam died there were just the two of them left, Mali and her father, sacked from the works for taking time off to nurse his wife. Mali felt she would never hate anyone as much as she hated Sterling Richardson, the young master of the Welsh copper town.

But Sterling had his own problems — bad ones — and not least was the memory of the young green-eyed girl who had spat hatred at him on the day of her mother's death.

COPPER KINGDOM is the first in a sequence of novels set in the South Wales copper industry at the turn of the century.

0 552 12387 0   £1.95

THE CHATELAINE
by Claire Lorrimer

Seventeen-year-old Willow, newly married to Rowell, Lord Rochford, believed she held not only the keys to a multitude of rooms, but also to her own happiness . . .

'The book, CHATELAINE, is not actually a sweeping romance. Instead the characters build and build becoming more real on every page. The plot which features hidden babies, a beautiful girl marrying the wrong man and a corrupted doctor, zings along packed not only with action but with information. Miss Lorrimer has done her research and the book is not just a good read; it is a slice of life' George Thaw, *Daily Mirror*

0 552 11958 8   £2.50

OTHER FINE NOVELS AVAILABLE
FROM CORGI BOOKS